SOCIETY AND SENTIMENT

SOCIETY AND SENTIMENT

GENRES OF HISTORICAL WRITING IN BRITAIN, 1740–1820

Mark Salber Phillips

PRINCETON UNIVERSITY PRESS   PRINCETON, NEW JERSEY

Published by Princeton University Press, 41 William Street,
Princeton, New Jersey 08540
In the United Kingdom: Princeton University Press,
Chichester, West Sussex

Library of Congress Cataloging-in-Publication Data

Phillips, Mark, 1946–
Society and sentiment : genres of historical writing in Britain,
1740–1820 / Mark Salber Phillips.
p. cm.
Includes bibliographical references (p.) and index.
ISBN 0 691-03179-7 (cloth: alk. paper)—
ISBN 0-691-00867-1 (pbk. : alk. paper)
1. Historiography—Great Britain—History—18th century.
2. Historiography—Great Britain—History—19th century.
3. Great Britain—Social life and customs—18th century.
4. Great Britain— Social life and customs—19th century.
5. Historiography—Social aspects—Great Britain. 6. Sentimentalism—
Social aspects—Great Britain.
7. Great Britain—Historiography. 8. Literary form. I. Title.
DA1 .P53 2000
907'.2041—dc21 99-048753

This book has been composed in Times Roman

The paper used in this publication meets the minimum
requirements of ANSI/NISO Z39.48-1992 (R1997)
(*Permanence of Paper*)

www.pup.princeton.edu

Printed in the United States of America

10 9 8 7 6 5 4 3 2 1

For Ruth, Sarah, Emma

Contents

Preface

THERE IS A story I like about an avid fisherman who spent every spare moment down on the public dock engaged in his favorite sport. Sometimes other fishermen joined him, but most days he had the waterfront to himself. On one particular day, however, he soon noticed that he was not alone. Up on the boardwalk overlooking the dock, a man was leaning on the railing watching him fish. Time went by, but the bystander showed no signs of leaving. Naturally, the fisherman grew irritated at being watched in this way. Still, there wasn't a lot he could do about it, so he did his best to keep his mind on the fish. Finally, at the end of the day (which really had not gone too badly, despite everything) the fisherman gathered up his catch and his tackle and made his way up to the road. As he passed by the stranger, the fisherman gave him a brief nod and asked civilly, "Fish much yourself?" "Oh no, not me," the other man replied; "I'd never have the patience!"

Among other things, this story appeals to me as a sort of metaphor for the way many historians see their relationship with students of historiography. Professional historians generally see themselves as skillful fisherman, and though they certainly have no objection to swapping a few good stories now and again, they are sometimes puzzled by colleagues who actually seem more interested in watching than fishing. Nor has it helped that in recent decades a good deal of writing on historiography has been inspired by the unfamiliar methods of literary criticism, so that the activities of the anglers and the language of the watchers seem further apart than ever before. In fact, for nearly a generation now students of historiography have effectively divided themselves into two camps. On one side stand those who approach the subject primarily as a problem in intellectual history; on the other we find those for whom historical writing is at bottom an act of imagination to be understood in literary (and especially narratological) terms. Valuable work has been done on both sides of this methodological divide, but it has not proven easy to marry the two approaches. In the first camp we can locate all those whose interest in historiography lies primarily in the opportunity it gives to study the expression of political or philosophical ideas, as well as those who approach the subject in light of the history of scholarship.[1] Historians of this school have often been

[1] Among many other important works of this character, see Felix Gilbert, *Machiavelli and Guicciardini* (New York: Norton, 1984); John Burrow, *A Liberal Descent* (Cambridge: Cambridge UP, 1981); Joseph Levine, *The Battle of the Books* (Ithaca: Cornell UP, 1991), and *Humanism and History: Origins of Modern English Historiography* (Ithaca: Cornell UP, 1987); John Pocock, *Virtue, Commerce, and History* (Cambridge: Cambridge UP, 1985), and *The Ancient Constitution and the Feudal Law*, rev. ed. (Cambridge: Cambridge UP, 1987); Philip Hicks, *Neoclassical His-*

people of real literary gifts, and this sensitivity has enriched their readings of earlier historians. Even so, their interest generally lies in the doctrines and commitments that link history to other disciplines, and their first impulse has been to investigate a realm of ideas, rather than to disclose narrative structures. In short, historiographical studies of this sort operate without much attention to what Hayden White calls a "theory of the historical text," and insofar as history is felt to possess its own distinctive practices, these are generally identified with its methods of argument and evidence, rather than its formal, textual qualities.

A very different set of assumptions grounds the work of those who view history primarily as a textual construction and an act of imagination. Their first impulse has been to challenge the matter-of-factness with which most historians still approach virtually all questions of historical representation. Wanting to "get the story crooked,"[2] these critics have sought to understand underlying imaginative structures that often appear remote from the more explicit concern of the text with questions of fact and argument. Writers of this school have seldom given us the extended examination of intellectual context that most intellectual historians identify with the methods of their discipline. Indeed, as I will explain a little more fully in the initial chapter, the pioneering work in this mode, Hayden White's *Metahistory* pursued a "theory of the text" that so detached a small number of great histories from surrounding literatures and institutions that intellectual history in the ordinary sense was rendered unnecessary.

As an intellectual historian, I begin with a sense that my subject should include the full range of historical writing, noncanonical as well as canonical, and a commitment to understanding all of this in a broad context of contempo-

---

tory and English Culture (New York: St. Martin's, 1996); Laird Okie, *Augustan Historical Writing* (Lanham, Md.: University P of America, 1991); Daniel Woolf, *The Idea of History in Early Stuart England: Erudition, Ideology, and the "Light of Truth" from the Accession of James I to the Civil War* (Toronto: U of Toronto P, 1990); David Womersley, *The Transformation of the Decline and Fall of the Roman Empire* (Cambridge: Cambridge UP, 1988); and Colin Kidd, *Subverting Scotland's Past* (Cambridge: Cambridge UP, 1993). Karen O'Brien, *Narratives of Enlightenment: Cosmopolitan History from Voltaire to Gibbon* (Cambridge: Cambridge UP, 1997) unfortunately reached me too late for me to make any detailed use of its findings, but readers will find a number of points of convergence.

[2] For a fine overview of this approach, see Frank Ankersmit's introduction to *A New Philosophy of History*, ed. Ankersmit and Hans Kellner (Chicago: U of Chicago P, 1995). Some of the most important works of this school include Hayden White, *Metahistory: The Historical Imagination in Nineteenth-Century Europe* (Baltimore: Johns Hopkins UP, 1973); and Hans Kellner, *Language and Historical Representation: Getting the Story Crooked* (Madison: U of Wisconsin P, 1989); Linda Orr, *Jules Michelet* (Ithaca: Cornell UP, 1975); among Stephen Bann's several works on this area, see in particular *Romanticism and the Rise of History* (New York: Twayne, 1995). More generally on the literary dimension of historiography, see Lionel Gossman, *Between History and Literature* (Cambridge: Harvard UP, 1990); and Robert Canary and Henry Kozicki, eds., *The Writing of History* (Madison: U of Wisconsin P, 1978).

rary intellectual life. At the same time, since histories are not treatises or manifestos, I do not want to abstract works of history into systems of ideas nor attempt to understand them apart from their literary structures. Further, in earlier work on the chronicles and histories of late medieval and Renaissance Italy as well as in occasional forays into problems of method, I have come to feel that there is a greater range and diversity in historiographical practice than we generally acknowledge. In my view, much of what has been written about historiography displays a peculiar kind of present-mindedness that narrows our sense of earlier traditions and flatters the professionalism of our own times with a false sense of its own distinctive accomplishments.[3] Not only philosophers and literary critics, but historians themselves have too often failed to subject their own assumptions about history to the modesty of historical reflection.

In short, I have attempted to respond to two kinds of methodological challenges. First, I have tried to find ways to join the contextualizing methods of intellectual history to the formalist concerns of literary analysis. Second, I have tried to capture something of the range of eighteenth-century practices by working with a deliberately liberal definition of the subject that does not limit us to one or two prestigious genres of historical writing. Both considerations have led me to shift attention away from the customary focus on a few great, individual works—the canonical histories of Hume, Robertson, Ferguson, or Gibbon—to wider questions of genre and audience as they affect a larger group of historical literatures. As I will explain in more detail in the introduction, recent discussions of genre have set aside the idea that genres are abstract fixities. On the contrary, it is argued, genre should be seen as an important instrument of literary communication that always remains open to revision as authors respond to current social interests and compete for the attention of readers. In my view, the communicative function of genre combined with its historical changeability promise to make genre study an approach to historiography that is both sensitive to literary structure and a guide to wider contexts and debates.

The standard narrative of the "rise of modern historiography" centers on continental Europe in the nineteenth century. In one version, we honor the objectivity and protoprofessionalism of Ranke's Berlin seminar, in another the philosophical depth or imaginative power of Hegel or Michelet. Either way, the historiography of the Enlightenment is no more than a preliminary: at best a foreshadowing, at worst an obstacle to the achievement of methodological or philosophical maturity. Such simplifications are probably unavoidable in historical schemas built on quests for the origins of modernity, and I have no

[3] See the recent volume by Joyce Appleby, Lynn Hunt, and Margaret Jacob for a particularly up-to-date version of this professional self-celebration: *Telling the Truth about History* (New York: Norton, 1994).

desire to enter a counterclaim for the distinctive modernity of eighteenth-century Britain. My intention, rather, is to underscore the importance of history to many of the salient intellectual enterprises of the Enlightenment and, reciprocally, to explore the ways in which those who read history as well as those who wrote it responded to the social and sentimental interests of the age. It seems to me unquestionable that the eighteenth century was a critical moment in the adaptation of classical understandings of history to the needs of a modern, commercial, and increasingly middle-class society. Eighteenth-century social analysis no longer permitted a definition of history that restricted itself to the conventional narrative of politics—the story of the public actions of public men. The result, it is important to emphasize, was not only a need to reconceptualize many traditional assumptions about historical knowledge, but also a good deal of formal experimentation that changed the shape of historical accounts and altered the character of historical reading. This book examines these adaptations in light of the intensified interest in both social and interior experience that characterized the philosophical and literary interests of the British Enlightenment. Its central chapters explore the ways in which historians, biographers, antiquarians, memorialists, literary historians, and others sought to represent the social world of everyday life as well as the inward world of the sentiments. History did not abandon its traditional concern with public life, but it significantly widened its scope as it created a new social narrative that could stand beside and even subsume the conventional account of political action. At the same time, new subjects made new demands on historians and their readers alike. For the first time, evocation became an important goal of historical narrative, and sympathetic identification came to be seen as one of the pleasures of historical reading.

Scholars have generally associated the sentimental concerns of this period not with history, but the novel, a new genre that quickly became one of the preeminent literatures of social description. For this reason, it may be useful to say something about the relationship between my historiographical concerns and the very rich literature on the "rise of the novel."[4] Students of the novel will certainly find parts of this landscape familiar, and they may be tempted to read this book as an essay on the relations between history and fiction. Indeed, at an early stage I too was inclined to see the problem in this light. As my knowledge of the material grew, however, I came to realize that the social and sentimental questions that I saw as transforming the reading of history were registered right across eighteenth-century letters and should not be identified solely with any particular genre. In fact, to reduce the question to a matter of

[4] I have taken my bearings on this subject especially from two important works, both of which in different ways have helped to shape my approach here: Paul Hunter's *Before Novels* (New York: Norton, 1990); and Michael McKeon, *The Origins of the English Novel* (Baltimore: Johns Hopkins UP, 1987)

the interplay of history and fiction would be to fall into the problem I saw in many studies of the novel, which remap the literary system around one favored genre, to which they assign an experimental energy denied to all other forms of writing—most notably history.

No one doubts that the rise of the novel carries enormous significance as an event in European culture, but by making the novel somehow both emergent and central, modern criticism has helped to obscure the dynamism of other contemporary literatures. (A good way, I think, to gauge the problems we create by reading later literary hierarchies into an earlier period is to imagine for a moment an eighteenth-century equivalent of the Pulitzer Prize, with David Hume or Edward Gibbon nominated for the award in "nonfiction.") Unfortunately, the modern restriction of literature to works of "imagination" has divided history and other "nonfictional" genres from a redefined literary field, thus obscuring history's importance to the literary system of an earlier day. One consequence has been that there is simply no counterpart for historical writing of the extraordinary mass and quality of criticism on the novel. As a result, though students of the early novel have recently become increasingly interested in texts outside of their traditional domain, they lack the resource of equivalent bodies of literary history or practical criticism for other genres. Ironically, then, the sheer weight of critical intelligence that modern scholarship has brought to fiction continues to work against the opening out to a wider contextualization that students of the novel are seeking.

At the risk of some oversimplification, I want to remark on two assumptions that I think remain embedded in much of our thinking about the rise of the novel as it relates to historiography. First, in celebrating the inventive novelty of an emergent form, critics have a tendency to construct the older genre, history, as monumental and unchanging. It is as though the rise of the novel were itself a kind of bildungsroman in which history is left to play the static and subordinate role of the parent. Second, studies of eighteenth-century fiction often appear to treat history more as an epistemological category than as a literary genre in its own right—a body of writing, in other words, with its own formal problems to solve and its own opportunities for experimentation and generic change. Since in criticism of this sort history figures as a kind of truth claim that the novel both emulates and ironizes, students of the novel have felt little need to investigate historiographical practices in any detail.[5] Once again, the result is that the novel is particularized, while history is generalized.

[5] A recent example of literary critics' avoidance of detailed investigation of historiographical texts is Everett Zimmerman's *The Boundaries of Fiction: History and the Eighteenth-Century British Novel* (Ithaca: Cornell UP, 1995). Zimmerman's study of eighteenth-century fiction claims also to be centrally concerned with the historiography of this period, but it is notable that among eighteenth-century historians, only Hume, Robertson, and Gibbon are mentioned. Of these, only Hume is discussed at any length, and his work is represented by the *Treatise*, not the *History of*

It would be foolish, however, for historians to complain about the critical attention fiction naturally attracts. The point, rather, is to emulate this success by creating a denser and more sophisticated history of the neglected genres of "nonfiction." If we could explore the many ages and varieties of historical writing with even a small part of the loving attention that generations of critics have brought to fiction, we would surely have an enormously valuable reflection of the historical discipline itself. But here, perhaps, lies the underlying reason why the body of historiographical criticism is not weightier. Diffident as historians generally are about the theoretical pronouncements of philosophers and literary theorists, they have also been wary of applying the usual methods of history to retelling the history of their own discipline. For some reason, historians who would not doubt that past practice is constitutive of present possibility in any number of other realms hesitate to think this way of their own activity. Accordingly, the history of historiography, though never wholly discounted (especially in pedagogical settings) generally lives a kind of marginal existence as a poor cousin to more serious historical enterprises. To revert to the earlier metaphor, we still want to divide the historical world into fishermen and spectators and choose to see the history of historiography as a hobby best suited to those who lack the patience to get out there themselves and catch a few fish. As a very distinguished historian once said to me in an unguarded moment, "I always think of historiography as something we do when we can't get to the archives."

A generation ago Louis Mink urged both historians and philosophers to give up the idea that narrative is a sort of literary grace added, so to speak, after the fact. Rather, Mink argued in a series of influential essays, narrative itself constitutes a "primary cognitive instrument" that is "particularly important as a rival to theoretical explanation or understanding."[6] Mink also stressed the complexity and diversity of narrative forms, and he observed that "only a beginning has been made toward understanding the structure of complex narratives and the classification of kinds of narratives."[7] With these views Mink effectively set an agenda for a new program of historiographical studies, and it is one on which a good deal of progress has since been made. Oddly, however, it seems to have been Mink's assumption that the challenge of disclosing the complexity and diversity of narrative form would be the work, if not of philosophers, then at least of theoretically minded critics. This assumption, no

---

England. Among exceptions to the general lack of interest in practical criticism of historiographical texts, see Leo Braudy, *Hume, Fielding, and Gibbon* (Princeton: Princeton UP, 1970); and W. B. Carnochan, *Gibbon's Solitude* (Palo Alto: Stanford UP, 1987), but the focus on Hume and Gibbon tells its own story.

[6] Louis Mink, "Narrative Form as a Cognitive Instrument," in *Historical Understanding*, ed. Brian Fay et al. (Ithaca: Cornell UP, 1987), 185.

[7] Mink, "The Divergence of History and Sociology in Recent Philosophy of History," in *Historical Understanding*, 179.

doubt, reflects Mink's assessment of the interests of the historical discipline in the 1970s; nonetheless, it seems in clear conflict with his own defense of narrative as a cognitive instrument. Surely as a subject for investigation, narrative itself is as much open to a historical mode of understanding as it is to a theoretical (or structural) one. Indeed, historical narrative has had a long and complex history, which, like any other great subject, calls for retelling in all its variety and detail. Such a history, of course, would necessarily encompass questions of literary structure and classification, where much could be learned from conversation with the work of literary theory. But literary structures do not live in isolation from social ones. Thus a properly historical account also needs to find ways to embed formalist concerns in a larger context that includes the conceptual debates and social interests that are the domain of intellectual history. Only then, I think, can we claim to have made the attempt to bring historical writing into focus under the light of its own "modes of cognition."

In the introduction that follows, I have tried to articulate in some detail my own approach to both the intellectual history and literary form of eighteenth-century writing on history; here I wish only to acknowledge a few of the book's most obvious limitations. This book is by no means intended as a survey of British historiography. Rather it traces two dimensions of historical writing—the "society and sentiment" of the title—through what I hope is a sufficient number of works and genres to show a reframing of historical thought and writing in this period. The story as I have told it is a British one, particularly a Scottish one. But there is no doubt in my mind that it is also a European episode and especially a French one. The justifications for drawing a boundary around a national literature are certainly as much pragmatic as intellectual, and I can only say that I hope the picture as I have sketched it will be complemented by others more cosmopolitan in scope. By the same token, I have chosen to focus primarily on histories concerned with the national past. Among other omissions, this concentration accounts for Gibbon's absence from the book, though almost every theme considered here could well be raised in connection with his great work. It might be added that the *Decline and Fall* has recently been the subject of a great deal of scholarly attention—so much so that it now ranks with some of the minor novels of the age. No other narrative, however, not even Hume's, has been analyzed in anything like this detail, and the approach I have chosen requires me to examine a range of texts that are far less often read. Accordingly, I have chosen to begin with Hume as the single figure who most centrally marks out the ambitions and vocabularies of the historiography of Britain, before moving on to consider a large number of other writers, many of them working in "minor" historical genres or even in genres not normally considered historical at all. Investigating these genres, as I explain in the introduction, seems to me essential to any consideration of historical writing in Hume's generation and after.

Finally, I must acknowledge that I have often allowed myself an old-fashioned luxury of extensive paraphrase or quotation. As academics, I know, we live in a hurried and argumentative age, and some readers may well lose patience with an expository method that they might not feel is required by my need to explore little-known works or to convey the textures of larger ones. In the end these are matters more of tact than of argument, but it seems worth saying that I have tried in this way to blunt the sense of coerciveness that often accompanies even the best of analyses. My hope, in short, is not simply to present my own views, but also to interest the reader in a wide, but often neglected field of texts and ideas. For this kind of engagement to be possible, I believe, there needs to be some space to look around.

I came to an interest in the eighteenth century after an extended apprenticeship in the historiography of the Italian Renaissance. I am particularly grateful to those who opened up this rich new world to me and were patient with the first steps of a neophyte. At a very early stage, the late Felix Gilbert, long a mentor in Italian subjects, responded with enthusiasm to this enlargement of my historiographical interests. John Burrow, Stefan Collini, and Donald Winch did a great deal, both by the force of their example and by the generosity of their friendship, to shape my interest in the intellectual history of Britain. April London first opened up for me in a concrete way some possibilities for enlarging the conversation between those of us interested in the historiography of this period and those who study the novel. Mary Catherine Moran, once a student, soon became a colleague in many areas of shared interest; later Michael White, Matt Lauzon, and Dale Smith followed suit. Ed Hundert not only read the entire manuscript, but also sustained the spirits of the author in the long, slow process of revision. Many other friends, too, have shown me paths that I have tried to explore, especially Robert Goheen, Martin Golding, Richard Kroll, Joseph Levine, Blair Neatby, and Gordon Schochet. Mary Catherine Moran, Dale Smith, and Sarah Phillips gave invaluable help with the notes and bibliography. I am most grateful to the two readers for the Princeton University Press, Paul Hunter and John Burrow, whose generous and detailed comments contributed so much to the final revisions. My largest debt, however, is certainly to my wife Ruth, whose intellectual companionship has, as always, sustained this project and whose gentle nagging helped bring it to a close.

I am much indebted to the Master and Fellows of Peterhouse, Cambridge for electing me a Visiting Fellow at the opening stage of this research, to Carleton University and to the Social Sciences and Humanities Research Council of Canada for research grants that supported the work, to the Folger Library for the Folger Long Term Fellowship that gave me a year free of teaching to complete a full draft, and to the University of British Columbia for support in preparation of the final manuscript. I am pleased also to have this opportunity to acknowledge the invaluable help of Callista Kelly and Laurie

Campbell of Carleton University Library, of Pam Cremona of the Peterhouse Library, and of the librarians and staff of the Folger Library, who made its collections an ideal setting for research and writing.

Some parts of chapter 3 appeared in an earlier version, as "Adam Smith and the History of Private Life: Social and Sentimental Narratives in Eighteenth-Century Historiography," in *The Historical Imagination in Early Modern Britain,* ed. D. Kelley and D. Sacks (Woodrow Wilson Center Press/Cambridge University Press, 1997). Portions of chapter 4 appeared in earlier form as " 'If Mrs. Mure Be Not Sorry for Poor King Charles': History, the Novel, and the Sentimental Reader," *History Workshop Journal* 43 (1997): 111–13. An earlier version of chapter 12 was published as "William Godwin and the Idea of Historical Commemoration: History as Public Memory and Private Sentiment," in *Shifting the Boundaries: Transformation of the Languages of Public and Private in the Eighteenth Century,* ed. D. Castiglione and L. Sharpe (Exeter: Exeter University Press, 1995), 196–219.

Abbreviations

BL	British Library
DNB	*Dictionary of National Biography,* 1898 ed.
ER	*Edinburgh Review*
MR	*Monthly Review*
NLS	National Library of Scotland

SOCIETY AND SENTIMENT

Introduction

"The More Permanent and Peaceful Scenes of Social Life"

ROBERT HENRY'S *History of Great Britain from the Invasion by the Romans under Julius Caesar* (1771–93) has never enjoyed the reputation of David Hume's more polished *History* and now is all but forgotten. Yet in many ways this large work, as laborious in its researches as it was inventive in its narrative arrangements, is more revealing of the tensions that shaped eighteenth-century historiography. Henry (1713–1790), a prominent minister of the Church of Scotland, brought out the first edition at his own expense, but the eventual success of the history allowed him to sell the rights for a considerable sum. After his death, the history was republished with a continuation by James Petit Andrews; there was also a French translation, and even a Victorian revision.[1]

From the start, the distinctive feature and selling point of this history was the "new plan" on which it was written. Henry's self-imposed program required him to compose seven simultaneous narratives for each of the periods his history recounted:

> Each book begins and ends at some remarkable revolution, and contains the history and delineation of the first of these revolutions and of the intervening period. Every one of these ten books [i.e. the successive chronological epochs of his history] is uniformly divided into seven chapters, which do not carry on the thread of the history one after another, as in other works of this kind; but all the seven chapters of the same book begin at the same point of time, run parallel to one another, and end together; each chapter presenting the reader with the history of one particular object. (xxxi)

Each of the seven parallel narratives pursued its own special theme. As outlined in the preface, these are (1) civil and military history; (2) ecclesiastical history and the history of religion; (3) history of our constitution, governments, laws, and courts; (4) history of learning, of learned men, and of the chief seminaries of learning; (5) arts, useful and ornamental; (6) history of commerce, and of prices and commodities; (7) manners, virtues, vices, remarkable customs, language, dress, diet, and diversions.

[1] Robert Henry, *The History of Great Britain, From the First invasion of it by the Romans under Julius Caesar. Written On A New Plan,* 6th ed. (London, 1823). Subsequent citations appear in the text. Henry's sixth volume, edited by Laing, appeared posthumously with a "Life" of the

Henry's arrangement was governed by two strong, but contradictory impulses. On the one hand, his work aimed to expand the sphere of historical understanding to incorporate a range of social activities well beyond the limits of traditional historiography as written on humanist lines. On the other, Henry wanted as far as possible to save the appearances of linear narrative, which was the identifying marker of that earlier, still authoritative tradition. For this reason, he promised to pursue each of his separate narratives in ways that fully respected and even improved upon the traditional demand for perspicuousness in narrative order—all the while juxtaposing these narratives in a fashion that demonstrates the utter inadequacy of the humanist framework.

Henry's plan for seven simultaneous narratives represented an ingenious experiment with narrative conventions designed to solve the problems brought on by an expanded definition of history's object of study. Where once it had been sufficient to pursue a narrowly defined narrative of public action, history now needed to comprehend a whole range of experiences that are best defined as social. This redrawing of boundaries on so much wider a scale certainly did not mean the elimination of political-military history, and in the most literal sense, political narrative retained its priority. But in this enlarged context, there was an inevitable displacement of the older narrative within the broadly drawn horizons of a new history that took society, not politics, as its definition. As a result, political and military events, once the whole frame of humanist historiography, now figured as simply one theme in a multiplicity of plots.

Henry joined a chorus of voices in the second half of the century who celebrated the contemporary expansion of the horizons of historical study. By this plan, he wrote, "the sphere of history will be very much enlarged" (xxxiii) and many useful and entertaining subjects, hitherto excluded, will be added. Most historians, he explained, have restricted themselves to detailing civil, military, and ecclesiastical histories. A few have included dissertations on the constitution, government, or law; but none had even pretended to give "any thing like a history of learning, arts, commerce, and manners" (xxxiv). Are these subjects, he asked rhetorically, unworthy to be included in the history of a country where learning, arts, and commerce flourish? Should history be written

> without ever attending to their conduct and condition, in the more permanent and peaceful scenes of social life? Are we now in possession of prodigious stores of natural, moral, and religious knowledge; of a vast variety of elegant and useful arts; of an almost unbounded trade, which pours the productions of every climate at our feet, to all which our forefathers were once strangers? And have we no curiosity to know, at what time, by what degrees, and by whose means, we have been enriched with these treasures of learning, arts, and commerce? (xxxv)

---

author. The French translation by Rowland and Cantwell appeared in 1789–96. Andrews' continuation appeared in 1794, with successive expansions and editions in 1796 and 1806.

As these comments indicate, Henry addressed his enlargement of history's social vision to the needs of present-day audiences in a great commercial and polite nation. And as an author who had incurred risks that were financial as well as literary, he might well express a hope that his attempt to comprehend "these important objects within the bounds of history, will be received by the Public with some degree of favor" (xxxv). He says nothing, however, that explicitly connects the expanded scope of his history to another salient feature of his work, its insistence on utmost symmetry in its narrative arrangements. It is left to us as readers to draw the conclusion that this rigorousness of outline indexes the need to bring an extra measure of discipline to a history written on this enlarged basis.

Henry promised to pursue his program in all possible strictness, so that within its chronological limits each of the ten books would be complete in itself, while at the same time being a "perfect pattern and model" of the whole work.

> To render this plan still more perfectly regular and uniform in all its parts, the author has disposed the materials of all the chapters of the same number, in all the ten books, in the same order, as far as the subject treated of in these chapters would permit. For example: The arts, which are the subject of the fifth chapter of every book, are disposed one after another in the same order of succession, in all the fifth chapters throughout the whole work. (xxxii–xxxiii)

The rigid symmetries of this arrangement, Henry acknowledged with some pride, meant putting himself under an obligation to examine every part of his subject with the same "constant anxious attention" (xxxix). In truth, as he later remarked to Walpole, the demands of such an undertaking were beyond any individual historian.[2] Yet remarkably, Henry also saw that this degree of self-discipline in the writer opened a kind of freedom for his readers. For them, it meant the possibility of following their own interests, choosing those "particular subjects" that seemed "most useful and agreeable in themselves, or most suitable to their respective ways of life" (xxxvii).

Jane Austen caught the sense of this invitation and responded with her own characteristic spirit. "I am now laying in a stock of intelligence to pour out on you as *my* share of Conversation," she told a friend, announcing that she was now reading Henry's *History,* "which I will repeat to you in any manner you may prefer, either in a loose, disultary, unconnected strain, or dividing the

[2] Robert Henry to Horace Walpole, March 3, 1783, *The Yale Edition of Horace Walpole's Correspondence,* ed. W. S. Lewis et al., 48 vols. (New Haven: Yale UP, 1952), 15:169. Henry pronounced his own plan "too bold and too extensive, I believe, for any one man." Walpole praised Henry's work, especially its "plan": "You have helped us, Sir, to read every period of our story with a map of the understandings of each age in our hands; and the plan of your work is so new and so just, that whencesoever you took materials, the design, arrangement and utility can be claimed by no man" (H. Walpole to R. Henry, March 16, 1782, *Correspondence,* 42:7).

recital as the Historian divides it himself, into seven parts . . . so that for every evening of the week there will be a different subject."[3] Austen counted off each branch of Henry's sevenfold narrative, remarking, "The Friday's lot, Commerce, Coin and Shipping, You will find the least entertaining, but the next Eveng:'s portion [i.e. manners] will make amends."

If individual readers had the freedom to single out themes most appropriate to their private occupations, Henry clearly expected that the work as a whole would reflect the broad interests of the contemporary British public. And in a country rich in trade, in arts, and in knowledge, what could be more "natural, laudable, and useful" than the enlarged curiosity about the past. The historical horizon, in short, would stretch to match contemporary experience, incorporating for the first time "the more permanent and peaceful scenes of social life." At the same time, Henry's comments indicate that he also expected his readers' curiosity to be enlarged by a corresponding recognition that the social experiences of earlier generations differed substantially from many features of present-day life—"to all of which our forefathers were once strangers." Thus, in Henry's view, contemporary interest in the economy and the arts was joined to an associated awareness of a kind of historical distance that separated current readers from social life in the past. Such an audience would want something more than a narrative of statecraft because it was eager to understand how the modes of contemporary social life first sprang into being.

Henry's remarks about his need to address his audience in terms of contemporary social realities make explicit a process of historical rewriting that we can take as axiomatic. Every society, it is clear, rewrites its history in ways that allow it to recognize itself in the mirror of its own past. But the rigidities of Henry's "new plan" also remind us that there is a historiographical corollary to Marx's dictum that while we make history, we do not make it under conditions of our own choosing. Not simply the outline of events, but in some ways even more compellingly the instruments of historical thought and representation are an inheritance of earlier social needs. In short, Henry and his audience shared a historical language and a set of narrative conventions that, to use the jargon of hermeneutics, were pregiven. Even the most thoroughgoing radicalism could not have changed the fundamentals beyond recognition, but for Robert Henry, a sober-minded churchman with a full printing of his book to sell, no innovation would be desirable that did not also reaffirm the tradition.

I will return to Henry's *History* in a later chapter in the context of eighteenth-century debates over linearity in historical composition and other experiments with narrative form. I have introduced it now because no other work I know of exhibits so plainly the full range of issues that constituted the problem of historical narrative in this period, especially the conjunction of questions of

[3] Jane Austen to Martha Lloyd, November 13, 1800, *Jane Austen's Letters,* ed. Deirdre Le Faye, 3d ed. (Oxford: Oxford UP, 1995), 59.

narrative structure with those of audience and social understanding. Much of this study will be preoccupied with formalist questions of the kind raised by Henry's experiment; and I will confess that these questions are made all the more enjoyable to explore because they contradict the received wisdom that sees historical writing in this period as anything but innovative, reserving that honor for that favored child of eighteenth-century literary studies, the novel, or to what are thought of as the "novelistic" practices of Romantic historians, which amounts to much the same thing.

But equally, Henry's *History* points to the ways in which consideration of narrative form opens out onto larger issues that are social and historical. For Robert Henry, experiment with narrative was hardly an end in itself. The impetus sprang from his desire to overcome the inadequacy of the inherited instruments of historical writing when measured by the needs and questions of the contemporary audience. His effort to broaden the historical horizon signals his recognition that history had to participate in the reconceptualization of social knowledge that was so pervasive a feature of contemporary thought.

In this sense, the challenges to historical writing were not so different from those that faced political economy, moral philosophy, or even the novel. What did set history apart from most other literatures, however, was the extent to which this reconceptualization complicated the central conventions of the genre, shaped as they had been for so long by an ancient and authoritative tradition of political narrative. For no other literature of social description, in short, was the formal problem of narrative so significant to the continued identity of the genre itself.

It needs to be said that the fundamental elements of the tension I have pointed to in historical composition had been present in British society for a very long time. Thus there is no question of a sudden revolution in social outlook producing a wholly new situation for historical writing. Since at least the middle of the seventeenth century, Britain had not only been a commercial society, but also one in which there was an increasing recognition that commercial interests constituted a new focus for political understanding, as well as for state action.[4] Nor was the course of intellectual change any more abrupt if we turn our attention from social to sentimental themes, to introduce a shorthand that will be useful in subsequent discussion. Exploration of inward and everyday experience was a growing preoccupation of postrevolutionary Britain, hence an important part of the interest that a historian like Robert Henry might expect to encounter in his readership.[5]

[4] On the economic thought of the earlier period, see for instance Joyce Oldham Appleby, *Economic Thought and Ideology in Seventeenth-Century England* (Princeton: Princeton UP, 1978).

[5] As we have already seen in Austen's comments, interest in the history of manners was a prime element in the appreciation of Henry's work. See, for example, the appreciative comments of Joseph Berington, a Catholic medievalist of decidedly sentimental interests, who in discussing his own appendix on manners, arts, and learning, calls Henry's work "far the most valuable compi-

My purpose, however, is not to fix an exact moment when new ideas of economy or new understandings of personality first appeared on the horizon of historical writing. It is enough to know that the middle of the eighteenth century represented a moment of particular richness for the central genres that expressed what I have called the social and sentimental interests of this culture. Hume's economic essays in *Political Discourses* (1752) were the first classics of Scottish political economy, followed by Smith's *Wealth of Nations* (1776). Philosophical history came into its own with the appearance of Hume's *History of England,* the first two volumes of which were published in 1754 and 1757, and with Voltaire's *Essai sur les moeurs* (1756), while for conjectural history, the equivalent milestones were Montesquieu's *De L'Esprit des lois* (1748), Ferguson's *Essay on the History of Civil Society* (1767), and Kames's *Sketches of the History of Man* (1774). The midcentury was equally engaged in exploring the sentiments. Richardson's *Clarissa; or the History of a Young Lady* (1748–49) and *Sir Charles Grandison* (1753–54) are obvious landmarks, as is Adam Smith's *Theory of Moral Sentiments* (1st ed. 1759). And yet—crucially for the situation of historical narratives—the prestige of these works was not accompanied by a movement to jettison classical models of historical narrative. On the contrary, in many ways the polite taste of the eighteenth century heightened the requirement for elegant composition. If this no longer meant the strictest adherence to conventions that were purely classical, it continued to entail that the best productions of modern letters would be held up to standards still deeply imbued with classical ideals, including the linearity and perspicuity that Henry strained so hard to achieve.

My point, then, is not that the tensions we see manifested in Henry's *History* are novel, but that they were deeply characteristic of the literary and philosophical culture of this period. Moreover, the fertility of this period in a variety of genres of historical writing suggests that these tensions may also be an important clue to its productivity. In particular, we need to consider the way in which Henry's sense of having successfully faced a distinctive set of challenges operated not only to stimulate innovation but also to confer a sense of concrete and indisputable progress. Nothing else, I believe, can so fully explain that sense of collective achievement that attaches to eighteenth-century pronouncements on historiography. When Hume asserted that "this is the historical age and this the historical nation," he surely had such accomplishments in mind.[6]

---

lation we possess." *The History of the Reign of Henry the Second* (Birmingham, 1790), xxvii. Berington is discussed further in chapter 5.

[6] Hume wrote a favorable review of Henry's *History* intended for the *Edinburgh Magazine and Review,* but it was suppressed by the editor, Gilbert Stuart, who was hostile to Henry. The text of the review is published in David F. Norton and Richard Popkin, eds., *David Hume: Philosophical Historian* (Indianapolis: Bobbs-Merrill, 1965), 377–88.

Defining a New Perspective

Unfortunately, there is not much in recent historiographical study that offers immediate help with the problems of narrative suggested by works like Henry's. British historiography in the eighteenth century has generally been studied in terms of the lives and opinions of a narrow canon of great authors: Hume and Gibbon, principally, but sometimes expanded to take in Robertson or Ferguson. The range of questions, too, has often been equally narrow. On the one hand, students of the classical tradition, preoccupied with the evolution of scholarly methods, have studied eighteenth-century historians primarily in terms of their contribution to a metanarrative of disciplinary development.[7] On the other, intellectual historians engaged in tracing the fortunes of political or philosophical ideas have read historical texts in terms of their doctrinal commitments. Neither approach has a stake in exploring narratological issues, nor, speaking more generally, much interest in examining the particular textual features that distinguish historical writing as a body of literature.

From the perspective of narrative, Hayden White's broad theoretical challenge to traditional scholarship seems more hopeful. Ironically, however, White's theorization of the literary character of historical texts built on prevailing modes of literary study that were themselves ahistorical; thus the impulses that fed the theoretical boldness of *Metahistory* also worked against its claim to be considered as a history of historical writing.[8] In practice, White's analyses prove to have much less to do with the "narrative prose discourses" that histories "most manifestly are" than his opening program indicates.[9] Rather his focus is on the "poetic act" by which the historian "prefigures" the historical field. The accompanying emphasis on "deep structure" shifts attention from what is most manifest in historical narratives to what is often most hidden, even from the historian himself. For this reason White's analysis turns to philosophers of history, arguing that there is no essential difference between the

[7] Levine, *Battle of the Books;* and Arnaldo Momigliano, *Studies in Historiography* (London: Weidenfeld, 1966). On some problems in Momigliano's conception of disciplinary progress in this period, see Phillips, "Reconsiderations on History and Antiquarianism: Arnaldo Momigliano and the Historiography of Eighteenth-Century Britain," *Journal of the History of Ideas* 58 (1996): 297–316.

[8] For a contrary view, see Frank Ankersmit, "Bibliographical Essay," in Ankersmit and Kellner, *New Philosophy of History.* Ankersmit argues that in White's hands historical theory lost its "abstract, aprioristic character" and became instead "a new and highly sophisticated form of historiography (i.e., the history of historical writing)" (281). I have outlined my unease with White's methods at greater length in "Historiography and Genre: A More Modest Proposal," *Storia della storiografia/Histoire de l'historiographie* 24 (1993): 119–32.

[9] "In this theory," he stated flatly in the preface, "I treat the historical work as what it most manifestly is: a verbal structure in the form of a narrative prose discourse" (White, *Metahistory,* ix).

works of the great historians and their counterparts in philosophy. In fact, for White's purposes, the "deep structures" of historical thought are actually clearer in nonhistoriographical texts than in the histories themselves.[10] The result is that *Metahistory* restricts itself to a tiny canon of philosophically elite "masterworks" and studiously ignores all other arts and literatures, even those most resembling history as "narrative prose discourses."[11]

In contrast to these approaches, this book shifts the focus away from the individual text to a concern with the features that for eighteenth-century readers distinguished history as a genre—or, more precisely, a group of overlapping and related genres. Thus I would begin by recognizing that history no more constituted a single, unified genre than did the novel or the drama.[12] And since genres cannot be studied isochronically or in isolation, my real concern is the development of the broader system of genres in which all historiographical texts participated. In short, my interest is not (to quote White again) so much in the individual text as an "icon" of the past, as in the ways in which historical understanding structured and was in turn structured by a historically dynamic literary system.

I do not mean to downplay the appreciation of individual histories, which constitutes much of the pleasure of historiographical study. But in reading individual narratives, "masterworks" or otherwise, I am especially interested in the articulating signals by which authors reached out to unseen readers and sought to position their writings in relation to the conventions of genre. Powerful works, of course, might revise or combine existing conventions or even initiate new genres and subgenres. But unlike "deep structures" that seem to enjoy a transhistorical life, genres are historical formations that mediate the communication of readers and writers. For this reason, the marks of genre, though certainly susceptible to complex interpretation, had to lie within the grasp of the "ordinary" competent reader, as he or she was shaped by the literary conventions of the day.[13]

For this reason, genre-study presumes a reader who is historically situated, not the universal reader presupposed by grand taxonomies like those presented in *Metahistory.* We need, in fact, to join in with the eighteenth-century writer,

[10] "What remains implicit in the historians is simply brought to the surface and systematically defended in the works of the great philosophers of history" (ibid., xi).

[11] In a history of the historical imagination in nineteenth-century Europe, practically no attention is given to the novel, to the Gothic revival in architecture, to history painting, to the influence of archeology or geology, or to many other topics of compelling interest. See Raphael Samuel's exasperated outburst in his recent *Theatres of Memory* (Verso: London, 1994), 41–42.

[12] It is not always easy to make this plural sense explicit; "the genres of historical writing" makes too awkward a phrase to repeat very often. I would like, however, to be understood as referring to history in this more inclusive way.

[13] My view of genre as a historical formation (and by implication as an index to changes in literary history) has been much influenced by Alastair Fowler, *Kinds of Literature: An Introduction to the Theory of Genres and Modes* (Oxford: Clarendon, 1982); and Ralph Cohen, "History and

who, in the conditions of an expanded and anonymous book market, was also engaged in an effort to imagine the audience for whose attention he or she competed.[14] In this respect, we will be helped by the notable self-consciousness characteristic of this moment in the history of authorship, when the relationship of writer and reader often betrays uneasiness and writers seem to need to make sure that someone is still listening. Hence the recurring apologies for venturing into publication, the convention of anonymous publication, the continued importance of dedications, though with new meanings, and the recurrent invocation of readers through various forms of addresses in advertisements, prefaces, and textual interruptions. Much of this apparent anxiety disappeared in the following century, or became bad manners to display, presumably because both sides were more used to the idea that writers were engaged in a commerce of ideas with unknown others, that there was a market for words, and that ideas had become a kind of property.[15]

Examining these sorts of gestures will not, with some exceptions, give a picture of the responses of actual readers, for which evidence must be sought elsewhere. But it will point to what we might call the historically specific ideal reader. Such a figure, albeit still an ideal type, has to be grounded in the reading habits of this time. It matters a good deal, for example, that the idea of a female readership for history became a point of issue in just this period. (See chapter 4.) It is important, too, not to imagine this reader in too restrictive a literary context; the audience for history did not confine itself to reading histories alone. For this reason, I am particularly interested in understanding how the cluster of genres most closely associated with historiography was constituted in the eighteenth century and how it changed over time to admit new genres or to acknowledge the power of other, competitive literatures.

Genre, of course, is not a self-contained system. It is a way of mediating and ordering experience, literary and extraliterary. An investigation of eighteenth-century historical writing must obviously ask what subjects eighteenth-century writers and their audiences considered appropriate to historical representation, and it must be alert to changes in the focus of historical interests. Conversely, signals of tension and competition within the cluster of historiographical and

Genre," *New Literary History* 17 (1986): 203–18. On problems of literary classification more widely conceived, see also Claudio Guillen, *Literature as System* (Princeton: Princeton UP, 1971).

[14] The best guide to the complex of issues connecting eighteenth-century prose genres and audience is Hunter's *Before Novels,* a book that has helped shape a good deal of my approach here. .

[15] Recent scholarship has given us a great deal better sense of the expansion of the book market and its consequences for writing in many genres. See, among others, James Raven, *Judging New Wealth: Popular Publishing and Responses to Commerce in England, 1759–1800* (New York: Oxford UP, 1992); Mark Rose, *Authors and Owners: The Invention of Copyright* (Cambridge: Harvard UP, 1993); Trevor Ross, "Copyright and the Invention of Tradition," *Eighteenth-Century Studies* 26 (1992): 1–27; and Cheryl Turner, *Living by the Pen: Women Writers in the Eighteenth Century* (London: Routledge, 1992).

parahistoriographical genres can be an important clue to the ways in which historical experience was understood, and especially to the tensions that arose when new areas of experience were being annexed to the traditional competencies of historical narrative. For a modern historian, one of the most intriguing aspects to be revealed by this kind of genre-study may be what it can tell us about how an ancient literary "kind" subtly and often silently transformed itself to remain relevant to the needs and interests of ever-new audiences.[16]

In short, the writer's need to imagine and create readership links the various genres that competed for the contemporary audience to a wider literary system. For my study it also stands as the point of connection between its formalist concerns and a broader intellectual history concerned with revisions in the contemporary framework of social understanding. Much of this book details the ways in which the formal repertory of historical representation responded to new images of the social world, but it is important to stress the reciprocities involved in this process. The genres of historical writing were not simply receiving an imprint of a problem articulated elsewhere. Rather, historical writers must be understood as actively engaged in revising the social questions that complicated their own formal activity.

Continuities and Reframing

Historians as well as students of other literatures often proceed on the assumption that the period around 1790 marked a sharp break in the history and literature of western Europe. There are advantages, however, to adopting a vantage point that permits us to discern enduring features in literatures so often divided into separate epochs. To a surprising extent, we have continued to see eighteenth-century historical concerns through nineteenth-century eyes, often uncritically accepting the complaints of early-nineteenth-century writers, without taking note of their need to distance themselves from their fathers and grandfathers. Some of the thinnest passages in Collingwood's *Idea of History,* for example, as well as in White's *Metahistory,* can be cited as evidence of this kind of prejudice—one that can only be corrected if we try to hold the writings of both periods at the same critical distance. (See chapter 2.)

A related advantage of the longer view is the opportunity it affords to examine the assumption of continuity itself. If continuities are to be found across this long and eventful period, these must have been continually reinscribed as

[16] In this context, it is worth considering the contrasting fates of history and epic. With hindsight, it is too easy simply to assume that history would inevitably reshape itself as a modern discipline, while traditional epic became more or less impossible to write. On epic and the mock-heroic, see Claude Rawson *Satire and Sentiment, 1660–1830* (Cambridge: Cambridge UP, 1994).

well as subtly reshaped. In fact, one of the prime tasks that challenges a more historical understanding of historiography is an investigation of the processes of reassertion and adaptation that enabled (and still enable) historians simultaneously to claim the prestige of an ancient art and the authority of a modern discipline.

Key to the way in which lines of continuity are asserted and controlled is the creation of authoritative textual canons, a process little studied for historiography. It is evident that eighteenth-century Britain not only saw a continuing revaluation of ancient authors, but also the establishment of a modern national canon. In the first part of the eighteenth century it is common to find worried reference to England's weakness in historical writing, but by the later decades of the century a rapidly formed consensus confidently declared that Hume, Robertson, and Gibbon had removed this stigma.[17] We need both to take note of the sources of the earlier unease about English historiography and to explore the grounds of the growing conviction that Britain now possessed a modern historical literature that had outstripped its French and Italian rivals.

Faced with the baffling combinations of persistence and movement that constitute the real challenge of intellectual history, we need more differentiated conceptions of change than those we usually work with—especially the ideas of "origin," "discovery," and "invention" that are still the intellectual historian's stock in trade. As metaphors for historical change, these notions focus attention on the enunciation of new truths: they assume, in other words, the autonomy of the statement and hence a world of positive knowledge. It is better, I believe, to begin with a figure that takes the situatedness of understanding as its point of departure. For this reason, I prefer to think in terms of "reframings" rather than inventions.

The idea of reframing suggests that statements identical in form may bear very different weights or meanings, depending on the context of questioning. For this reason, I would argue that the primary way in which the movement of ideas takes place is not through the formulation of ideas that are unambiguously novel, but through a repositioning that responds to changing contexts and needs. Reconfigurations of this kind may well be the result of a desire to accommodate new discoveries (e.g. the expanded geographical and ethnographical knowledge of the eighteenth century), but at a more profound level they are also a reflection of the hermeneutics of historical interpretation as it shapes our conversation with history and tradition. In the process, familiar but subordinated notions may acquire a new centrality, thereby taking on new meaning and seriousness in relation to other concerns. (The centrality of "manners and customs" in eighteenth-century thought, discussed in chapter 5, is a

[17] On the English sense of inferiority in historical writing, see Hicks, *Neoclassical History* and chapter 1 below.

prime example.) Equally, older ideas may slip to the side, though without in any real sense disappearing. This has frequently been the fate of prestigious literary genres, for example, as they are relegated within the literary system to places of prestige that no longer hold responsibility.

Classical Eloquence and a Postclassical Subject

The questions I want to raise concern the ways in which history was reframed by eighteenth-century writers working in a variety of related genres. No simple answer is possible since this reframing involved shifts in the underlying conception of the object of historical study as well as in the modes of representation and tools of analysis. As a start, let us examine two contrasting characterizations of history's purposes and concerns, each of which presents itself as the common sense of the age. The obvious differences that emerge have to do with the way in which the initial question is phrased.

If we approach eighteenth-century sources seeking an answer to the question, "What is the purpose of History"—especially if the context is literary or one that indicates the need for abstract definition—the answer is likely to run along the following lines:

> As it is the office of an Orator to persuade, it is that of an Historian to record truth for the instruction of mankind. This is the proper object and end of history, from which may be deduced many of the laws relating to it. . . . As the primary end of History is to record Truth, Impartiality, Fidelity, and Accuracy, are the fundamental qualities of an Historian.[18]

This passage opens Hugh Blair's description of historical composition, a discussion undertaken as part of a larger, formal discussion of belles lettres as a whole. In the more detailed description that follows, Blair will go on to modify the classical outline in a number of important ways (see chapter 1), but the gravity of this initial pronouncement well represents his rather traditional sense of history's high moral purpose and decorum.

If, however, we change the angle of questioning by placing under discussion a text that clearly belongs to a different part of this period's historical interests, we get a very different idea of the consensus of the age. Here is the *Monthly Review* on Sir John Sinclair's *History of the Public Revenue* (2d ed. 1790):

> History, till of late, was chiefly employed in the recital of warlike transactions. . . . The *people* were not known; the circumstances that affected *their* domestic prosperity

[18] Hugh Blair, *Lectures on Rhetoric and Belles Lettres,* ed. H. F. Harding (London, 1783; rpt., Carbondale: U of Southern Illinois P, 1965), 259–60. Subsequent references will be given in the text.

and happiness were entirely overlooked; and the records of many ages might have been perused without obtaining the least information concerning any fact that led to a knowledge of the internal economy of the state, or the private situation of individuals.

Thanks, however, to the more enlightened spirit of modern times, things are much altered in this respect. Readers now expect to find, not only the *warlike* exploits, but the *civil* transactions, of princes, recorded in the historic volume. The *people* claim their share of attention; the progress of arts is considered as an object of importance; industry, agriculture, manufactures, commerce, manners, population, and personal security, are now viewed as objects that deserve a particular degree of investigation. Finance is become a science, and *begins* to be studied as an object of primary importance, by those who aspire to dignified offices in the state.[19]

The easiest way to reconcile these two views of historical writing would be to accede to the reviewer's assertion that the second framework had simply succeeded the first. But, as we will see in examining Adam Smith's views on historical narrative, the wide social understanding called for by the *Monthly* is not necessarily incompatible with Blair's literary conservatism. (See chapter 3.) Accepting the idea that both outlooks are, in fact, characteristic expressions of this time involves some complications, but it surely offers a more rounded understanding of the expectations that eighteenth-century audiences brought to their historical reading.

This juxtaposition of eighteenth-century views makes the obvious point that frameworks of historical understanding depended to a considerable extent on the nature of the occasion that called for such a framework to be articulated. For readers coming to such texts two centuries later, this means that a great deal will depend on the genres that we study and the questions that guide our research. It is important to recognize, too, that although significant aspects of the challenge to traditional practices expressed by the *Monthly* can be traced right across the spectrum of historiographical genres, this challenge is often registered most distinctly in the "minor" genres. That is, it is frequently on the margins of formal historiography, not at its more prestigious and conservative center, that we find the clearest clues to the new demands and interests that operate in modified ways right across the cluster. By the same token, the literary conservatism for which Blair speaks must also be taken as exerting its influence across this whole spectrum, including those genres like biography or the novel that take history as a countergenre against which to define their own audience and identity.

The most easily identifiable reason for the eighteenth century's reframing of historical narrative came from the self-evident power of commerce in contemporary Britain. As Robert Henry put it, "No apology is necessary for introducing the history of Commerce into the history of Britain, which hath derived

[19] *Monthly Review,* 2d ser., vol. 3 (1790): 93–94 (henceforth *MR*).

so many advantages from that source."[20] Behind this unapologetic apology we hear the echo of a deeper difficulty. This was a distinctively modern subject, since commerce had no place in classical definitions of politics and history. As Hume pointed out in the *Essays,* even the Italians, who pioneered the modern study of politics, had barely taken trade into account, though it had since become a preeminent concern for all governments (see chapter 1). Nor was this a casual exclusion; classical historiography, as well as its early modern humanist revival, was predicated on a sharply drawn separation between public and private concerns. Commerce—which we now see as a principal agent in blurring the division between private and public and creating the new form of commonality that Hannah Arendt calls "the social"—had no place in historical narrative because it had no legitimate place in the pursuit of the *vita activa.*[21]

Despite the continued prestige of classical literary models, this exclusion of commerce could not survive the conditions of writing in a modern commercial nation. At stake was the self-recognition of a society keenly aware of how much it owed to the power of trade. Inherited traditions of historical narrative needed to be reshaped so that the political class of a commercial empire could examine and celebrate a history recognizably their own. The only real alternative was that some of the central functions of historical narrative might be taken over by other genres less tied to ancient prescriptions—and, in part, of course, this did indeed occur. Yet to abandon historical writing for more modern genres might mean losing the sense of dignity and consequence that came with incorporating oneself into history's ancient lineage. The larger outcome, therefore, was the incorporation of some aspects of classical tradition into a new, postclassical definition of the nature and subject of historical study.

The power of commerce, however, only gives us the beginnings of the eighteenth century's groping toward a new definition of its historical interests. A much wider spectrum of subjects is implied when the *Monthly* reviewer speaks, for example, of the need for "knowledge of the internal economy of the state, or the private situation of individuals." As is so often the case, it is easiest to say what was displaced: gone, certainly, was the old restriction of history to statecraft and military maneuver—and with it an easy accommodation to the clarity and linearity of classical ideals of narrative. In its place stood a much wider, but less easily defined set of concerns for which contemporaries did not really have a name, though *philosophical history* was a useful term for designating the literary form that did its best to encompass all the parts of this expanded subject. As the philosophical histories of Hume, Robertson, and others attest, the "matter" that history now needed to "imitate" (to adopt the

[20] Henry also stressed that, given the lack of "genuine authentic materials," this was a history that would be difficult to write for many periods of British history (*History of Great Britain,* 6:255).

[21] Hannah Arendt, *The Human Condition* (Chicago: U of Chicago P, 1958).

terms of Aristotle's *Poetics*) had enlarged itself enormously. It incorporated not only commerce and navigation, but the history of literature, of the arts and sciences, of manners and customs, even of opinion and sentiment. It needed to consider the experiences of women as well as of men, of "rude nations" living without the institution of property, as well as of those of commercial societies. But this diversity of subject matter was only a part of the problem; a further challenge was added by the belief that to write history at its highest level would mean being able to describe the underlying connectedness of all of these different aspects of life in the past, each of which was acquiring a literature of its own.

The simple, but fundamental point is that in light of this enlargement of the boundaries of the historical, it was increasingly hard to think of history as exclusively concerned with the narrative of political action. The consequence was not, of course, a loss of interest in politics as such, which continued to occupy a large (though no longer exclusive) place in most forms of historical writing, especially in its most prestigious genres. But Montesquieu, Hume, Smith, Ferguson, Millar, and others made it clear that the possibilities of political action were shaped in a hundred ways by the often invisible movements of economy, custom, or opinion. Considered in relationship to the social framework argued for by these writers, politics as it had been conceived by classical histories—the *vita activa* as a narrative subject—could no longer be thought of as an autonomous field of activity. To an alert eighteenth-century reader, its traditional terms had become superficial, if not unintelligible.

This realization stands behind the repeated observation that Greek and Roman historians failed to concern themselves with much that modern readers would like to know about the conditions of life in the ancient world.[22] Of course, the eloquence of classical narratives was still much admired, and this admiration continued to be linked to the notion that history serves as a literature of moral instruction. But the humanist conviction that this ethical content also amounted to an effective political analysis could hardly stand up when history could no longer define its terms as exclusively concerned with either males or public actions. Indeed, as a definition of history's subject matter, "action" itself would need to give way to more inclusive categories of experience.

The challenges posed by this expanded subject were severe, and they still confront historians two centuries later. But for a culture that remained so close to its classical inheritance, the fact that history confronted a task that seemed largely unknown to the ancients also had a liberating effect. Historians, like

[22] See for example Blair's remarks on the insufficiency of the ancient historians: "From the Greek historians, we are able to form but an imperfect notion, of the strength, the wealth, and the revenues of the different Grecian states; of the causes of several of those revolutions that happened in their government; or of their separate connections and interfering interests" (*Lectures on Rhetoric,* 269).

other writers, felt the "burden of the past" that eighteenth-century literatures inherited with their classicism.[23] Indeed, the problem of belatedness was particularly powerful for British historiography, which suffered not only by comparison to the great histories of the ancient world, but also (as already mentioned) to the modern classics of Italy and France. (See chapter 1.) The construction of a new, definitively postclassical subject for historical narrative meant, therefore, that a new generation of historians could find a useful distance on the still-revered models of antiquity and bring a new confidence to their own distinctive forms of historical inquiry.

Society and Sentiment: The Eighteenth Century's Discourse of the Social

The argument for examining the reframing of historical practice in the eighteenth century can now be given a clearer focus. The reconfiguration I wish to explore is bound up with what I would like to call the eighteenth century's discourse of the social. In using this rather awkward designation, I am following Hannah Arendt's lead in using *social* as a shorthand to identify the characteristically postclassical interpenetration of private and public life, which gave new meanings to both;[24] at the same time, by *discourse* I mean to indicate something wider, if less easily located than a term like "the Scottish enquiry," though Hume, Smith, and their contemporaries certainly played a central part in this reconfiguration. It is important, however, to avoid the impression that these philosophers were the discoverers of a brave new commercial world that was then translated, already formed, into historiographical terms. Equally, it is crucial to understanding the environment in which history was written not to separate disciplines like political economy from contemporary developments in biography or the novel.

[23] Walter Jackson Bate, *The Burden of the Past and the English Poet* (Cambridge: Harvard UP, 1970). This newfound confidence is evident in proliferating celebrations of the historiographical achievements of the age: "Among the various improvements of the eighteenth century, the advances in historical composition deserve a principle rank. Men of genius and philosophical reflection have disentangled the chaos, and, by pursuing a route hitherto unknown, have destroyed the fictions and romances of monkish ignorance and credulous superstition. . . . Latter [*sic*] historians have not contented themselves with a sterile narrative of facts, but, by investigating the causes of the facts they relate, and having discovered them in the passions and interests of men, they assign the true motives which influenced to action, those who make a figure in the history of nations. . . . Such are the writings of a Hume and a Robertson, of a Gibbon, Gillies, and several others, both British and foreigners, who, having written as philosophers, and not as annalists, their histories are a pleasing and instructive picture of the human mind." George Thomson, *The Spirit of General History, in a series of lectures, from the eighth to the eighteenth century,* 2d ed. (London, 1792), iii–iv.

[24] See Arendt, *The Human Condition,* chap. 1.

The discourse of the social incorporates two dimensions of enquiry, which might be thought of schematically as the social and the sentimental. On the one hand, reexamination of the social was directed to the material and moral life of humankind; on the other, to the play of the passions and sentiments in the individual mind. In the final analysis, however, what most fully characterizes the historical understanding of this period is its reliance on the reciprocities linking the social and the sentimental as two complementary kinds of knowledge—the belief that human beings are naturally led by their passions to form communities, and, conversely, that the way to understand society is to picture it as a place shaped by the meeting of experiencing and sociable minds. These reciprocities encouraged the conjectural historian to speculate on the sentiments of the ancient Britons out of his reading of contemporary missionaries, just as they led the "philosophical" traveler to intersperse his notes on foreign places with observations on manners and the lessons of history.

A key unifying element was this pervasive eighteenth-century interest in manners (see chapters 6 and 7). The phrase *manners and customs* is ubiquitous in widely differing genres, where it bridges the most individual questions of conduct and the most remote customs of distant peoples. And, crucially, the language of manners not only brought the hitherto excluded experiences of women into history, but it also made both men and women creatures of custom and habit. These and other reciprocities mean that the literatures most adapted to exploring inward and affective experience—biography, the novel, and various forms of lyric most obviously, but also conduct literature, pedagogy, and even rhetoric—must also be read as part of the formation of this larger social discourse.

For the student of historical writing, the broad range of this discourse and the reciprocities that hold it together are especially important because of the strategic place the historical genres hold between so many didactic and narrative literatures, "low" as well as "high." This means that in considering the evolution of historiography we need to break the habit of consulting only "serious" works of philosophy and politics and search more widely through the literary system. Clues to the reframing of historiographical practice lie in all the surrounding genres and disciplines.

No one will have trouble identifying the ways in which the displacement of political action in eighteenth-century historical writing brought social questions to the fore; the inwardness of history, however, may raise more doubts. The answer to this skepticism lies in the suggestion made earlier that the reframing of historical understanding meant that historical writing would need to grapple with representing something wider, but less easily defined, than action. Poetry, Aristotle says, is the imitation of action, but when we undertake the biography of a poet (as dozens of eighteenth-century biographers pointed out) there is often very little in the way of "action" to recount. Nonetheless, one of the achievements of eighteenth-century literature was to find ways to make compelling reading of lives lived in thought and private conversation. (Boswell's *Johnson* is the outstanding example.) As a result, the emerging genre of literary history became a prime vehicle for those who wanted to evoke the textures of life in another age (see chapters 10 and 11). But the problems of literary history were not unique in this respect: ancient tribes, women at all stages of history, and most men in private life also lacked the capacity to act in this traditional sense. Nonetheless, the new frameworks of social discourse demanded that their experiences somehow be included. In this reorientation from action to experience lay some of the most interesting challenges to history's narrative resources. (See chapter 3.)

Genre and Reframing

It was not very long ago that genre-study was generally understood as an attempt to discover distinct and enduring formal characteristics beneath the fluctuations of literary history. More recently, however, these assumptions about the unity and fixity of genres have been discarded in favor of approaches emphasizing precisely the opposite qualities of instability, mixture, and historical specificity. Reconsidered in this light, genre-study emerges as a prime avenue for exploring historical change and one that lends itself particularly to the idea of "reframing" that I outlined earlier.

Summarizing the changed emphasis in genre-study from fixity to historicity, Alastair Fowler writes that "if we describe the genres in fuller detail, we find ourselves coming to grips with local and temporary groupings, perpetually contending with historical alterations in them. For they everywhere change, combine, regroup, or form what seem to be new alignments altogether." He goes on to say that the instability of genres may upset our aspiration to build systems. "But it is just the activity that genre's communicative function should have led us to expect. If literary meaning works by departing from generic forms, successions of meanings over a long period are bound to change them extensively."[25]

This emphasis on the communicative functions of genre is helpful because it makes it clear that we are not dealing with something either arbitrary or passive, a purely conventional structure confined to a separated world of purely literary usage. On the contrary, genre is a central part of the capacity literature gives us for questioning and ordering the world. Genre, to put it in the terms already used, is a key element of literary framing. As such, genres, like other communicative frameworks, must necessarily remain open to reframing, if they are to stay in active use.

[25] Fowler, *Kinds of Literature,* 45–46.

Thus the communicative function of genre leads us to the historicity of genres; it also points to a recognition that what is communicated is simultaneously something about the world and about the literary system itself. Because of this element of reflexiveness, generic self-definition necessarily involves contrasts and hierarchies that establish the place of a particular genre in the wider literary system. Without such contrasts, in fact, readers would have no way of understanding the terms that mark an individual "kind." Since genre is by nature a contrastive category, it follows that individual genres cannot really be examined on their own. But contrast is only a part of the picture. This same logic of contrast and competition leads to the frequency with which genres combine and recombine, which is a further element in their historicity.

The results of this contrastive and combinatory dynamic may be the formation of new genres or something more individual and temporary. The outcome obviously depends on the responses of readers, a central consideration for any investigation of genre. In fact, everything I have said about genre could be restated in terms of the activity of readers—their competence to recognize the markers of genre, their ability to adapt to new demands, their understanding of a wider literary system, the sense of status or even membership that comes from constituting oneself as an audience to a given literature. From the writer's point of view, then, much of what is at stake in working within an existing genre or attempting to move beyond it can be seen as a matter of selecting or creating an audience.

History as Instruction and Mimesis

To make this general framework relevant to the history of historical writing it is necessary to bring into relief some of the characteristic features of historical writing as they were identified in contemporary discussions. Though the effort is likely to seem overly schematic, as definitional exercises always are, it would be worse to begin by simply assuming that we know what histories are and what place they held within the literary system of another time.

In the classical tradition, persisting well into modern times, a perpetual feature of debates over the nature of historiography was a division between those who identified history primarily as a faithful narrative and those who saw it above all as a literature of instruction. Faced with the possibility of conflict between two versions of history's fundamental purpose, most commentators chose to elide the choice, while in practice giving emphasis either to the instructive or mimetic function.[26] Thus Greek historians generally emphasized

[26] I have discussed tensions between mimetic and didactic thrusts in historiography with particular reference to Italian Renaissance texts, in "Representation and Argument in Renaissance Historiography," *Storia della storiografia* 10 (1986): 48–63.

the idea of history as a strict mimesis, while the Romans—reframing the idea of mimesis to mean political impartiality—gave most weight to the instructive value of history. The Renaissance was heavily indebted to Roman rhetorical traditions, and most writers continued to value history primarily for its persuasiveness and didactic power. This stress on instruction continued to be dominant in the eighteenth century, when it was given a famous formulation in Bolingbroke's phrase, "philosophy teaching by example." But alongside of arguments for "exemplary history," strongly antirhetorical views also flourished in early modern Europe.[27] This counterlineage was associated especially with antiquarian studies, whose practitioners insisted that history's function had less to do with eloquence than with the need to establish a strict record of the past.

Bolingbroke's formula is not only a memorable example of definitions emphasizing history's didactic purpose, but also a useful instance of the way in which classical and neoclassical writers successfully glossed over the differences between mimesis and instruction, ignoring as best they could the potential conflicts between the two goals they set for historical composition. It was not until the end of our period that writers in the Romantic tradition reversed this aspect of their classical inheritance and built a newly heroic image of the historian as a genius capable of meeting and transcending a contradiction that was now treated as self-evident.[28]

The persistent interplay between mimetic and instructive definitions of history provides a useful heuristic in dealing with questions of genre because it points to a range of choices facing eighteenth-century writers and readers. As conceived by classical and postclassical audiences, historiographical narrative emerges as a kind of mixed genre governed by two distinct principles that must be reconciled in practice, but that always stand in some tension.[29] These ten-

[27] For "exemplary history," see George Nadel, "The Philosophy of History before Historicism," *History and Theory* 3 (1963): 291–315.

[28] Macaulay wrote that the contrary demands of truthfulness and imagination make great history even more difficult to achieve than great poetry. Only the truly great historian will be able to reconcile the analytic power of political economy with the poetry of Herodotus. Michelet's famous definition of the goals of history is equally pertinent and even more self-aggrandizing. "Thierry called it a *narration* and M. Guizot *analysis.* I have named it resurrection, and this name will remain." Both passages can be conveniently consulted in Fritz Stern, *Varieties of History* (New York: Random House, 1972), 72–88, 117.

[29] It is interesting to note how thoroughly this tension persists even in our own times where doubling formulas still continue to be required in definitions of history. Stuart Hughes's description of history "as art and science" is an obvious example. Hayden White, too, expresses this tension—as well as the desire to overcome it—when he defines the work of history as purporting to *explain* the past by *representing* it. For White, a history purports to be a "model, or icon" of the past, but Nancy Struever, criticizing White, argues that history is primarily a discipline and a body of argument. White and others have reduced rhetoric to poetics, Struever writes. Yet in fact "the discipline of history is argument," so that the appropriate rhetorical analysis should be "a topics, rather than a tropics of historical discourse." See Nancy Struever, "Topics in History," in

sions were not, of course, unique to historiography—they also reflect the long history of efforts to define the purpose of poetry—but in the terms I have underlined they evidently had a special relevance to historical writing.[30]

In general, as narratives move toward a focus on the mimetic, they concentrate on recording the concreteness of events. Given the breadth of eighteenth-century interest in history, historical mimesis might involve anything from a chronicle of battles to the manners of "savages." Most often presenting the past in this way means emphasizing the satisfactions of detailed narrative, but the mimetic impulse, when taken further, can also result in dissolving the connected narrative in favor of compiling diverse or discrete data. Encyclopedias and biographical dictionaries, as well as the many forms of antiquarian publication, exemplify these possibilities. Perhaps the greatest challenge to historical mimesis in this period, however, came from the desire to represent experience as well as action, and the many narrative experiments that register this ambition stand among the most interesting histories of this time. They also stand, it should be added, among the most neglected, since they do not conform to our conception of what historians should be about in a neoclassical age.

Didactic impulses, too, can take many forms, but in general they involved privileging intellectual order over representational concreteness. This means paring and shaping the narrative to give it coherence and point, endowing narrative with some of the clarity of argument. Pursued far enough, however, the argumentative impulse, like the mimetic one, could break down narrative structures, with the result that the text is reorganized into a set of dissertations. This is a characteristic tendency of eighteenth-century philosophical histories, which generally include dissertations appended to the main body of narrative. By extension, conjectural histories—the intellectual avant-garde of Enlightenment historiography—abandoned conventional narrative entirely in favor of didactic formats, thus bringing history into line with other literatures of instruction.

The heuristic I have outlined can be useful in two ways. First, by bringing into relief the implicit tension between two foci of historiographical practice, the schema helps to account for the range and variety of historical writings in this period. Second, since it seems to be a distinctive characteristic of historical narrative that it acknowledge *both* purposes, the schema also allows us to identify more clearly the lines that connected the historical genres to wider families of mimetic and didactic genres.

"Metahistory": Six Critiques, History and Theory Beiheft 19 (Middletown: Wesleyan UP, 1980), 66–67.

[30] Given the isolation in which historiographical analysis has often been conducted, it is important to underline the point that definitions of history like Nadel's "exemplary" tradition are incomprehensible outside of the larger tradition of efforts to define the purpose and value of poetry. I have explored this idea and pointed to the ways in which the "expressive" literary views of romantic criticism shifted the grounds on which history and fiction competed, in my essay,

Eighteenth-century historiography encompassed a wide and diverse body of writing, but the same interests and structures that created or expressed this diversity also tied history to other literatures.[31] Historical narrative, in other words, constituted a broad middle ground on which mimetic and instructive impulses were worked out, but a fuller picture must take account of other genres that carried further the didactic or mimetic practices that, in more moderated forms, characterized historiography itself. Over time, both literary sensibilities and social discourses shifted, and these neighboring literatures played their part in determining which frameworks of historical representation now seemed adequate to historians and their publics.

The Dignity of History

All genres are not, of course, born equal. An important feature of eighteenth-century definitions of history is their stress on decorum. Witness this definition, taken from Thomas Sheridan's pronouncing dictionary of 1780: "History . . . A narration of events and facts delivered with dignity; narration, relation; the knowledge of facts and events."[32] In Sheridan's formulation, history is both a body of knowledge and a form of narration, but its instructive and mimetic purposes are both subordinated to his emphasis on "genre height." In fact, decorum was inseparable from history's instructive and mimetic purposes. When people spoke in a commonplace way of the "dignity of history," they implied that history should be concerned only with representing events of a certain order of public importance and, correspondingly, that its lessons were addressed primarily to those in a position to profit by them. In the end, then, these definitions were as much social as formal, and, in keeping with the contrastive nature of genre, they were also hierarchical. Thus eighteenth-century readers defined history by the rank and gender of its audience, while "lesser" genres, like romance or biography, had equivalently lower audiences.

As I will show in some detail in the chapters that follow, this definition came under considerable pressure during this period, a result of the expanded tasks set by changing visions of the social, as well as of the presence of new audiences wanting to assert their competence to read history (see chapter 4). Nonetheless the idea that history enjoyed the privileged position of a "high" genre remained important to ways that the genre-map was drawn—perhaps espe-

"Scott, Macaulay, and the Literary Challenge to Historiography," *Journal of the History of Ideas* 50 (1989): 117–33.

[31] This point is made very nicely by John Burrow, who insists that narrative historiography is a "mixed mode" that incorporates a variety of kinds of writing: "It touches on one side the abstraction of constitutional law and political theory, on the other the full-bodied representations of the novel. It demands correspondingly eclectic treatment" (*A Liberal Descent,* 4).

[32] Thomas Sheridan, *A General Dictionary of the English Language* (London, 1780).

cially as "History" was seen from the vantage of competitive literatures and audiences.

Given the prestige of history in this period, writers working in a group of contrastive genres found it a prime referent for their own efforts to secure an audience; or, to be more precise, they constructed an image of history (now too often taken as innocent) against which to produce the formal and social outlines of their own literatures. In this sense, history served as a kind of countergenre helping to define a cluster of related literatures. This strategy of appropriation is common in novels, but it was also a feature of biography, travel, and memoir, as well as literary history, antiquities, political economy, and conjectural history.

The signals given off in this game of maneuver can tell us a great deal about the reciprocities and pressures shaping the historical genres. These genre-signals should not be read literally, though some twentieth-century critics have rushed in to perpetuate the image of history that suited the genre strategies of the eighteenth-century novelist, endorsing an image of a pompous and monolithic history against which to celebrate the agile and populist genre of the novel. This is a form of presentism that, despite all its protestations, fails to take into account the very different relationship between genres before the novel achieved its later centrality. Critics would do well to consider whether—although our current designation of history and biography as "nonfiction" tells much about a *subsequent* literary history—eighteenth-century fictions might not better be defined as "nonhistory."

We need to be better readers of Jane Austen, for example, when in *Northanger Abbey* Catherine Morland confesses she cannot bear to read history, "real solemn history": "The quarrels of popes and kings, with wars or pestilences in every page; the men all so good for nothing, and hardly any women at all." This passage has been treated as an encapsulation of Jane Austen's view of history, but that it clearly is not. Rather it is a lovingly ironic characterization of a girl who still lacks the maturity and education of her companions, the history-reading Tilneys. The deftness of Austen's irony is all her own, but the amount of information that she could convey by so quick a device speaks to the fact that the history/novel contrast was part of the understanding of the literary hierarchy that every novel-reader possessed.

Catherine Morland's reading habits may not say much about Austen's personal views of history, nor about the "deep structures" of the historical imagination. But the reading habits of young women, fictional or real, do tell us a good deal that we might want to understand about how both histories and novels were seen in Austen's time. By extension, they point to questions that need to be considered across a broad spectrum of mimetic and instructive genres before we can understand what history—"real solemn history"—meant to British readers.

The Politics and Poetics of Historical Distance

I want, finally, to introduce one more analytic frame, which is the idea of historical distance. Distance is not explicitly mentioned in eighteenth-century prescriptions for writing history, nor has a concept of distance been a tool of twentieth-century scholarship. Even so, I would argue for its interpretative value, since almost every feature of eighteenth-century practice will prove to have some bearing on the way in which distance is managed. Some degree of temporal distance is, of course, a given in historical writing, but temporal distance may be enlarged or diminished by other kinds of distances, which we might think of as formal, conceptual, and affective. Historical distance in the full sense I want to give it refers to the sense of temporality constructed by every historical account as it positions its readers in relation to the past. Distance includes political as well as emotional engagement (or disengagement) and is the consequence of ideological choices, as well as formal and aesthetic ones. In this enlarged sense, historical distance is an intrinsic feature of all historical accounts, though (for the very reason that it is implicit in so much of what we do when we write history or when we read it) it is one that has been neglected by historians and literary scholars alike.

I began by suggesting that every historical account must position its audience in some relationship of closeness or distance to the events and experience it recounts. Historical distance, in other words, is an issue that confronts everyone who writes in the historical genres and one that is registered in every reading of a historiographical text. But we must also recognize that no single location is proper for all works of history. Rather, norms of distance vary both by genre and by period, and even within a single narrative, effective distance is never uniform. It is important to stress, too, that what I am calling distance necessarily incorporates the full range of positioning, both *near* and *far*. In this sense, distance incorporates the desire to make past moments close and pressing—in order to intensify, for example, the affective, ideological, or commemorative impact of an event—as well as that of stepping back from the historical scene—perhaps to emphasize the objectivity, irony, or philosophical sweep of the historian's vision.

In practice, historical distance is determined by the balance between these opposing impulses, and, as I have said, even within a single work, the tensions between engagement and disengagement will shift and adjust. These variations may register different ideological or emotional responses to events; they may also reflect the ways in which the historian constructs an authorial voice, or chooses to vary the rhythms of a narrative. Unfortunately, we lack a vocabulary for describing these choices and tensions. For want of better English words, I will label the opposing impulses *approximative* and *distanciating:* what matters, however, is not the terms we use, but rather the recognition that the concept of historical distance must be capable of incorporating *both* the desire to figure the past as close or present and (in the more normal sense of distance) the opposing impulse to seek detachment or removal.

The push and pull of historical distance is observable at every level of narrative construction, beginning with the dynamics of the individual work and moving on to broader questions of genre and period. At each of these levels—text, genre, period-style—issues of distance will be explored much more fully in the body of this book; here, I want only to provide a preliminary outline of the sorts of issues that thinking about distance will help to illuminate.

Let me begin with the study of individual texts. Distance is not the property of any single dimension of historical writing. Rather it is a complex response that results from the workings of a whole range of formal, rhetorical, and ideological structures. Thinking about distance, then, involves a broad inquiry into the variety of features of historical accounts that shape the reader's relationship to past events. Stated so abstractly, however, the question may give the misleading sense that I am speaking of universal qualities that uniformly produce effects of proximity or distanciation in some equally universalized reader. On the contrary, questions of distance should be addressed to the specific vocabularies of historical thought in a given time, as well as to all the particular conditions of literature and social life that shape the expectations of specific reading publics.

On another level, distance is also an important feature of historiography considered as a genre, or as I prefer to think of it, as a family of related genres and subgenres. Variations in distance—whether formal, conceptual, or affective—appear to be important to the ways readers distinguish between competing genres of historical writing, or differentiate history from its nearer neighbors. A recent example that will be familiar to most readers is the popularity of microhistory, a form of narrative that is principally distinguished by a flexible combination of the distanciated perspectives associated with general histories and the strong approximative impulses of biography and contemporary anthropology. Similarly, the eighteenth century's taste for biography and memoir clearly owed a good deal to a sentimentalist desire to endow the past with strong evocative presence. But conceptual distance also had a strong appeal in this period: the philosophical and conjectural histories that were such a marked feature of the Enlightenment were generally thought to promise a deeper understanding of the past than conventional narratives of statecraft, a claim that was principally based on the longer perspectives opened up by philosophical judgment.[33]

[33] Hume was typical of his age in expressing the superior power of general explanation. (See chapter 1.) On the ways in which eighteenth-century writers and painters associated the capacity to take a broad view with social prestige and gentlemanly wealth, see John Barrell, *English Literature in History, 1730–1780: An Equal, Wide Survey* (London: Hutchinson, 1989).

Variation in distance affects period-style as well as genre. I do not mean to suggest that each period possesses one invariable norm of historical distance. But it has gone largely unnoticed that such norms do change over time and that changes of distance may have considerable impact on the way in which readers in one period respond to the writing of another. Clearly there was a notable shift in the predominant sense of distance between the generation of Hume and Robertson and that of Macaulay and Carlyle (though not one that was unprepared for in the earlier writers). In the interval, historical accounts lost the air of aloof generality that eighteenth-century readers associated with the dignity of history as historians sought to capture some of the evocative closeness that in an earlier time had been associated primarily with the minor genres of biography and memoir. This change of distance erected considerable barriers between nineteenth-century readers and the historical writers of the previous century. Indeed, the changes in reception proved so powerful and so enduring that (as will be explored in more detail in the conclusion) nineteenth-century assumptions about distance have continued to shape the reputation of eighteenth-century historiography ever since.

Historians of early-nineteenth-century Britain have registered such changes primarily in aesthetic terms, that is, as an extension of Romantic currents of feeling into the literature of historical writing. I want to suggest, however, that if we think of the new historical climate of the early nineteenth century in terms of the framework of distance, we can give the question both a longer history and a more concrete political setting. In the longer perspective I am working with it should be clear that eighteenth-century sentimentalism played an enormously important role in encouraging the idea that we go to history in order to experience a sense of the evocative presence of other places and other times. What is more, I will also argue that the nineteenth century's desire to make history compellingly immediate has as much to do with the ideology of Burkean traditionalism as with the specifically literary influence of romanticism (see chapter 9).

The choices historians make regarding historical distance structure the relationship of the past to the present on every level. Distance, in other words, is both a formal and a social construction, a place where the poetics and politics of narrative combine in ways impossible to separate. As a result, distance has the potential to be an integrating notion in historiographical studies, one that helps us to frame questions that cut across some of the conventional divisions of textual analysis and makes it easier to align the formal features of narrative construction with the figurative dimensions of language and the ideological implications of historical representations.

To this point, I have said nothing about the political frameworks of historical writing that preoccupy so many students of early modern historiography. Indeed, since the central theme of this book is the displacement of political action as the central subject of historical narrative, it might appear that the ideological dimension of historical writing will receive little notice. But the fact that the most remarkable developments in eighteenth-century historiography involve a displacement of the classical *vita activa* hardly means that historical writing lacked a politics. On the contrary, it is important to recognize that the move to reframe historical experience in terms that contemporary philosophical, social, and aesthetic ideas made compelling had important ideological as well as narratological implications. Hume's sentimentalist depiction of the execution of Charles I and Burke's famous invocation of the memory of Marie Antoinette are just two examples of the way in which, despite an apparent turning away from politics, an aestheticized history can carry a powerful ideological current.

There is certainly no difficulty in identifying political commitments in early modern historiography. Historians were often men of party, and their histories were frequently published in the context of partisan debate. In fact, the conventional criticism of British historical writing before its philosophic expansion in the midcentury was that it was entirely too partisan. But pinning party labels on historians (was Hume really a Tory or a special sort of Whig?) is not one of the more interesting questions that confronts students of historiography. It simply continues a long established habit of setting historical writing into already established lines of political debate and thereby obscures the deeper challenge of investigating ideological dimensions intrinsic to any attempt to frame a narratable past.

At another level, the politics of historical narrative can be approached as a dimension of the "fusion of horizons" that Gadamer argues all historical understanding demands.[34] Gadamer's well-known phrase suggests a double engagement with history that joins opposed acts of comprehension and self-recognition in a dialectic of distance. To comprehend history means framing it in ways that aim to give us a sense of meaningful oversight. When this is achieved, we are rewarded with the comforts of moral, intellectual, or aesthetic coherence, even when there is no possibility of turning any of these understandings into action. Yet our comprehension of the past would have little meaning if it were not also joined to some form of self-recognition that makes the history our own. In this way we insert ourselves into the larger narrative, allowing ourselves to be comprehended by history as well as comprehending of it. Thus self-recognition takes its place next to comprehension as two parts of an essential dialectic of historical understanding.

In ideological as well as sentimental terms, this dialectic can be understood to define the need every society has for a usable past. From this point of view, we can say that the reframing of historical writing that took place in this period

[34] *Truth and Method,* trans. Joel Weinsheimer and D. G. Marshall (New York: Continuum, 1995), 306. Gadamer, of course, was certainly not interested in tracing signs of this fusion in the poetics of historical narrative, and he can be criticized for failing to clarify the ideological dimensions of his own work.

is the sign that neither comprehension nor self-recognition was really possible within the framework of traditionally sanctioned narratives. Thus the eighteenth century's reluctant acceptance of the fact that classical forms, though eloquent in themselves, no longer comprehended the sorts of understanding that a modern, commercial society required can be taken as a point of departure for asking more specific questions about what eighteenth-century audiences felt was missing, which literatures they looked to for answers, what kinds of historical frames were in the process of being constructed, and whose need for self-recognition they served.

These are not questions that can be responded to simply by invoking broad generalizations about social structures and ideological positions. Rather, the answers should be traced in concrete problems of narrative construction, where this same dialectic of comprehension and self-recognition takes the form, already mentioned, of the determination of historical distance. Clearly, we should not expect to find a single politics characterizing all the historical productions of this age, any more than we expect to encounter narratives of only a single type. Nonetheless, questions of distance do offer a common focus for an investigation of the widest range of formal and stylistic practices. The play of ironic and sentimental constructions; the seductive power of vast conjectural histories as well as that of unmediated documents; the persistence and prestige of classical narrative, even when overlaid by histories of the arts, manners, and letters; the fascination of ethnographies, literary anecdotes, and memoirs; the prominent use of notes and appendices to amplify the range of narrative; the explanatory power of stadial theories; occasional experiments in epistolary writing; the allure of philosophical fictions; the burgeoning interest in literary biography and literary history; the emerging ideas of public opinion and national tradition as frameworks of historical narration and explanation: all these and still other features of eighteenth-century historical practice play a part in this essential dynamic of presence and distanciation. Whatever other purposes or meanings each of these features of historical narrative reveals, they are also key elements in the ways eighteenth-century historical writings offered their readers possibilities for both comprehension and self-recognition.

THE ENGLISH PARNASSUS

One

David Hume and the Vocabularies of British Historiography

LET ME BEGIN by looking forward for a moment from David Hume to Walter Scott, the great legatee of the Scottish Enlightenment's vision of history. When Scott gave his famous subtitle *'Tis Sixty Years Since* to the first of his historical novels, he called attention to the extraordinary transformation of Scotland since 1745. In the course of two generations, a new Scotland had emerged that was almost unrecognizable from its earlier history. "There is no European nation," he wrote, "which, in the course of half a century or little more, has undergone so complete a change as this kingdom of Scotland. The effects of the insurrection of 1745 . . . commenced this innovation. The gradual influx of wealth and extension of commerce have since united to render the present people of Scotland a class of beings as different from their grandfathers as the existing English are from those of Queen Elizabeth's time."[1]

Along with the rapid transformation of eighteenth-century Scotland, Scott's subtitle also calls attention to an important dimension of historical perception that is more universal: the span of two generations to which he refers not only witnessed remarkable changes, it also provided Scott and his audience with a privileged distance from which to observe this transformation. Two generations put the '45 just on the horizon of living memory. At this remove, when events are still close enough to recall, yet distant enough to have been overtaken by other developments, there is a need both to recover past events and to begin to resolve their singularity into the wider patterns and plots of history. At just such a distance, in short, both recuperation and resolution seem possible. Hence, as many a commentator on Scott's novels has affirmed, the genuine engagement with the past that sets the Waverley novels apart from so many imitative historical costume dramas; hence, too, Scott's ability to celebrate the distinctive textures of other times while affirming the present social order, which is also the product of history.[2]

[1] Walter Scott, *Waverley,* ed. Andrew Hook (New York: Penguin, 1972), 492.

[2] Among many important studies on Scott and the historical novel, see Harry Shaw, *The Forms of Historical Fiction: Sir Walter Scott and His Successors* (Ithaca: Cornell UP, 1983); Alexander Welsh, *The Hero of the Waverley Novels: With New Essays on Scott* (Princeton: Princeton UP, 1992); Ina Ferris, *The Achievement of Literary Authority: Gender, History, and the Waverley Novels* (Ithaca: Cornell UP, 1991); and Peter Garside, "Scott and the 'Philosophical' Historians," *Journal of the History of Ideas* 36 (1975): 497–512.

The commemorative experiences of recent years confirm the value of Scott's perception and may, I believe, help us to view David Hume's historical task with more sympathy than Enlightenment historiography has usually received. The half century that now separates us from the closing acts of World War II has brought with it a flood of remembrance, often mixed with bitter controversy. Fifty years have certainly not resulted in consensus on the significance of Auschwitz or Hiroshima, much less in resolution and forgetfulness. On the contrary, the stunned silence that followed the end of the war has been replaced in recent decades with an ever growing literature in both history and fiction, accompanied by an equally urgent need both to remember and to reconsider. Daily we are coming closer to the poignant moment when living memory cedes, finally and without possibility of appeal, to the constructed narratives provided by histories, novels, movies, and museums. As we absorb this realization, on which one could say all writing of history is founded, with respect to the most terrible events of this century, we may perhaps reach a better understanding of the ways in which earlier generations responded to their own irrevocable passages.

I am not, of course, trying to assert some sort of comparability between the Regicide or Culloden and the Holocaust. Rather, I want only to enlist our present heightened sensitivity to the complexity and importance of historical memory as an aid to understanding the historical outlook of a period when Britain, both north and south of the Tweed, looked back upon a particularly difficult and divisive heritage. In this context, it seems reasonable to call attention to the fact that Hume and his audience stood at much the same remove from the Revolution of 1688 as Scott stood from Culloden. More particularly, I want to suggest that Hume's Stuart volumes can be read as seeking a kind of historical distance that would allow the turbulent epoch that closed in 1688, "sixty years since," to be both accepted and transcended.

This chapter and the one that follows will examine the various frameworks of historical understanding and representation available to Hume and trace the ways in which his *History of England* seeks to find a kind of mastery over the complex narrative problem of historical distance. As indicated in the introduction, historical distance (in the sense I am using it here) does not imply simple detachment. It incorporates a desire to recuperate aspects of the past and make them temporarily present, as well as the reciprocal need to establish longer perspectives or to impose a kind of closure. Nor is historical distance an abstraction. In Hume's history, as much as in Scott's novels, it is an effect of a complex and varied narrative practice: one might even say that it constitutes an important dimension of the meaning of Hume's narrative. This being the case, I will begin with a broad discussion of Hume's vocation as a historian and follow with an exploration of neoclassical and philosophical history, the two principal frameworks of historical understanding in his time. The balances and tensions between these two modes of historical thought and writing, complicated by Hume's attraction to both sensibility and irony, make up the fundamental vocabulary of his *History of England*.

"My Own Life"

In "My Own Life," the brief autobiography he wrote shortly before his death, Hume summed up for the last time his sense of his own accomplishments as a historian:

> I was, I own, sanguine in my expectations of the success of this work. I thought that I was the only historian, that had at once neglected present power, interest, and authority, and the cry of popular prejudices; and as the subject was suited to every capacity, I expected proportional applause. But miserable was my disappointment: I was assailed by one cry of reproach, disapprobation, and even detestation; English, Scotch, and Irish, Whig and Tory, churchman and sectary, freethinker and religionist, patriot and courtier, united in their rage against the man, who had presumed to shed a generous tear for the fate of Charles I and the Earl of Strafford.[3]

This brief autobiography was intended, it is clear, not only as a record of the philosopher's life, but also as a testament to a philosopher's death. His parting summary of his career as a historian carries, therefore, all the poignancy of this moment, when it had become proper, as he puts it, to speak of himself in the past tense.[4] Yet for all Hume's characteristic composure, there is a good deal more than simple acceptance in his retrospect on his first steps as a historian. Though he had long since established himself as the preeminent historian of England, he invoked once more the disappointment of the *History*'s first reception in order to restate his central conviction about his aims and achievements. With all the sincere conviction imparted by the situation in which he wrote, Hume reiterates his faith in his own impartiality and presents his superiority to faction as his highest aim and greatest success as a historian.

The claim to write, as Tacitus famously said, "sine ira et studio" had long been enshrined in the classical tradition as the chief duty of the historian. Nonetheless, Hume's claimed indifference to "present power" and "popular prejudice" bears little real resemblance to Tacitus's impartiality. The story Hume wanted to tell, in fact, reverses that of imperial Rome, moving toward the establishment of liberty, not away from it. The real threat to an impartial account of English history was not subservience to an imperial tyrant, but

[3] David Hume, "My Own Life," in *Essays, Moral, Political, and Literary,* ed. Eugene F. Miller (Indianapolis: Liberty, 1987), xxxvi–xxxvii.

[4] Ibid., xl.

the blind prejudice of party. As Montesquieu had put it, whereas in absolute monarchies historians betray the truth because they are unable to speak out, in free states they do so "because of their very liberty," which enslaves them to the prejudices of faction.[5]

The consequence of factionalism, Hume believed, was that eighteenth-century Englishmen had been unable to achieve a proper detachment from their past—a reflective distance that, wisely managed, would confer a balanced understanding of the weaknesses as well as the strengths of their much admired, much mythologized constitution.[6] Nor did Hume exempt himself from feeling the power of this mythology: in his autobiography he stressed that his own emancipation had only come in stages and had occupied a process of many years. This is the meaning, I take it, of his declaration—so often used against him—that his revisions to the history, undertaken after "farther study, reading, or reflection," had all worked against the preconceptions of the reigning Whig establishment.[7]

In part, of course, all this is no more than Hume's proud insistence that his work owed nothing to the patronage of the great. But the detachment Hume seeks is more than personal; it is also historical. It speaks to his conviction that the conflicts of the previous century could finally be left behind because they had resulted in a new order of government as well as, more comprehensively, in accompanying changes in manners and opinions. This new order was not the work of any single party, but emerged as an indirect consequence of the irregular and self-contradictory politics of the times. "It is ridiculous," he concludes flatly, "to consider the English constitution before that period as a regular plan of liberty."[8]

Perhaps the most striking phrase, however, in Hume's brief rehearsal of his first steps as a historian, sounds a rather different note, which must also be taken into account. Hume's self-dramatization as "the man who had presumed to shed a generous tear" for King Charles and Strafford stands as a further claim to independence of mind, but the personal and sentimental tone seems to move in quite the opposite direction from the reflective distance sought in earlier and later passages. Yet there is no real contradiction. As readers of the

[5] Montesquieu, *The Spirit of the Laws,* trans. and ed. Anne M. Cohler, Basia Carolyn Miller, and Harold Samuel Stone (Cambridge: Cambridge UP, 1989), 333.

[6] For Hume's views on party, see especially his essays "Of the Coalition of Parties," "Of Passive Obedience," and "Of the Protestant Succession," in *Essays.* In a letter regarding publication of the last-mentioned essay, Hume offers a good example of the search for philosophic distance that made up one element of his historiography: he explains that he examines the issue of the succession "as coolly and impartially as if I were remov'd a thousand Years from the present Period: But this is what some People think extremely dangerous, and sufficient not only to ruin me for ever, but also throw some Reflection on all my Friends." *Letters of David Hume,* ed. J. Y. T. Greig, 2 vols. (Oxford: Clarendon, 1932), 1:112–13.

[7] Hume, "My Own Life," xxxviii.

[8] Ibid.

History we soon learn that our sympathy is free to respond to the individual dramas of Charles and Strafford precisely because, on another level, the historian's faculty of impersonal judgment has secured us the necessary distance. But Hume also knew from long experience that this capacity for generosity in detachment could not be taken for granted; it requires careful cultivation and certainly had not yet become general among readers when the *History* first appeared. For this reason, Hume also solicits our sympathy for his own situation as a writer, faced with the combined rage of so many and such different enemies, alike only in their shared inability to distinguish the events of the past from their own immediate interests. Thus the comprehensive list of his enemies—"English, Scotch, and Irish, Whig and Tory, churchman and sectary, freethinker and religionist, patriot and courtier"—becomes the final guarantor of his own claim to reflection, distance, and composure.

To David Hume, writing at the midpoint of the eighteenth century, two generations from the decisive events of 1688, it evidently seemed possible at last to write an impartial and reflective history of this earlier and more turbulent age. He set out to show that the settled liberties of England after the expulsion of the Stuarts were primarily an indirect consequence of the Commons's struggle to wrest powers from the Crown, not—as the Whigs contended—a direct consequence of their defense of traditional powers guaranteed by an "ancient constitution." Of the political results of this irregular and often unprincipled struggle, Hume had no doubt. He believed that the commercial society of Hanoverian England enjoyed a new constitutional order whose liberties were wider and more systematic than was ever the case under the Tudors or Stuarts. In this sense, despite his criticism of Whig prejudices or his sentimentalizing of Tory heroes, Hume remained substantially Whiggish in his politics.

My main concern, however, is not with party labels. Hume's recognition of an evolving constitutional and social order entailed historiographical consequences that go well beyond the issues of political allegiance that so often have monopolized assessments of his work. His overwhelming ambition was to compose a history of lasting value, one raised above its predecessors not only by the elegance of its style, but also by its intellectual clarity and critical distance. But poise and detachment alone would not be enough; a successful narrative that eventually grew to encompass all of British history from the Roman conquest to the Glorious Revolution would need to cultivate a variety of ways of relating to the past, incorporating sympathy as well as philosophic elevation, actuality and vivacity as well as irony.

To accomplish all this, Hume called upon some of the most traditional elements of Western historical thought, as well as many of its most recent and innovative features. The still authoritative conventions of classical narrative historiography, dating back to Herodotus and Thucydides, the new tools of philosophical history to which Hume himself was a major contributor, eighteenth-century wit and sensibility: all these historiographical and literary modes contributed in essential ways to the richness of Hume's narrative. Other historians, as we will see, developed separate elements of this historiographical inheritance further, displaying more openly the tensions that underlay it. Hume's temperament, however, led in the opposite direction, establishing harmony between the several frameworks he had at hand. In the end, the greatness of the *History* lies both in the richness of its intellectual resources, new and old, and in the apparently easy mastery with which Hume summoned them to support his vision of England's past.[9]

The Prospect of Parnassus

"My Own Life" possesses the complexity of retrospect; the prospective view was simpler. In January 1753, writing to his friend Clephane, Hume described his hopes for the history:

> As there is no happiness without occupation, I have begun a work which will employ me several years, and which yields me much satisfaction. 'Tis a History of Britain, from the Union of the Crowns to the present time. I have already finished the reign of King James. My friends flatter me (by this I mean that they don't flatter me), that I have succeeded. You know that there is no post of honour in the English Parnassus more vacant than that of History. Style, judgement, impartiality, care—everything is wanting to our historians.[10]

For all the characteristic self-deflating wit, Hume speaks here without disguise or reservation about his desire for fame in English letters. More to the point, he makes it clear that his hopes rest as much on an absence in English letters as on confidence in his own literary powers. Style, judgment, impartiality, care—these were the hallmarks of the classical tradition, to whose continued authority in historiography Hume seems not to want to offer the slightest challenge. On the contrary, the failure of England to produce a suitable national history beckons to him, offering the promise that a literary Scotsman of no particular political connection might reasonably make his mark as a historian of England.

[9] All students of Hume's historical work are indebted to the scholarship of Duncan Forbes: *Hume's Philosophical Politics* (Cambridge: Cambridge UP, 1975). Other important studies include Giuseppe Giarrizzo, *David Hume, politico e storico* (Torino: Einaudi, 1962); Victor Wexler, *David Hume and the History of England,* Memoirs of the American Philosophical Society, vol. 131 (Philadelphia: Philosophical Society, 1979); David Fate Norton and Richard H. Popkin, *David Hume: Philosophical Historian* (Indianapolis: Bobbs-Merrill, 1965); Nicholas Phillipson, *Hume* (London: Weidenfeld and Nicholson, 1989); David Livingstone, *Hume's Philosophy of Common Life* (Chicago: U of Chicago P, 1984); David Wootton, "Hume, 'the Historian,' " in *The Cambridge Companion to Hume,* ed. David Fate Norton (Cambridge: Cambridge UP, 1993), 281–312; Kidd, *Subverting Scotland's Past;* Hicks, *Neoclassical History.*

[10] David Hume to John Clephane, January 5, 1753, *Letters,* 1:170.

Hume's ambitions were personal, but they also coincided with a long-felt need.[11] Critics agreed that England possessed no national histories that could be compared to the modern classics of France and Italy, much less the best of the ancients. "Our writers had commonly so ill succeeded in history," wrote one reviewer of Hume's *History,* "the Italians, and even the French, had so long continued our acknowledged superiors, that it was almost feared that the British genius, which had so happily displayed itself in every other kind of writing, and gained the prize in most, yet could not enter in this. The historical work Mr. Hume has published discharged our country from this opprobrium."[12]

Britain's lack of dignified and correct histories made for a notable absence. In general, the country's slowness to develop national schools of arts or letters aggravated a sense of inferiority to France that is a persistent theme of British cultural history. It is worth speculating, however, on the particular anxieties that attach themselves to historical writing, since it is hard to silence the doubt that a nation lacking a great national historian also lacks a great history. Indeed, it had long been a rhetorical commonplace that without the eloquence of a poet or a historian to praise them, the deeds of even the greatest heroes would soon be forgotten. Writing in just this vein, Adam Ferguson observed that much of the fame of Greece and Rome could be attributed, not so much to the substance of their history, "but to the manner in which it has been delivered, and to the capacity of their historians, and other writers." If the Greek world had come to us only in the trivial factual records of "the mere journalist," Ferguson concludes, we would never have distinguished the Greeks from their barbaric neighbors.[13]

Hume's own circle in Scotland shared this disparaging view of English historiography. In his *Lectures on Rhetoric,* first delivered in 1748, Adam Smith heaps praises on the classical historians, but dismisses Clarendon, Burnet, and Rapin with brief and unfavorable remarks.[14] (See chapter 3.) Hugh Blair, Smith's successor as lecturer on rhetoric, offered similar views. To him it was evident that in modern times the "Historical Genius" had shown itself most prominently in Italy, though France, too, had made great contributions. Britain, however, "till within these few years," has had little to show (284). But Blair's

[11] Hicks, *Neoclassical History,* chap. 1.

[12] *Annual Register* 4 (1761): 301–4, quoted in Hicks, *Neoclassical History,* 197–98.

[13] Adam Ferguson, *An Essay on the History of Civil Society,* ed. Fania Oz-Salzberger (Cambridge: Cambridge UP, 1996), 185. It should be added that Ferguson's recognition of the power of eloquence takes a form very characteristic of his age. His meditation on the historical fame of the Greeks and Romans reflects a conflict between his veneration of the classics and the new stadial view of history that he pioneered. In light of the Enlightenment's historical sociology, it was difficult to assert that "the character of civility pertained even to the Romans" until late in their history.

[14] Adam Smith, *Lectures on Rhetoric and Belles Lettres,* ed. J. C. Bryce (Indianapolis: Liberty, 1985), 115–16. Subsequent references will be given in the text.

Lectures on Rhetoric was published late enough to reflect the reversal of this old deficiency. "During a long period, English Historical Authors were little more than dull Compilers," he adds, "till of late the distinguished names of Hume, Robertson, and Gibbon, have raised the British character, in this species of Writing, to high reputation and dignity" (285).

The New Rules of Historical Composition: Hugh Blair

As his letter to Clephane indicates, Hume's ambition to write a national history that would earn lasting fame meant that he would largely work within the prestigious idiom of the classical tradition. What was at stake, then, as Hume set out to accomplish his task, was not so much whether he would model his work on classical lines, but how successfully he could adapt the conventions of ancient historiography to the needs of a society whose commitment to commerce and modern manners rendered the task of the historian decisively different from what it had once been. In fact, though recent commentary has had surprisingly little to say about the classicizing strain of Hume's historiography, there are many signs of the *History of England*'s filiation to a long tradition of classical narratives. Its elevated diction, its pairing of "speeches" or analyses on significant occasions, its retrospective summations of character at the end of reigns, its annalistic structure, the linearity of the narrative, combined with strong didactic motifs, all mark out the importance of this lineage.

In the next chapter, I will examine in detail some of the ways in which Hume adapted classicizing conventions to his own purposes and audience. For the present, I want to look more programmatically at what it meant to work within the broad compositional or rhetorical structures set by contemporary prescriptions for historical writing. A helpful resource here is Hugh Blair's *Rhetoric* (1783), a work that better than any other tells us about the expectations that both Hume and Clephane would have had in mind when imagining the sort of history that could earn a post of honor in the English Parnassus.[15]

Blair's *Lectures* not only sets out the broad assumptions of the age regarding historical composition, but also shows how easily its conventional classicism absorbed other contemporary influences. His opening definition, speaking in long-familiar terms, attempts to fix the nature of history as a mix of mimetic and didactic purposes:

[15] Blair was less original a rhetorician than Smith, whose work will be discussed in chapter 3. For this very reason, Blair's popular and influential work seems a better guide to opinion. The book was not published until 1783, but it began life as a course of public lectures in 1759–60 and apparently underwent very little revision after 1760—six years after the first volume of Hume's *History* appeared. See Wilbur S. Howell, *Eighteenth-Century British Logic and Rhetoric* (Princeton: Princeton UP, 1971), 648–74.

> As it is the office of an Orator to persuade, it is that of an Historian to record truth for the instruction of mankind. This is the proper object and end of history, from which may be deduced many of the laws relating to it. . . . As the primary end of History is to record Truth, Impartiality, Fidelity, and Accuracy, are the fundamental qualities of an Historian. He must neither be a Panegyrist, nor a Satyrist. He must not enter into faction, nor give scope to affection: but, contemplating past events and characters with a cool and dispassionate eye, must present to his Readers a faithful copy of human nature. (259–60)

To this point, the emphasis rests on truthful imitation, but in the course of further discussion, the balance shifts from imitation to instruction. A faithful record of facts, Blair goes on to say, is not enough; properly speaking, history is the kind of "record as enables us to apply the transactions of former ages for our own instruction." What is more, the facts recorded must be "momentous and important," and they must be "unfolded in a clear and distinct order" so that events are connected to their causes and their consequences. "For wisdom is the great end of History" (260).

Like his classical mentors, from whom the idea of history as both imitative and didactic literature derives, Blair seems unself-conscious about this shifting emphasis, and certainly he has no inclination to probe the possible tensions between the two. In practice, the mixture is stabilized by his sense of decorum. History as a public discourse is endowed with its own particular obligations and responsibilities: witness, in the passage just quoted, the connection that is assumed between great events, the tracing of causes and consequences, and the wisdom that history teaches. History, Blair goes on to say, serves "to enlarge our views of the human character, and to give full exercise to our judgment on human affairs." Accordingly, the historian "must sustain the character of a wise man, writing for the instruction of posterity" (260).

In short, history's public responsibilities determine its style, structure, and decorum. The historian must maintain a proper dignity, avoiding colloquialism, vulgarity, or affectation of wit. Equally, his narrative must be clearly articulated and tightly controlled. "The first virtue of Historical Narration," writes Blair, "is Clearness, Order, and due Connection" (272). The history should not seem to be made up of unconnected parts. Rather it should be held together by "some connecting principle"—an effect that is easiest in histories of the Sallustian type that trace a single episode, but one that it is still possible to achieve even in general history. In larger narratives of this type—Polybius is cited as the preeminent example—unity in the story depends on a wider intellectual clarity. The historian must master his subject, seeing it whole and comprehending "the chain and dependance of all its parts, that he may introduce every thing in its proper place" (273).

All this stands as a summary of the qualities of rationality, linearity, and dignity that continued to define narratives written in the classical tradition—

the same qualities Hume had evoked in his letter when he spoke of "style, judgment, impartiality, care." But there are elements in Blair's longer description that indicate the presence of other literary and rhetorical ideas, largely sentimentalist in inspiration. These elements blend with the dominant classicism to produce a mix highly characteristic of the literature of the second half of the eighteenth century.

Some of the most telling examples come from passages written in praise of the ancient historians. It is only to be expected, of course, that Blair's aesthetic vocabulary would be that of the age of Gray or Goldsmith; even so, it is striking to see the great ancient histories applauded as "picturesque" or "interesting."[16] Tacitus in particular comes in for praise voiced in distinctively sentimentalist terms: Blair salutes him as a writer "eminent for his knowledge of the human heart . . . sentimental and refined in a high degree" (270). Tacitus's descriptions of the deaths of several of his characters are deeply affecting. "He paints with a glowing pencil; and possesses, beyond all Writers, the talent of painting, not to the imagination merely, but to the heart" (279).[17]

Blair stresses that historical narrative needs to create interest through the sort of details that give a sense of actuality to events: "It is by means of circumstances and particulars properly chosen," he writes, "that a narration becomes interesting and affecting to the Reader. These give life, body, and colouring to the recital of facts, and enable us to behold them as present, and passing before our eyes." This facility is what is "properly termed Historical Painting" (274–75).

Sentimentalist judgments of this sort were a common feature of historical criticism in this period. They appear to reduce the traditional stress on truthful mimesis and public instruction in favor of other qualities that bring the historical scene before the reader's eyes. In fact, spectatorial criticism of this sort does not so much abandon mimesis and instruction as redefine both in important ways. Blair's remarks on "Historical Painting" establish actuality (or presence) as the guiding principle of mimesis, while redefining instruction as dependent upon readerly interest or sympathy. Yet Blair, like other critics who wrote in the same vein, says nothing to indicate that he saw any conflict between these sentimental revisions and his general view of the dignity and rationality of historical writing—a genre that he continues to insist is "addressed to our judgment, rather than to our imagination" (260–61).[18]

Blair also found some important deficiencies in the ancient historians—deficiencies that reveal other pressures to revise the canons of neoclassical

[16] Despite some defects, Blair writes, "it may be safely asserted, that we have no such historical narration, so elegant, so picturesque, so animated, and so interesting, as that of Herodotus, Thucydides, Xenophon, Livy, Tacitus, and Sallust" (*Lectures on Rhetoric,* 257).

[17] Blair is probably echoing Smith's views on Tacitus. On which, see below, chapter 3.

[18] For spectatorial views in Smith and Kames, see below, chapter 3.

taste. While the ancients excelled in the art of narrative, it was also clear to Blair that they lacked the "political knowledge" that the modern world, with its wider horizons, possessed. Their distrust of foreigners, their narrowly confined political experience, and the limited audience for which their histories were written meant that they gave little attention to explaining the questions of "domestic policy" that interest modern readers:

> From the Greek Historians, we are able to form but an imperfect notion, of the strength, the wealth, and the revenues of the different Grecian states; of the causes of several of those revolutions that happened in their government; or of their separate connections and interfering interests. (269)

Here we see the impact of new understandings of society on conventional definitions of historical knowledge. Traditionalist though he was in so many ways, Blair felt sure that it was the historian's task to describe "the political constitution, the force, the revenues, the internal state" of the country (270). For the same reasons, he praised Thucydides, Polybius, and Tacitus, while pronouncing Livy an elegant writer, but one who is little help in understanding the real causes of Roman greatness or decline (269). Even so, Blair remained faithful to the narrative traditions of classical historiography, and he cautioned against allowing excessive didacticism to interrupt the flow of narrative. In doing so, he demonstrated clearly, if unwittingly, the added strain that the philosophical tone of much eighteenth-century writing put on the customary compromise between mimesis and instruction. "But when we demand from the Historian profound and instructive views of his subject," he writes, "it is not meant that he should be frequently interrupting the course of his History, with his own reflections and speculations" (270–71). When a historian is too ready to "philosophize and speculate," the reader will suspect that he has shaped his "narrative of facts" to the needs of a favorite system. In short, history must instruct us through the medium of narrative itself; only rarely is it advisable for the historian to deliver his instruction "in an avowed and direct manner" (271). Even so, Blair rejected the Thucydidean convention of inserted orations, which he felt solved the problem of maintaining narrative continuity only by introducing fiction into its pages. In this regard, he went against the judgment of his predecessor, Adam Smith, who—still more the classicist—firmly maintained the propriety of this device.

Blair completes his review of historiography by examining "the inferior kinds of Historical Composition"—an indication of the contemporary popularity of these minor historical genres, which so diversified the literature of history in the eighteenth century.[19] Annals he quickly dismissed as mere compilations of fact—mimesis, we might say, without instruction. Memoirs, on the other hand, held more interest, though of a rather dangerous kind. A few

[19] Blair also discusses "Fictitious history" (i.e. the novel) in a subsequent section.

memoirs approach the dignity of legitimate histories, but in general Blair was contemptuous of the negligence and self-display of the lesser genre—one that, significantly, he associates with French tastes and talents (285–86). In contrast, Blair warmly praised the usefulness of biography. Less formal and stately than history itself, biography is no less instructive for most readers. The biographer is concerned as much with the private life of his subject as with public actions and may legitimately "descend" to giving an account of small and intimate details: "nay, it is from private life, from familiar, domestic, and seemingly trivial occurrences, that we often receive most light into the real character" (287).

Blair does not characterize the biographical reader, but other texts of the time make it clear that biography's concern with private life makes it more suitable than history for women, youths, and a wide variety of other readers looking for private, rather than public, instruction. In these ways, biography occupies its own sphere of understanding, where it stands in a complementary relationship to history (see chapter 7). This distinct, if subordinate, dignity of biography contrasts with the less reliable qualities of memoir, where the division between private and public life is far less clear and the writer is tempted—or, as Blair says, "witched"—into self-revelations that lead him to wander capriciously through matters high and low, without due dignity or decorum. Biography also had the sanction of antiquity, particularly as practiced by its great ancient exemplar Plutarch, who was "fond of displaying his great men to us in the more gentle lights of retirement and private life" (288).

Having explored this hierarchy of lesser genres, Blair has not quite finished with his subject. "I cannot conclude the subject of History," he writes, in a passage whose placement at the end of this section seems to indicate a modification of his earlier views,

> without taking notice of a very great improvement which has, of late years, begun to be introduced into Historical Composition; I mean a more particular attention than was formerly given to laws, customs, commerce, religion, literature, and every other thing that tends to show the spirit and genius of nations. It is now understood to be the business of an able Historian to exhibit manners, as well as facts and events; and assuredly, whatever displays the state and life of mankind, in different periods, and illustrates the progress of the human mind, is more useful and interesting than the detail of sieges and battles. (288)

This concluding remark returns us to the unacknowledged tensions running through the discussion of history in his time, but does so characteristically with an air of imperturbable balance. Blair seems well aware of the innovative character of contemporary historical interests, but he found no difficulty in appending this discussion to a lecture that in so many ways reflected traditional prescriptions for historical narrative. Examined closely, the passage might be read either as recognizing a substantial disruption of historical studies or as assuming a smooth continuity. The placement of the passage and its emphasis on the "improvement" in historical composition succeed in conveying the sense of effective continuities within an ancient and respected tradition. Yet Blair names vast areas of study that in classical or Renaissance practice were at best the domain of antiquarians. In doing so, he indicates clearly that these are not now matters of peripheral concern, but are as much the "business of an able Historian" as facts and events, and he concludes by insisting that the military subjects that had formed the core of ancient narratives have only a trivial interest by comparison.[20]

A Matter of Balances

Hume's practice, like Blair's prescriptions, can be read as pointing to new, disruptive demands on historical writing or to the remarkable adaptiveness of older traditions. In the remainder of this chapter I will examine some of the balances in Hume's writing, but my purpose is not simply to point out that Hume's narrative depends on classical models even while it incorporates important elements of "philosophical" history, that his theory of politics makes him a "scientific whig" while his political commentary often has the appearance of Toryism, or that new readings of Hume have discovered sentimentalism in a style once regarded as typically ironic. These elements are all important, as is their diversity, but there seems limited value in simply pointing to their presence in the text. Rather, as I indicated at the outset, I want to trace the ways in which these different elements in Hume's historical vocabulary come together and especially to note the way each contributes to Hume's control of both the politics and the poetics of historical distance. To restate this point in the manner of an earlier distinction, I want to indicate how in the *History of England* the modes of representation as well as the forms of argument combine to establish the sense of critical distance that, I believe, was a central objective of Hume's historical studies.

When he had completed work on the second volume of this history, which covered the period of Charles II and James II, Hume summed up for his publisher the differences that the public might find between the two volumes: "I have always said to all my Acquaintance that if the first Volume bore a little

[20] On the importance of antiquities in ancient and early modern historiography, see the classic articles by Arnaldo Momigliano collected in successive volumes of his *Contributi* and reprinted in *Studies in Historiography,* as well as *The Classical Foundations of Modern Historiography* (Berkeley and Los Angeles: U of California P, 1990). I have offered a critique of these views in "Reconsiderations on History."

of a Tory Aspect, the second wou'd probably be as grateful to the opposite Party." The difference, he explained, was owing to a fundamental shift in the way government was understood:

> The two first Princes of the house of Stuart were certainly more excusable than the two second. The Constitution was in their time very ambiguous and undetermin'd, and their Parliaments were, in many respects, refractory and obstinate: But Charles the 2d knew, that he had succeeded to a very limited Monarchy: His long Parliament was indulgent to him, and even consisted almost entirely of Royalists; yet he cou'd not be quiet, nor contented with a legal Authority. I need not mention the Oppressions in Scotland nor the absurd Conduct of K. James the 2d. These are obvious and glaring Points.[21]

The passage is a useful compression of Hume's views on the politics of this crucial period and especially of his verdict on the policies of the Stuart kings. Hume's judgment on these rulers as individuals clearly rests on his central constitutional thesis, namely that the English constitution before 1688 (and especially before 1660) was an uncertain and irregular arrangement, not to be compared to the better-regulated mix of liberty and prerogative initiated by the Glorious Revolution. Equally, the passage reminds us that in Hume's eyes many of the failures of English historiography sprang from the willingness of both Whig and Tory historians to ignore the changing foundation of English government, so strongly did both sides share a desire to make of the constitution a firm and transhistorical entity. Characteristic, too, is the lesson Hume drew for the success of his own work. Attentive as always to audience and reputation, he writes that he now wished he had published the two volumes together: "Neither one Party nor the other, wou'd in that Case, have had the least Pretext of reproaching me with Partiality."[22]

In a letter of the following year, Hume returned to much the same concern, but found a new way to formulate his commitment to impartiality: "With regard to politics and the character of princes and great men, I think I am very moderate. My views of *things* are more conformable to Whig principles; my representations of *persons* to Tory prejudices. Nothing can so much prove that men commonly regard more persons than things, as to find that I am commonly numbered among the Tories."[23]

Unlike the previous letter, this passage says nothing about specific historical interpretations, but its apparently simple division between things and persons points to fundamental balances that give the *History* some of its most character-

[21] David Hume to Andrew Millar, April 12, 1755, *Letters,* 1:217–18.

[22] Ibid., 218

[23] David Hume to John Clephane, 1756 (month uncertain), ibid., 1:237. Hume begins with the still more dangerous question of religious partisanship, an area where he now admitted to have demonstrated a lack of judgment in appearing *too* detached.

istic qualities. Hume's explicit meaning, of course, has to do with the issues of party politics, which I have touched on several times. But beyond these political questions, Hume's distinction carries implications for historiographical method that for our purposes are still more important. Hume's phrasing suggests that he has had in mind two quite different kinds of histories, which he has tried to marry in a single work. On the one hand, the *History* offers philosophical "views of things"; on the other, it showcases several brilliant "representations of persons." Thus, in this quickly drawn distinction between modes of writing appropriate to personal and to impersonal subjects, Hume signals the tension emerging in his day between two historiographical conventions: the exemplary narrative of humanist or neoclassical historiography and the newer, more systematic arguments of philosophical history. Historiographically, then, as well as politically, he represents himself as having to balance two large and seemingly antithetical frameworks, neither of which alone is sufficient for the work he wants to do.

Unfortunately, the scholarly literature on Hume does not make it easy to assess this balance. Intellectual historians have given more thought to Hume's political and philosophical views than to the complex achievement of his narrative. This prejudice in favor of those elements of history that can be reduced to abstract doctrine ("my view of things") is all too common in historiographical studies, but it has seemed almost irresistible in dealing with a philosopher of Hume's eminence. In consequence, scholars have particularly stressed Hume's contributions to the new eighteenth-century genre of philosophical history, leaving a virtual silence about the large proportion of the *History of England* that is so evidently founded on classical models of historical narrative.[24]

It is not hard to understand why this selective picture has come into being. In recent decades historians of ideas have reacted against the long-standing prejudice that dismissed Hume's social and historical concerns as irrelevant to his philosophical career. The result has been a new recognition that his interest in historical subjects did not date from 1752, when serious work on the history began, but was in fact lifelong.[25] Not surprisingly, however, many commentators engaged in reintegrating Hume's historical interests into his philosophical career have focused on the explicitly philosophical elements in his thinking about history. Several scholars, for example, have stressed the importance of skeptical and conjectural methods in both the *Essays* and the *History*.[26] At the same time, the recent upsurge of interest in the Scottish Enlightenment's "contribution" to the development of the human sciences has brought with it

[24] Hicks's recent study is an exception: on Hume as neoclassical historian, see his *Neoclassical History,* chap. 7.

[25] On Hume's early interest in history, see Ernest Campbell Mossner, *The Life of David Hume* (Oxford: Clarendon, 1980), 301–2.

[26] See especially Norton and Popkin, *David Hume;* Phillipson, *Hume;* and Wootton, "Hume, the Historian."

a new sense of Hume's significance as a social and economic thinker. As a result, Hume can now be seen much more clearly as a practitioner as well as a theorist of the "Scottish enquiry."[27]

From a historiographical point of view, these revisions have brought some losses as well as gains. As I have already noted, renewed interest in Hume's historical career has come with an unbalanced reading of the *History* in which the "philosophical" elements capture all our attention at the expense of other, apparently less innovative features of the work. At the same time, to substantiate this picture of the philosopher-historian, scholars have drawn heavily on more plainly stated arguments found in the *Enquiries* and the *Essays,* overlooking important distinctions of genre. In consequence, those elements of Hume's historical thought that can be reduced to philosophical or political doctrines have been emphasized, at the cost of neglecting the complex understandings embodied in a variety of narrative practices.

The "Philosophical Eye"

It is well beyond my scope to carry out an extensive review of Hume's philosophical writings. Rather I want to restrict discussion to the ways in which philosophical history enters into the overall narrative structure of the *History of England.* But before we turn to the *History,* it may be useful—especially for readers less familiar with this aspect of the Scottish Enlightenment—to indicate some of the main lines of Hume's thinking with regard to philosophical history.

Hume's distinction between "persons" and "things" can serve as a useful point of departure. We have already seen that this dichotomy implied the need to reconcile two modes of composition, summarized by Hume as "views" and "representations." In the essay "Of the Rise and Progress of the Arts and Sciences," however, the problem of history is reformulated as a matter of possibilities for philosophical understanding. "What depends upon a few persons is, in a great measure, to be ascribed to chance, or secret and unknown causes: What arises from a great number, may often be accounted for by determinate and known causes." The effective division, however, is not really between chance and causality, since Hume sets aside chance as an analytic dead end; instead, his real concern has to do with a contrast between causes operating

[27] For an early appreciation of Hume's contribution to political economy, see the editor's introduction to David Hume, *Writings on Economics,* ed. Eugene Rotwein (Madison: U of Wisconsin P, 1970). Somewhat earlier, A. F. Tytler gave his opinion that Hume was wrong to assign more lasting success to his philosophy than to his political essays, "which have served as the basis of that enlarged system of polity, which connects the welfare of every nation with the prosperity of all its surrounding states." *Memoirs of the Life and Writings of Henry Home of Kames,* 2 vols. (Edinburgh, 1807), 1:104–5.

on the many and those affecting the few. "The latter are commonly so delicate and refined, that the smallest incident in the health, education, or fortune of a particular person, is sufficient to divert their course . . . ; nor is it possible to reduce them to any general maxims or observations."[28]

Thus, the difference between what affects the few and what affects the many (a distinction close to the earlier division between persons and things) has a good deal to do with what can be known in general terms and what must be understood in more contingent ways—implicitly the particularized world of narrative. "To judge by this rule," he continues, "the domestic and the gradual revolutions of a state must be a more proper subject of reasoning and observation, than the foreign and the violent, which are commonly produced by single persons, and are more influenced by whim, folly, or caprice, than by general passions and interests."[29] For this reason, Hume continues, the rise of commerce is more easily accounted for than that of learning, since avarice is a more universal passion than curiosity for knowledge. Hume's point, however, is obviously not to discourage an investigation of "the rise of the arts and sciences," but to treat a subject dear to his heart with the caution it requires. In short, under the rubric of his general point about knowledge, Hume wants to indicate that historical knowledge incorporates a spectrum of understanding. Experiences common to all of humankind—those responding to "general passions and interests"—are simply those most susceptible to philosophical observation.

The "domestic and the gradual revolutions of a state," the rise of commerce, the progress of learning, these subjects were open to the possibility of systematic understanding, and for that reason they were the proper territory of the philosophical historian. But there was another key reason to focus on questions concerning gradual change and the "general passions and interests" of humanity. This is Hume's conviction that ultimately all government is founded on opinion, a view that turns all history, in effect, into a history of the human mind.

"Nothing appears more surprizing to those, who consider human affairs with a philosophical eye," writes Hume in another essay, "than the easiness with which the many are governed by the few; and the implicit submission, with which men resign their own sentiments and passions to those of their rulers." Force, he continues, is always on the side of the governed, while the governors have nothing to support their position but opinion. "It is therefore, on opinion only that government is founded; and this maxim extends to the most despotic and most military governments, as well as to the most free and most popular."[30] Opinion in this sense is necessarily a very capacious term, and in this brief

[28] Hume, *Essays,* 112.

[29] Ibid.

[30] Hume, "Of the First Principles of Government," in *Essays,* 32.

essay Hume includes under it "opinion of interest" and "opinion of right"; the former amounts to a recognition of social utility, the latter incorporates ideas of power, property, and tradition ("sanction of antiquity").[31] Hume admits that fear, affection, and self-interest also enter into governing, but they suppose the "antecedent influence" of opinion; they are, he says, the secondary principles of government, not the original.[32]

Hume's "axiom" that beneath the appearance of force lies the reality of opinion carries large implications not just for origins of government, but for the writing of history. Historical writing, after all, had traditionally focused on the actions of the few, whereas Hume suggests that a history written with a "philosophical eye" would depict the changing climate of opinion as it affected the interests, fears, and affections of humankind. How, in practice, would such a history be written? A model of a kind, though one remote from politics, might be Adam Smith's remarkable (and very Humean) early "History of Astronomy": a survey of astronomical doctrines from the Egyptians to Newton in which all such systems are considered "as mere inventions of the imagination."[33] Among Hume's own works, the *Natural History of Religion* is certainly a history of opinion, though as a conjectural history of religious feeling in the earliest stages of history, it lacks the concreteness of Smith's essay. In this respect Hume's essay "On the Populousness of Ancient Nations" is perhaps a better candidate. Though cast in the form of a treatise rather than a narrative, the essay examines a wide range of historical evidence concerned with the "moral causes" of population increase in order to cast doubt on the idea that the ancient world was more heavily populated than the modern.

Hume's essay on population has been applauded as an example of his antiquarian abilities and his concern for source criticism.[34] But Hume shows very little of the antiquarian's concern for textual criticism or recondite learning. Rather, as a reader of ancient sources, he most impresses us with his ability to pursue clues to the social habits of antiquity by asking questions that are oblique to the literal messages of the text. In turn, this ability to read texts symptomatically reflects the real strength of the essay, which lies in its resourceful pursuit of a simple but powerful hypothesis about the conditions affecting population levels. For Hume, the causes are not primarily physical

[31] For further discussion of Hume and the idea of tradition, see below, chapter 9.

[32] In the essay "Whether the British Government Inclines More to Absolute Monarchy, or to a Republic," Hume repeats the central assumption of the earlier essay: "It may farther be said, that, though men be much governed by interest; yet even interest itself, and all human affairs, are entirely governed by *opinion*. Now, there has been a sudden and sensible change in the opinions of men within these last fifty years, by the progress of learning and of liberty" (*Essays,* 51).

[33] Smith, *Essays on Philosophical Subjects,* ed. W. P. D. Wightman and J. C. Bryce (Indianapolis: Liberty, 1982), 105.

[34] Wootton, "Hume, the Historian," 288.

but "moral"—a matter of mind and manners (opinion), not of physical limitation. Since almost "every man who thinks he can maintain a family will have one," Hume speculates, population will naturally increase, unless limited in some way.[35] For Hume, this question of limitation implies important consequences since it involves "their whole police, their manners, and the constitution of their government." Accordingly, much of Hume's effort is concerned with investigating the widespread ancient practice of slavery and establishing the depressing effect slavery must have had on the fertility of this broad sector of ancient populations.[36]

Two additional features of this essay should be mentioned. First, as a comparison of ancient and modern societies, the "Populousness of Ancient Nations" necessarily works with an extensive chronology, but the time-scale of the essay is owing to something more than its subject alone. In essence, the essay stands as a fragment of a universal history—a study of fertility in all times and places—and this distanciating frame is essential in establishing many of the particular judgments it contains. Second, the essay is avowedly skeptical in its stance. "If I can make it appear," writes Hume, "that the conclusion is not so certain as is pretended, in favour of antiquity, it is all I aspire to."[37] This deliberate methodological skepticism in the face of received truths is also characteristic of the "philosophic eye."

We could pursue these themes much further in Hume's nonnarrative works, but my real interest lies in examining the philosophical outlook as it helps shape the *History of England*. Before exploring the *History,* however, it may be useful to summarize some of the basic features that have already been mentioned. The essence of philosophical history is the desire to move toward more general truths and systematic methods in the study of history. As a result, the philosophical method does not stand wholly apart from traditional narrative, but is linked to it as a form of critique. In a positive vein, the philosophic method links the possibility of systematic knowledge to the historian's engagement with the most general of causes, namely the "general passions and interests" of humankind. Reciprocally, by establishing historical understanding on the basis of the passions, the philosophical historian can be said to put the human mind at the center of the story, thus shifting the ground of history from action to experience and perception ("opinion"). Clearly the new approach shifts the center of historical concern away from statecraft to a wider terrain that incorporates both everyday activity and inward life: what Hume calls the "domestic and the gradual revolutions of the state." At the same time, by appealing as far as possible to the most general causes, philosophical history

[35] Hume, "Of the Populousness of Ancient Nations," in *Essays,* 381.

[36] Ibid., 383 ff.

[37] Ibid., 381.

constitutes itself as a kind of universal history, encompassing (potentially) not only the fullest chronologies and geographies, but also the widest range of human experience in society.

Philosophical History and the *History of England*

Both the manner and the materials of the philosophical historian can be found throughout the *History of England,* but since Hume gave particular prominence to these concerns in four appendices, I will begin with them. In these four chapters, Hume surveys the constitutional order, manners, commerce, and arts in Saxon, feudal, Elizabethan, and Jacobean England. Hume composed his *History* in reverse order, however, beginning with the Stuart volumes and working his way back to the earliest times, so these sections were composed in reverse order. Not surprisingly, the appendices pursue many of the same themes as the essays and exhibit many essaylike features. Yet despite the obvious similarities in content, the change in context creates very significant differences. Here the arguments of the philosophical historian, though frequently relished in themselves, inevitably take on a narrative function, if not always an explicitly narrative form.

The appendices should not, then, be taken as so many essays dropped into the body of the history. Rather, they are part of Hume's attempt to solve some of the pressing difficulties he faced in moving between two very different concepts of historical composition. The appendices make it possible for the historian to give full attention from time to time to aspects of society that in the main stream of political narrative could find only a limited scope. At the cost of violating the decorum of humanist narrative in this way, Hume's procedure—one of a number of such experiments in this time—establishes sight lines that run through the work as a whole, connecting together a distinctive set of themes and observations. The effect is to ensure that every reader will understand that the *History* always requires attention to more than one level of narrative and explanation. Yet by labeling these chapters "appendices," an innovation that he settled on only in the second edition, Hume also paid deference to the primacy of narrative as prescribed by classical tradition. Sometimes the narrative implications of Hume's philosophical "views" are quite clear. In the third appendix, for instance, which closes the Tudor volume, we encounter again the distinction between particular and general causes already familiar from the essay "Of the Rise of the Arts and Sciences." In the context of the *History,* however, albeit in one of its nonnarrative sections, the observation inevitably takes on new concreteness. "There were many peculiar causes in the situation and character of Henry VII. which augmented the authority of the crown: Most of these causes concurred in succeeding princes; together with the factions in religion, and the acquisition of the supremacy, a most important article of prerogative: But the manners of the age were a general cause, which operated during this whole period, and which continually tended to diminish the riches, and still more the influence, of the aristocracy, anciently so formidable to the crown."[38]

Even where the fit between philosophical instruction and mimetic narrative is less obvious, Hume's philosophical "views" necessarily carry narrative implications, since, for all their didacticism, the appendices are to be read as representations of manners and customs of the times. As such, they describe four crucial moments of English history: Saxon barbarity, Norman feudalism, Elizabethan absolutism, and finally the confused progress of constitution, arts, and manners that marked off early Stuart society from its successor in the eighteenth century. Static when read singly, these four nonnarrative chapters are linked together as a history of a different sort—one that moves above or below the ordinary level of political action to constitute a kind of sketch for a history of civilization in England.

I have spoken of four historical moments, but a crucial fifth stage, the mid-eighteenth-century present, is implicit throughout. In the fourth appendix, which falls after the death of James I, comparison to the present is particularly frequent and explicit. (This section, we should remind ourselves, though it deals with the most recent period of history, was the first in order of composition.) Here, in the absence of the high degree of thematic unity that would mark his first and second appendices (examinations of barbaric and feudal societies), the comparison between the present and the relatively recent past becomes a major organizing principle of the chapter.

Whether silent or voiced, reference to the present is particularly useful to Hume in discussing manners, in part perhaps because contrastive distance provides a kind of thematic unity to a discussion of everyday life that is hard to unify in any other way. "High pride of family then prevailed," Hume writes, "and it was by a dignity and stateliness of behaviour, that the gentry and nobility distinguished themselves from the common people. . . . Much ceremony took place in the common intercourse of life, and little familiarity was indulged by the great" (5:132). In such descriptions, the manners of the past are only visible against the backdrop of present assumptions. "The country life prevails at present in England beyond any cultivated nation of Europe; but it was then

[38] There is no critical edition of the *History;* I cite the most available edition: *The History of England from the Invasion of Julius Caesar to the Revolution in 1688,* foreword by William B. Todd, 6 vols. (1778 ed.; rpt. Indianapolis: Liberty, 1983), 4:383–84. Subsequent citations are given in the text. For more on Hume's explanation of the ascendancy of the crown and the decline of aristocratic power, see chapter 9 below.

much more generally embraced by all the gentry. The encrease of arts, pleasures, and social commerce was just beginning to produce an inclination for the softer and more civilized life of the city" (5:133). A similar structure underlies much of what Hume has to say about the history of commerce, as, for example, when Hume asserts that a "catalogue of the manufactures, for which the English were then eminent, would appear very contemptible, in comparison of those which flourish among them at present" (5:143).

Such passages may remind readers of Macaulay's famous review of the state of British society at the accession of James II. Macaulay's chapter is often cited as a forerunner to the social concerns of modern historians, an honor not extended to Hume. But the real difference between their surveys of British society has less to do with the nature of their fundamental questions than with their different attitudes toward historical change and what I have been calling historical distance. In Macaulay the signs of material change serve to give tangible evidence to support his vision of pervasive progress. Hume, for his part, saw signs of rupture as well as of progress. Accordingly, the appendices insist on the essential differences that make it unwise to draw any direct lines from past to present.

The fourth appendix, for example, begins with just this note: "We may safely pronounce, that the English government, at the accession of the Scottish line, was much more arbitrary, than it is at present; the prerogative less limited, the liberties of the subject less accurately defined and secured" (5:124). Similarly, mention of the "ancient constitution" at the beginning of the third appendix is followed by the explanation that in fact there was a still more ancient constitution before that, and yet another before that (4:355). Nor should we see these ruptures as confined to some abstraction called the constitution. Witness Hume's remark in the fourth appendix that the "manners of the nation were agreeable to the monarchical government, which prevailed; and contained not that strange mixture, which, at present, distinguishes England from all other countries" (5:132).

At the opening of the fourth appendix, Hume writes that without a knowledge of the constitution and manners of the age, "history can be little instructive, and often will not be intelligible" (5:124). Beyond this, however, he offers almost nothing on the way in which the history sketched in the appendices would relate to the main body of the narrative that surrounds and contains it. Yet it is perfectly clear that he aligned these two elements of his work with great self-consciousness. In the first edition of the Stuart volume, for example, this same survey of government and manners appears in the body of the work, where it is introduced with a brief apology for "departing a little from the historical style." In later editions this apology was dropped, but the survey became the "Appendix to the Reign of James I." This change obviously brought the narrative proper closer to classical models, but it also indicated Hume's preference for a structural solution to the problem of balancing his two histories. Henceforward, he left the counterpoint between the two elements entirely unspoken.

The placement of the first appendix is also instructive. Here Hume surveys the customs and manners of the Anglo-Saxons, making little distinction between the Germanic tribesmen described by Tacitus and the rulers of England many centuries later. Yet Hume positions this rather static overview of barbaric society very precisely between the close of the battle of Hastings and the further stages of Norman conquest that followed the death of the Saxon king. For the space of twenty-five pages, the narrative is temporarily suspended, while the character of the defeated people is anatomized.[39] This digression into early ethnography does not suggest, however, that Hume intended to emphasize the disjunction between these two elements of his work. Rather, the placement of the appendix bears considerable resemblance, in function as well as form, to the character sketches that historians traditionally inserted at the end of the reigns of important monarchs—an impression that is reinforced by the similar placement of the other appendices. Indeed, it may well be that for a writer who had his eye on Parnassus, this analogy with an older convention made the formal innovation possible, against the objections of purists, like his friend Adam Smith, who thought that in historical writing any deviation from narrative was simply unacceptable.

The Philosophical Method: Criticisms and Constraints

I want to end this discussion of the various historiographical programs of the eighteenth century by looking at some objections that were raised against the philosophical method. These criticisms had much to do with the way in which this innovation in historiography was absorbed into practice. In the absence of any explicit commentary from Hume, once again it will be necessary to look to his Scottish contemporaries, Smith and Blair, whose views on historical composition shed some light on Hume's intentions.

In this connection, it is worth reminding ourselves of the extent of the contradiction between the two predominant modes of historical representation. As an innovation in historical understanding, the philosophical method ran counter to many of the assumptions of humanist historiography. The new emphasis on manners and opinion as the foundation of social experience radically undercut

[39] "The Norman army left not the field of battle without giving thanks to heaven, in the most solemn manner, for their victory: And the prince, having refreshed his troops, prepared to push to the utmost his advantage against the divided, dismayed, and discomfited English" (1:159). So ends chapter 3, which immediately precedes the first appendix.

It should be noted that Hume includes smaller surveys of arts and manners at the ends of a number of reigns.

the authority of the traditional narrative of public events. As a result it became a commonplace to decry the emptiness of conventional histories with their stories of kings and generals. It is characteristic, however, of the sideways movements of intellectual history that the answer to the philosophical critique was not pitched at this level of historical understanding; rather, it came effectively in continued discussions of rules of historical composition, such as Smith's and Blair's, where the norms of Thucydidean narrative, however modified, remained predominant. Traditional historiography, in short, was defended as a matter of genre, not of social analysis, and on this level there was as yet no real reply.

Adam Smith's *Lectures on Rhetoric* is highly critical of philosophical innovations. "The Dissertations which are everywhere interwoven into Modern Histories," writes Smith, "contribute among other things and that not a little to render them less interesting than those wrote by the Ancients" (102). Smith has primarily in mind the interruption of the narrative to prove a learned or controversial point—an objection also shared by Hume—but he is just as severe about philosophical as about learned digressions:

> The same objections that have been mentioned against Long Demonstrations hold equally against Reflexions and observations that exceed the length of too [*sic*] or three sentences. If one was to point out to us some interesting spectacle, it would surely be very disagreeable in the most engaging part to interrupt us and turn our attention from it by desiring us to attend to the fine contrivance of the parts of the object or the admirable exactness with which the whole was carried on. (102)

This is a nice parody of the excesses of the "philosophical eye," but for Smith this sort of inappropriate kibitzing is exactly what is produced by philosophical digressions: "The historian who brings in long reflections acts precisely in the same manner, he withdraws us from the most interesting part of the narration" (103).

Smith connects the modern habit of intruding dissertations into historical narration to the spread of political and religious sectarianism. Since all parties now make arguments from history, the "Truth and Evidence of Historicall facts" has come to be more closely scrutinized (102). This is an astute observation, which makes particular sense in relation to the kind of inelegant and contentious factional narratives Hume thought typical of English historiography. Smith's observation misses the possibility, however, that—in reaction to these same sectarian battles—a historian might very well wish to "withdraw us" from some parts of history that others have found all too "interesting." As I have already indicated, just such a distanciating motive was, in fact, fundamental to Hume's procedures.

Smith's view derives in part from a kind of purism about ancient practices, as well as from the strict division he maintains between historical and demonstrative writing. (See chapter 3.) But a further element here is his assumption that the main aim of historical narration is to cultivate in the reader a kind of immediate engagement that digressions can only undercut. Hume's practice suggests that he did not share Smith's view, or—more accurately—that rather than prescribing a single historical style or normative distance, as Smith seems to do, Hume wanted to balance passages that aim at cultivating sympathetic engagement with others that deliberately foster a kind of reflective detachment.

Hugh Blair was far less the purist than Smith on the matter of narrative, and his comments on philosophical history place him considerably closer to Hume's practice. Blair, we remember, speaks unequivocally in favor of philosophical method, which he considered a recent and "very great improvement" in historical composition. Though he attributed the change to Voltaire rather than Hume, Blair embraced the attention now given to laws, customs, commerce, religion, literature "and every other thing that tends to show the spirit and genius of nations" (288).

Still, Blair too had some doubts about the literary consequences of this new emphasis, and his comments on this score tell us something of the dangers as well as the advantages of the new method. In a passage I have already quoted, he writes: "But when we demand from the Historian profound and instructive views of his subject, it is not meant that he should be frequently interrupting the course of his History, with his own reflections and speculations." The historian should inform us about the "political constitution, the force, the revenues, the internal state of the country"—all characteristic topics of Hume's appendices. He should "place us, as on an elevated station, whence we may have an extensive prospect of all the causes that co-operate in bringing forward the events which are related" (270). Occasionally, too, Blair concedes, the narrative may be held in suspense while the historian enters into some weighty discussion. But for Blair, the philosophic historian's invitation to us to enjoy his "elevated station" and his "extensive prospects" also comes with a considerable risk to his credibility, and he warns that the historian should be careful to avoid too much airing of his own opinions. History should instruct by judicious narration rather than by too much explicit instruction: "When an Historian is much given to dissertation, and is ready to philosophise and speculate on all that he records, a suspicion naturally arises that he will be in hazard of adapting his narrative of facts to favour some system which he has formed to himself" (270).

The difference between Blair's objections and Smith's are instructive. Smith had warned that argumentative interruptions would distract attention from the narrative, resulting in a loss of the sense of actuality on which, so he believed, historical representation relies. Blair, for his part, worries that if the didactic intention is too strong, the mimetic dimension of the narrative of events will lose its appearance of fidelity. In effect, the reader will suspect that the narrative is contrived and one-sided: that is to say, not so much a faithful representation of events as a disguised argument. By extension, the history would also lose much of its power of instruction if its credibility as a faithful representation were lost.

In short, while Smith thought philosophical histories risked being dull, Blair suspected readers would find them strained or even false. In fact, in the case of David Hume, Blair's comments came very close to the mark, since a particularly vociferous group of contemporary critics read Hume's work as a work of irreligious propaganda. No doubt, Hume's reputation as a freethinker made such an attack more or less inevitable, but it is worth noting the way in which his stance as a philosophical historian unwittingly contributed to the particular angle of attack. One of the qualities of the history that gave enormous offense was Hume's air of lofty detachment in discussing matters of religion. Behind the historian's pose of detached, philosophical observation, Protestant critics like the Edinburgh clergyman Daniel MacQueen saw only a propagandist's attack on the Protestant Church and the party that supported it. MacQueen's outraged response is worth dwelling on for a moment, since—beyond the specifics of religious controversy—it serves to confirm the general tendency of the "philosophical" approach to produce a sense of historical detachment and distance.

Daniel MacQueen was offended by two passages in particular.[40] In the first, Hume applied his customary typology of religious behavior to the Reformation, seeing it as a contest between "two species of religion, the superstitious and the fanatical." Hume's characterization of the leading reformers as "men inflamed with the highest enthusiasm" was certainly not calculated to please, nor did he bother to veil his irony when he speaks of how they "preached the doctrine of peace, and carried the tumults of war through every part of Christendom."[41] But as much as anything else, what enraged these critics was Hume's pose of disengaged neutrality regarding the Reformation. The "elevated station" Hume occupied in matters of religion, already clear in the methods of his historical sociology, was made utterly explicit in a second passage attacked by MacQueen. The principal subject this time is the Roman Church:

> Here it may not be improper in a few words, to give some account of the Roman-Catholic superstition, its genius and spirit. History addresses itself to a more distant posterity than will ever be reached by any local or temporary theology; and the characters of sects may be studied, when their controversies shall be totally forgotten.[42]

[40] Daniel MacQueen, *Letters on Hume's History of Great Britain* (1756; rpt. Bristol: Thoemmes, 1990), 7–11.

[41] Hume, *History of Great Britain* (Edinburgh, 1754), 8.

[42] Ibid., 25.

This elevation of history over theology understandably infuriated MacQueen, but another of Hume's critics, Joseph Towers, responded with an irony that was still more effective. It was indeed fortunate, Towers observed, "that the memory of these two inconsiderable sects should be transmitted to posterity through the channel of Mr. Hume's history."[43]

Hume eliminated both offending passages in subsequent editions, a recognition that in matters concerning England's national church, too much distance might be a dangerous thing.

[43] Joseph Towers, "Observations on Mr. Hume's *History of England,*" in *Tracts on Political and Other Subjects* (1796), 319.

Two

Hume and the Politics and Poetics of Historical Distance

IN A LETTER written to his old friend William Mure not long after he had begun his history, Hume summed up the challenges he faced in his new vocation. "The first Quality of an Historian," Hume writes, "is to be true and impartial; the next to be interesting. If you do not say, that I have done both Parties Justice; and if Mrs Mure be not sorry for poor King Charles, I shall burn all my Papers, and return to Philosophy."[1]

Here, once again, Hume defines history as a meeting of contrarieties, though not this time of "things" and "persons" or of "views" and "representations," but of two sorts of readers and two qualities of reading. And how deftly he divides his tasks between the couple: priority, not surprisingly, is assigned to the male, but Hume makes it plain that both Mures are essential to the way in which he conceives his task. As a magistrate and member of Parliament, Mr. Mure (later Baron Mure) is well suited to symbolize history's public responsibilities. Truth and impartiality, so long enshrined as history's highest duty, are addressed to him. Mrs. Mure, as a woman and a private person, commands the secondary, but still essential dimension of "interest." William Mure, as judge of the historian's obligation to truth—which for Hume as for his classical mentors meant impartiality more than exhaustive research—would be in the best position to pronounce whether justice had been done to both parties. Mrs. Mure, for her part, could be relied upon to know that history is often most engaging when the fate of an individual, not the clash of parties or principles is at issue; at least, she might be more likely to see that when our sympathies are captured by the sufferings of another human being, abstract notions of justice or reason may give way to more immediate human emotions.

The Mures, of course, were real readers, but the swiftness with which Hume transforms his friends into "implied readers" is characteristic of eighteenth-century writing, with its unabashed didacticism and its sometimes extravagant self-consciousness in handling the conventions of literary representation. With readers like the Mures in mind, he could reconfigure the problems of historical composition in essentially social terms. To write history effectively would be a matter of addressing two audiences, differing in taste, interest, and gender—

[1] Hume to William Mure, October 1754, *Letters*, 1:210.

a challenge that, as we are reminded by his joking threat to burn his papers, was not an issue for the philosopher.[2] Characteristic, too, is this use of gender (whose terms are always both real and symbolic) to indicate the distribution of his tasks and especially to explain the presence of new ones. Truth versus interest, impartiality versus compassion, justice versus pity, parties versus persons: Hume embraces the differences between male and female reading to give direction to his writing—to give it warmth as well as clarity, variety as well as order, presence as well as distance.

Once again it is apparent that control of historical distance occupies a central place among the several balances Hume seeks to establish in his work. Mrs. Mure, he believes, will pay attention to the human foreground of events, while her judicious and public-spirited husband will take in a more remote, but wider horizon. The Mures, with their contrasting reading-habits and characteristic interests, signify his desire not only to revivify the experiences of the past, but also to subject them to rational understanding and control.

All historical narratives have to confront the problem of finding an appropriate distance on the past, but for Hume there were particular challenges that made this issue especially prominent. For reasons that had to do with literary ambition as well as political conviction, he wanted to speak to the central chapters of national life, yet in crucial respects he also aimed to undercut the prescriptive authority of those same events. Accordingly, he emphasized the changes in constitution and society that created a substantial *dis*continuity between that earlier time and his own. The Civil War, the Regicide, the Commonwealth, the Glorious Revolution: for most readers, these events continued to be charged with the highest ideological significance. Hume knew that to succeed in rising above the faction-ridden historiography that had preceded him he would have to tame the crude ideological force of his subject, without also robbing it of all its life and present drama. It should be possible, in short, not only to declare that the English Revolution was over, but also to "shed a generous tear" for its victims.

As Hume's appeal to the Mures indicates, his sense of historical distance was the product of competing impulses: a desire to bring the past before us as an unmediated presence, along with a contrary need to seek closure and intellectual order. Since distance is created by the interaction of both impulses, it is not a contradiction to speak of proximity as a mode of historical distance, nor a redundancy to call the opposite end of this spectrum "detachment." Nor should we assume a simple parallelism between narrative distance and historical experience. On the contrary, the relationship is as likely to be reversed:

[2] In "Of Essay-Writing," one of the early essays Hume later withdrew, he defined the essayist's task in somewhat similar terms: he would be an ambassador from "the Dominions of Learning to those of Conversation" (*Essays*, 535).

troublesome memory may produce a need for ironic narratives, while effective discontinuity with the past often results in a stress on evocation and revived immediacy.

It should be clear, then, that in talking about historical distance I do not mean simple withdrawal, though much of what has been said against Hume, both in the nineteenth century and in the twentieth, has amounted to just such an accusation. I will return to this issue at the end of this chapter, but the point is worth flagging early on, since part of the value of this discussion may be to clarify a misunderstanding that has had much to do with Hume's reputation as a historian. In very simplified terms, it can be said that much nineteenth-century historical thought, responding to romantic and historicist influences, privileged the idea of reenactment of past experience. This understanding of history, which constituted both a philosophical and a literary ideal, favored proximity over detachment, evocation over irony. The consequence for Hume and other eighteenth-century writers was an unfavorable revision of the ground rules of historical writing that continues to have its effect in twentieth-century discussions. In short, as in so many aspects of eighteenth-century life, large obstacles to our understanding of eighteenth-century historiography have come from the habit of viewing the century from the point of view of its immediate successors. Ironically, to the extent that we remain the heirs of the nineteenth century's view of the previous century we will continue to have difficulty in assessing the historical vision of the Enlightenment in the more sympathetic and historicized terms that historicism itself demanded.

Orations and Documents

In the last analysis, Hume has to be thought of as a postclassical historian, not a classical one. Nonetheless, he worked easily with structures whose fundamentals were still set by neoclassical convention and he showed no sign of restlessness with a tradition that afforded him wide opportunities to shift his stance and to express a variety of forms of engagement with the past. Stately periods reminiscent of classical oratory, inserted letters and speeches, and death-bed portraits live easily beside sentimental scenes of suffering or farewell, a scattering of philosophical "views," and a host of ironies, verbal and historical. These and other devices shape the impact of Hume's lengthy narrative and allow for a varied play of presence and distance.

There would be little point in attempting to analyze Hume's management of historical distance across every aspect of his narrative. Rather, I want simply to illustrate something of the variety that exists within a narrative whose first and lasting impression is always one of balance, moderation, and critical detachment.

A case in point is Hume's use of the oration. Invented speeches, often arranged in pairs, have long been taken as a salient feature of the classical tradition. In Hume's day this convention was already a subject of controversy. Blair, as we have seen, regarded such speeches as no longer usable, since they introduce an unacceptable element of fiction into history. Adam Smith, on the other hand, defended speeches as a useful convention that allowed the historian to "illustrate" the narrative with reflections and observations. Unlike philosophical digressions, Smith argues, speeches do not "interrupt the thread of the narration, as they are not considered as the authors [*sic*], but make a part of the facts related" (*Rhetoric,* 103). Hume's practice, once again, seems closer to Blair. Though he marks significant occasions again and again by presenting the arguments of the opposing sides, Hume generally avoids staging oratorical contests in the classical manner. Instead he often reports the substance of an argument in abbreviated form, sometimes as a series of parallel clauses in which each point of the argument is introduced by *that*. The effect is to emphasize the argumentative structure of a given position while checking its rhetorical flow.

Speeches reported in this indirect manner may still be attributed to specific speakers and backed by reference to historical sources, but often Hume chose to set the debate in wider terms and to attribute the arguments to groups rather than individuals. On such occasions, the contesting positions are given us in the form of synthetic statements whose purpose is to characterize the division of opinion at a critical moment. Such "speeches" echo the Thucydidean convention, while maintaining a critical separation from it. Here for example is Hume's setting for a discussion of responses to the principles set out in the Petition of Right:

> While the committee was employed in framing the petition of right, the favourers of each party, both in parliament and throughout the nation, were engaged in disputes about this bill, which, in all likelihood, was to form a memorable aera in the English government.
>
> That the statutes, said the partizans of the commons, which secure English liberty, are not become obsolete, appears hence, that the English have ever been free, and have ever been governed by law and a limited constitution. (5:192–93)

A full page of such reasoning is then followed by the equivalent arguments advanced by their opponents ("the partizans of the court"), succeeded by a neutral summary emphasizing the complexity of the issues.

However one feels about the stiffness of this way of anatomizing opinion, it is perfectly clear that Hume has no intention of actualizing the terms of debate so as to involve us in its conflicting passions. Quite the contrary, his procedures imply a deliberate distance and an appreciation of complexity beyond the grasp of most contemporary observers. Yet although this cultivated detachment may be the predominant note in Hume's handling of such occasions, it is far from invariable. And when Hume chooses to give us more direct access to opinion, the unmediated documents have a greater impact in re-creating the emotional texture of the past.

The Petition of Right, which has already provided an example of abstracting synthesis, also offers a ready instance of the contrasting approach. Just prior to the passages already quoted regarding the division of opinion in the country, Hume details the debate that led up to the Petition. In this instance he employs direct quotation to suggest the responsibility of the king for the growing confrontation with his Parliament, as well as to portray the dignity of the parliamentary response. "Take this not for a threatening," James says to the Commons, "for I scorn to threaten any but my equals," while his lord keeper, in echo of his master, adds: "Remember his majesty's admonition, I say, remember it" (5:188). More pointed still is Hume's handling of the parliamentary response, which mixed a determination to pursue their policies with a judicious desire to avoid violent confrontation. "Nothing," writes Hume, "can give us a higher idea of the capacity of those men, who now guided the commons, and of the great authority, which they had acquired, than the forming and executing of so judicious and so difficult a plan of operations" (5:188). Accordingly, through a series of direct quotations, Hume then offers a picture that is anything but abstract of this high-minded and resolute parliamentary leadership. Here, for instance, is a part of what he quotes from Sir Francis Seymour:

> He, I must confess, is no good subject, who would not, willingly and chearfully, lay down his life, when that sacrifice may promote the interest of his sovereign, and the good of the commonwealth. But he is not a good subject, he is a slave, who will allow his goods to be taken from him against his will, and his liberty against the laws of the kingdom. By opposing these practices, we shall but tread in the steps of our forefathers, who still preferred the public before their private interest, nay, before their very lives. It will in us be a wrong done to ourselves, to our posterities, to our consciences, if we forego this claim and pretension. (5:189)

Clearly, in this instance Hume intended to convey something quite different from the summaries of public opinion that follow only a page or two later. Direct quotation gives us, as summarized abstractions could not, a glimpse of individual character and a sense of the vocabulary of parliamentary opposition. But beyond these specifics, Hume also means to convey the emotional resonance of the "spirit of liberty" that, he says, carried "the whole house" to embrace the "sentiments" of the popular leadership (5:191).

A similar point can be observed in relation to other documents inserted in the narrative. For example, when Hume prints a fatal letter from one of the conspirators in the Gunpowder Plot warning a Catholic peer to absent himself from Parliament (5:28–29), it is clear that his intention is not "documentary" in the usual sense; rather he aims to exploit the expressive immediacy that such documents possess. On the other hand, Hume carefully avoids choking his narrative with the more conventional type of constitutional or diplomatic documents, a clear sign of his commitment to classical ideals of narrative. Like his friend and historiographical rival, William Robertson, Hume knew that the best way to maintain the elegant clarity of his narrative was to make use of notes at the end of his volumes for anything that smacked of learned compilation or antiquarian controversy.[3]

Character and Sensibility

Another feature of classical historiography is the portrait, generally introduced postmortem as a final assessment of the balance of virtues and vices exhibited in the life of an important man. The prominence of such portraits is more than simply conventional; it reaches into the very basis of historical study as conceived by classical writers. Humanist and neoclassical tradition viewed history as preeminently a training for public life, and since public life was taken to be the highest sphere of moral choice, history's lessons were as much ethical as political. Thus history's concern with character is twofold. As mimetic narrative, history is largely the story of the revelation of character in action, while as instruction, it is an effective form of teaching that uses compelling examples to train readers to aspire to virtue and to shun the temptations of vice.

Many of the assumptions underpinning formal portraiture were losing conviction in the eighteenth century, but portraits remained a prominent feature of narratives like Hume's, where formal enumerations of virtues and vices serve, as they had always done, to bring closure to prominent lives. Recent readings of Hume, however, have emphasized a less traditional feature of his presentation of character, namely his sentimentalism. Hume himself called attention to this side of his work when he described himself as the man who dared to shed a generous tear for King Charles and the earl of Strafford. In this sense it is surprising, in fact, that it has waited almost to the present moment for historians and literary scholars to begin to notice the presence of sentimental motifs in his narrative. Once the sentimental side of Hume's writing has been called to our attention, however, it is hard to miss how often Hume paints scenes of "virtue in distress."[4] All this, of course, is perfectly in keeping with

[3] A good example of the way that the notes offered space for a more complex investigation that would have unbalanced the narrative is Hume's discussion of the grounds for the condemnation of Raleigh in note 1 to vol. 5.

[4] On Hume as sentimentalist, see J. C. Hilson, "Hume: The Historian as Man of Feeling," in *Augustan Worlds: Essays in Honour of A. R. Humphreys*, ed. J. C. Hilson, M. Jones, and J. Watson (Leicester: Leicester UP, 1978); Donald Siebert, *The Moral Animus of David Hume* (Newark: U of Delaware P, 1990), chap. 1; and O'Brien, *Narratives of Enlightenment*, 60–67. In a wider context, the literature on sentimentalism or sensibility is now a large one. See R. F. Brissenden,

the opportunities provided by his subject as well as the literary values of his age. The difficulty, however, is that scholars have tended to read these sentimental passages in isolation, with little sense of how they relate to other aspects of his handling of character or the wider balances of his narrative.

On one level, uncontextualized response is precisely the kind of reading that sentimental writing invites. The moments of intensified sympathy that sentimentalism encourages have a tendency to weaken the connectedness of narrative. In a fully sentimental narrative, the result is that the story largely dissolves into loosely connected scenes as we accompany the hero in becoming spectators to a series of affecting tableaux. In a narrative like Hume's, however, where sentimental themes are subordinate or intermittent, a different economy obtains. Here the cultivated pathos of an isolated scene leaves us to indulge a moment of feeling that seems free of the stricter imperatives of the larger work. Nonetheless, the moment passes and the narrative resumes its more exigent and complex tasks. In such a narrative, then, it is important both to appreciate the temporary release of feeling allowed by the sentimental moment as well as to understand the broader conditions governing the play of character in history.

Hume's convictions, as well as his subject, provided many opportunities for invoking sentimental sympathy. Not only did history offer its usual abundance of innocent victims, but Hume's own feelings were especially open to those who suffered at the hands of political and religious zealots. In this light, it would be wrong to underestimate the depth of Hume's commitment to Mrs. Mure's compassion.

Some of these sufferers were low-born women of simple faith; some were anonymous victims of persecution or mindless savagery.[5] Without question, however, as Hume's self-characterization emphasizes, the outstanding examples are his depictions of royal or aristocratic executions—including not only Charles and Strafford, but also the deaths of Mary, Queen of Scots, the earl of Montrose, and even of Harrison and the other regicides. Here the victim's high status, personal attractions, and reversal of fortunes heighten the pathos of death.

Virtue in Distress: Studies in the Novel of Sentiment from Richardson to Sade (New York: Harper and Row, 1976); Janet Todd, *Sensibility: An Introduction* (London: Methuen, 1986); John Mullan, *Sentiment and Sociability: The Language of Feeling in the Eighteenth Century* (Oxford: Clarendon, 1988); J. G. Barker-Benfield, *The Culture of Sensibility: Sex and Society in Eighteenth-Century Britain* (Chicago: U of Chicago P, 1992); and Anne Jessie Van Sant, *Eighteenth-Century Sensibility and the Novel: The Senses in Social Context* (Cambridge: Cambridge UP, 1993).

[5] See Hume's pathetic description of the execution of two women (Scottish Covenanters) who refused to say "God save the king" (6:418). These victims of political zeal were tied to stakes on a beach and left for the sea to come in. A classic instance of virtue in distress is that of a young woman who sacrifices her honor to save her brother's life; when she discovers that her brother has been killed nonetheless, she goes mad (6:462–63). The massacre of the English in Ulster offers another example of extreme, but anonymous distress (5:341–42).

Though Hume worked hard to investigate the "crimes" of the Scottish queen, Mary remains one of the most consistently sentimentalized figures in this narrative, as we sense from the moment of her arrival in Scotland as a young queen. People of all ranks, Hume writes, flocked to the shore as soon as they saw the approach of the French galleys carrying her: "She had now reached her nineteenth year; and the bloom of her youth and amiable beauty of her person were farther recommended by the affability of her address, the politeness of her manners, and the elegance of her genius. . . . men prognosticated both humanity from her soft and obliging deportment, and penetration from her taste in all the refined arts of music, eloquence, and poetry" (4:38). Mary's "politeness" as well as her youth and gender mark her for sympathy. But as much as her personal attractions, Mary's loyalty to Catholicism, despite a general campaign to convert her, sets the tone of Hume's treatment. "Soon after her arrival she dined in the castle of Edinburgh; and it was there contrived that a boy, six years of age, should be let down from the roof, and should present her with a bible, a psalter, and the keys of the castle. Lest she should be at a loss to understand this insult on her as a papist; all the decorations expressed the burning of Corah, Dathan, and Abiram, and other punishments inflicted by God upon idolatry" (4:39–40).

Mary's many persecutors make their own contribution to the sentimental scene. Among the cruelest in these early days is John Knox, a man Hume stigmatizes in equal measure for his zeal, his boorishness ("this rustic apostle"), and his misogyny. Hume calls attention to Knox's authorship of *First Blast of the Trumpet against the Monstrous Regiment of Women,* written against Mary Tudor, and comments that his conduct toward his young queen ("this amiable princess") showed that he thought no more civility than loyalty due to any of the female sex (4:40–42).

Mary's later life is hardly a story of simple virtue, but in its last scenes especially, her powerlessness and the calm resolution with which she confronts her enemies bring a renewed innocence. Again, the character of her persecutors, who persist in their malignancy to the final moment, does much to fix our sympathies on the unlucky queen:

> Before the executioners performed their office, the dean of Peterborow stepped forth; and though the queen frequently told him, that he needed not concern himself about her, that she was settled in the ancient catholic and Roman religion, and that she meant to lay down her life in defence of that faith; he still thought it his duty to persist in his lectures and exhortations, and to endeavour her conversion. The terms, which he employed, were, under colour of pious instructions, cruel insults on her unfortunate situation; and besides their own absurdity, may be regarded as the most mortifying indignities, to which she had ever yet been exposed. (4:249)

The emotional character of the scene is reflected in the eyes of the spectators who crowded the room:

> She now began, with the aid of her two women, to disrobe herself; and the executioner also lent his hand, to assist them. She smiled, and said, That she was not accustomed to undress herself before so large a company, nor to be served by such valets. Her servants, seeing her in this condition, ready to lay her head upon the block, burst into tears and lamentations: She turned about to them: put her finger upon her lips, as a sign of imposing silence upon them: and having given them her blessing, desired them to pray for her. One of her maids, whom she had appointed for that purpose, covered her eyes with a handkerchief; she laid herself down, without any sign of fear or trepidation; and her head was severed from her body at two strokes by the executioner. He instantly held it up to the spectators, streaming with blood and agitated with the convulsions of death: The dean of Peterborow alone exclaimed, "So perish all queen Elizabeth's enemies": The earl of Kent alone replied "Amen": The attention of all the other spectators was fixed upon the melancholy scene before them; and zeal and flattery alike gave place to present pity and admiration of the expiring princess. (4:250–51)

This is one of many instances where Hume shows the power of human sympathy over all but the most vicious souls.[6] Yet in speaking of "present pity" Hume also seems to be saying that this momentary withdrawal from enthusiasm and barbarity could not be expected to last and that it would not be long before "zeal and flattery," though temporarily disarmed, would regain their customary power in Elizabeth's court. As for Elizabeth herself, when the narrative resumes she is shown as reacting to Mary's death with a spectacle of mourning that counterpoints the genuine sentiments evoked by the actual scene of Mary's death. Upon being brought the news, the queen "affected the utmost surprize and indignation. Her countenance changed; her speech faltered and failed her; for a long time, her sorrow was so deep that she could not express it, but stood fixed like a statue, in silence and mute astonishment" (4:252). Only after grief had abated a little could silence (the highest tribute of sensibility) give way to other manifestations of sorrow. At this point the queen's feelings "burst out in loud wailings and lamentations . . . and she was seen perpetually bathed in tears, and surrounded only by her maids and women" (4:252).

Elizabeth's superb management of the weaponry of sentimental gesture—a language generally associated with women—here becomes a part of statecraft too. The combination is part of what makes her so formidable a politician, though it adds nothing to her reputation for sincerity. In this sense, the counter-

[6] See, for example, the execution of Lord Strafford, when the populace melts into tears and the executioner himself falters: "Twice he lifted up the ax, with an intent to strike the fatal blow; and as often felt his resolution to fail him. A deep sigh was heard to accompany his last effort, which laid Strafford for ever at rest. All the spectators seemed to feel the blow. . . . Pity, remorse, and astonishment had taken possession of every heart, and displayed itself in every countenance" (6:395).

pointing of Mary's death with Elizabeth's stagey mourning not only comments on the possible abuses of sentimentalism, it also speaks to a split between personal virtue and public office that, in the last analysis, makes humanist assumptions about history as a lesson in character difficult to sustain.

This conclusion is supported by some of Hume's most prominent portraits, including those of Mary, Elizabeth, and Charles I. Mary's portrait follows immediately upon the scene of her death, and should be taken, I think, as in part a kind of correction to it. In this parting view of the Scottish queen Hume must, of course, consider the whole conduct of her life, not just its final pathos; even so he manages a delicate mixture of judgment and apology that retains a good bit of his chivalric attitude toward womanhood.[7] Hume's fullest assessment, however, can only be accomplished by resort to a typically Humean chiasmus: "An enumeration of her qualities might carry the appearance of a panegyric; an account of her conduct must, in some parts, wear the aspect of severe satire and invective" (4:252).

As so often in Hume, the crisply antithetical formulation can be read, depending on one's point of view, either as resolving a tension or making it permanent. In this instance, the effect is to exonerate Mary's private character at the cost of splitting her "qualities" from her "conduct." Thus, despite her actions, she retains a kind of magdalene purity, the quality that shines through in her final scenes of life and makes the sentimentalism of the death scene possible. At the same time, however, Hume alerts us to the severe limitations that surround the sentimental portrait when considered in the larger structures of history. It is evident that in this more restricted setting, personal virtue has limited relevance to the historian's ordinary business of understanding and motivating events. By the same token, if, as readers, we nonetheless appreciate scenes of pathos or sentiment—moments in which our sympathies are engaged with an immediacy that is capable of leaping over differences of time and manners—then the meaning of this way of reading must be found somewhere else than in the old humanist convictions.

I am not arguing that Hume believed individual personality had no bearing on history. Much of this narrative, like so many others in the classical tradition, concerns judgments about the intersection of temperament and opportunity, about the successes or failures owing to calculation or imprudence. What I do believe, however, is that Hume could not sustain the humanist's conviction of the (ideal) congruence of private and public character. In fact, his portraits generally work on the opposite principle and retain what explanatory

[7] To form a "just idea" of Mary's character," he says, we must set aside one part of her life when, "enraged" by her husband's conduct and "seduced" by treacherous counsel, "she was betrayed into actions, which may, with some difficulty, be accounted for, but which admit of no apology, nor even of alleviation" (4:251–52).

power they have by stressing the discontinuity between the office and the man.[8] On the other hand, though Hume certainly felt the attractions of the sentimentalist's vision of transparent private virtue, the resulting understanding of character has little explanatory relevance. The reader's experience of the text is certainly enlivened by these moments of heightened presence, but, in the absence of other justifications (justifications that romantic historiography would later provide), such evocations of character can play only a limited role in his history.

Other royal portraits in the Tudor and Stuart volumes may help to clarify this point. Of Elizabeth, for example, Hume writes that her "singular talents for government were founded equally on her temper and on her capacity. Endowed with a great command over herself, she soon obtained an uncontrouled ascendant over her people" (4:352). But, he quickly adds, though Elizabeth's "real virtues" merited her people's loyalty, "she also engaged their affections by her pretended ones."

In the case of Elizabeth as of Mary, Hume identified the essentials of character in terms of an ideal of femininity that offered no space for public life. Thus Mary's underlying virtues and attractions are inseparable from her femaleness, while in Elizabeth it is precisely the absence of these female virtues that brings political success.[9] If we contemplate Elizabeth as a woman, writes Hume, we admire her capacities, but we also feel the absence of something of the "softness of disposition" and "those amiable weaknesses" that distinguish the female sex. "But the true method of estimating her merit," Hume concludes, "is to lay aside all these considerations, and consider her merely as a rational being, placed in authority, and entrusted with the government of mankind. We may find it difficult to reconcile our fancy to her as a wife or a mistress; but her qualities as a sovereign, though with some considerable exceptions, are the object of undisputed applause and approbation" (4:352–53).

The exemplary function of historiography in the classical tradition was supported by an ideal conception of disinterested male virtue.[10] In Hume's male portraits, however, personal virtue seems largely disconnected from public ac-

[8] See for example his summation of Shaftesbury: "It is remarkable that this man, whose principles and conduct were in all other respects, so exceptionable, proved an excellent chancellor; and that all his decrees, while he possessed that high office, were equally remarkable for justness and for integrity. So difficult is it to find in history a character either wholly bad or perfectly good; though the prejudices of party make writers run easily into the extremes of panegyric and of satire!" (6:427).

[9] Of Mary, Hume writes in the portrait that she "seemed to partake only so much of the male virtues as to render her estimable, without relinquishing of those soft graces, which compose the proper ornament of her sex" (4:251).

[10] On exemplary history, see Nadel, "Philosophy of History." On the classical ideal of citizenship and its transmission to eighteenth-century Britain, see Arendt, *The Human Condition;* and Pocock, *Politics, Language, and Time* (New York: Atheneum, 1971).

tion. Though Hume pays a good deal of attention to the private affections of some of the principal figures, the exploration of private character often ironizes the public role. Hume presents Charles II, for example, in terms of a simple dichotomy between the attractions of his character as a man and his dangerous deficiencies as a sovereign.[11] Regarding Charles I, though the underlying contrast is the same, he builds a more complex and interesting case. "A kind husband, an indulgent father, a gentle master, a stedfast [*sic*] friend; to all these eulogies, his conduct in private life fully intitled him" (5:220). This description comes early in Charles's reign, and the same virtues, retained under conditions of increasing distress, make possible the glowingly sentimental image of Charles that Hume paints at the king's execution. But with respect to the king's public character, Hume cannot permit us the same satisfactions. "The moderation and equity, which shone forth in his temper, *seemed* to secure him against rash and dangerous enterprizes: The good sense, which he displayed in his discourse and conversation, *seemed* to warrant his success in every reasonable undertaking." Much good was promised also by his learning and good taste, as would indeed have been in the case in "any other age or nation." But Charles's too rigid view of his own authority and the spirit of liberty that "*began* to prevail" made for a different conclusion. "And above all, the spirit of enthusiasm, being universally diffused, disappointed all the views of human prudence, and disturbed the operation of every motive, which usually influences society" (5:221).

In the event, as every reader knew, Charles proved incapable of meeting the extraordinary and unforeseeable challenges of his time. But by his deliberately ironic presentation of the king's public character, in which defeated expectations of the king are set against the enduring virtue he possessed in private life, Hume brings new pointedness to the division of character and conduct. Once again it is easy to see why Hume thought it appropriate to shed a generous tear for the man, and why, on another level, it seemed to him a mark of shallow reading that so much of his audience accepted this kind of personal tribute as defining the essential meaning of his history.

Irony and the "Unaccountable" Spirit of Religion

There was a time when Hume's irony figured largely in his reputation as a historian, generally very much to its detriment. More recently, a sentimental reading of Hume has coincided with a new appreciation of his value as a

[11] "With a detail of his private character we must set bounds to our panegyric on Charles. . . . When we consider him as a sovereign, his character, though not altogether destitute of virtue, was in the main dangerous to his people, and dishonourable to himself" (6:446–47).

historian. But if we think of both irony and sentiment in relation to the problem of historical distance, it becomes evident that although these two modes of representation pull in different directions, neither can be understood separately from the other. I would argue, in fact, that any of the sentimental scenes I reviewed earlier in this chapter could be recast in distanced, ironic terms simply by shifting the spotlight from the helpless innocence of the victims to the inhuman grotesquery of the victors. Thus while it is natural for us to open our hearts to the suffering queen of Scots, it is equally natural to draw back from the implacable dean of Peterborough or that "rustic apostle," John Knox. Yet the movements of irony are never simple: in distancing the object it observes, irony may also bring us closer to the narrator, who implicitly invites us to share a privileged vantage on the past.[12]

If sentimentalism suspends the historical narrative from time to time with scenes that make the past seem simple and transparent, irony forces a retreat from this illusion. A good part of Hume's irony, in fact, amounts to a recognition that there is something puzzling or inaccessible in the way people acted in the past. Nothing was more opaque to Hume in past ages than religion. The religious spirit, he says, when it mingles with faction, "contains in it something supernatural and unaccountable," and "in its operations upon society, [its] effects correspond less to their known causes than is found in any other circumstance of government" (5:67). Much of Hume's explicit irony in the *History* is occasioned by this baffling spirit of religion, both as it infects the actions of individuals and as it shapes the manners of the whole age. Like other skeptical rationalists before and since, Hume can well see that individuals inspired by deep attachment to faith are sometimes capable of extraordinary acts of strength or courage; still, it seems to take a genuine effort on his part to remind himself that the attractions of Puritanism were not confined to persons of weak understanding: "Some men of the greatest parts and most extensive knowledge, that the nation, at this time, produced, could not enjoy any peace of mind; because obliged to hear prayers offered up to the Divinity, by a priest covered with a white linen vestment" (5:159).

Much of Hume's irony is overtly satirical. Witness his comments on James I, who, out of timidity and indolence, maintained "a very prudent inattention" to foreign affairs, until roused to action by "a dangerous rival in scholastic fame," a Dutch professor of divinity (5:46). In a similar vein he remarks that although James II understood the power of religious feeling in his own heart, he never could conceive that it might "have a proportionable authority over his subjects" (6:489). Carried to extremes, this sort of irony can so diminish the sense of any authentic consciousness in the historical

[12] On narratorial irony as an invitation to intimacy, see Gossman, *Between History and Literature*, 243.

agent that no exchange of sympathies is conceivable. In Hume's narrative, this more or less complete denial of sympathy is particularly likely to hold for those who represent the extremes of religious "enthusiasm": the Puritans, for instance, who renamed themselves with unlikely religious tags ("Accepted, Trevor of Northam"—"Fight the good Fight of Faith, White of Emer" (6:62); the Quaker James Naylor, who in imitation of Christ entered Bristol mounted on a horse, "I suppose from the difficulty in that place of finding an ass" (6:145); the Scottish clergy to whom everything seemed "impious, but their own mystical comments on the Scriptures, which they idolized and whose eastern prophetic style they employed in every common occurrence" (5:69).

One of Hume's consistent targets is anti-Catholicism, a form of "bigotry" to which not just "enthusiasts" but the widest circles of English Protestantism unhesitatingly subscribed. Witness the following remarks on the trial of a woman accused of complicity in a poisoning:

> It may not be unworthy of remark that [Sir Edward] Coke, in the trial of Mrs. Turner, told her, that she was guilty of the seven deadly sins: She was a whore, a bawd, a sorcerer, a witch, a papist, a felon, and a murderer. And what may more surprize us, Bacon, then attorney general, took care to observe, that poisoning was a popish trick. Such were the bigotted prejudices which prevailed: Poisoning was not, of itself, sufficiently odious, if it were not represented as a branch of popery. (5:62)

Hume's target here is obviously not the personal religious character of Coke and Bacon. Rather the narrow prejudice of two men famous for law and literature is intended once again to support Hume's view that the English were the most bigoted of European nations.[13] In this case, however, Hume seems unable to sustain the ironic tone, and the passage slips from irony into earnestness. It is hard to know whether Hume's need for explicitness here is simply evidence of the intensity of his convictions or—since irony depends upon being sure of one's audience—a sign of his faltering confidence whether, when it came to anti-Catholicism, even in the polite eighteenth century, Englishmen could yet be trusted to draw the moral themselves.[14]

[13] "And it plainly appears from this incident, as well as from many others, that, of all European nations, the British were at that time, and till long after, the most under the influence of that religious spirit, which tends rather to inflame bigotry than encrease peace and mutual charity" (5:164).

[14] The passage illustrates my earlier point that the difference between a sentimental and an ironic treatment has much to do with whether the focus is on the victim or the tormentor. Hume keeps our attention focused on Coke and Bacon, and there is no question of our developing sympathy with the victim. For another example of persecution where the victims are not characterized, see Hume's comments on the rage to stamp out witchcraft in Scotland (6:27–28).

Constitutional Change and the Manners of the Age

It would be very hard, then, to find in Hume any element of sympathy for the religious spirit of the seventeenth century. Even so, the fractious religiosity of the times served as a constant reminder that those days were very different from his own and that they required a particular effort of understanding.

In good part, Hume approached the question of difference by reference to a scheme of constitutional change, allied to a wider conception of the manners and "genius" of the times. There is no need to outline once again Hume's view of the English constitution under the Stuarts, or its differences from the more perfect system of liberties that had prevailed since 1688.[15] In the context of the present discussion, however, it is important to observe the way in which Hume accepts the logic of his constitutional argument as requiring us to lend a kind of tolerant understanding to both parties, neither of which—from the vantage of the present—could be expected to avoid entanglement in the ironies of history.

I am not here referring to the ironies arising from local and specific misjudgments: in the history of a turbulent era, when participants were often blind to the consequences of their actions, opportunities for dramatic irony were sure to arise. Both the historian and the reader knew, for example, as Charles I could not, that it would prove a disastrous mistake to prevent the emigration of Hampen, Pym, and Cromwell, who had decided to abandon England for America, "where they might enjoy lectures and discourses of any length or form which might please them" (5:242).[16] But beyond such specific ironies we are always aware of Hume's view of the seventeenth century as a time when England was undergoing a political and social transformation whose dimensions none of the participants could be expected to grasp.[17] Hume raises the question, for example, of the Commons's persistent recalcitrance in providing adequate financing to the Crown, even though the burden of government "at

[15] See especially, Forbes, *Hume's Philosophical Politics;* and Phillipson, *Hume.*

[16] See, similarly, his comments on James II's escape to France: "As if this measure had not been the most grateful to his enemies of any that he could adopt, he had carefully concealed his intention from all the world" (6:516).

[17] Hume explicitly embraces the need for a historically flexible standard of judgment in discussing Laud's abuse of Star Chamber. "The severity of the star-chamber, which was generally ascribed to Laud's passionate disposition, was, perhaps, in itself, somewhat blameable; but will naturally, to us, appear enormous, who enjoy, in the utmost latitude, that liberty of the press, which is esteemed so necessary in every monarchy, confined by strict legal limitations. But as these limitations were not regularly fixed during the age of Charles, nor at any time before, so was this liberty totally unknown, and was generally deemed as well as religious toleration, incompatible with all good government. No age or nation, among the moderns, had ever set an example of such an indulgence: And it seems unreasonable to judge of the measures, embraced during one period, by the maxims, which prevail in another" (5:240).

that time" was surprisingly light. In his view, however, "that very reason, which to us, at this distance, may seem a motive of generosity, was the real cause why the parliament was, on all occasions, so remarkably frugal and reserved" (5:22). Parliament had not yet become accustomed, he writes, to supplying the Crown more generously.

Conversely, when Charles I threatened the Commons for its attacks on the duke of Buckingham, his favorite, Hume stresses the novelty of the shifts in social and economic power that underlay the new relationship of power:

> No one was at that time sufficiently sensible of the great weight, which the commons bore in the balance of the constitution. The history of England had never hitherto afforded one instance where any great movement or revolution had proceeded from the lower house. And as their rank, both considered in a body and as individuals, was but the second in the kingdom; nothing less than fatal experience could engage the English princes to pay a due regard to the inclination of that formidable assembly. (5:170)

In part, Hume's warning against unconsidered judgment aims to head off the possibility that we might find ourselves so out of sympathy with either of the parties as to lose a sense of the contest. More broadly, however, the result of his coaching is not to engage us with particular individuals or parties, but rather to involve us in a larger process that necessarily lies beyond the actions or understanding of the participants themselves.

In such instances, it is implied, the mistake belongs less to the historical actors than to the historian who fails to benefit from the perspective of history. Thus it is entirely possible for Hume, without abandoning his habitual perspectives, to urge us toward more tolerant standards of judgment, or even at times to speak in favor of what sounds like a kind of historical relativism. It "seems unreasonable," he writes at one point, "to judge of the measures, embraced during one period, by the maxims, which prevail in another" (5:240). In marking these views, however, I am not arguing that Hume was a nineteenth-century historicist before the fact.[18] My point, rather, is to emphasize once again the continual interplay of distance and presence, of judgment and acceptance. Hume's distance, in fact, is never merely detachment—though, as we will see shortly, that continues to be the view of some hostile readers even in this century.

Much the same point can be made about his present-mindedness, for which he, like other Enlightenment historians, has been much criticized. It should be considered, however, that when the vantage of the present is as self-conscious as it is in Hume and when the emphasis also falls upon a pervasive change in the nature of society and government, the resulting cultivation of historical

[18] Here I have to disagree with Livingstone, who appears to construct Hume as a kind of early Collingwoodian. See Livingstone, *Hume's Philosophy*, chap. 8.

distance allows the historian to credit both sides with good faith and even to enter into their opposing causes with some degree of sympathy.

Beyond constitutional change, however, a still longer perspective on the seventeenth century was opened up by philosophical history's interest in manners and customs. I have already discussed Hume's philosophical framework at some length, particularly as projected by the appendices: I want only to direct attention to a striking passage in volume 6 that can serve as a reminder of the importance of the philosophical frame to matters of historical distance. Hume sums up the effect of the Civil War and the Restoration on English society as follows: "No people could undergo a change more sudden and entire in their manners than did the English nation during this period. From tranquillity, concord, submission, sobriety, they had passed in an instant to a state of faction, fanaticism, rebellion, and almost frenzy. The violence of the English parties exceeded any thing which we can now imagine" (6:141). The transformation produced a social rupture so deep that there resulted a cessation of all social intercourse between the two sides. "The manners of the two factions," he writes, "were as opposite as those of the most distant nations."

The terms in which Hume contrasts the manners of the Royalists and their enemies were hardly meant to evoke sympathy, and he is particularly hard on the "gloomy enthusiasm" of the defeated parliamentarians. Nonetheless, we should not miss the effect of Hume's resort to the language of philosophical history. The only way to understand the profound transformations of the past century, he seems to be saying, is to work in the very widest terms available, to adopt, in fact, the anthropological framework with which Enlightenment writers had learned to understand remote civilizations or barbaric tribes. How else to think about a habit of violence that he finds beyond present imagination? How else to imagine a social divide so deep that the English seemed split not merely into two nations, but distant ones at that?

What, then, is Hume's vantage on this generation-long eruption of violence beyond imagination, on this nation split into two warring cultures? Once again, it seems useful to invoke Scott's sense of looking back over an epochal divide—of describing a society so transformed that he could say that "the present people of Scotland [are] a class of beings as different from their grandfathers as the existing English are from those of Queen Elizabeth's time." Hume, of course, was writing his history at the time of those Scottish grandfathers. Thus he experienced in his own lifetime a part of the transformation of Scotland that Scott would later try to recapture. In his *History of England,* he himself looked across an earlier divide and wrote to an English audience two generations closer to the time of Elizabeth. Their need, as Hume saw it, was to understand the revolution of manners and constitution that *their* grandparents had accomplished in the previous century and, like Edward Waverley, to accept the burdens of living in a new historical age.

Distance and Proximity as Historiographical Norms

By the time Hume composed his history there was already a considerable tradition of English historical writing, and though Hume keeps his references to earlier historiography quite general—saving more specific discussion for the notes—no reader of the *History of England* will be unaware that the present account has been *constructed* by an author whose work, in part, has been a matter of weighing and sifting earlier accounts. This sense of a tradition of narratives seems to me an important undercurrent in the text. Among other things, it is a part of the way in which Hume tunes his narrator's voice, which is itself a considerable factor in his control of historical distance. Nothing in the history itself, however, offers so explicit an insight into Hume's awareness of his relationship to prior historiography as a remark in the essay "Of Tragedy" concerning Clarendon's *History of the Rebellion*. Hume observes that as Clarendon approaches the final and most tragic parts of his history, the trial and execution of King Charles, his narrative becomes thinner, and he "hurries" through the king's death, without giving any of its circumstances:

> He considers it as too horrid a scene to be contemplated with any satisfaction, or even without the utmost pain and aversion. He himself, as well as the readers of that age, were deeply concerned in the events, and felt a pain from subjects, which an historian and a reader of another age would regard as the most pathetic and most interesting, and, by consequence, the most agreeable.[19]

Here Hume points to an irony that is central to the ways in which historical continuity and discontinuity change historical distance. For Clarendon and his generation, evidently, proximity had required an effort to push away the painful side of living memory, while two generations later, it had become possible for another generation, one not as "deeply concerned in the events," to recognize and even enjoy previously untouched possibilities for pathos.

Hume does not comment on the possibility that the general norms of historiography might change—that new generations of readers might have a taste for new modes of historical writing. But his remarks do stand as an important recognition that historical distance is itself a product of history. Hume clearly saw that Clarendon did not freely and individually choose his stance in relation to the Regicide; rather he shared with his readers a proximity to the event that made a sentimental representation of Charles's death unthinkable. By the same token, Hume knew that the passing of the pain of events had meanwhile opened up for his readers as much as for himself possibilities for finding new meaning.

Unfortunately, Hume's understanding of the legitimate variability of historical distance has been lost on many modern commentators who seem to believe

[19] *Essays*, 223–24.

that "historical imagination" can only take the form of an attempt to recapture the immediacy of the past. This is an important point with respect to Hume's reputation, which—in common with so much else in his period—has been obscured by the imposition of nineteenth-century criteria on eighteenth-century practices. Even in the present century, historians as diverse as R. G. Collingwood and Hayden White have disparaged Hume's stance, first by drastically simplifying his views and then by insisting, in effect, that genuine historical understanding requires a narrative that foregrounds historical presence.

I will return in the conclusion to the question of the ways in which shifting norms of distance have shaped the reception of Hume's historical work.

NARRATIVES AND READERS

Three

Tensions and Accommodations: Varieties of Structure in Eighteenth-Century Narrative

THE IDEA that history should be written as a linear narrative of public matters is an enduring legacy of the classical tradition. The link between linearity and public life was deeply held and far from trivial. Statecraft provided history with a coherent and dignified subject, while clarity of form made history a worthy instrument of public instruction. In eighteenth-century Britain these assumptions retained enormous prestige, but characteristic tensions emerged between an ideal conception of historical narrative and a multiform practice responsive to a wider range of questions. This was an age that paid the highest tribute to the literary artistry of ancient historians while undermining some of the central assumptions on which classical politics and historiography were founded. The resulting experimentation with a variety of forms and modes of historical representation clearly reveals the pressure of new interests not easily assimilated to a unitary history of public events.[1]

It comes as something of a surprise that the most penetrating contemporary account of the formal dilemmas of eighteenth-century historical representation was written by Adam Smith, a crucial thinker for this period, but one seldom discussed in relation to historiography. Smith's unpublished *Lectures on Rhetoric and Belles Lettres*—a reconstruction of Smith's classroom teaching from student notes—offers a brilliant, if neglected commentary on the history and problems of historical composition. Here Smith probes the tensions between his own deeply felt commitment to classical literary procedures and an equally strong interest in realms of experience difficult to represent within the conven-

[1] On the expansion of the range of historical writing in the late eighteenth century, see Arnaldo Momigliano, "The Eighteenth-Century Prelude to Mr. Gibbon," in *Sesto Contributo allo studio degli studi classici* (Rome: Edizioni di Storia e Letteratura, 1980), as well as my comments on Momigliano's approach in Phillips, "Reconsiderations on History." See also Peter Burke, "Reflections on the Origins of Cultural History," in *Interpretation and Cultural History*, ed. J. Pittock and A. Wear (London: Macmillan, 1991), 5–24. Thomas Peardon, *The Transition in English Historical Writing* (New York: AMS, 1966), remains a broad and valuable survey of the period under discussion, as is R. J. Smith, *The Gothic Bequest* (Cambridge: Cambridge UP, 1987). Important background on humanist or neoclassical assumptions about history is to be found in Anthony Grafton, *Defenders of the Text: The Tradition of Scholarship in an Age of Science* (Cambridge: Harvard UP, 1991); James Johnson, *The Formation of English Neoclassical Thought* (Princeton: Princeton UP, 1967), as well as Momigliano, *Studies in Historiography;* Levine, *Battle of the Books* and *Humanism and History;* Woolf, *Idea of History;* and Hicks, *Neoclassical History.*

tions of this tradition. The resulting exploration of the limits and potential of historiographical narrative illuminates the central issues facing historical writers in this period.

Taking its cue from Smith's analysis of the underlying tensions in eighteenth-century historiography, but without limiting itself to the solutions that Smith himself would have endorsed, this chapter explores the range of narrative forms that characterized historical representation in this period. Such a sketch, I hope, will prove useful as an orientation to the more detailed discussions of the forms and thematics of historiography that follow in later chapters.

Adam Smith's *Lectures on Rhetoric*

Even without the recovery of his early teaching on rhetoric, Smith would, of course, stand as an important figure in the background of contemporary historiographical thinking. Smith played a crucial part in redefining the map of social knowledge for eighteenth-century audiences. His *Wealth of Nations* (1776) was the paradigmatic work of the new political economy, while his *Theory of Moral Sentiments* (1st ed. 1759) was this period's most comprehensive treatise on the philosophical psychology of morals. More than any other writer of the time, then, Smith embodies the aspiration to comprehend both dimensions of what (guided by Arendt) I am calling the social: the everyday world of work and custom as well as the inner one of the sentiments. But for the student of literature and history the *Lectures on Rhetoric* adds a whole new dimension to Smith's importance. The work contains an extensive commentary on problems of historical composition in which Smith shows himself to be a literary conservative who insisted that historians should stick to narrative in the manner of the ancients and avoid the notes and demonstrations that had become a good part of the didactic style of modern historiography. "It is not [the historian's] business to bring proofs for propositions," Smith says, "but to narrate facts" (101). This stance puts Smith in the fascinating position of condemning precisely those experiments in contemporary historical writing that would appear to be best adapted to expressing the new insights of political economy and philosophical history. At the same time—and for reasons closely connected to this literary purism—the lectures also include a striking analysis of subjective effects in narrative that reflects his deep interest in issues of sympathy and spectatorship. The sum of both approaches is a searching examination of the formal problems challenging historical writing in his day.[2]

[2] Smith lectured on rhetoric from 1748 to 1763. For a discussion of his teaching of rhetoric and of the manuscript sources for this text, see the editor's introduction to the *Lectures on Rhetoric*. On Smith's teaching career, see also Ian Simpson Ross, *The Life of Adam Smith* (Oxford: Clarendon, 1995), 87–96, 128–31.

Smith's rhetoric lectures were never published (our text comes from student notes of 1762-63) but the strictness of his views on narrative was not lost on his immediate successors. In discussing the achievements of William Robertson, Dugald Stewart noted that Smith was hostile to any device that compromised the continuity of narrative. He "carried to such a length his partiality to the ancient forms of classical composition," wrote Stewart, "that he considered every species of note as a blemish or imperfection; indicating either an idle accumulation of superfluous particulars, or a want of skill and comprehension in the general design."[3]

By 1762, Smith's hostility to anything that would detract from the narrative character of historical writing put him at odds with the most innovative developments in contemporary writing. Yet it seems fair to say that it was precisely because Smith would not abandon history's commitment to classically prescribed forms of narrative that he produced a fertile reexamination of the way in which a narrative of private life might be constructed. His desire to reconcile his spectatorial analysis of historical writing with the stringent formal demands of linear narrative produces the creative tension animating his discussion of historiography—and it adds a further dimension to the story that he believed that the greatest of the classical historians, anticipating his own theory of narrative, had already shaped their narratives along sentimental lines.

The four lectures that are at the center of Smith's description of history show his classical tastes most clearly, including his uncompromising condemnation of philosophical digressions. Despite the incorporation of the doctrine of sympathy, which would become so central to his work as a moral philosopher, the first impression is certainly that Smith's review of historiography proceeds along lines completely familiar in the classical tradition. Similarly, in the discussion of the history of historiography that follows, his judgments strongly favor the ancients over the moderns, leaving us little reason to dissent from Dugald Stewart's picture of Smith's rigid classicism. A more balanced and also a more interesting picture emerges, however, if we frame this discussion in wider terms.

Smith joined Kames and other proponents of the "new rhetoric" in attempting to put the study of literature on a more "philosophic" footing. This meant redirecting attention away from conventional discussions of the rules of composition and toward an examination of the effects of art on the mind of the viewer. But Smith recognizes that literature not only has the capacity to trigger emotional response; it also aims to represent emotional states. Given Smith's commitment to narrative, he then has to ask himself how narrative, which is normally concerned with actions, can also represent invisible inward feeling.

[3] Dugald Stewart, *Account of the Life and Writings of William Robertson*, 2d ed. (London, 1802), 141–42.

This question, which I find so revealing and so fertile, grows out of the way in which Smith divides his material. Every discourse, he writes, aims either to relate some fact or to prove some proposition (62). In the latter case we have either didactic or rhetorical discourse; in the former we have narrative, which he also calls "the historical style."[4] Smith's unwillingness to mix different modes of writing leads to his antipathy to the philosophical historian's incorporation of didactic discourse into a historical text. Having characterized narrative in this strict way, Smith then adds a second fundamental division according to whether the events to be narrated are external or internal. The "Design of History," he adds, is compounded of both of these (63). Thus for Smith history is not only an account of observable events, but also in some measure the narrative of things unseen—"to wit the thoughts sentiments or designs of men, which pass in their mind" (63). Smith strongly emphasizes the difficulty of narrating these "dispositions of mind," a difficulty that is compounded by the fact that the causes of internal events may themselves be either internal or external.[5]

Smith's next step is to divide narrative technique along similar lines. He distinguishes between direct description, which represents the object itself, and indirect description, which represents the object as it is registered in the response of a spectator. The symmetry between objects and techniques, however, is not complete. Internal events, such as the passions and affections, can only be described by the indirect method, that is, "by the Effects they produce either on the Body or the mind" (68). Often, however, the same indirect technique is also the best resource for evoking external objects.[6] Here Smith cites Addison as an example: by describing the effect of St. Peter's on the beholder, he had succeeded far better in conveying a notion of the size and proportions of the church than if he had provided exact dimensions of all its parts (74).

[4] See lecture 17, for example, where Smith refers to the "rules for narration in generall, that is for the historical Stile" (*Lectures on Rhetoric*, 89). History, then, for Smith is both a fundamental literary mode (i.e. narrative) and a literary genre. It is notable the historical genre provides him with a very large portion of his literary examples. Fictional narratives, in verse or prose, are much less prominent. This focus on works of history was noted in a contemporary account written by one of his auditors, James Woodrow. See *Lectures on Rhetoric*, 11.

[5] "The internall are such dispositions of mind as fit one for that certain passion or affection of mind; and the external are such objects as produce these effects on a mind so disposed" (ibid., 68). He adds: "But whatever difficulty there is in expressing the externall objects that are the objects of our senses; there must be far greater in describing the internal ones, which pass within the mind itself and are the object of none of our senses. . . . The easiest way of describing an object is by its parts, how then describe those which have no parts" (68).

[6] "That way of expressing any quality of an object which does it by describing the severall parts that constitute the quality we want to express, may be called the direct method. When, again, we do it by describing the effects this quality produces on those who behold it may be called the indirect method. This latter in most cases is by far the best" (ibid., 67).

Clearly Smith's narratology, like his moral philosophy, depends upon notions of sympathy and spectatorship.[7] Like other sentimentalists, too, Smith stresses that narratives describing misfortune are the most affecting of all. For this reason, an impartial historian, wanting to describe the effects of battle, would be more likely to dwell on the "lamentations" of the defeated than the "exultations" of the victors. But even in respect to the most affecting events, direct description produces a "very languid and uninterresting [*sic*]" impression; "when we mean to affect the reader deeply we must have recourse to the indirect method of description, relating the effects the transaction produced both on the actors and Spectators" (86–87).

This is the heart of Smith's revaluation of the problem of narrative in the light of his idea of sympathy. The fertility of his discovery may not be fully evident, however, until we reach those lectures—in some ways the most conservative—where Smith reviews the history of historical writing and extols the virtues of the ancients against the inadequacies of the moderns. His judgments on the ancient historians consistently apply sentimentalist readings built on the divisions of narrative outlined earlier. Both Thucydides and Livy are analyzed in this way.[8] Smith's most extensive comments, however, are reserved for Tacitus, whom he credits, in effect, with anticipating his own understanding of narrative.[9] This remarkable reinterpretation is worth quoting at length:

> He had observed that those passages of the historians were most interesting which unfolded the effects the events related produced on the minds of the actors or spectators of those; He imagined therefore that if one could write a history consisting

[7] "As it is mankind we are chiefly connected with it must be their actions which chiefly interest our attention. . . . 'Tis therefore the actions of men and of them such as are of the greatest importance and are most apt to draw our attention and make a deep impression on the heart, that form the ground of this species of description" (ibid., 85). Smith's explanation here of history's concern with important men hints at the fuller discussion elsewhere in these lectures—as well as in *Theory of Moral Sentiments*—of the sympathetic basis for deference and the way in which this natural deference to our superiors underpins the classical rules for tragedy. See *Lectures on Rhetoric*, 124. For a helpful discussion of the spectatorial elements in Smith and in Scottish literary culture more generally, see John Dwyer, *Virtuous Discourse: Sensibility and Community in Late Eighteenth-Century Scotland* (Edinburgh: John Donald, 1987), as well as his "Enlightened Spectators and Classical Moralists: Sympathetic Relations in Eighteenth-Century Scotland," in *Sociability and Society in Eighteenth Century Scotland*, ed. John Dwyer and Richard Sher (Edinburgh: Mercat, 1993).

[8] Thucydides, for example, writes a "crowded" narrative, "accounting for every event by the externall causes that produced it. . . . He renders his narration at the same time interesting by the internall effects the events producd [*sic*] as in that before mention'd of the Battle in the night" (*Lectures on Rhetoric*, 106). So too Livy, the best of the Roman historians, "renders his descriptions extremely interesting by the great number of affecting circumstances he has thrown together" (108–9).

[9] I have examined Smith's revaluation of Tacitus (as well as the similar interpretation presented by Arthur Murphy's translation) in another context in "Reconsiderations on History."

> entirely of such events as were capable of interesting the minds of the Readers by accounts of the effects they produced or were themselves capable of producing this effect on the reader [*sic*]. (111–12)

Smith connects the qualities of Tacitus's narrative to the peace and orderliness of his age. In the absence of pressing public affairs, Tacitus realized that the incidents of private life, though less important than public ones, "would affect us more deeply and interest us more than those of a Publick nature" (113). In calamities of a private nature, Smith adds, "our passions are fixt on one," rather than dispersed over the wider set of figures involved in common misfortunes. Accordingly Tacitus largely disregards the question of the importance of events, considering instead their affective power. In doing so, he follows the techniques of indirect narration, describing events "by the internall effects" and accounting for them "in the same manner" (113).

Using these techniques more fully than any other historian, Tacitus created a kind of narrative that Smith clearly finds both disturbing and intriguing. Though the events of his history may often be considered secondary, "the method [by which] he describes these is so interesting, he leads us far into the sentiments and mind of the actors that they are some of the most striking and interesting passages to be met with in any history" (113). And when Tacitus does concern himself with more important (that is, public) events, he disregards external causes in favor of the internal ones. The consequence is that his account may not instruct us in the causes of events, "yet it will be more interesting and lead us into a science no less usefull, to wit, the knowledge of the motives by which men act; a science too that could not be learned from [lacuna in text]" (113).

It is impossible to know how this intriguing sentence was completed when Smith spoke this lecture. But the "science no less useful" taught by Tacitus's history of private life clearly has some affinities to the one explored in these lectures and perfected in the *Theory of Moral Sentiments*. The comparison Smith wants to draw, however, is to the literature of contemporary France, where he finds the same luxury and refinement that marked the Roman Empire in the age of Trajan:

> Sentiment must bee what will chiefly interest such a people. . . . Such a people, I say, having nothing to engage them in the hurry of life would naturally turn their attention to the motions of the human mind, and those events that were accounted for by the different internall affections that influenced the persons concerned, would be what most suited their taste. (112)

It is for this reason, Smith concludes, that Tacitus so much resembles Marivaux and Crebillon—"as much as we can well imagine in works of so conterary [*sic*] a nature" (112).

As Smith well knew, this is an extraordinary comparison to make; after all, Tacitus's name had long been a byword for a ruthless, *un*sentimental acceptance of political reality, while in Britain more recently Tacitus had figured as the scourge of tyrants and the champion of lost republican virtue. Smith obviously felt the novelty of what he was doing, and he closes the lecture with an uncharacteristic flourish: "Such is the true Character of Tacitus," he proclaims, "which has been misrepresented by all his commentators from Boccalini down to Gordon" (114).

What, then, had Adam Smith discovered about Tacitus? He had discovered a sentimentalist, where others had seen a terse, tough, realistic politician. He had found an analysis of private life, where others had seen a critique of politics. He had turned traditional readings of Tacitus inside out. But from the present perspective, he had also found something larger—the possibility of a history registered in the eyes of spectators, a sentimental history concerned less with outward acts and public occasions than with the private passions and experiences of men. And all this without for a moment relinquishing his decided preference for linear narrative as practiced by the great historians of antiquity.

Narrative Structure and History's Expanded Subject: Dugald Stewart and William Robertson

Smith's analysis of narrative provides an opening to examine the ways in which eighteenth-century historians responded to the practical challenges implicit in narrating events and experiences outside the sphere of the *vita activa*. In the remainder of this chapter, I would like to sketch two lines of discussion. First, since in practice very few historians shared Smith's purism, it is useful to explore some of the accommodations that permitted historical narratives to incorporate the questions about commerce, manners, and everyday life that were being brought into prominence by conjectural and philosophical historians. Second, Smith's analysis of indirect narrative suggests a broader look at techniques of spectatorial narrative. Taken together, the two sorts of narrative—one, broadly speaking, concerned with manners, the other with the sentiments—helped bring into history the investigation of two distinct, yet allied aspects of social life. (As a shorthand, I will refer to them as the *social* and the *inward*.) The challenge of narrating both of these dimensions of the social was, I believe, a crucial part of the Scottish Enlightenment's widening exploration of human nature and experience.

In practice, few historians were prepared to keep to the strictly classical model Smith upheld. In an age that stressed the didactic uses of literature, writers were generally hostile to a view of narrative that excluded all overtly argumentative elements. A revealing exception is the fragmentary *History of the Early Part of the Reign of James the Second* (1808) written in retirement by the great Whig politician Charles James Fox and published posthumously by his nephew, Vassall Holland. In his apologetic introduction, Holland explains that one of the reasons for the slow progress of the work was the rigor of his uncle's classicism, which led him to oppose the "modern practice of notes" and to insist that "all which an historian wished to say, should be introduced as part of a continued narration."[10]

Holland illustrates his uncle's strict standards by recounting a conversation about the literature of the period of James II in which Fox had lamented his inability to devise a method of "interweaving" any account of these authors. When Holland suggested the example of Hume and Voltaire, who had discussed such topics either in a separate chapter or at the end of a reign, Fox firmly rejected the precedent: "such a contrivance might be a good mode of writing critical essays, but . . . it was, in his opinion, incompatible with the nature of his undertaking, which, if it ceased to be a narrative, ceased to be a history."[11]

Holland's tone here is as interesting as Fox's old-fashioned views on narrative. As his uncle's executor and editor, Holland's purpose was not to express his own opinion, but to present the fragment in its best light. Yet he feared that the work might be misjudged unless readers understood Fox's conception of the historian's "duties"; otherwise "some passages, which according to modern taste, must be called peculiarities, might . . . pass for defects which he had overlooked, or imperfections which he intended to correct."[12] Evidently, Holland had difficulty believing that Fox's strict classicism was still tenable, or even fully recognizable: despite Fox's well-known admiration for classical letters, readers might simply mistake the character of his uncle's style. Even in Smith's day this sort of purism had been a conservative stance, but apparently by 1808 it had become truly eccentric.

Unsympathetic as they were to the mixed narrative form, neither Smith nor Holland says much about the reasons for its utility in modern compositions, though Fox's frustrated desire to incorporate a discussion of English literature into his history of the Glorious Revolution speaks for itself. Henry Steuart of Allanton, author of an extensive commentary on Sallust, took up a middle

[10] Charles James Fox, *A History of the Early Part of the Reign of James the Second* (London, 1808), xxviii–xxix. Holland writes that Fox "formed his plan so exclusively on the model of ancient writers, that he not only felt some repugnance to the modern practice of notes, but he thought that all which an historian wished to say, should be introduced as part of a continued narration, and never assume the appearance of a digression, much less of a dissertation annexed to it."

[11] Ibid., xxix.

[12] Ibid., xxviii.

position. Reviewing the progress of historical composition in Britain, Steuart praises the "wide, and philosophic views" open to the modern historian. But he is also troubled by the consequences:

> Amidst these improvements, however, some doubts may be entertained, whether the Philosophy of History . . . have [*sic*] not been cultivated to the prejudice of Narrative. History, whatever other means it may adopt for instruction, should never depart from its essential and primary character, as a *relation of facts*.[13]

The danger is that instead of "naturally giving rise to the reflections," narrative will seem to be nothing more than a platform for metaphysical speculation (a caution we have also heard voiced by Hugh Blair).

Dugald Stewart was alive to the same tensions, but he approached the problem firmly in the spirit of the "moderns." In his brief life of William Robertson, Stewart gives particular praise to Robertson's skill in balancing the contradictory demands of narrative history and philosophical enquiry. The modern historian's task has become more difficult, Stewart remarks acutely, because of the new fashion for combining political histories with a philosophic view of manners and conditions. "In consequence of this innovation, while the province of the historian has been enlarged and dignified, the difficulty of his task has encreased in the same proportion; reduced, as he must frequently be, to the alternative, either of interrupting unseasonably the chain of events, or, by interweaving disquisition and narrative together, of sacrificing clearness to brevity."[14]

In Stewart's view, Robertson's success in retrieving the traditional excellence of narrative in the face of this challenge stemmed from his plan of "throwing" into notes and illustrations whatever discussions appeared "to interfere with the peculiar province of history." By this device, and by the "felicity" of his transitions, Robertson was able to sustain an uninterrupted narrative, giving his works "that unceasing interest which constitutes one of the principal charms in tales of fiction; an interest easy to support in relating a series of imaginary adventures, but which in historical composition, evinces, more than anything else, the hand of a master."[15]

Stewart understood Smith's opposition to Robertson's way of saving the continuity of narrative, but he himself was convinced of the advantages gained

[13] Henry Steuart, *The Works of Sallust; to which are prefixed two essays; with notes by H. S.* (1806), 273.

[14] Stewart, *Account of Robertson*, 139.

[15] Ibid., 140–41. Compare Priestley: "By the use of *notes* the moderns have a considerable advantage over the ancients, who had no idea of such a convenience. By the help of notes a history may go on without interruption, and yet a great variety of *incidental things*, worth recording, and which cannot be introduced with ease into the body of a work, may have a place assigned to them, where they may be attended to at the reader's leisure." *A Course of Lectures on Oratory and Criticism* (London, 1777), 39.

by the moderns. In fact, he feels that the absence of notes considerably diminished the value of the ancient historians, and he adds that readers of the *Wealth of Nations* had reasons to regret Smith's reluctance to use notes and appendices.[16] Gibbon, on the other hand, goes too far: "The curious research and the epigrammatic wit so often displayed in Mr. Gibbon's notes, and which sometimes render them more amusing than even the eloquent narrative which they are meant to illustrate, serve only to add to the embarrassment occasioned by this unfortunate distribution of his materials."[17]

Robertson's *History of Charles V* (1769) is, indeed, a case study of the conflicting demands on historical composition in the eighteenth century. But, unlike his biographer, Robertson chose not to call attention to the problems he had worked to overcome. Rather he points to divisions in his subject and in his audience to explain his procedures. In the modern period, Robertson writes, which began with the reign of Charles, Europe's history stands as an interconnected whole, regulated by such principles as the balance of power. The long epoch between the fall of Rome and the emergence of the modern balance of power, on the other hand, lacked this unity, and its detailed history could only be of interest to separate nationalities. Yet taken as a whole, this history had enormous importance as the foundation for everything that followed. Accordingly Robertson came to write the long prefatory essay that is now the best-known portion of his work: "A View of the Progress of Society in Europe."[18] For this early period a true history would not be possible since a political narrative would be too particular and a "view" sufficiently general could not be narrative. His solution, in other words, was to frame the history proper with a philosophical history quite different in its structure, scope, and lessons.

It is evident that Robertson (and his readers) took for granted the primacy of narrative, with its traditional dignity, unity, and didactic force. Even so, the early history of Europe could not support such a narrative not only because it lacked unity, but also because the obscurity of the evidence would involve the historian in reasoning too complex or technical to interest the general reader. By its very nature, the "general view" stood halfway to antiquarianism—"the province of the lawyer or antiquary"—and introduced considerations better

[16] Stewart, *Account of Robertson*, 148–49.

[17] Ibid., 143–44.

[18] William Robertson, *The History of the Reign of the Emperor Charles V. With a view of the progress of society in Europe, from the subversion of the Roman Empire to the beginning of the sixteenth century*, 3 vols. (London, 1769). The introductory "view" is conveniently available in Robertson, *The Progress of Society in Europe*, ed. Felix Gilbert (Chicago: U of Chicago P, 1972), from which I quote. For Robertson and his milieu, see Richard Sher, *Church and University in the Scottish Enlightenment* (Princeton: Princeton UP, 1985). And see now the valuable collection of essays edited by Stewart J Brown, *William Robertson and the Expansion of Empire* (Cambridge: Cambridge UP, 1997); as well as O'Brien, *Narratives*.

kept separate from the text, even in this introductory book. Hence the need for the "Proofs and Illustrations" attached to the "View."

It would be rewarding to examine in detail the range and variety of problems and sources that Robertson felt he needed to handle in this manner, but it may be enough to say that the forty-three notes that make up this appendix could be read as a kind of index of excluded questions. "Many of my readers will, probably, give little attention to such researches," Robertson writes. "To some they may, perhaps, appear the most curious and interesting part of the work."[19] Thus Robertson envisioned the problem of structure as a matter of mediating between two audiences. The general literary public was the traditional audience for the instruction and entertainment provided by history, and it still carried the highest prestige. Yet, as Robertson states several times in his works, he is not satisfied with the level of evidence or argument customarily addressed to such readers. He expects his history also to interest a more limited, expert audience, whose antiquarian tests of evidence as well as "philosophical" sense of causation must also be addressed. Even so, the wider audience remains central, and—having completed his philosophical prelude along with its antiquarian addenda—Robertson is free to commence the history proper with the birth of the great emperor.

Robertson had rejected the exclusivity of classical narrative advocated by Smith and replaced it with a new narrative order incorporating a hierarchy of narrative and nonnarrative elements based in part on the needs of distinct audiences. Robert Henry's experiment in simultaneous narrative, examined at the opening of this book, carried these changes considerably further. Henry offers his own disciplined, systematic procedure as a strict discipline for the historian and a model for a new, more comprehensive way of writing. Even so, it is evident that his simultaneity possesses less unifying power than Robertson had achieved through hierarchy. In Henry's account, the traditional narrative of politics still comes first, but public life only has priority in a literal sense, while histories of religion, learning, arts, commerce, and manners occupy a larger horizon. Perhaps the most radical sign of the displacement of the narrative of statecraft, however, is Henry's suggestion that the reader might want to take advantage of the systematic arrangement of his chapters to construct his own path through the history. This invitation offered a striking new possibility—a history whose comprehensiveness does not so much enlarge the scope of history's traditional public concerns as open the way for specialist readers to reconstruct the narrative according to their own particular needs. This "readerly" narrative would not only be a history of social life, but also one open to being read for private purposes. (This was the kind of reading Austen evoked when—in a passage already cited—she joked about the choice of discussing the book "either in a loose, disultry, unconnected strain, or dividing the recital

[19] Robertson, *Progress of Society*, 5.

as the Historian divides it himself, into seven parts . . . so that for every evening of the week there will be a different subject.")[20] And beyond Henry's valiant attempt to retain some unity in the multiplicity of his social descriptions lie any number of dispersed and particular histories, each contributing to the wide array of historiographical genres that characterized the historical reading of this time. Writers of biography, for instance, often claimed that to men in private station individual lives are more interesting than general history because readers find in biography a reflection of their own concerns.

Inward Narratives and Epistolary Form: Helen Maria Williams and Samuel Ancell

Adam Smith would surely have disliked Henry's experiment for the ways in which it undermines the traditional unities of historical narrative. Yet Smith's idea of indirect narrative could be taken as licensing some equally radical alternatives. The works that I now want to discuss have a frankly (even extravagantly) sentimental character, which may lead some to set them aside as peripheral to more traditional forms of historical writing. Nonetheless, these experiments in spectatorial narrative help to establish the range of questions and methods that characterize the full spectrum of historiographical representation. In this way, they are important to our understanding of even the most canonical works of the time.

One narrative mode that was well adapted to expressive uses of the sort Smith had analyzed under the category of indirect narrative is the epistolary. Epistolary narrative has been well studied in eighteenth-century fiction, but is seldom thought of as a historiographical convention, nor have the implications of its popularity been examined in relation to the historical genres.[21] In fact, the epistolary convention was widely used in many eighteenth-century literatures of instruction. The letter form is common in travel literature, for example, while in literary biography compiling a poet's letters became a prime mode of "life writing." In historical writing, as we will see, it remained relatively unusual as a vehicle for narrative, but some prominent exceptions do exist: Catherine Macaulay's *The History of England from the Revolution to the Present Tine, in a Series of Letters* (1778), for example, or William Russell's popular *History of Europe . . . in a series of letters from a nobleman to his son* (new ed. 1788).[22]

[20] Austen, *Letters*, 59; see above, introduction.

[21] For epistolarity in other contexts, see Bruce Redford, *The Converse of the Pen: Acts of Intimacy in the Eighteenth-Century Familiar Letter* (Chicago: U of Chicago P, 1986).

[22] Another example, aimed at instructing young women, is Charlotte Smith's *History of England from the Earliest Records to the Peace of Amiens. In a series of letters to a young lady at*

Even without these nonfictional uses, however, epistolary fiction (along with the allied convention of the found manuscript journal) should have a real interest for students of historiography. The popularity of epistolary and journal fictions is not only a sign of contemporary interest in interiority, but also a striking indication of the scrupulousness with which writers, even when creating fictions, treated the difficulty of gaining access to interior feeling. In essence, these novels begin by creating a fictional archive and then construct the reader as a true historian. In this way, epistolary and journal fictions overcome the problem of insight into other minds by means that in crucial respects parallel the procedures used by historians. In short, until free indirect discourse became commonly accepted in the novels of the next century, history and fiction largely operated under common rules of evidence with respect to interiority—a fact of considerable importance for understanding the evolving relationship between historical and fictional narratives.[23]

Epistolarity, it should be said, had other attractions besides the access letters give to inward feeling. Both Catherine Macaulay and William Russell, for example, use the letter form simply as a didactic instrument and have no interest in its sentimental potential. The opposite was true, however, of another politically radical female historian, Helen Maria Williams. Williams was powerfully drawn to the affective possibilities of epistolary narrative. Her *Letters Written in France, in the Summer of 1790, to a Friend in England* stands as a remarkable illustration of the affective possibilities that Smith had described in connection with indirect narrative.[24]

Williams is far less concerned with establishing a coherent outline of events than with conveying the stirring atmosphere and emotional impact of the dawn

school, 3 vols. (London, 1806). Letters were also used to comment on historical subjects, as for example MacQueen's *Letters on Hume's History.*

[23] On the problem insight presents to the writing of history in an era of novelistic omniscience, see my "Scott, Macaulay." On omniscience and free indirect discourse, see Dorrit Cohn, *Transparent Minds: Narrative Modes for Presenting Consciousness in Fiction* (Princeton: Princeton UP, 1978).

[24] This was the original title, one meant, evidently, to emphasize the spectatorial and contemporaneous character of the account. The work was continued as *Letters from France* in eight volumes published serially between 1790 and 1796. The first two volumes, in particular, were very widely read. I cite Helen Maria Williams, *Letters from France*, ed. Janet Todd, 2 vols. (London, 1796; rpt. New York: Scholar's Facsimiles, 1975). On Williams, see Gary Kelly, *Women, Writing, and Revolution, 1790–1827* (Oxford: Clarendon, 1993), chap. 6; Mary Favret, *Romantic Correspondence: Women, Politics, and the Fiction of Letters* (Cambridge: Cambridge UP, 1993); Vivien Jones, "Women Writing Revolution: Narratives of History and Sexuality in Wollstonecraft and Williams," in *Beyond Romanticism: New Approaches to Texts and Contexts, 1780–1832*, ed. Stephen Copley and John Whale (London: Routledge, 1992), 178–99; Eleanor Ty, *Unsex'd Revolutionaries: Five Women Novelists of the 1790s* (Toronto: U of Toronto P, 1993); and William Stafford, "Narratives of Women: English Feminists of the 1790s," *History* 82 (1997): 24–42. On the popularity of the work, see Robert Mayo, *The English Novel in the Magazines, 1740–1815* (Evanston, Ill.: Northwestern UP, 1962), 259–56.

of revolution. To do so, the *Letters* makes use of a number of expressive devices—including the epistolary form, eyewitness reportage, and an embedded memoir—that mediate the responses of the reader through the eyes of local witnesses. Most prominent among these mediators is the narrator herself. As a woman, a foreigner, and a letter writer, she is perfectly placed to occupy the role of historical spectator: neither an active participant in events, nor a detached narrator as conventionally required, she is an ideal spectator, universal rather than impartial in her sympathies.[25] Such a narrator can give voice to interior feelings that (as Smith had argued) could not be described by more ordinary means:

> I promised to send you a description of the federation: but it is not to be described! One must have been present, to form any judgment of a scene, the sublimity of which depended much less on its external magnificence than on the effect it produced on the minds of the spectators.[26]

For Williams, places as much as people act as witnesses to the great scenes of the Revolution, and she writes with a prescient sense of the evocative power of these historic sites. In a key passage she imagines herself as simply the first of many in a new kind of secular pilgrimage. In years to come, she imagines, strangers will follow in her footsteps: "I see them eagerly searching for the place where they have heard it recorded, that the National Assembly were seated! I think of these things, and then repeat to myself with transport, 'I, was a spectator of the Federation.' "[27]

Williams also makes use of a second narrative form that contrasts with the predominant epistolary structure: an embedded biographical memoir, recounted by the author herself, concerning the unfortunate friends whom she had traveled to France to meet. The lengthy history of Mons. du F., persecuted by his aristocratic father because of his marriage to a woman of the middle class, stands as a sort of sentimental tale set into the larger narrative. It is

[25] Favret makes the point that Williams avoids overt partisanship and rarely refers to her meetings with influential Girondins and Jacobins. "In order to raise the letters 'beyond dispute,' all feeling and desire must be general and universal ('you will rejoice with me'). . . . This identification with the 'people,' reinforces Williams' democratic aspirations for France, and for England" (Favret, *Romantic Correspondence*, 65).

[26] Williams, *Letters from France*, 1:5. In the same vein, she adds: "I may tell you of pavilions, of triumphal arches, of altars on which incense was burnt, of two hundred thousand men walking in procession; but how am I to give you an adequate idea of the behaviour of the spectators? How am I to paint the impetuous feelings of that immense, that exulting multitude? Half a million of people assembled at a spectacle, which furnished every image that can elevate the mind of man; which connected the enthusiasm of moral sentiment with the solemn pomp of religious ceremonies; which addressed itself at once to the imagination, the understanding, and the heart!" (1:5–6).

[27] Ibid., 1:107. On Williams's sense of place, see Elizabeth Bohls, *Women Travel Writers and the Language of Aesthetics, 1716–1818* (Cambridge: Cambridge UP, 1995), chap. 4; and chap. 12 below.

presented as a microcosm of the system of tyranny, domestic as well as public, from which France had been liberated by the Revolution, and in telling it, Williams is at pains to point out the ways in which the old baron's cruelties to his son required official support and aristocratic complicity. But the memoir is more than a metonymic representation of the evils of the old regime; it also represents a kind of personal knowledge that, as a female spectator, Williams could hold with entire confidence in her own judgment. The reasonings of philosophers might confuse her, she acknowledges, but when a proposition is addressed to her heart she has no doubts; "nor could I be more convinced of the truth of any demonstration in Euclid, than I am, that, that system of politics must be the best, by which those I love are made happy."[28]

The memoir of Mons. du F. re-creates the conditions of the ancien régime against which the events of the summer of 1790 must be understood. In this way it extends the temporal and geographical range of Williams's *Letters,* overcoming two of the most obvious restrictions of the epistolary form. But on a more fundamental level the two parts of Williams's history unite in their assertion of the importance of direct experience and personal knowledge, even in the face of enormous public events. Thus, like so many others on both sides of the Revolution debate, Williams embraced the view that the deepest meaning of the Revolution would be felt in private life, a perception difficult to express within the restraints of linear narrative.[29]

Another sentimentalist experiment in contemporary history—one that combines the epistolary and journal forms—is Samuel Ancell's *A Circumstantial Journal of the Long and Tedious Blockade of Gibraltar* (1783). This work of an Irish military agent and editor is perhaps harder to place.[30] As an account of things military, the *Circumstantial Journal* is closer in obvious ways to the traditional historical interests. Ancell's military history, however, has little to do with generalship and strategy. The running title calls the work an "An Authentick Journal," and the anonymous narrator signs himself simply "an Officer," signaling that this is war as experienced close to the ground.[31] Throughout, Ancell emphasizes the actuality of his record. The entries are set down and dated in the manner of a daily journal, a framework that allows for an

[28] Williams, *Letters from France*, 1:196.

[29] See chapter 10 below for a discussion of private life and the importance of "opinion."

[30] [Samuel Ancell], *A Circumstantial Journal of the Long and Tedious Blockade and Siege of Gibraltar, from the Twelfth of September 1779, to the third Day of February, 1783. By An Officer* (Manchester, 1783). The British Library Catalogue lists five editions of this work: 1783, 1784, 1786, 1793, 1802. I have also consulted a 1785 edition (Liverpool). Evidently the book enjoyed considerable popularity. Ancell was the editor of a military publication, *Ancell's Monthly Military Companion* (see below, n. 32).

[31] In a prefatory letter to the Liverpool edition of 1785, Ancell asks the reader to make allowance for circumstances. "The circumstances are authentic, and were penned during a long and laborious Siege, amidst the Roar of Guns, Mortars, Howitzers, and the bursting of Shells."

engaging and sometimes dramatic mix of information about the long siege. In consequence, "reality effects" abound, but the reader has no way of knowing how many are owing to novelistic imagination, or indeed whether the *Circumstantial Journal* might be an outright fiction. In the end, only Ancell's biography stands as a kind of guarantor of the work.[32]

Ancell details all the expected elements of a military campaign—troop strengths, naval maneuvers, rumors of a fleet ready to relieve the besieged, brave sorties, sudden calamities, and patriotic messages. But thanks to the journal convention, public matters are easily combined with circumstantial details designed to bring the reader closer to the front lines. He is quick to report apparently trivial events, such as the execution of a private soldier for theft or the consequences of a stray shot.[33] He comments on the fluctuating price of foodstuffs and inserts garrison orders that told the men what to expect from the commissary or from enemy action.[34] Above all, the journal format allows the fiction of a continuous present, so that every hope and every danger—often indicated in terse and fragmentary entries—can be held in suspense.[35]

Ancell chose to combine his "circumstantial journal" with epistolarity—for reasons that are indicated by a note attached to the opening letter:

> Epistolary correspondence always affords pleasure to a mind fraught with sensibility; but it becomes an absolute duty in persons at a distance, to inform their relatives who are apprized of their being in dangerous situations, of every event, in order to allay the well grounded anxiety of a father, and the pangs of an affectionate mother or sister.[36]

[32] Ancell's obituary reads: "Mr. Samuel Ancell, commission and half-pay agent. He was born in England, and entered into the army at an early age. He was in Gibraltar during the late memorable siege; and, on the return of the 58th regiment (in which he was) to England, he published 'A Journal of the Blockade and Siege of Gibraltar, from the 12th of September, 1779, to the 10th of March, 1783; containing a minute Detail of the memorable and interesting Events of that important Investment and Defense, written in the Garrison during the passing Transactions.' This work is possessed of considerable merit, and has run through five editions in England and Ireland; the last was published a few months ago. About 18 months since, he published proposals for a periodical work, under the title of 'The Monthly Military Companion,' the first number of which appeared on the 1st of October, 1801. Previous to his death he had put the twelfth number to the press, which finishes the second volume. In this work he was assisted by some military characters of eminence in Ireland; and, from the encouragement it met with, and the materials in his possession, there is little doubt but it would have been a valuable addition to the library of military men, and lucrative to him." *Gentleman's Magazine* 72 (Dec. 1802): 1161.

[33] The shot, falling through the roof of "Mr Quartin's house . . . drove a splinter into a lady's heel" (Ancell, *Circumstantial Journal of Gibraltar*, 25). The execution is reported on p. 48.

[34] An example: *Garrison Orders. "The men to receive to-morrow, two pounds of salt fish, one ditto of pork, and half a pound of beef. N.B. This is for the week's allowance"* (ibid., 75).

[35] Occasionally, too, this effect is further dramatized by breaking off the narrative in midpassage by a military emergency. "A call to arms prevents my further writing . . . Adieu, dear Father, I must hasten to the alarm post" (ibid., 122).

[36] Ibid., 1.

Neither the anonymous soldier who writes these letters, nor the man who receives them—designated simply as "Honor'd Father"—is in any way individuated.[37] Emotions, too, are generalized, yet apparently intensely felt, providing the reader with easily read tableaux of filial duty, friendship, or the loss of comrades.[38]

Thus in the midst of a description of a sortie, the narrator writes, "my comrade falls by my side, and with a tender regret gazes on me, while I push forward to the battery or guard, and leave him to groan out his last accents, weltering in blood! My acquaintance receives a wound, and my best of friends looses the arm that was ever ready to cherish and supply. Sympathetic feeling melts my soul! I dare not weep."[39] Then, unexpectedly the passage moves on to encompass a death that is simultaneously the officer's own expected end and the reader's:

> Pangs, sufferings, and bleeding spectacles, with a military man, is denied operation: Probably with a bosom overloaded with the most poignant grief and anguish, a heart pierced with excruciating woes, you sally forth to meet the daring foe, you receive a wound; you are left to bleed; the foe pursues; your detachment retreats; you find Death busy; the lamp of life faintly burns; your friends are absent; the foe shows no tenderness; you sigh, weep, groan, pray, beg, intreat, and in the bitter agonies of death implore Almighty God to be merciful to a poor sinner—life hangs on a hair—the cordage of your heart cracks, and you drop into an unknown world where the secrets of all hearts are disclosed.[40]

It would be hard to find a microhistory of the late twentieth century that has taken history further toward the attractions of sentimentalism.[41]

[37] Among the many changes that Ancell made in later editions was a change in the addressee. In the 1785 edition, the letters are addressed "Dear Brother" and the subtitle is suitably altered to read, *In a series of letters from the Author to his Brother.* There was no change, however, to the claim to truthfulness.

[38] The narrator conjures up the inevitable scene of the soldier returning from war to find his wife and children dead: "On his return (O sensibility) what a ravaging scene is presented to his view! Let imagination conceive" (*Circumstantial Journal of Gibraltar*, 128–29).

[39] Ibid., 127.

[40] Ibid., 127–28.

[41] An interesting eighteenth-century parallel comes from Tobias Smollett's *Continuation*, a history designed to continue the narrative of English history where Hume's account left off. Here is Smollett's description of the Black Hole of Calcutta: "By this time, a profuse sweat had broke out on every individual, and this was attended with an insatiable thirst, which became the more intolerable as the body was drained of its moisture. In vain those miserable objects stripped themselves of their clothes, squatted down on their hams, and fanned the air with their hats, to produce a refreshing undulation. The dreadful symptom of thirst was now accompanied with a difficulty of respiration, and every individual gasped for breath. Their despair became outrageous: Again they attempted to force the door, and provoke the guards to fire upon them by execration and abuse. The cry of "Water! Water!" issued from every mouth." *Continuation of the complete History of England* (London, 1791), 3:512–13; I cite this from the thesis of my student Dale Smith, who is

Documentary Sentimentalism

As contemporary historians, Williams and Ancell could offer themselves as immediate witnesses to the emotions generated by revolution and war. For historians concerned with earlier times, the eighteenth-century audience's desire for a more inward understanding of personality and experience posed a problem of sources as well as of narrative structures. To put it simply, a sentimental narrative—one focused on subjective reflections of historical experience—required documents that seemed to offer authentic access to inward feeling. This was one of the reasons for the popularity of literary biography: an age attracted to quotidian experiences and private life often found the words of poets more interesting than the actions of politicians. Similarly, "naive" narratives, such as medieval chronicles, were prized for their presumed sincerity. But best of all, perhaps, were letters and memoirs, documents whose first-person vantage seem to promise unmediated access to past experience.

In a later chapter I will explore the ways in which a historical biographer might use the letters and memoirs of earlier times in ways that parallel the effects Williams and Ancell sought in their contemporary histories. For the moment, however, I want to turn to a related way of capturing inwardness that is easily overlooked and that will always be difficult to measure. What I have in mind is the sort of transformative reading of older texts of which Smith's interpretation of Tacitus is such a startling example.

Though reading practices are notoriously hard to recapture, there is good evidence that eighteenth-century Britons were moving away from the idea that history should be read strictly for its public and didactic purposes and were beginning to relish the evocative possibilities open to the historical reader. (See chapter 4.) For such readers, memoirs, letters, and other first-person documents held a particular attraction, because they promised unmediated access to the experiences of another time. If sufficiently expressive, such documents held out the possibility that a historian might abandon the attempt to write narrative altogether and overcome the problem of gaining access to inwardness by offering himself as an editor, not an author. This was, of course, a familiar strategy of eighteenth-century fiction, but it may also have been a larger motive in the historical and antiquarian publication of the time than we have yet noticed.

A case in point is Lucy Hutchinson's *Memoirs of the Life of Colonel Hutchinson,* a memoir of the Civil War first published in 1806. Students of English

---

preparing a longer study on Smollett and contemporary history: "Impolite Atoms and Polite Histories: Tobias Smollett, Contemporary History, and the Republic of Letters in Eighteenth-Century Britain," M.A. thesis, Carleton University, Ottawa, 1996.

history who read this important seventeenth-century narrative in later, more scholarly editions will miss what earlier readers encountered in the first edition, a finely printed quarto, edited by the Reverend Julius Hutchinson in a spirit of family piety and modest antiquarianism.[42]

In the aftermath of the French Revolution, British political culture was dominated by counterrevolutionary hysteria. Julius Hutchinson's first concern, therefore, was to protect the political respectability of his ancestors, the republicans and regicides of an earlier revolution.[43] To condemn their actions would be presumptuous, Hutchinson argued, considering "the tempest and darkness which then involved the whole political horizon" (ix). Such a judgment would also amount to an act of ingratitude on the part of those who could now enjoy a balanced constitution thanks to the virtues and "even the mistakes" of their ancestors (ix). With these apologetics (adaptations, essentially, of Hume's view of the seventeenth century) Julius Hutchinson does what he can to remove the taint of revolution from the history of his family. But partisan conflict is not really his chosen ground, and, having vindicated the reputation of his ancestors, he moves on to another sort of politics that builds on historical presence rather than distance. Much of the remainder of the preface (as well as a number of sentimentalizing editorial footnotes)[44] is devoted to guiding the reader to an appreciation of the *Life* that diminishes its political content in favor of its social and domestic elements. Reverend Hutchinson begins by recommending the book as "a faithful, natural, and lively picture, of the public mind and manners, taken sometimes in larger, sometimes in smaller groupes" (xi), but proceeds to emphasize more than anything else its evocative power. The greatest appeal will be to "lovers of biography," which he calls the most numerous class of readers, since they will, "in fancy, have lived in times, and witnessed scenes

[42] *Memoirs of the Life of Colonel Hutchinson*, ed. Julius Hutchinson (London, 1806).

[43] "That avowed predilection for a republican government, which is conspicuous in this history, as it was in the lives of the persons who are the principal subjects of it, may perhaps give a momentary alarum," Hutchinson conceded; "but a little reflection will dissipate it" (ibid., iv–v).

[44] Regarding Lucy Hutchinson's account of a siege, he comments that it is "told in the most affecting, manner; the scene with which it finishes is surely as striking and as singular as any that story or imagination can furnish, not excepting the death of Le Fevre in the Sentimental Journey" (ibid., 258). Similarly, the death of the colonel from a fever elicits the following: "We now hasten to the conclusion of our tragedy, and accordingly here are all the principal characters in their proper places and attitudes: our hero suffering with fortitude, calmness, and dignity; the kind hearted brother, the idolizing devoted wife, the observant son and daughter soothing him with their assiduities, and the constant friends procuring and sending alleviations. Evils so endured, so consoled, almost begin to partake of the nature of enjoyments; but even this state of things will prove very transient, and like the last gleams of departing day, and we must speedily descend into the vale of tears."

the most interesting that can be imagined to the human mind, especially the mind of an Englishman."[45]

Up to this point, the gender of the author has not been particularly stressed and the reader remains conventionally male. But the preface moves toward an increasingly sentimental appreciation of the *Life* that inevitably concludes by linking its female author to a female readership and a presumptively female genre. Pointing to Lucy Hutchinson's talent for portraiture—"the delicate touch of the pencil of a female"—he ends his preface with a direct appeal to an audience of women:

> The ladies will feel that it carries with it all the interest of a novel, strengthened with the authenticity of real history: they will no doubt feel an additional satisfaction in learning, that though the author added to the erudition of the scholar, the research of the philosopher, the politician, and even the divine, the zeal and magnanimity of a patriot; yet she descended from all these elevations to perform in the most exemplary manner, the functions of a wife, a mother, and mistress of a family. (xiv)

Clearly this editor's sentimentalist strategy was shaped by his female subject as well as by anti-Jacobin fears. As a female history, the "memoir" could be nudged toward biography and novel, where more easily than in history proper the narrative could be depoliticized and the objectifying distances customary in historiography could be blurred or collapsed.[46] Accordingly the editor invited his readers—especially his female readers—to respond to those elements that allowed the *Life* to be read above all as a document of social custom and private feeling, the record of a virtuous female offered in devotion to the memory of a brave husband.

And what of the other side in the Civil War? Here, too, political interests and family pieties could be expressed as a program for rereading the documents of the great conflict. Two generations before the publication of Lucy Hutchinson's *Life,* Thomas Carte, a prominent and well-supported royalist historian, initiated a campaign that resulted in the publication of the lives and papers of a number of prominent Cavalier families.[47] Carte's clear purpose was to counter Whig views of the Civil War (and, more secretly, to promote the restoration of the Stuarts), but the terms in which he urged the public to read his documents carry implications far beyond his own Jacobite politics:

[45] Ibid., xii. "Perhaps the prevalence of this predilection [i.e. for biography] may be traced to the circumstances of the reader's thus feeling himself to be, as it were, a party in the transaction which are recounted. A person of this taste will, it is hoped, here have his wishes completely gratified" (xii).

[46] The title of "memoir" given to works of this kind is, of course, a first signal to the reader to expect something distinct from the conventional public framework of history.

[47] On Carte's Jacobite program, see Hicks, *Neoclassical History,* 159–69.

> Letters wrote in the scene and at the time of actions and negotiations, especially when wrote by persons present at those actions, and employed in those negotiations, are with reason deemed the most proper means of obtaining, and conveying down to posterity, just and authentick accounts of the transactions to which they relate. These accounts are generally more enlivening than narrations purely historical on the same subject, representing things (which Poets choose to do to render them more agreeable as well as moving) in the very action, bringing us as it were either back to those times, or exposing them so naturally to our view, that we are in a manner present at them; so that they are often as entertaining as any poetical descriptions.[48]

These letters, the editor goes on to say, "afford us the same pleasure which the fiction of a warm and fine imagination in a Poet is able to create," yet with the advantage of having truth on their side.

Twentieth-century readers encountering this passage are less likely to think of poetry than the novel; Carte's preface, in fact, strikingly anticipates the terms in which, just a few years later, Richardson introduced *Clarissa:* "the letters on both sides are written while the hearts of the writers must be supposed to be wholly engaged in their subjects: the events at the time generally dubious—so that they abound not only with critical situations, but with what may be called instantaneous descriptions and reflections, which may be brought home to the breast of the youthful reader: as also with affecting conversations, many of them written in the dialogue or dramatic way."[49]

The parallel attractions of Carte's historical archive and Richardson's fictional one—albeit addressed (nominally) to different classes of readers—suggest a more complicated genealogy of documentary research than the one historians generally subscribe to. The cornerstone of modern historiography, it has long been taught, is the primacy of document study—a primacy that is generally identified with the objective methods of nineteenth-century German historians, beginning with Leopold von Ranke. It is hard to look beyond profession shibboleths of this sort, most of all for the professionals themselves. Carte's preface, along with similar evidence from later in the century and the early part of the next, suggests, however, that historians might well rethink this part of their own history and consider the sentimental as well as the scientific value of the historical document.[50]

[48] Thomas Carte, *A Collection of Original Letters and Papers, Concerning the Affairs of England, from the year 1641 to 1660*, 2 vols. (London, 1739), 1:iii.

[49] Samuel Richardson, *Clarissa, or The History of a Young Lady*, ed. Angus Ross (Harmondsworth: Penguin, 1985), 35.

[50] Smollett's experiment with contemporary history in the *Continuation* once again provides an interesting parallel. An anonymous reviewer in Smollett's own periodical, the *Critical Review* comments: "In writing the history of the present times, Dr. Smollett has encountered difficulties which will vanish before a future historian; but he hath likewise experienced very peculiar advantages. . . . Our author sympathizes with the distress, and exults in the prosperity of his country,

Certainly, within the narrower limits of eighteenth-century historiography, Carte and Richardson together indicate that the most traditional forms of antiquarian publication could serve as occasions for the most "advanced" experiments in reading. Taken together with other evidence such as Adam Smith's rereading of Tacitus or Julius Hutchinson's editing of Lucy Hutchinson's *Life,* Carte's program suggests that in some remarkable ways reading outran writing in giving expression to a new historical outlook. Well before Britons could *narrate* a sentimental history of the social, it appears that they could already *read* one in the documents and narratives of an earlier age.

---

with heart-felt emotions that must appear counterfeit, should they be expressed by a writer of the future age." *Critical Review* 12 (1761): 284, cited from Smith, "Impolite Atoms," 80.

Four

History, the Novel, and the Sentimental Reader

HISTORIANS have argued that in the early modern period reading was conceived as an essentially public and active process. Though it seems unlikely that reading habits in all situations and genres followed the same pattern, this view of reading was certainly apt for works of history, and it is no coincidence that the idea of active, public reading is often illustrated by reference to historiographical texts.[1] In the latter half of the eighteenth century, however, an important shift took place in the way historical reading was described. History's reference to public matters did not disappear, nor did the reading habits associated with public instruction. Even so, there is evidence that many writers reconceived the reader's engagement with the historical narrative in more inward and sentimental terms. This shift in understanding of reading style had far-reaching implications. It worked against long-held assumptions about the value of historical instruction and so helped to reshape not only the formal but also the moral dimensions of historiographical practice.

One cannot pursue the question of eighteenth-century reading-styles very far without considering important questions of genre and audience—and especially, in this period, of a gendered audience. Contemporary thinking about historical writing relied on a series of contrasts that helped define the genre and set its place in the hierarchy of literatures; that is to say, history was defined by continual reference to other, associated genres—especially biography, memoir, or novel—which in turn derived much of their identity from their relations to history. The same contrastive habit operated with respect to audience, a key element of genre definition. History was defined by its appropriateness to an active, adult, male reader, whose interests and capacities were contrasted to the youthful, female, and private readership ascribed to the novel (and, to some extent, to biography as well). In this setting, the tension between active and sentimental reading I have spoken of was inevitably understood in

[1] On active reading, see Anthony Grafton and Lisa Jardine, " 'Studied for Action': How Gabriel Harvey Read His Livy," *Past and Present* 129 (1990): 30–78. Grafton and Jardine do not comment on genre and the ways in which it may condition reading styles, though much of their material in fact concerns historical reading. See also Paul Hunter, "The Loneliness of the Long-Distance Reader," *Genre* 10 (1977): 455–84. A good recent discussion, with notes to the growing literature on this subject, is Steven Zwicker, "Reading the Margins: Politics and the Habits of Appropriation," in *Refiguring Revolutions: Aesthetics and Politics from the English Revolution to the Romantic Revolution*, ed. Kevin Sharpe and Zwicker (Berkeley and Los Angeles: U of California P, 1998), 101–15.

reference to a series of other contrasts, making it difficult to discuss historical reading without also exploring history's relationship to the novel or its appeal to the female reader.

It is useful to recall for a moment Hume's letter to his friend William Mure, quoted at the opening of chapter 2, since it presents us with a very brief and engaging instance of the way in which such tensions were characteristically displayed and resolved by a male writer. As we saw, Hume refers the highest obligations of the historian, namely truth and impartiality, to Mure himself, while Mrs. Mure commands the subordinate, but still necessary quality of interest. As a man and a public figure, Mure would be able to judge whether justice had been done to both sides in the Civil War, while his wife's attention would be absorbed by the fate of individuals, more than the clash of principles.

No doubt Hume addressed himself to actual female readers, for whom Mrs. Mure is a kind of surrogate, but his invocation of her sympathy for "poor King Charles" also signals his desire to experiment with sentimental possibilities usually associated with female readership and the fictional genres. The Mures, it is clear, stand in for a range of conflicting values Hume wished to reconcile in his writing: truth versus interest, impartiality versus compassion, justice versus pity, parties versus persons. By extension, from the point of view of reception, the Mures represent two different forms of attention to history, thus two different ways of understanding the activity of reading history. Evidently, translating these forms of reading into the familiar terms of gender provided a useful sense of order among a range of conflicting demands. At the same time, by displacing on to the female reader an essential, if subordinate element of his own historical outlook, Hume found a place for a part of his history that would otherwise be hard to reconcile with strict neoclassical prescriptions. Less explicit in this context, but no less important are parallel issues of genre, since female readers were conventionally regarded as forming the audience not for history but fiction. As a result, the unspoken effect of Hume's homage to Mrs. Mure is to move his history still further from his earlier writings in philosophy toward the nominally female realm of novelistic fiction.

In other hands, these reciprocities of genre and gender could also be invoked for a very different purpose. If the female reader possessed symbolic value, so too did the act of reading history. In fact, women who were ambitious to be recognized as capable of reasoning about public matters had reasons to resist inclusion on Hume's terms. For them, it was important that history should retain its customary dignity, if women were going to consider it a worthwhile prize. As a result, historical reading needed to remain diligent and accountable, even if insistence on these qualities had once been an instrument of female exclusion. Ironically, then, such women invested in the traditional associations of genres, even as women's presence as a newly recognized reading audience inevitably exerted a pressure for change. Reading history, as we are continually reminded by such discussions, meant more than having access to a few shelves in the library.

Reading History Diligently; Reading History Sympathetically

Treatises on the "art of history" make it plain that history written in the classical tradition assumed an active and accountable reading-style. The best-known English example of this common seventeenth-century genre is Degory Wheare's treatise, translated and enlarged by Edmund Bohun as *The Method and Order of Reading both Civil and Ecclesiastical Histories* (1685).[2] Wheare conducts a methodical survey of ancient historians and accompanies this program of systematic reading with a view of the reading process that is correspondingly orderly and laborious. Three things are necessary, he writes, for the student to receive the greatest benefit from his reading of history:

> First, that the Order he observe be Right and Constant, that he be not confused, wandring and desultry in his Reading. Secondly, That he have a clear and good Judgment, that he may with dexterity apprehend what he reads, and well discern what is to be selected. Thirdly, There ought to be employed a diligent and exact industry, that gathering Stores of all sorts, they may be regularly disposed as it were in a Granary.[3]

This diligent style of reading demands a great deal from the reader, and Wheare devotes the second part of the treatise to considering the question, "who is to be esteem'd a competent, well qualified reader of history" (297). His conclusion is that history, like moral philosophy, is beyond the reach of children and ignorant men. (It is a sign of the times that female readership—so prominent in eighteenth-century discussions—does not arise at all.) Such people may reap a measure of delight from "remembering some pretty stories," but they lack the capacity to use the examples history presents. His intended reader—"the reader we are now forming" (308)—studies histories for improvement, not pleasure, so it is absolutely necessary that "the reader of histories be studious and diligent, serious and attentive, constant and steady" (315).

[2] Wheare's *Reflectiones hyemales, de ratione et methodo legendi utrasque historias, civiles et ecclesiasticas* (Oxford, 1637) was translated by Edmund Bohun as *Method and Order of Reading Both Civil and Ecclesiastical Histories* (1685). I have used the third edition (London, 1678), which includes Dodwell's "Invitation to Gentlemen to acquaint themselves with Antient History." On Wheare and Bohun, see Woolf, *Idea of History*, 186–90; and Levine, *Battle of the Books*, 278–80.

[3] Wheare, *Method and Order*, 19–20.

Wheare's conception of "studious and diligent" reading attaches itself to the idea that history offers public lessons and therefore must be of the greatest use to readers engaged in public business. This was a fundamental of the classical tradition and was restated many times in early modern writings. Thus later editions of Bohun's volume appeared with a prefatory essay by Henry Dodwell, who insisted that the best reader of history would be a gentleman, not a scholar. The study of history works "to the accomplishment, not of the Speculative, but the Practical, Reader, that is of such a one as for the future should be engaged in Civil, or Military Affairs."[4]

In the eighteenth century, however, the conjunction of classes of readers and modes of reading assumed by Wheare and Dodwell came under pressure both from those who would widen the circle of readers as well as those—not always the same—who invested the reading process with new, more interiorized meaning. I will return to the question of audience later in this chapter, but for the moment I want to focus on the reading process itself. Here there are many signs that another view of reading had gained ground, according to which readers were invited to cultivate sympathetic identification and even dreamy self-forgetting.

The idea of sympathetic reading is set out with particular clarity in several of the essays William Godwin collected under the title of the *Enquirer* (1797). In discussing the moral effects of literature, Godwin recognizes a degree of autonomy for the reader's experience that undercuts any possibility of a strictly accountable reading process. "It seems that the impression we derive from a book," Godwin argues, "depends much less upon its real contents, than upon the temper of mind and preparation with which we read it."[5] Similarly, in an essay on childhood reading, he celebrates readers who, totally absorbed in their books, take on the full coloration of the author's mind:

> It is impossible that we can be much accustomed to such companions, without attaining some resemblance of them. When I read Thomson, I become Thomson; when I read Milton, I become Milton. I find myself a sort of intellectual chameleon, assuming the colour of the substances on which I rest. (33)

The poor reader, for Godwin, is one who resists this self-seduction, perhaps because he read little as a child or came to reading late. Such a reader never allows himself to become intimate with the author. "Stiffness and formality are always visible between them. He does not become the creature of the author: neither bends with all his caprices, nor sympathizes with all his sensa-

[4] Dodwell, "Invitation to Gentlemen," par. III (unpaginated). On Dodwell, see Levine, *Battle of the Books*, 93–101.

[5] William Godwin, *The Enquirer* (London, 1797; rpt. New York: A. M. Kelley, 1965), 135, and 144–45.

tions" (34). Rapt absorption is the gift of those who read avidly as children. Only those who grew into "this mode of reading" early can receive their full share of its blessing of self-improvement.[6]

In reading Godwin we need to bear in mind that earnest books of advice continued to urge young readers to practice an accountable reading style,[7] while contemporary moralists loudly denounced sentimental fiction for inducing just this sort of dreamy self-forgetting, especially in young and female readers. But Godwin not only applauds the unchecked flow of sympathies, he makes no distinction between classes of readers or of genres. As a result, though neither history nor the novel is mentioned, one feels that his self-portrait as reader applies equally to the wide range of writing in history, biography, and historical fiction that made up Godwin's own literary career. It seems appropriate, for instance, that in his essay "Of the Study of the Classics," also published in the *Enquirer,* he urges us to read the Roman historians in a spirit of intimacy.[8]

Godwin's views on reading might be set aside as a "precursor" of romanticism, yet a full generation earlier central figures of the British Enlightenment recognized similar connections between historical narrative and sympathetic response. Though Kames, Ferguson, or Priestley did not focus so explicitly on the activity of reading itself, their analysis of the moral powers of literature implies a historical reader much like the one Godwin portrays.

[6] Though politically much opposed to Godwin, Thomas Green gives an account of childhood reading much like Godwin's: "It is not merely that in early youth we are blind to defects, but that we enter with an *entire* and cordial interest into whatever captivates the imagination. When I first read Robinson Crusoe—(the remembrance of it is still delightful, and refreshing to the spirits)—I went along with him completely—I was absorbed in his adventures: I sailed with him on the raft; I saw the print of the foot upon the sands; I prattled with Friday. The most devoted novel-reader, in maturer life, I should suppose, never attains to such a perfection of illusion and interest. It is indeed scarcely possible that he should." *Extracts from the Diary of a Lover of Literature* (Ipswich, 1810). Godwin's recollection of his own childhood passion for reading follows the same lines: "it was scarcely possible for any preceptor to have a pupil more penetrated with curiosity and a thirst after knowledge than I was when I came under the roof of this man. All my pleasures were sedentary; I had scarcely any pleasure but in reading; by my own consent, I should sometimes not so much as have gone into the streets for weeks together." Quoted in *Caleb Williams*, ed. M. Hindle (Harmondsworth: Penguin, 1988), xxix.

[7] See, for example, John Trusler, *Principles of Politeness, and of Knowing the World* (London, 1775), 82–83: "Take up some valuable book, and continue the reading of that book til you have got through it; never burden your mind with more than one thing at a time: and in reading this book don't run over it superficially, but read every passage twice over, at least do not pass on to a second till you thoroughly understand the first, nor quit the book till you are master of the subject; for unless you do this, you may read it through, and not remember the contents of it for a week."

[8] "We must watch their minutest actions, we must dwell upon their every word. We must gain admission among their confidents [*sic*], and penetrate into their secret souls" (*Enquirer*, 41).

Adam Ferguson outlines the moral importance of history's power to evoke sympathetic emotion in a brief, but comprehensive passage in his *Essay on the History of Civil Society* (1767).

> As actors or spectators, we are perpetually made to feel the difference of human conduct, and from a bare recital of transactions which have passed in ages and countries remote from our own, are moved with admiration and pity, or transported with indignation and rage. Our sensibility on this subject gives their charm, in retirement, to the relations of history, and to the fictions of poetry; sends forth the tear of compassion, gives to the blood its briskest movement, and to the eye its liveliest glances of displeasure or joy.[9]

For Ferguson, history, like poetry or other forms of narrative, stirs in us a current of sympathy that (combined, as he is careful to stipulate, with the workings of reason) stands as the basis of our moral natures. His emphasis on the universality of the principle of sympathy points to the ubiquity of spectatorial relationships in literature as in life. Ferguson brings art and lived experience into a single frame of analysis. At the same time he makes no distinction between the genres, at least for purposes of moral education, since both the "relations" of history and the "fictions" of poetry have the power to turn "human life into an interesting spectacle" (36).

The source of Ferguson's views on the moral psychology of literary response was, more than likely, Lord Kames's influential *Elements of Criticism* (1762). Kames argues that the passions are moved by fiction, as well as by truth. Verbal representations ("fiction") have the same power as actual experience—or the memory of experience—to stir the passions. Neither memory nor representation can have this effect, however, unless the scene represented carries with it a degree of vividness that results in a loss of critical distance, a kind of "waking dream." Kames calls this crucial effect "ideal presence."

It is a key point for Kames that the effect of ideal presence requires a reader who is wholly receptive. The playgoer willingly loses himself in the spectacle; so too, the absorbed reader loses all sense of the separation of art and life and enters the pages as if in a dream:

> The reader's passions are never sensibly moved, till he be thrown into a kind of reverie; in which state, losing the consciousness of self, and of reading, his present occupation, he conceives every incident as passing in his presence, precisely as if he were an eye-witness.[10]

Much of what Kames has to say about composition comes back to this central requirement to enhance the reader's absorption in the "scene" before him.

[9] Ferguson, *History of Civil Society*, 36.
[10] Henry Home, Lord Kames, *Elements of Criticism*, 3 vols. (Edinburgh, 1762), 1:112.

Nothing, he insists, should be done to jar the illusion of actuality.[11] Narration and description should aim to present clear and lively images. Unnecessary detail should be suppressed, but whenever particularity is needed to carry the sense of actuality, description must be as minute as possible. The force of writing lies in "raising complete images; which cannot be done till the reader, forgetting himself, be transported as by magic into the very place and time of the important action, and be converted, as it were, into a real spectator, beholding every thing that passes."[12]

I need hardly say how important this idea of transporting the reader to "the very place and time" would become to historical narrative and its allied arts—historical novel, biography, historical painting, and all the rest. The phrase carries with it, in fact, an implication of the transformation of historical distance that becomes pervasive in historiographical criticism in succeeding generations. But Kames, it is clear, was not thinking specifically of *historical* evocation. The point, rather, is that he did not recognize any limit to the principle of ideal presence, so that he could apply it with equal force to epic, drama, and even *The History of the Peloponnesian War*. For Kames, in fact, as for rhetorical theorists in our own day, history seemed an attractive proving ground for an argument that stresses the universality of the processes of the literary imagination:

> In support of the foregoing theory [i.e., ideal presence], I add what I reckon a decisive argument. Upon examination it will be found, that genuine history commands our passions by means of ideal presence solely; and therefore that with respect to this effect, genuine history stands upon the same footing with fable. To me it appears clear, that our sympathy must vanish so soon as we begin to reflect upon the incidents related in either. The reflection that a story is a pure fiction, will indeed prevent our sympathy; but so will equally the reflection that the persons described are no longer existing. It is present distress only that moves my pity.[13]

For Kames, ideal presence was much more than a source of rules for effective composition, though it is that too. Above all, ideal presence furnished him with an explanation of the moral purposes of literature, though one that differed in some significant ways from traditional mimetic conceptions. "It is wonderful to observe," he wrote,

> upon what slight foundations nature sometimes erects her most solid and magnificent works. In appearance at least, what can be more slight than ideal presence of objects? And yet upon it entirely is superstructed, that extensive influence which language

[11] See, for instance, Kames's comment on suspension of disbelief in drama: "The spectator once engaged is willing to be deceived, loses sight of himself, and without scruple enjoys the spectacle as a reality" (ibid., 3:254).

[12] Ibid., 3:174.

[13] Ibid., 1:115.

hath over the heart; an influence, which, more than any other means, strengthens the bond of society, and attracts individuals from their private system to exert themselves in acts of generosity and benevolence.[14]

Kames obviously relished his success in discovering so important a principle, one whose operations he saw as further evidence of a benevolent creation.[15] Yet it remains unclear how Kames regarded ideal presence in relation to more traditional notions of the didactic powers of history and other literatures. There are certainly some important differences between the idea that we grow in moral power through repetitive exercise of our sympathies and the ancient doctrine of instruction summed up by Bolingbroke when he said that history is philosophy teaching by example. I will return to this issue at the end of this chapter.

History and the Female Reader

Few writers joined Kames in giving so wide a scope to sympathetic reading. In theory, at least, most acknowledged the need to subordinate sentimental identification in history to more rational forms of understanding. Both Priestley and Campbell, for example, inclined in this direction.[16] But rather than pursue their discussions of the rhetoric of history, I want to explore another way in which sentimental reading was both promoted and limited: namely through the conventional association between sentiment and the female reader—a strategy we have already seen demonstrated in Hume's letter to William Mure.

A good illustration is provided by John Bennett's *Letters to a Young Lady on a Variety of Useful and Interesting Subjects. Calculated to Improve the Heart, to Form the Manners and Enlighten the Understanding* (1789), a work whose title says much about the sentimental framework of his views on female education. "Cultivate then, such studies, as lie within the region of sentiment

[14] Ibid., 1:121.

[15] In the theodicy that underpins all of Kames's writings, the broad application of this principle confirms the design of the moral world: "It therefore shows great wisdom, to form us in such a manner as to be susceptible of the same improvement from fable that we receive from genuine history. By this admirable contrivance, examples to improve us in virtue may be multiplied without end" (ibid., 1:127).

[16] Joseph Priestley reviews the same kinds of "reality-effects" that interest Kames in his *Course of Lectures*. See, for example, his discussion of the power of circumstantial description (84–85). Like Kames, too, he insists that in mobilizing the passions history and fiction stand on much the same footing. "The faithful historian, and the writer of romances, having the same access to the springs of the human passions, it is no wonder that the latter generally moves them more forcibly, since he hath the choice of every circumstance that contributes to raise them; whereas the former hath nothing in his power but the *disposition* of them, and is restricted even in that." In his *Lectures on History and General Policy* (Birmingham, 1788), however, Priestley subordinates sentimental reading to higher and more rigorous ways of learning from history.

and taste," he counsels his female reader: "Let your knowledge be feminine, as well as your person. And let it glow within you, rather than sparkle upon others about you."[17] Bennett's prescription entirely excluded metaphysical interests, but he did not put history beyond the reach of women. On the contrary, he believed that women should know something of the history of their own country—including a general character of the kings and queens, the manners and customs of the primitive Britons, the ways in which the present state of civilization was introduced, the causes of the Reformation, and the development and advantages of the British constitution. These topics point to a perhaps surprisingly up-to-date view of historical understanding. It is evident, in fact, that Bennett regarded the "philosophical" view of history as especially suited to female readers, since for women, history is not so much the study of politics—"a mere detail of names, facts, epochs, and events"—as a portrait of human nature and a lesson in God's providence (173).

Bennett fills out the picture with practical advice on particular authors and texts. He comments on histories that offer a good understanding of manners and customs. He also favors works of abridgement and synthesis, a concession to the limits of female application. "Knowledge thus epitomized is what I would recommend," he writes in relation to Dodd's *The Beauties of History.*[18] But his principal suggestion has to do with a different way of epitomizing history:

> That species of history, which describes the lives and characters of particular persons, and is included under the name of biography, is by far the most useful and interesting to a woman. Instead of wars, sieges, victories or great achievements, which are not so much within the province of a female, it presents those domestick anecdotes and events, which come more forcibly home to her bosom and her curiosity. (184)

Clearly, Bennett's gesture of welcome to the female reader—predicated as it was on an opposition between public and sentimental reading—confirmed rather than denied that women would approach history in their own distinctive manner. Nonetheless, Bennett did not exclude women from historical reading, and the partial opening that he and others provided served as an opportunity to claim a wider definition of female competence. Just as for Hume gender could be an instrument for redefining the historical genre, so for feminist writers like Chapone or Wollstonecraft, the historical genre seemed a prize worth pursuing in their struggle to raise the status of their sex.

Men "allow us Poetry, Plays, and Romances, to Divert us and themselves," wrote Mary Astell early in the century; "and when they would express a particular Esteem for a Woman's Sense, they recommend History." But Astell waves

[17] John Bennett, *Letters to a Young Lady* (Warrington, 1789), 169.

[18] On ancient history, for example, he recommends Rollin over the original authors, who "are too voluminous for a female." He also recommends Goldsmith and Robertson (ibid., 177–80).

away the condescending gesture, saying, "History can only serve us for Amusement and a Subject of Discourse. For tho' it may be of Use to the Men who govern Affairs, to know how their Fore-fathers Acted, yet what is this to us, who have nothing to do with such Business?"[19] When a few women do make their way into histories, Astell continues, they are regarded as having acted beyond their sex: "By which one must suppose they wou'd have their Readers understand, That they were not Women who did those Great Actions, but that they were Men in Petticoats!"

For Astell, then, the gendering of reading ultimately required a complex gesture of renunciation. If history had little meaning for a sex excluded from public life, women's reason had higher objects to contemplate in religion and the sciences. Even so her remarks indicate the strong association between reading history and the exercise of reason that would make later writers insist that women too could achieve competence in history. But this change, as we will see, depended not only on a greater assertiveness among female readers, but also on a widening definition of history that was less tied to the exclusively male domain of political action.

Hester Chapone, a member of Samuel Richardson's circle and later of the Bluestockings, is remembered principally for her *Letters on the Improvement of the Mind* (1773). A pious and high-minded conduct book, the *Letters* includes a letter "On the Manner and Course of Reading History," as well as one on geography and chronology. Chapone's prescriptions for women's education seem in many ways closer to Degory Wheare's diligent reading-process than to the looser, sympathetic reading of Godwin. "When you have gone through Rollin's "Histoire Ancienne" *once,*" she remarks, "then will be the time to fix the ancient Chronology deep in your mind, which will very much enhance the pleasure and use of reading it a *second* time; for you must remember that nobody reads a history to much purpose who does not go over it more than once."[20]

This is not to say that Chapone's view of history is without sentimental elements, or that she recognizes no difference between male and female reading style. She frequently comments, for example, on the "interesting" contents of the histories she reviews. On the other hand, she also emphasizes the need for a regular plan of reading, so that histories of different times and places are not indiscriminately mixed. Significantly, she stresses the value of repeating to a friend important parts of what has been read, so that striking particulars

[19] [Mary Astell] *The Christian Religion, as Profess'd by a Daughter of the Church of England* (London, 1705), 292–93. On Astell, see Gianna Pomata, "History, Particular and Universal," *Feminist Studies* 19 (1993): 9.

[20] Hester Chapone, *Letters on the Improvement of the Mind, Addressed to a Young Lady,* 3d ed. (London, 1774), 170–71.

will be fixed in the memory and can be refreshed in a second reading.[21] This way of reading is obviously not public in the same sense as Wheare's lessons for young men who would someday be statesmen; even so, it might be thought of as seeking an equivalent sense of accountability within its own much more restricted community.

Chapone's program for female readers, like Bennett's, favors philosophical history over the narrower confines of political narrative.[22] In particular, the broad horizon of Britain's imperial history—a topic requiring an understanding of "the amazing progress of navigation and commerce"—offered her scope to comment on a wide range of topics, including the dangers of hero worship, the contrast of East and West, the barbarity of European conquests in Africa and America, the swift progress of the American colonies and the concomitant dangers of corruption (201–8). Evidently, the opportunity for moral commentary was one of the attractions of the philosophical approach.

The obvious preference that both Chapone and Bennett show for philosophical history over political narrative invites a further comment. Their interest in the history of manners gives evidence of the way in which manners constituted a mediating discourse in this period. Since manners were regarded as a legitimate female sphere, as well as a link between the domestic and the social worlds, the concept of manners opened a wide, new path for the female reader.

The customs of the primitive Britons, or the introduction of civilization into England appear far removed from cloistered female interest or experience. But these topics are not taken in isolation; rather they stand in implicit counterpoint to another kind of history writing whose preoccupations were seen as exclusively public and male. Paradoxically, then, in the library of female reading, the primitive Briton stood closer to the interests of women than a contemporary dispute over parliamentary politics.

One might also pursue the thought a step further. Considered in the light of the conjectural history of humankind, the primitive Briton and the contemporary Englishwoman, in fact, had much in common. Both were creatures governed by the passions and swayed by extremes of sensibility. In fundamental ways, both stand outside of the structures of history, which only properly commences when men become possessors of property, acquiring and extending the means of domination over other men and, of course, women. In short, primitive man shares with women in all states of rudeness and refinement a common condition as "other" to the world of political action. However wide, therefore,

[21] Ibid., 186.

[22] In a cautious discussion of the way in which English historiography has suffered from political partisanship, she offers the advice that "as *you* will not read with a critical view, nor enter deeply into politics, I think you may be allow'd to choose that which is most entertaining; and, in this view, I believe the general voice will direct you to Hume" (ibid., 212).

the "objective" distance between them, the savage Briton and the female reader share their common exclusion from the high ground of classically conceived historical narrative. Neither one, it is fair to say, has a narratable history.[23]

History and Novel: Wollstonecraft and Hamilton

If history was flanked on one side by the philosophical history of manners, it was challenged on the other by the attractions of the novel. Given the conventional linkage of young women and fiction, the polarity of history and novel was sure to find its way into any discussion of the taste and capacity of female readers.[24] Though the reading habits of actual readers were far more varied, in the simplified symbolisms that such polarities evoke, the choice between histories and novels often stands for the essentials of male and female reading, and even in more complex discussions, neither genre ever entirely loses this symbolic valence.

In her passionate advocacy of women's rationality, Mary Wollstonecraft employed the symbolism of genres in just this way. Since women are denied all political privileges, she argues in the *Vindication of the Rights of Women* (1792), their attention is drawn from the good of the whole community to that of its smallest parts. In their resulting ignorance and isolation, they cultivate sentiment at the expense of more profound and active forms of understanding:

> But, confined to trifling employments, they naturally imbibe opinions which the only kind of reading calculated to interest an innocent frivolous mind inspires. Unable to grasp anything great, is it surprising that they find the reading of history a very dry task, and disquisitions addressed to the understanding intolerably tedious, and almost unintelligible? Thus are they necessarily dependent on the novelist for amusement.[25]

Wollstonecraft, a novelist herself, did not condemn all reading of fiction. Women need to be "led by degrees to proper studies," a process of improvement of understanding in which novel reading can play a part.[26] By the same

[23] On this point I have learned much from discussions with my former student Mary Catherine Moran. See " 'The Commerce of the Sexes': Civil Society and Polite Society in Scottish Enlightenment Discourse," in *Paradoxes of Civil Society: New Perspectives on Modern German and British History*, ed. Frank Trentmann (Providence: Berghahn Books, 1999).

[24] See Jane Spencer, *Rise of the Woman Novelist: From Aphra Behn to Jane Austen* (Oxford: Blackwell, 1986); Janet Todd, *Sign of Angellica: Women, Writing, and Fiction, 1660–1800* (London: Virago, 1989); and Ros Ballaster, *Seductive Forms: Women's Amatory Fiction from 1684–1740* (Oxford: Oxford UP, 1992).

[25] Mary Wollstonecraft, *Vindication of the Rights of Woman* (1792) (Harmondsworth: Penguin, 1985), 306.

[26] In illustration she offers the story of a wise man left in charge of two young women. His niece, who had considerable abilities, he encouraged to read history and moral essays, but his

token, Wollstonecraft saw that reading history in anything less than a diligent manner meant conceding ground to a restricted sense of female capacities. Women should study politics, she writes, "and settle their benevolence on the broadest basis; for the reading of history will scarcely be more useful than the perusal of romances, if read as mere biography; if the character of the times, the political improvements, arts, etc., be not observed. In short, if it be not considered as the history of man" (261). For her, significantly, philosophical history does not figure as an extension of women's domestic interest in manners and an alternative to the study of politics. On the contrary, in Wollstonecraft's campaign against the gendering of reading, philosophical history evidently stands for a wide understanding of politics and history that should be open to all rational observers, male and female alike.

Wollstonecraft's *Vindication,* it should be added, does not demonstrate any deep interest in history itself, only in what it symbolizes for women. In this context, history's function is inseparable from its habitual pairing with the novel. Thus it was not so much history that mattered, actually or symbolically, to Wollstonecraft, but the larger scheme in which history and novel stand for active and passive intellect, for rational responsibility and sentimental confinement. In essence she adopted the Aristotelian and humanist doctrine that active engagement amplifies the powers of individuals, but denied the classical premise that men alone are fit to enter the contest for civic honors. Only when women win full rights and responsibilities will history be truly, unsentimentally *interesting;* only then, we must assume, will ignorant women cease to "allow their imagination to revel in the unnatural and meretricious scenes sketched by the novel writers of the day, slighting as insipid the sober dignity, and matron graces of history."[27]

Elizabeth Hamilton is most often remembered for her novel *Memoirs of Modern Philosophers* (1800), a satire on Godwin and his circle. Despite her reputation as an anti-Jacobin, however, Hamilton's educational politics in many ways align her with, not against, Mary Wollstonecraft's radical assertion of women's rationality. Her *Letters on the Elementary Principles of Education* (1801) is a program for educational reform based on principles of philosophical psychology largely taken from Dugald Stewart.[28] But Hamilton sets her own

---

daughter—too much indulged by a fond mother and consequently "averse to everything like application, he allowed to read novels . . . saying that if she ever attained a relish for reading them, he would have some foundation to work upon" (ibid., 308).

[27] Ibid., 309.

[28] Elizabeth Hamilton, *Letters on the Elementary Principles of Education*, 2 vols. (Bath, 1801). See also *A Series of Popular Essays, illustrative of principles essentially connected with the improvement of the understanding, the imagination, and the heart* (Edinburgh, 1813). On Hamilton, see Kelly, *Women, Writing, and Revolution*, chaps. 4, 8. On the intersections (especially regarding questions of education) of radical and conservative writers at the century's end, see Chris Jones, *Radical Sensibility: Literature and Ideas in the 1790s* (London: Routledge, 1993).

stamp on the discussion by the attention she gives to women and the poor, topics that engage her feminist and Evangelical sympathies.

Hamilton's indignation at the miseducation of women in a society that encourages "beautiful imbecility"[29] matches Wollstonecraft's. She protests that "from the cradle upwards every possible pains have been taken to destroy the rational faculty. Without judgment, there can be no knowledge of first principles; without first principles, there can be no rule of conduct or of duty."[30] The mental habits of childhood are not, of course, the only determinants; reading, too, has a role in reinforcing or counteracting other influences. In one of her letters, Hamilton writes that minds cramped in early life, "as is generally the fate of my sex," are likely to remain static. People in this condition will make no attempt to rise above the intellectual condition of those around them, unless a love of reading counteracts their situation. "A lively imagination creates a sympathy with favourite authors, which gives to their sentiments the same power over the mind, as that possessed by an intimate and ever-present friend: and hence a taste for reading becomes to females of still greater importance than it is of to men."[31]

Hamilton's comment both endorses and reverses common assumptions about women's lives. A great deal of eighteenth-century commentary on reading is, in fact, directed to women. Plainly, this attention to women's reading is part of a general anxiety to police the "purity" of their lives, but more particularly it reflects the idea that women, possessing a more delicate sensibility than men, are more easily corrupted through the imagination. For her part, Hamilton gives the importance of reading a sociological and feminist coloration. Women, it appears, are not less rational than men, but they are more restricted in their activity and thus more dependent on the wider society of books. But the same is true, Hamilton adds in a nice twist, of men who are not in a position to choose their own associates: country squires and fox-hunters (absolute types of maleness!) are in just the same straits as women, since they are "tied down to the society of little minds."

A successful novelist and the author of an ambitious historical biography, Hamilton had more than an abstract interest in assessing the rival claims of history and fiction. Her *Memoirs of Agrippina, Wife of Germanicus* (1804) was written expressly to illustrate the psychological principles expounded in her work on education,[32] and the *Letters* includes "Observations Upon the Method

[29] Hamilton, *Elementary Principles of Education*, 2:212.

[30] Ibid., 2:213.

[31] See Elizabeth Benger, *Memoirs of the Late Mrs. Elizabeth Hamilton. With a selection from her correspondence, and other unpublished writings* (London, 1818), 142–43.

[32] See the preface to *Memoirs of Agrippina, the Wife of Germanicus*, 3 vols. (Bath, 1804), 1:vii: "To point out the advantages which are to be derived from paying some attention to the nature of the human mind in the education of youth, was the object of a former work; the Author's aim in

To Be Pursued in Reading History." Here Hamilton takes the "diligent" view of historical reading we have come to expect of feminist writers. The advantages gained from the study of history seem obvious: "under the direction of a judicious preceptor, it cannot fail to enlarge the conceptions, to increase the number of ideas, to improve the judgment, and to strengthen moral and religious principle in the heart."[33] The presence of the preceptor and the stress on intellectual growth indicate that Hamilton, like Wollstonecraft, sees history primarily as an exercise of the rational faculties. For these purposes, however, the ordinary business of names and dates has little value, nor—contra Bennett—does she believe women have anything to gain from abridgements.[34] The novel, on the other hand, symbolizes the kind of loose exercise of the imagination that destroys our rational capacities: "The swarm of heterogeneous absurdities that daily issue from the press under the appellation of Novels, would . . . afford the most convincing proof of the effects produced upon the mind by calling forth the imagination, while the powers of judgment are suffered to lie dormant."[35]

History, too, holds its perils, which are connected, significantly, to its power to evoke the reader's sympathies. History presents us with an "instructive portrait of the human passions," she writes—a formula that summarizes her program in writing the *Agrippina*. Unfortunately, the passions history depicts are generally those connected to ambition. For this reason, the "interest which [history] excites in the fate of heroes and conquerors" may mislead an "ardent mind" with images of false glory.[36]

Hamilton's objection is wide-ranging, applying as much to the humanist's trust in imitation as to the sentimentalist's mobilization of sympathy. Nor does she think that historians can easily evade the problem of misplaced sympathies and perverted heroism, since the attractions that lead to moral danger

---

the present is to give such an illustration of the principles that were then unfolded, as may render them more extensively useful."

[33] Hamilton, *Elementary Principles of Education*, 2:226.

[34] Instead, Hamilton recommends that even the young can learn by studying a detached period of history. As long as it is supplied with clear and distinct conceptions, she writes, "the mind may be capable of forming very just and accurate ideas concerning particular instances of human conduct, long before it is capable of embracing a series of complicated and successive events" (ibid., 2:231–32).

Hamilton does offer the point that abridgments are useful to the older and more learned, who already possess the materials of history. For them, every event recorded "awakens a chain of associations, and revives ideas which had become in a manner extinct" (ibid., 2:228).

[35] Ibid., 2:237. The passage continues: "We see invention on the stretch to produce effects to which the causes assigned are totally inadequate; the laws of nature violated; the course of the passions misrepresented; the principles of morality set at defiance; and the whole mixed up with a jargon of sentiment, which is incomprehensible to plain common sense" (237–38).

[36] Ibid., 2:224.

are implicit in the needs of narrative itself.[37] In (partial) reply, Hamilton stresses the real lessons of history, which depend neither on sentimental identification nor humanist emulation, but on exercising the judgment in search of more fundamental principles of understanding. "Were the judgment to be exercised in tracing *cause* and *effect,* as they are delineated in the historic page; the ardent youth, instead of being dazzled by the false lustre of splendid atchievements, would pursue their consequences to the human race, and see widespread ruin, pain, misery and devastation, the awful price of short-lived glory" (2:225–26).

"History and Romance": Godwin and Hamilton

Though Hamilton was much concerned with the special circumstances of women, her discussion of history and fiction, it is clear, goes far beyond the symbolism of the genres for female readers. Most fundamentally, she was concerned to defend the powers of rational judgment, including a rigorous reading of history, against an overreliance upon the powers of the imagination stimulated by fiction—a danger especially for education of the young.

I will return to Hamilton shortly, but to understand the threat she felt and the passion with which she defended historical knowledge, it is helpful to look to the other side of the debate. In particular, I want to turn to Godwin's "Of History and Romance," one of a group of manuscript essays that he intended as a second volume to the *Enquirer* (1797).[38] Here Godwin argues for a view of history and fiction that not only brings them very close to each other, but for some purposes elevates the claims of fiction over those of history. This brief essay remained unpublished until very recently, but it stands as a striking representation of the view of history that so alarmed Hamilton; at the same time, the essay can also be taken as working out the implications for genre of the sympathetic view of reading Godwin had articulated in the earlier set of essays.

Godwin opens with an attack on the rational abstractions of philosophical history, against which he presents a contrary demand for a history that is detailed, concrete, and emotionally compelling. For the sake of self-knowledge as well as knowledge of society, Godwin strongly prefers history that focuses

[37] "The historian who does not catch a portion of his hero's spirit, and enter with warmth into his interests, will be cold and inanimate. He who does, will be apt to throw false colours over actions that are in their natures base and vile" (ibid., 2:225).

[38] William Godwin, "Of History and Romance," in *Caleb Williams*, 359–73. Though the essay remained unpublished, Godwin did return to some of its ideas in the preface to *Mandeville*, though in ways that eliminated the tensions I point to below.

on the individual life and the individual mind. But he insists on the need to see the individual in his full particularity, which means exploring his private self as well as his public role:

> I am not contented to observe such a man upon the public stage, I would follow him into his closet. I would see the friend and the father of a family, as well as the patriot. I would read his works and his letters, if any remain to us. I would observe the thoughts and the character of his phraseology. . . . I should rejoice to have, or to be enabled to make, if that were possible, a journal of his ordinary and minutest actions.[39]

Godwin's hesitation over the thought that it might be possible to construct a journal if none already existed offers the first hint that knowledge so detailed and even intimate might call for an imaginative license not given to historians. In these early pages, Godwin looks to classical literature, not the novel, as the place where such possibilities are best realized; in the larger view, however, Godwin recruits both Plutarchan biography and modern fiction into an alliance against the thin abstractions of Enlightenment historiography (365–66).

Fifteen years before *Waverley,* Godwin pointed to the "historical romances" of Prévost as indicating a path for the historical imagination that might restore to history the richness of the great classical narrators. In fact, he insists, there is no essential division between the two genres. Romance is simply "one of the species of history."[40] The difference is that the conventional historian is "confined to the individual incident and individual man," while the romance writer can call upon the widest range of sources and experience, which the author generalizes and selects to have the greatest impact on the reader's heart and mind. In this sense, Godwin concludes, romance is a "bolder" species of composition than history.

Godwin refuses to be distracted by the criticism that romance corrupts our knowledge of history by mixing fact with fiction. History itself, Godwin insists, cannot possibly be accepted as a narrative of fact: "there is no darkness, if we consider the case maturely, as that of the historian."[41] Even direct witnesses to public events are hopelessly contradictory. More desperate, though, is the historian's conjectural knowledge of character—a subject on which we are all blind with respect to each other and even to ourselves. The fiction-writer, on the other hand, has complete knowledge of his own creation. "He must be permitted," Godwin writes, "to understand the character which is the creature of his own fancy" (372).

[39] Ibid., 364.
[40] Ibid., 370.
[41] Ibid., 371.

This is a remarkable moment. Godwin's observations seem a prescient recognition that the new and still uncertain techniques that allowed novelists to display unmediated access to other minds would be epoch making for the relations of history and fiction.[42] Certainly Godwin saw authorial omniscience as offering him a decisive argument to overturn the conventional hierarchy that placed the truths of history above the inventions of fiction: "The writer of romance, then, is to be considered as the writer of real history," while the historian must concede his place to his rival. Worst of all, the historian must be recognized as "a romantic writer without the arduous, the enthusiastic, and the sublime licence of imagination that belong to that species of composition."[43]

But the techniques of omniscient narrative were only in their infancy and even Godwin could not see very far into the possibilities that they would open up for writers of fiction. Just at the point at which he seems most insistent on sacrificing all other kinds of knowledge to privileged insight, Godwin retreats to a formulation that would not have been out of place in a conventional philosophical history. True history, he goes on to say, "consists in a delineation of consistent human character, in a display of the manner in which such a character acts under successive circumstances." Although a moment before he had emphasized the mysteriousness of character, here he speaks neither of its spontaneity nor opacity, but of consistency and the play of circumstance.

This "retreat" prepares the final reversal of this brief essay in which Godwin restores history, if not to its former dignity, at least to some of its utility. To write romance (in the ideal sense he gives it) is in fact too great a task for a human author since precise knowledge of how an individual would act in a series of settings would require an almost divine understanding. The historian's situation is quite different: he "does not understand the character he exhibits, but the events are taken out of his hands and determined by the system of the universe, and therefore, as far as information extends, must be true. The romance writer, on the other hand, is continually straining at a foresight to which his faculties are incompetent, and continually fails."[44]

In the end, then, Godwin accepts that the truths of history are open to inspection and correction in a way that inward truths are not. But this recognition that fiction is ultimately a more fragile form of knowledge than history does not fundamentally alter his sense that romance pursues deeper and more desirable forms of understanding. Thus having opened his essay with an attack

[42] I have explored some aspects of this important (and, I think, neglected) realignment in my essay "Scott, Macaulay." On the techniques of authorial omniscience, see again Cohn, *Transparent Minds*.

[43] Godwin, "Of History and Romance," 372.

[44] Ibid.

on the empty abstractions of philosophical history, Godwin leaves us with a justification for a new philosophical history of the individual, for which fiction, not history, is the ideal vehicle.

Very similar issues of history and fiction preoccupied Elizabeth Hamilton in writing the *Memoirs of Agrippina,* but she held fast to conclusions that Godwin only reluctantly conceded. The *Memoirs* was originally intended to initiate a series of historical biographies aimed at delineating the actual operation of the passions, a project much like the one Godwin assigns to the novel. Hamilton's program expresses her view that psychological study must go beyond philosophical introspection and be more aware of individual and dynamic factors in character. Metaphysicians, she writes, may be capable of separating the passions, but in life the passions blend together, showing their tendency to good or evil in the combinations they form with each other. This amounts to an argument that narrative, not philosophical abstraction, stands as the best method for the study of character.

To this point, Hamilton and Godwin share common ground, but Hamilton is not prepared to exchange the speculations of the metaphysician for those of the philosophical novelist:

> A work of the imagination, in which the characters are of the author's own creation, and in which every event is at his disposal, may be so managed, as to be admirably calculated to promote the reception of a favourite theory, but can never be considered as a confirmation of its truth. Nor will the theory built upon such a basis be of long duration; for though the brilliant illusions of fancy may affect the sensibility of the heart, and so far captivate the understanding as to render it unwilling to exert itself in detecting the fallacy of arguments which have spoken so powerfully to the feelings, the chasm will at length be broken, and then the system which had been supported by its influence, will inevitably sink into disgrace.[45]

Since philosophical novels were closely identified with Jacobin politics, Hamilton's disapproval is in good part political, but it is also clear that—as in her earlier work—she continues to hold fiction suspect because of its appeal to a youthful audience that lacks the strength of judgment to scrutinize stories addressed to the imagination.[46] Against fiction's acknowledged attractions, Hamilton argues for the more lasting rhetorical power that comes with the truth-telling claims of history. In biography, she writes, unlike the novel,

> expectation of amusement is chastened by the solemnity of the ideas attached to truth. The emotions produced will, on this account, be probably less vivid, but the interest will be deeper; while the impression made upon the mind by a belief in the

[45] Hamilton, *Memoirs of Agrippina*, 1:xi.

[46] Ibid., xi–xii.

> reality of the scene will give a peculiar force to whatever is calculated to operate either as warning or example.[47]

These considerations, she concludes firmly, determined her choice of biography. Yet as an honest biographer and especially as a student of mental life, she fully acknowledges that her choice for history over fiction brings with it some inevitable frustrations—the kind of frustrations, in fact, that preoccupied Godwin. Biography requires more than an effort to "trace the progress of an extraordinary mind,"[48] more than a study of the influences and circumstances that shaped the understanding. Creatures of the passions as well as the intellect, human beings never leave a full record of their own inner lives, and they can never be fully known to other human beings.

This is not, I think, a renunciation on Hamilton's part of the essential tasks of historical biography, much less an acknowledgment that her work has shifted in method, becoming (as has recently been said) a "quasi-novel."[49] On the contrary, it is a restatement of Hamilton's opposition to the philosophical novel in terms that, transcending the objections already raised, are complete and absolute. For Hamilton, it is essential to accept that a limit is placed on all our knowledge of other souls, however much we may desire to know more:

> for however possible it may be to trace the progress of talents, and to take the measure of the understanding, He who made the heart can alone appreciate its frailties and its virtues. Their record is on high, but the memorial that remains is imperfect, and the manner of their growth has eluded observation. To special acts of benevolence many may indeed give testimony; but the secret trials of the heart . . . are not of a nature to be disclosed.[50]

In this sense, the arrogance of the philosophical novelist goes far beyond political utopianism. For Hamilton, it amounts to a form of blasphemy.

James Mackintosh on Fiction and History

For all their differences, Hamilton and Godwin share a powerful desire to portray the complexity of the individual mind, and in consequence they give a new, more inward sense to the traditional ideal of exemplary history. Their

[47] Ibid., xiii. The passage begins: "Hence arises the advantage which the biographer possesses over the novelist. Amusement is expected by the reader from both; but in sitting down to peruse the memoirs of a fellow being, in whose past existence we have assurance, in whose eternal existence we have hope . . ."

[48] Ibid., xvi.

[49] See Kelly, *Women, Writing, and Revolution*, 269.

[50] Hamilton, *Memoirs of Agrippina*, 1:xvii–xviii.

heroes—real or fictitious—would not likely be patterns of virtue or vice, in the manner of humanist history. Rather, the sign of the hero is the depth of his emotions and the way in which his life gives the reader access to knowledge of the human mind.

This shift from the ideal to the actual, which is implicit in the entire sentimentalist outlook, is carried further in another contemporary essay on history and the novel, an unpublished fragment by the well-known Whig politician and historian, James Mackintosh.[51] (For more on Mackintosh's life, see chapter 8.) At the heart of Mackintosh's essay is the Kamesian view of literature as a vicarious exercise of moral sentiments, though curiously Mackintosh, a man of very wide reading, seems unaware of this influence and proudly stresses the originality of his own ideas. As we have already seen in discussing "ideal presence," the consequence of this concept of reading is to shift attention from the character of the hero to the mind of the reader. Consequently, though Mackintosh was a great admirer of the modern novel, his stress on spectatorial sympathy did not lead him to speculate that fiction might achieve superiority over history—the view that Godwin championed and Hamilton feared—but to emphasize the common ground of readerly sympathy uniting the two genres.

Mackintosh begins with Bacon's argument in the *Advancement of Learning* that poetry satisfies the human mind's need for events that are greater and more heroic than true history. Without refuting this humanist view, with its stress on imitation as a response to the ideal, he gives all his attention to a separate and parallel argument based on eighteenth-century doctrines of sympathy. The core of the argument is that fictions work to interest us in the lives of their characters and that the resulting feelings of sympathy promote benevolence. "Every fiction therefore in proportion as it delights, teaches us a new degree of fellow-feeling with the happiness or misery of other men; it adds somewhat to the disposition to sympathise, which is the Spring of benevolence; and benevolence is not only the Queen and Sovereign Lady of all the virtues, but that virtue for whose sake every other exists."[52]

The idea is plainly sentimentalist. In making it, Mackintosh drew on the eighteenth-century doctrines of sympathy that he took from Hume and Smith, and (as I have already said) his specific arguments for the moral value of fiction closely parallel those of Kames. Yet he clearly felt that he has added something important of his own; with a flourish that is rare in Mackintosh's writings (one

[51] Mackintosh's "essay" on the moral powers of fiction is found in his manuscript journal for August and September 1811, written while returning from India. See British Library, Add. mss. 52438B, 128r–156v. His son, Robert Mackintosh, reproduced a judiciously edited version of this material in *Memoirs of the Life of Sir James Mackintosh*, 2 vols. (Boston, 1853), 2:127–35. Mackintosh broached the same subject in a fragmentary journal written on his way out to India in 1804: see below, chapter 8.

[52] Mackintosh, BL Add. mss. 52438B 132r–132v.

that was suppressed in his son's posthumous publication of parts of the journal) he concludes: "That an operation of so much importance as this last should have escaped the attention of Philosophers seems extraordinary."[53]

So impressed is Mackintosh with this connection between fiction and benevolence that, in the manner of his Scottish mentors, he offers a brief natural history of the moral effects of fiction. The real importance of fiction would be much clearer if we could transport ourselves back into the "first abject condition of the human brute." Sometime in the dimness before all memory, he conjectures, a rare act of valor was celebrated in song. Although the motive of the savage poet was simply diversion, "something of the Sentiment which produced the virtue steals into his soul." In this way, isolated acts of virtue, "multiplied by a thousand mirrors of rude fiction," worked their way into the savage imagination and humanized what was brutal in their nature.[54]

The moral power of fiction is also demonstrated by its misuse, particularly in the way that writers can enlist our sympathies on behalf of characters who are morally flawed. This was a worry that critics expressed in relation to Richardson's Lovelace, for example, whom many readers found too attractive a villain. But Mackintosh extended the problem in a way that reflects his historical sense. Granting that fictions are more powerful teachers than moral treatises, he writes, we must recognize an important drawback. As works primarily of feeling, fictions must reflect "the prevalent feelings of the age." Thus it is natural that the *Iliad* glorifies not only the courage of Achilles, but also his cruelty. At the same time, since Homer has played a major role in civilizing Europe, the poem has inescapably altered its own moral position. Thus later readers of Homer need to read more selectively, seizing on the *Iliad*'s truly admirable qualities and turning away from its ferocity.[55]

Mackintosh's real interest, however, is not ancient poetry, but the modern novel, a genre of writing that he identifies firmly with modern England, female authorship, and the experiences of everyday life. In the brief time since *Clarissa* and *Tom Jones,* he writes, twelve novels of the first rank had appeared, an astonishing record in any chapter of literature, and in consequence the novel has acquired more influence on the public than all other kinds of books combined. This popularity is not, for Mackintosh, a minor point: "Nothing popular can be frivolous; whatever influences multitudes, must be of proportionable importance."[56]

[53] Ibid., 133r.

[54] Ibid., 133r–133v. The younger Mackintosh suppressed this excursus on "the great civilizing effect of fiction." Perhaps he disagreed with his father's view that fiction, not property and the division of labor, had been responsible for the progress of mankind.

[55] Ibid., 134r–136r.

[56] Ibid., 137r.

How had the novel acquired such a position? Mackintosh stresses the importance of its solid grounding in common life. The moral powers of fiction prove greatest "when the fiction most resembles that real life which is the sphere of the duties and feelings of the great majority of men." In consequence of these developments in the novel, there had been a "literary Revolution" that Bacon and Turgot would have looked upon with admiration, though "a foolish pedant sneers and a commonplace Moralist rails."[57]

We might follow several more themes in Mackintosh's discussion—his sense that the novel has marked an era for female writers, his counter to the antisentimentalist argument that novels dissipate rather than stimulate moral feeling, his reliance on associationalism to argue for the deepening of moral feeling through vicarious experience. But what is more critical here is to examine the implications he discovers in these arguments for the literary field where his own ambitions lay, the writing of history.

To defend the seriousness of the novel, a new genre, it was common to associate it with older and more dignified literatures, like history. Mackintosh, however, works in the opposite direction. History is not summoned to the defense of fiction; on the contrary, since the moral seriousness of the novel has already been well established, it is history, if anything, that seems to gain by the comparison:

> It should be observed that for the purpose of this argument, history and fiction are on a footing. Both present distress not occurring in our own experience. The effect does not at all depend on the particular or historical Truth, but on that more general or philosophical Truth of which Aristotle speaks, and which consists in a conformity to human nature. The effect of the death of Clarissa, or of Mary Stuart on the heart by no means depends on the fact that the one really died, but on the vivacity of the exhibition by the two great pathetic painters, Hume and Richardson.[58]

Mackintosh's affective poetics works against the neoclassical emphasis on the hierarchy of genres, focusing attention instead on the universality of reading. On this view, the link between every reader and writer lies in the way writing stimulates the play of the passions. This is the bridge that every writer must cross to find a reader, and here all genres necessarily draw close to one another.

Once this affective structure has been identified, history is easily assimilated to the general pattern. At the beginning of his essay, Mackintosh had generalized his argument by substituting "fiction" for poetry; now, in a further expansion, he restates his argument in its widest terms and replaces "fiction" with "narrative":

[57] Ibid., 137v.

[58] Ibid., 153v–154r.

> The honour and applause bestowed on Pity in Pathetic narrative is a means of moral discipline. I substitute narrative for fiction as if the matter be well considered the very same minute circumstances rendered present by the powers of imagination affect the mind when the outline is historical as when it is invented. All the Interest of the Story and all the charm of the Stile produce subordinate Sentiments which in a pathetic narrative flow into the main Stream of Pity, sweeten its composition, increase its pleasurable ingredients and strengthen the disposition towards it.[59]

Sympathetic Reading and Humanist Emulation

Godwin, Hamilton, and Mackintosh all responded, with varying degrees of enthusiasm or restraint, to the contemporary desire for inwardness that is as much a part of the history of historiography as of poetry or the novel. More particularly, these writers, along with many others of the latter part of the eighteenth century, all accepted the importance of sympathy, not only as the basis of social relations, but also as the essential bond that shapes the way readers enter into and experience a text. In concluding this chapter, I want to indicate very briefly some implications of their sympathetic view of reading, contrasting it to the doctrine of emulation that underpinned the humanist concept of history.

Writers in the classical tradition had long recommended history for its power to shape both the mind and the will to meet the tasks of public life. A central assumption of this humanist teaching was that a reader who is confronted with effective representations of the ideal will be moved by a spontaneous desire for emulation—or, in the case of vicious example, by an equivalent feeling of

[59] Ibid., 154v. One more expansion remains, which carries his thoughts away from history, but adds further interest to his analysis of literary response. Replying to an Edinburgh reviewer who had denied the affective power of drama on the ground that any theater performance is necessarily brief and transitory, Mackintosh counters with some acute remarks on the factors that make the experience correspondingly intense. He draws attention especially to the ritual and public character of dramatic presentation, a setting in which spectators are "kindled into enthusiasm by the action and reaction of each others passions." He emphasizes, too, the ways in which both anticipation and memory will amplify the effect of the drama and concludes that "these observations may be applied with the necessary abatements to all popular and powerful fictions" (156r–156v).

Given this sensitivity to the atmosphere enhancing the moral effectiveness of theater, it is worth noting that Mackintosh offers nothing comparable on the special conditions surrounding the reading of history. Yet surely, as Hamilton points out, history gains a special impact by the force of its compact never to invent. Hume might be as much of a "pathetic painter" as Richardson, but the strength of Hume's portrait consciously builds on the reader's acceptance of the reality of the Scottish queen's life and death. In this sense, the affective power of Hume's history depends in good part on precisely those features by which it could assert and maintain its difference from fiction.

abhorrence. The doctrine of sympathy, on the other hand, did away with this assumed equation between the ideal and exemplary. Moreover the educative goal it proposed was not so much a readiness for action as a kind of spectatorial fellowship that, as James Mackintosh put it, "strengthen[s] the disposition" toward a generous pity. In this way the humanist idea of imitation ceded to a sentimentalist conviction that (if presented with sufficient vivacity) characters and experiences more ordinary than ideal can foster habits of benevolence.

If the proponents of sensibility saw it as offering a kind of vicarious strengthening of the moral faculties, its opponents believed that sentimental reading would only induce a state of excited passivity that had no outlet in effective action. As the young Anna Laetitia Aikin put it in reference to novels of sentiment, "That they exercise sensibility is true; but sensibility does not increase with exercise."[60] Indeed, it has often been remarked that sentimental plots center on the man of feeling, not of action. This means that, even in the midst of great events, we may sacrifice the sense of the "hero" as an agent, with the obvious loss (from the humanist standpoint) of that clarity of outline that makes a character exemplary.

From another perspective, however, it is important to see that sympathetic reading was part of a crucial expansion of the aims of historical writing in the course of which the traditional historical task of mimesis was reinterpreted to include the evocation of past experience. History enlarged its scope to incorporate the wider spectrum both of actors and experiences that made up a modern, commercial, and increasingly middle-class society. Needless to say, much of this expanded scope lay beyond the concerns of traditional historical narration, with its exclusion of private life or everyday matters. Thus the reorientation of history to the idea of evocation presumed new ways of representing the past, as well as new ways of reading the text.

There is no doubt that fiction responded with particular quickness to the needs of the new literary audience, including its preoccupation with inward

[60] See *The Works of Anna Laetitia Barbauld*, 2 vols. (London, 1825), 2:227–28. The passage comes from "An Inquiry Into Those Kinds of Distress Which Excite Agreeable Sensations," first published in 1773 as part of a miscellany of essays written by Anna Laetitia Aikin and her brother John. The passage continues: "But in these writings our sensibility is strongly called forth without any possibility of exerting itself in virtuous action, and those emotions, which we shall never feel again with equal force, are wasted without advantage. Nothing is more dangerous than to let virtuous impressions of any kind pass through the mind without producing their proper effect." Barbauld also argues that the reader of sentimental fiction grows to expect that distressed virtue will present itself with "a certain elegance of manners and delicacy of virtue" that is seldom found in genuine scenes of poverty. Vicesimus Knox makes a similar criticism: "but if a distress equally afflicting occurs in the obscure village where the mansion-house stands, no notice is taken of it, or no more than a regard to common decency requires." *Winter Evenings: Or Lucubrations on Life and Letters*, 3 vols. (London, 1788), 2:94. Knox focuses on the desire to win a reputation for sensibility, a need that is best served when the scene of charity is more public.

feeling. But though we often proceed as if the audience for history and the readership for fiction were entirely separate, they must, in fact, have been very largely the same, thus ensuring that both literatures would respond to the same broad interests and questions. These readers—Mr. and Mrs. Mure and their many descendants to this day—insisted that while the first quality of the historian continued to be justice and impartiality, deeper insight into personality and experience would be needed for history to remain truly *interesting*.

LIVES, MANNERS, AND "THE HISTORY OF MAN"

Five

Biography and the History of Private Life

TRADITIONALLY, history and biography occupied separate, but adjacent domains divided by a seemingly natural boundary, which was the distinction between public and private life. In theory, then, the relationship between history and biography was both clear and complementary, but in practice the eighteenth century saw a deepening interest in the domain of the social that rendered the assumed opposition between public and private matters more problematic. Without always being explicit in their strategies, biographers found a number of ways to undercut the traditional hierarchies of public and private knowledge and to broaden the range and appeal of life writing. As biography ceased to be exclusively identified with the private lives of public men, it necessarily concerned itself increasingly with other domains of experience. The lives of poets or women often contained little in the way of action, but letters, journals, and literary anecdote opened windows on everyday worlds hard to evoke by any other means. It is noteworthy that the most famous biographical work of the century memorialized the cut and thrust of coffeehouse conversation, not clashes of arms or feats of statesmanship. Carlyle was not speaking for the nineteenth century alone when he called Boswell's *Johnson* the true history of the eighteenth century.

Like history, biography is an ancient art with an honorable place in the map of literary kinds. Conventionally, of course, history occupied much the higher position. Its objects of study were matters of undoubted importance, and it remained necessary to defer to the "dignity of history." But not all classes of readers could come up to the standards of seriousness associated with history; indeed, eighteenth-century writers recognized that even adult males whose position in society entitled them to participate in public affairs would sometimes prefer something more intimate and less formal. If histories boasted of their "dignity," biographies kept their "interest."

The popularity of biography, especially biography concerned with the affairs of "common life," was noted by contemporaries as a particular characteristic of their own times:

> The lives and actions of illustrous warriors and statesmen have ever been esteemed worthy the attention of the public: but this age has been the first to enter the more private walks of life, to contemplate merit in the shades, and to admire the more silent virtues. Dazzled with the glare of military talents, or caught in the intricacies of state politics; the world seldom condescended to look upon literary accomplish-

> ments even of the highest order; but wholly disdained the study of common life, and those characters which it would be of the most general use to be acquainted with, because they lie most open to imitation.[1]

At stake, so this writer clearly thought, was a major shift in attention, which gave biography both a new subject and a new and wider utility. Equally significant, perhaps, is the prominent place he gives to literature among the "more silent virtues" that contemporary biographers sought to articulate. The association made here between literary accomplishment and the desire to penetrate the "more private walks of life" has important implications for literary history as well as biography.

Biography and "The Study of Common Life"

An anonymous advice book entitled *Letters to a Young Nobleman* (1762) usefully sets out a number of the conventions incorporated in the eighteenth-century discussion of biography, including assumptions about the division between public and private matters and associated views of audience and gender. The *Letters* contains two chapters on history and another on biography, rounded out by further discussions of "the influence of liberty on taste." In defining a plan of studies, the author/tutor addresses himself specifically to his pupil's high social position. A young nobleman needs to take a particular interest in history, he argues, because the nobility is entrusted with care of the public realm, which is also the sphere of the historian:

> If then history chiefly relates such actions, as the first men of a country have had, and must have, a principal share in; when a young nobleman is reading history, tracing back the great events and revolutions of human affairs to their springs and causes, considering the characters of legislators and heroes . . . he is as much busied and employed in studying his own profession, as a watchmaker, who is viewing the machinery of a clock, and considering its springs and movements; or an anatomist, who is dissecting a human body.[2]

The writer admitted, however, that history's concern with public affairs severely limits its interest in individuals, a need best met by reading biography. Since the "happiness of the world depends no less upon the conduct of men in

[1] Thomas Martyn's life of his father, John Martyn, *Dissertations upon the Aeneids* (1760), i, quoted from D. Stauffer, *The Art of Biography in Eighteenth Century England* (Princeton: Princeton UP, 1941), 541. This discussion is much indebted to Stauffer's comprehensive survey, as well as Richard Wendorf's *Elements of Life: Biography and Portrait Painting in Stuart and Georgian England* (Oxford: Clarendon, 1990).

[2] *Letters to a Young Nobleman* (London, 1762), 15. The work is sometimes attributed to Robert Bolton.

their private than in their public capacities," biography has an important educative role.[3] Reading lives, he contends, is like being introduced into the best company—an elite argument that contrasts with the tendency of other contemporaries to universalize biography's appeal. Autobiography possesses some particular advantages, and it is a sign of the times that he cites fictional autobiography as proof of its value (65). Familiar letters, too, have a special attraction: "When one is writing to a friend the heart is open, and discloses those opinions and sentiments, which prudence makes it improper that all the world should be acquainted with, or which perhaps less honourable motives make men cautiously conceal" (69).

It is worth noting how easily this writer passes over the dangers to privacy that seem inseparable from his desire to know what is "improper that all the world should be acquainted with." We will have to come back to this question a number of times, since—as the dark side of the growing interest in private life—it constituted the central tension in contemporary commentary on the attractions of biography. For the moment, however, I want to follow up on another feature so apparent in this text, which is the importance of audience in determining definitions of genre. In this respect the closeness of biography to history is particularly telling, since lives are often recommended on exactly the same terms as histories, but to more protected classes of readers. "Biography has, ever since the days of *Plutarch,* been considered as the most useful manner of writing," Goldsmith wrote in his introduction to an abridgement of Plutarch's *Lives*. Biography "not only removes the dryness and dogmatical air of precept, but sets persons, actions, and their consequences before us in the most striking manner."[4] Put in this way, biography makes its claim as a kind of metonymic history—philosophy teaching by the most select examples—and, for this reason, Goldsmith wrote, it was particularly suited to instructing the young. Others would make much the same point about women, another group of sheltered readers. "Instead of wars, sieges, victories or great atchievements," wrote John Bennett in his book on female education, "which are not so much within the province of a female, it [i.e. biography] presents those domestick anecdotes and events, which come more forcibly home to her bosom and her curiosity."[5]

The convention that confined historical reading to the care of well-born, male adults was deep seated and very persistent, yet its precise content was not frozen. Though neither Goldsmith nor Bennett would have put it in just these terms, we could summarize the development of life writing in the eighteenth century as gradually opening up to adult male readers the same interests and allowances as were more easily acknowledged in women and youths.

[3] Ibid., 57.

[4] Goldsmith, *Collected Works*, ed. Arthur Friedman, 5 vols. (Oxford: Oxford UP, 1966), 5:226.

[5] Bennett, *Letters to Young Lady*, 184.

In pursuit of a wider, more varied, and more prestigious audience, biographers made several related arguments to promote their art. In general, they began by accepting the traditional division between private and public, but endeavored to turn its hierarchical assumptions in their own favor. If history speaks to public men, they argued, then it is meaningless for the largest part of mankind. In contrast, biography encompasses everyone because it is the study of common life. "No species of writing combines in it a greater degree of interest and instruction than Biography," wrote Robert Bisset in 1793:

> Our sympathy is most powerfully excited by the view of those situations and passions, which, by a small effort of the imagination, we can approximate to ourselves. Hence Biography often engages our attention and affections more deeply than History. We are more concerned by the display of individual character than of political measures, of individual enjoyment or suffering, than of the prosperity or adversity of nations. Even in History, the biographical part often interests us more than any other.[6]

As these remarks make clear, the language of sympathy so prominent in this period made it easy to make claims for biography as a form of historical narrative that imposes relatively little distance between the subject and the reader. At the same time, arguments for the intimate pleasures of biography must always be read against a background of suspicion of an art whose interest in private life (taken in the old sense of that which is kept from public view) seemed all too likely to lead to prurience or scandal mongering. Thus, despite everything, an odor of Grub Street clung to life writing, whose dignity often seemed a little unsteady. Early in the century, for instance, Addison had written: "There is a Race of Men lately sprung up among this sort of Writers, whom one cannot reflect upon without Indignation as well as Contempt. These are our Grub Street biographers, who watch for the Death of a Great Man, like so many Undertakers. . . . He is no sooner laid in his Grave, but he falls into the hands of an Historian."[7]

Addison's slippage from "biographer" to "historian" speaks to the closeness of the two genres as well as the characteristically loose usage of the period. A half century later, Goldsmith used the two terms with similar ambiguity, but in a manner that strikingly contradicted Addison's assumptions about greatness. In the *Life of Richard Nash* (1762), Goldsmith argues that "history" owes its value to the understanding of the historian rather than the greatness of its subject: "whether the hero or the clown be the subject of the memoir, it is only man that appears with all his native minuteness about him; for nothing very

[6] Quoted from Stauffer, *Art of Biography*, 550. Bisset was an early biographer of Burke; on his work as a historian, see chapter 9 below.

[7] Ibid., 530

great was ever yet formed from the little materials of humanity."[8] Here the flexibility of terms corresponds to Goldsmith's conviction that in the end what counts in history writing is a kind of sympathetic understanding in both writer and reader that has little to do with worldly pomp:

> Thus none can properly be said to write history, but he who understands the human heart, and its whole train of affections and follies. Those affections and follies are properly the materials he has to work upon. The relations of great events may surprize indeed; they may be calculated to instruct those very few, who govern the million beneath, but the generality of mankind find the most real improvement from relations which are levelled to the general surface of life; which tell, not how men learned to conquer, but how they endeavoured to live; not how they gained the shout of the admiring croud, but how they acquired the esteem of their friends and acquaintance. (2–3)

The most instructive of all histories, he goes on to say, would be each man's honest autobiography—a move that takes us still further from Addison's clear-cut division between greatness and vulgarity. Few readers, writes Goldsmith, would not prefer Montaigne or Colley Cibber to the "stately memoirs" of kings and potentates.

To make space for their interest in common life, biographers were more inclined than historians to assert the common condition of mankind, once the outward trappings are set aside. This stress on common life, in the sense of what is done every day, easily carried over into another realm of common experience, the interior world of the passions. A good example of the tendency of biography to move between two versions of private life, the quotidian and the intimate, can be seen in the life of a London magistrate, Sir Thomas Deveil: "There seems to be no kind of writing more in favor with the present age, than memoirs," wrote the anonymous biographer, "or accounts of persons who have distinguished themselves in the world, by arms or arts, by wit or learning, in a civil, military, naval, or commercial capacity."[9] Deveil's biographer stresses this range of subjects in order to argue that biography could serve as a source of specialized knowledge for readers in many walks of life.[10] But the writer also has a wider and in a sense contrary claim to make, one that stresses universality rather than particularity. However men may differ in their public standing, he writes, "in their private characters, in their virtues and vices, inclinations and aversions, they stand much upon the same foot." For ordinary people, it is a matter of some pleasure to discover this truth. But the fact is that what-

[8] Goldsmith, *The Life of Richard Nash* (London, 1762), 2.

[9] Anon., *Memoirs of the Life and Times of Sir Thomas Deveil, Knight, One of his Majesties Justices of the Peace* (London, 1748), 1.

[10] Biography "shews us what kind of abilities are requisite in different professions" (ibid., 2).

ever differences may appear on the outside between men of different ranks, "yet follow them close, enter with them into their cabinets, or, which is still more, into their private thoughts, and the dark recesses of their minds, and they will be found pretty much on a level" (1).

In parallel with fictional writers of the same period, biographers experimented with narrative devices that would give readers the sense of gaining a more informal and intimate view of character. An important pioneer in this regard was William Mason, whose *Life of Gray* set a new pattern for biography by creating the poet's life as far as possible through letters and journals. In this way, Mason wrote, Gray would in effect become his own biographer, and his temperament would be expressed more clearly.[11] Mason's innovation, to put it in other terms, represented a notable shift in historical distance. It brought biography closer not only to autobiography, but also to Richardson's desire to create a "dramatic" narrative through epistolary fiction. In both cases greater inwardness was achieved at the expense of a narrative of action. In Gray's life, as in Clarissa's, events were few, and the sentiments became the focus of narration. Indeed, it is hard to think how Gray's quiet life of poetry and scholarship could have been recounted through more traditional narrative forms. As Goldsmith wrote in another context, "The life of a scholar seldom abounds with adventure. His fame is acquired in solitude, and the historian who only views him at a distance, must be content with a dry detail of actions by which he is scarce distinguished from the rest of mankind."[12] Presence, then, not the biographer's customary middle-distance, best suits the life-story of a man of letters.

Samuel Johnson was not the retiring figure Gray was, but even his well-populated, urban life could hardly have been the subject of a large book without his biographer's conviction that his real subject was not action, but Johnson's endless fund of conversation. Boswell followed Mason's method, and like his model (as well as Richardson and Carte) he stresses the actuality of the resulting portrait. This mode of presentation, he writes, not only gives a fuller picture of Johnson's life than most of his own acquaintances had, but enables readers "to see him live, and to 'live o'er each scene' with him, as he actually advanced through the several stages of his life."[13]

In his introduction, Boswell did his best to recruit the most famous of biographers to his side: "If authority be required, let us appeal to Plutarch, the prince of ancient biographers. . . . 'Nor is it always in the most distinguished atchievements that men's virtues or vices may be best discerned; but very often an

[11] *The Poems of Mr Gray, to which are prefixed Memoirs of his Life and Writings* by W. Mason (York, 1775), 5: "They will give a much clearer idea both of Mr. Gray and his friend, at this early period, than any narrative of mine. . . . They will ascertain, not only the scope and turn of their genius, but of their temper. In a word, Mr. Gray will become his own biographer."

[12] Goldsmith, "The Life of Thomas Parnell, D.D.," in *Collected Works*, 3:407.

[13] Boswell, *Life of Johnson* (London: Oxford UP, 1976), 22.

action of small note, a short saying, or a jest, shall distinguish a person's real character more than the greatest sieges, or the most important battles.' "[14] In fact, by Plutarchan standards, Boswell's book presented an odd ideal of biography: the total recuperation of the life of a private man, in all its petty encounters and endless talk over cups of tea or plates of steak. Nonetheless, the appeal to Plutarch nicely illustrates the way in which intellectual change takes place, not by a simple overthrow of authority, but by the recontextualizing of earlier views, so that central values are quietly shifted, while previously marginal ones are brought into a new focus closer to the center.

The very success of Boswell's work led to a backlash from those who found this hunger for knowledge of private life unseemly. (See chapter 11.) Even Boswell acknowledged that his quest for the smallest detail of Johnson's conversation was "adapted for the petty exercise of ridicule," and so it proved to be. Witness a fine parody entitled "Lesson in Biography; or, How to Write the Life of One's Friend":

> On my return to town, we met again at the chop-house. We had much conversation to-day: his wit flashed like lightning: indeed there is not one hour of my present life in which I do not profit by some of his valuable communications.
>
> We talked of *wind*. I said I knew many persons much distressed with that complaint. Pozz. "Yes Sir, when confined, when pent up." I said I did not know that, but I questioned if the Romans ever knew it. Pozz. "Yes. Sir, the Romans knew it." Bozz. "Livy does not mention it." Pozz. "No, Sir, Livy wrote History. Livy was not writing the Life of a Friend."[15]

From almost any point of view, including parody, Samuel Johnson stands at the center of eighteenth-century biography in Britain. The subject of the greatest biography of the age and himself a literary biographer of the first rank, he was the center of a literary circle that included an impressive number of biographers and autobiographers: Boswell (who was an obsessive autobiographer), Oliver Goldsmith, Arthur Murphy, Sir John Hawkins, Edmund Malone, and Dr. Burney.[16] Johnson himself had a passion for biographical knowledge, so much so that he sincerely felt "that there has rarely passed a life of which a judicious and faithful narrative would not be useful."[17]

[14] Ibid., 23–24.

[15] The satire was written by Alexander Chalmers and printed by John Wilson Croker in his edition of the *Life of Johnson* (London, 1831), 5:478. For more on Croker's edition, see chapter 11 below.

[16] This point is made by Robert Folkenflik in *Samuel Johnson, Biographer* (Ithaca: Cornell UP, 1978), 19–20. For Johnson and literary biography, see Annette Wheeler Cafarelli, *Prose in the Age of Poets: Romanticism and Biographical Narrative from Johnson to De Quincey* (Philadelphia: U of Pennsylvania P, 1990); and David Wheeler, ed., *Domestick Privacies: Samuel Johnson and the Art of Biography* (Lexington: U of Kentucky P, 1987).

[17] Samuel Johnson, *The Rambler*, ed. W. J. Bate and A. B. Strauss, 3 vols. (New Haven: Yale UP, 1969), 1:320.

"The biographical part of literature is what I love most," Johnson told Boswell.[18] This was a bond the two men shared; and when the younger man worried that he had freighted his journal with too many little incidents, Johnson reassured him: "There is nothing, Sir, too little for so little a creature as man. It is by studying little things that we attain the great art of having as little misery and as much happiness as possible."[19] At bottom, the power of biography was consolatory, a value that Johnson believed it could possess only if written honestly and in detail. Otherwise life writing would set a standard too high for the imitation of ordinary men. Biography that was too exalted would ignore the things that matter to ordinary life, with their power to instruct and to comfort. In this, we might add, it would resemble history: "The good or ill success of battles and embassies extends itself to a very small part of domestick life: we all have good and evil, which we feel more sensibly than our petty part of publick miscarriage or prosperity."[20]

Johnson presented a brief and influential account of the value of biography in the sixtieth paper of the *Rambler.*[21] The power of literature, he argued, lies in its ability to create an emotional identification with others, so that for a time we feel their happiness or their pains. But even the best of writers will find it hard to interest us in emotional states that lie outside of our experience. For this reason we can read the histories of the "downfal [*sic*] of kingdoms, and revolutions of empires" without disturbance. The opposite is true when we read the lives of "particular persons." Here "parallel circumstances, and kindred images" capture our interest, making biography the most delightful and useful sort of writing.[22]

History was the natural foil for this view of biography, one that so evidently depends on assumptions about questions of presence and distance:

> The general and rapid narratives of history, which involve a thousand fortunes in the business of a day, and complicate innumerable incidents in one great transaction, afford few lessons applicable to private life, which derives its comforts and its wretchedness from the right or wrong management of things which nothing but their frequency makes considerable, *Parva, si non fiant quotidie,* says Pliny, and which can have no place in those relations which never descend below the consultation of senates, the motions of armies, and the schemes of conspirators.

[18] Boswell, *Life of Johnson* (1976 ed.), 301; James Boswell, *London Journal, 1762–1763*, ed. Frederick Pottle (London: Heineman, 1950), 293.

[19] Boswell, *Life of Johnson* (1976 ed.), 307.

[20] Ibid., 269.

[21] For what follows, see Johnson, *Rambler*, 1:318–23.

[22] It is worth noting the parallel between such remarks on the "downfal of kingdoms" and those in Smith and others on the naturalness of the way in which we experience a small personal hurt as more disturbing than the deaths of a multitude of fellow creatures further afield. *The Theory of Moral Sentiments*, ed. D. D. Raphael and A. L. Macfie (Indianapolis: Liberty, 1982), 136–37.

Johnson knew, however, that everyday things might not seem important enough for study. To this objection he had two answers. First he stressed the common condition of mankind—our common stock of motives, deceptions, hopes, dangers, desires, and pleasures. This was the path taken by much of the philosophical psychology of the Enlightenment, which built its science of man on a study of the individual mind and temper. But Johnson was a moralist, not a philosopher, and he gave greater weight to a second response, which amounted to a counterattack on public measures of celebrity. The quiet life of the scholar, the merchant, or the ordinary priest, he wrote, is generally overlooked because it seems to lack public importance. But "the business of the biographer is often to pass slightly over those performances and incidents, which produce vulgar greatness, to lead the thoughts into domestick privacies, and display the minute details of daily life, where exterior appendages are cast aside, and men excel each other only by prudence and virtue."

At bottom Johnson's view of biography expressed a strongly religious sense of the value of everyday life, and his occasional attacks on the pomp of history should be read in this light. When Johnson praised biography above history he was not showing indifference to the whole range of activities and questions we think of as historical.[23] Rather he rejected the celebration of what Fielding called "bombast greatness" in favor of a deeper appreciation of the experience of ordinary humanity.[24] This is a legacy of Protestant individualism that Charles Taylor has nicely called the "affirmation of ordinary life"; through figures as different as Johnson and Carlyle it has come to constitute a central feature of modern sensibility.[25]

Biography and Foundations of History

Clearly, there was a broad tendency in eighteenth-century commentary to flatten out the hierarchies governing the relationship between history and biography. For the most part writers did not directly attack the "dignity of history," nor did they need to; instead they pressed the claims of common life and

[23] A number of scholars have tried to correct the stereotyped image of a Johnson who arbitrarily dismissed the value of history. They have shown instead that Johnson often wrote on antiquarian and historical subjects and that in his appreciation of literature particularly, he often thought in historical terms. See especially John Vance, *Samuel Johnson and the Sense of History* (Athens: U of Georgia P, 1984).

[24] Henry Fielding, *Jonathan Wild* (Harmondsworth: Penguin, 1982), 32–33: "Now as to that greatness which is totally devoid of goodness, it seems to me in Nature to resemble the *false sublime* in poetry; whose bombast is, by the ignorant and ill-judging vulgar, often mistaken for solid wit and eloquence, whilst it is in effect the very reverse. . . . This bombast greatness then is the character I intend to expose."

[25] Charles Taylor, *Sources of the Self: The Making of the Modern Identity* (Cambridge: Harvard UP, 1989), pt. 3.

inwardness so effectively that history's proverbial dignity comes to look like a mark of pompous weakness, not of strength. But there were other strands of opinion that, while remaining critical of older conventions, built toward a more positive commentary on the potential meaning of biography for history.

As we have seen, it was commonly argued that because it stands closer to individual experience than history, biography will be more "interesting" and more instructive than history. But biography's concern with individual lives also held another, perhaps deeper promise. It could be argued that the passions and sentiments lie more open to view in narratives of private life than in the public struggles and ceremonies of history. As a result, biography offers something more than a complement to the public concerns of history; it also stands as a gateway to a deeper sense of social life. And certainly to write history without the insights of biography would be to miss much of the real experience of the past.

Writers were also attracted by the flexibility the "minor" genre offered as a form for historical study. A case in point is the biography of Lord Kames by Alexander Fraser Tytler. Tytler saw that in Kames he possessed a subject who summed up a good deal of the character of his times, and he believed that the smaller scale and looser requirements of a biography offered him a manageable way to organize a history of the intellectual life of eighteenth-century Scotland. His aim, Tytler states, was not to write a narrow biography, but something "much more comprehensive in its plan." His aim was "to exhibit the moral and political character of the Times in which he lived, and to detail the progress of the Literature, Arts, Manners, and General Improvement of Scotland, during the greater part of the eighteenth century."[26] Adapting the language of the eighteenth century, we might indicate the broad scope of the book as well as its attempt to write a Humean history of opinion by calling Tytler's work an essay in philosophical biography. Such a work, Tytler wrote, "is not subjected to the laws of regular history, or of biography, strictly so termed. It admits easily of digressions, and is thus suited to the utmost variety of subjects."[27]

Tytler's subject belonged to the immediate past, but when the subject was more remote and the materials harder to come by, the flexibility gained by using this mixed form was especially attractive. The advantages seem very clear in two biographical works by Joseph Berington, a little-known Catholic writer, whose lives of Abelard and Eloise and of Henry II are shaped by the scarce, but evocative materials of medieval history. At a slightly later date, Godwin's *Life of Chaucer* (1803) presents an even more self-conscious use of historical biography.

[26] Tytler, *Memoirs of Kames*, 1:v–vi.

[27] Ibid., 1:viii–ix: "It professes not to exhaust the topics of which it treats; but rather to open and introduce them to the reader: And above all, it allows a varied tone of composition, and at times a familiarity of style, which greatly smooth the labour of a lengthened work." Tytler himself uses the French term, "memoirs pour servir a l'histoire."

Berington's *History of the Lives of Abeillard and Heloisa* (1787) makes use of the rich autobiographical writings of the two central figures not so much to trace the outward dramas of their lives as to create an intimate narrative of experience that stands at the core of a wider history. As so often in the eighteenth century, the emotional resonances of gender play a large role in explorations of inwardness. What engages Berington most is his desire to understand Heloisa's situation as she registered it with her own eyes and feelings. As a sentimental heroine, she is at once the central figure and the key spectator of the story. Accordingly, Berington skims close to his sources, making a narrative out of expressive passages of quotation that alternate with looser paraphrases and interpolated emotional responses attributed indifferently to the historian and his reader.[28] Often, of course, the evidence is thin or simply absent, but Berington is skillful in reading silences. He strains every resource to re-create the tenor of the lovers' relationship, often by exploring the omissions in Abelard's *Historia calamitatum* in counterpoint to Heloisa's more revealing letters, matching the theologian's public account of his "calamities" against his lover's devoted questionings, her combination of independent mind and female submission.

Berington stresses the authentic documents that differentiate his work of true history from Pope's poetic fable, but his allegiance to history is not in any real tension with the novelistic sentimentalism that infuses his portrait of Heloisa. On the contrary, Berington is most novelistic when he is closest to his documents. The book is completed with a substantial appendix of translated letters—another instance of the fusion between the methods and materials of antiquarian scholarship and the tones of epistolary novel.

The *History of the Reign of Henry the Second* (1790) continues the earlier history, changing the focus from the sufferings of a female heroine to the dramatic clash of masculine temperaments that culminated in the murder of Thomas à Becket. Here once again Berington pursues a story that could be evoked though expressive contemporary sources. The chronicles, memoirs, and letters thrown up by the Becket controversy permit Berington to reconstitute the conflict over ecclesiastical power in ways that bring to life the shape of individual experience in an age often left to the wide generalizations of philosophical historians.

To present this conflict Berington adopts what he calls the "*dramatic* style"—that is, the fiction of direct address—and in a series of well-staged scenes he presents Becket and Henry speaking directly to each other and

[28] "The reader, whom Heloisa's romantic epistle had left animated and greatly interested in her cause, will, I know, be sadly disappointed by this cold reply. To me it is all I looked for, and it stamps indelibly the character I had given to the man." Berington, *The History of the Lives of Abeillard and Heloisa* (Birmingham, 1787), 224–25. In a similar vein, he writes: "More reflections on this beautiful epistle will not be necessary. The reader must have made many as he came along; and he must have admired, have pitied, and have praised the lovely writer" (234).

to us.[29] In justifying this device, he avoids the obvious fictional precedents, citing instead the Greek poets and historians, whose way of allowing their characters to speak for themselves "insensibly transports the reader into the company of their heroes and sages, obliterating, by a momentary magic, the distance of years, and the consciousness of present existence" (xxvi).

Lord Kames would have been pleased to find so clear a confirmation of his doctrine of "ideal presence" in a historical work.[30] But in practice Berington did not want presence to prevail so entirely over distance; the reader must also be reminded of the unknowable darkness of history, which differentiates it from the simpler attractions of fictions. The book opens with a moody invocation of history as a quest for a past that is remote and almost unreachable:

> Awful is the impression which now falls on my mind, when, with the annals of times long passed open before me, I sit down to contemplate the manners of men and the events of their days, and to trace, through the maze of its progress, the meandring [*sic*], and often evanescent, line of truth. *History* is the narration of *facts;* but we receive them on the testimony of men like ourselves, whom want of evidence sometimes misled, or incaution, or credulity, or views of party, or inability of discernment, exposed to error.[31]

Berington wants us to understand that the student of the Middle Ages encounters particular difficulties and special charms. Accordingly he emphasizes the temporal and intellectual remoteness of his sources—men "whom the cowl covered, whom, in a dark age, genius did not illumine, nor science polish." Yet, by a sentimental logic that ranks inarticulate communication highest of all, the plain-speaking heroes and their "unadorned" testimonies possess a simple directness capable of shattering the barriers separating a polished age from its primitive past.

Controlling the poetics of presence and distance is clearly one of Berington's central concerns as a narrator. The price of failure would be to surrender either to flat factuality or sentimental fictionalization, while success, as Berington emphasizes, means an active sympathy with what is best in the past—a kind of nonphilosophical historicism. "The age, I own, was dark," he writes near the end of his book; even so,

[29] Berington, *Henry the Second*, xxvi: "I must notice the *dramatic* stile, which I have sedulously adopted, whenever the original writer had himself used it, and at other times, when the narration, from its circumstantial detail authorized the licence. Thus when the old writer related that such things were said in conversation or at interviews, I sometimes took the liberty to make the persons speak for themselves, as, on the occasion itself, they certainly had done."

[30] On Kamesian "ideal presence" in historiography, see chapter 4 above.

[31] Berington, *Henry the Second*, 1–2.

> the mind that divests itself of modern habits and modern prejudices, and goes back with some good temper into the times, I have described, will discover virtue that it may imitate. . . . The man is unequitable, who, possessing but one standard, measures by it all the characters and events of other days.[32]

In the preface to his *Abeillard and Heloisa,* Berington acknowledged the difficulty of connecting the ordinary chronicle of the times to the lives of a literary man and a cloistered nun; Godwin's choice of Chaucer was more accommodating, since the poet was a highly placed courtier as well as a great chronicler of vernacular life. But Godwin also surpassed Berington in the self-consciousness with which he pursued the widest historical dimension of biography. The reciprocity of biography and history was an essential part of his conception of the book.

The full life of the poet, Godwin wrote, would have to include an extensive survey of the manners and arts of the time:

> This is the only way in which we can become truly acquainted with the history of his mind, and the causes which made him what he was. We must observe what Chaucer felt and saw, how he was educated, what species of learning he pursued, and what were the objects, the events, and the persons, successively presented to his view, before we can strictly and philosophically understand his biography. To delineate the state of England, as Chaucer saw it, in every point of view in which it can be delineated, is the subject of this book.[33]

The first ten chapters of the book are given over to a wide survey of medieval manners, arts, and education, and many other chapters, even after the biography proper has begun, continue these concerns.

But Godwin did not see biography simply as an easy perch from which to eavesdrop on the manners of the age. He insisted that neither biography nor history would be complete on its own; each required the perspective of the other:

> But, while engaged in this study, the reader may expect an additional advantage, beside that of understanding the poet. If knowledge of contemporary objects is the biography of Chaucer, the converse of the proposition will also be true, and the biography of Chaucer will be the picture of a certain portion of the literary, political and domestic history of our country. The person of Chaucer may in this view be considered as the central figure in a miscellaneous painting, giving unity and individual application to the otherwise disjointed particulars with which the canvas is diversified.[34]

[32] Ibid., 645–66.

[33] Godwin, *Life of Geoffrey Chaucer, the early English Poet, including Memoirs of his near friend and kinsman, John of Gaunt, Duke of Lancaster: with Sketches of the Manners, Opinions, Arts, and Literature of England in the Fourteenth Century,* 4 vols. (London, 1803), 1:viii.

[34] Ibid., 1:viii–ix.

Biography and the Classics

Godwin spoke of his study of Chaucer as "a work of a new species." But perhaps the most striking evidence of the way in which what I have called philosophical biography entered into a reappraisal of history came not from new works, but rather from revaluations of the some of the oldest and most prestigious works in the historiographical canon.

I have already reviewed the transformation of Tacitus's reputation in connection with Adam Smith's *Lectures on Rhetoric*. Smith's lectures remained unpublished until the present century, but Arthur Murphy presented a very similar view of the Roman historian in his *Works of C. Tacitus with an Essay on His Life and Genius* (1793). Murphy was a member of Johnson's circle and is now most often remembered as one of Johnson's early biographers. In his day he was a popular playwright, but he was also enough of a classical scholar to translate Sallust as well as Tacitus. Murphy saw Tacitus as a brilliant judge of men and manners, and he lamented that there was no biography to do justice to the man whose life of Agricola was itself "a perfect model of biography."[35] For Murphy, Tacitus's strength as a historian lay in this biographical understanding, and he celebrated Tacitus above all as "the anatomist of the heart."

"The passions, and, if the expression may be allowed, their antagonist muscles, were perfectly known to him," Murphy wrote; "he saw their inward workings, however disguised."[36] As a historian of corrupt times, Tacitus depicted "the very inward frame" of vicious and profligate rulers (1:x). At the same time, he was a great portraitist who had the power to make the reader feel the immediate presence of these specimens of human nature, virtuous or evil. Tacitus's "Annals may be called an historical picture gallery. It is by that magic power that Tacitus has been able to animate the dry regularity of the chronologic order, and to spread a charm though the whole, that awakens curiosity and enchains attention" (1:lxv).

This understanding of human nature made Tacitus a great teacher of morals as well as of politics. "Every short description is a picture in miniature; we see the person acting, speaking, or suffering."[37] By placing these pictures before our eyes, the historian animates our own inward feelings: "our passions are

[35] Arthur Murphy, *Works of C. Tacitus by Arthur Murphy; with an Essay on the Life and Genius of Tacitus*, 8 vols. (London, 1811), 1:x. The work first appeared in 1793 with a dedication to Edmund Burke. ("To whom can Tacitus, the great statesman of his time, be so properly addressed, as to him, whose writings have saved his country? Scenes of horror like those which you have described, were acted at Rome, and Tacitus has painted them in colours equal to your own.") His play, *Arminius; a tragedy* (London, 1798), is worth noting in this connection for the way in which it plays out patriotic themes on the stage of gothic history. Murphy also published another translation of a classical historian: the *History of Catiline's Conspiracy* (1795).

[36] Murphy, *Tacitus*, 1:lxxvi.

[37] Ibid., 1:lxi.

kept in a tumult of emotion; they succeed each other in quick vicissitude; they mix and blend in various combination; we glow with indignation, we melt with tears" (1:lxi).

It is a measure of Tacitus's greatness that he could sustain such a reading. But he was not the only classical historian open to this kind of sentimentalist rereading. In 1806, Henry Steuart (a Scotsman known primarily for a later work on sylvaculture)[38] published a translation and a lengthy commentary on the works of Sallust in two quarto volumes. Steuart's case for Sallust is very similar to Murphy's view of Tacitus, but Steuart had a broader sense of the evolution of historiography, and his discussion brings out a wide-scale critique of classical historical outlook that is quite remarkable.

Much of the bulk of the book is made up of two long introductory essays and substantial notes intended to supply "such historical circumstances, as the author has withheld, in the parsimony of his narrative." These additions, he added, "may be read as the Memoirs of the times, of which the text constitutes the History."[39] In this usage, "memoir" stands for a wider social chronicle that could not be contained by the standard conceptions of historical narrative. In effect, then, Steuart wanted to provide retrospectively for his author something like the mix Tytler aimed to achieve in composing his life of Kames.[40] At the same time, the need for supplementary "memoirs" clearly signals Steuart's sense of the limitations attached to classical narratives. Much of his commentary, in fact, rests on his supposition that ancient historiography was generally silent on issues of deep concern to modern readers, especially private feeling and everyday life.

Steuart's critique of ancient historiography centers on biography, which, he argues, is "among the few branches of the fine arts, in which we may be said to have outstripped our masters."[41] Ancient biography might be instructive and even pleasing. But though the ancients might have had the ability to delineate the character of a prominent man, the subject always remains solitary, an object detached and isolated from the life that surrounds it. Modern biography, in contrast, has a broader social scope, joined to a wider ambition: "In the best specimens of the art, a view is . . . given of the age and nation of the person to be described; its political character is represented; and its state of advancement in arts, in manners, and in literature" (1:2).

Steuart shared with many others this belief in the wide social value of biography, but he went further than others in identifying the "philosophical" grounds for this conviction. "The fact seems to be," he wrote, "that those

[38] Henry Steuart of Allanton (1759–1836) was best known for his later work *The Planter's Guide* (1828).

[39] Henry Steuart, *The Works of Sallust*, 2 vols. (London, 1806), 1:xxx–xxxi.

[40] Steuart, in fact, dedicated his book to Tytler, whose biography of Kames was to appear in the following year.

[41] Steuart, *Sallust*, 1:2.

antient artists overlooked the relative importance, which the peculiarities of the individual bear to the history and knowledge of the species."[42] Thus, in Steuart's view, as in Tytler's, the case for biography becomes the same as that for philosophical history as Lord Kames had practiced it. Biography would no longer be restricted to telling the lives of the great, as in ancient times, but would take its subjects "alike from the summits of grandeur, and the scenes of privacy."[43] In short, like history itself, biography would move into the social realm, the vast and almost uncontainable domain of manners, material life, and social opinion, where every individual plays a part and enjoys an interest.

[42] Ibid.

[43] Ibid., 1:3: "Hence we see . . . how great an improvement has been made, in modern times, in this species of composition. On the antient plan, it was adapted chiefly to record the transactions of the great, and the illustrious. In the modern view, it comprehends, and gives lessons to every rank of life. It selects its subject alike from the summits of grandeur, and the scenes of privacy; or even from the tranquil shade of literary retirement."

Six

Manners and the Many Histories of Everyday Life: Custom, Commerce, Women, and Literature

IT WOULD be hard to find a phrase in eighteenth-century letters more characteristic than "manners and customs." Almost every discipline of thought or body of literature found a use for this flexible vocabulary, but for the historical genres in particular "manners" have a special interest. Imprecise though its usage was, the term pointed unmistakably to the domains of experience excluded by traditional concepts of historical narrative. Thus *manners* was immediately recognizable as the brief signature of the new concern with the social that set the interests of this period apart from those of its classical and Renaissance predecessors.

Concern for manners was a key place where a variety of moral discourses—classical republicanism, Addisonian politeness, sentimentalism—intersected with a number of philosophical or learned ones. Thus the idea of manners and its various extensions served as a common currency linking the themes of law, history, or ethnographic travel with other, more overtly moral languages of the times. In Addisonian moralists, for example, preoccupation with manners took the form of the idea of "politeness," a genial program of sociability and reform.[1] A darker view of the times was preached by John Brown in his popular jeremiad on contemporary effeminacy and corruption, the *Estimate of the Manners and Principles of the Times* (1757). Others were less apocalyptic, but when Britons thought about the future of their commercial empire, few could avoid entirely thoughts of imperial Rome, corrupted and effeminated by power and luxury.[2]

In relation to manners, ideas of wealth and gender took on strikingly similar burdens. Women, like commerce, were principal agents in polishing and softening social life, and the progress of women, like the advancement of trade, was regarded as either an index of refinement or an incitement to luxury. On

[1] On politeness, see Lawrence Klein, *Shaftesbury and the Culture of Politeness: Moral Discourse and Cultural Politics in Early Eighteenth-Century England* (Cambridge: Cambridge UP, 1994).

[2] On the theme of luxury and corruption, see John Sekora, *Luxury: The Concept in Western Thought, Eden to Smollett* (Baltimore: Johns Hopkins UP, 1977). For a wider economic framework, see Istvan Hont, " 'The Rich Country–Poor Country' Debate in Scottish Classical Political Economy," in *Wealth and Virtue: The Shaping of Political Economy in the Scottish Enlightenment*, ed. Hont and Michael Ignatieff (Cambridge: Cambridge UP, 1983).

one side, Brown and others saw luxury and feminization as more deadly threats to national vigor than the military force of any overt enemy. On the other, refinement of manners was taken as a kind of scientific measure of the progress of society. "Rude" nations, exhibiting human life at its greatest simplicity, were regarded as a natural laboratory for the study of the species. Authentic descriptions of the earliest stages of European history were, of course, few, but a vast contemporary literature of travel brought home news of the customs of far-off peoples. "The only certain means, by which nations can indulge their curiosity in researches concerning their remote origin," writes Hume at the opening of his history, "is to consider the language, manners, and customs of their ancestors, and to compare them with those of the neighboring nations. The fables, which are commonly employed to supply the place of true history, ought entirely to be disregarded" (1:4). In a modern context too, the manners of "neighbouring nations" were closely scrutinized, especially those of the French and Italians, who were generally regarded as more "polite" than the English. Thus manners, which had once marked the special something possessed by the courtier or the nobleman, came to stand for the equally undefinable essence of national character.

This range and diversity of usage is easily illustrated by a quick scan of book titles, which in the eighteenth century have a rambling attractiveness that makes simple shelf-reading an almost irresistible temptation. Even a small sample will give the flavor of what has been described, while indicating the variety of genres and contexts that made use of the idea of manners. Perhaps the widest category is travel; for example: Barrington, *A Voyage to New South Wales; with a description of the country; the manners, customs, religion, and of the natives in the vicinity of Botany Bay* (1796); Bartholomew Burges, *A series of Indostan letters by Barw. Burges containing a striking account of the manners and customs of the Gentoo nations* (1790); John Ogden, *A tour through Upper and Lower Canada. . . . Containing a view of the present state of religion, learning, commerce, agriculture, colonization, customs and manners, among the English, French, and Indian settlements* (2d ed. 1800).

Diplomacy was also a traditional context for the analysis of foreign ways, and a number of titles make reference to embassies, whether to nearby Holland or far-off China.[3] William Macintosh's *Travels in Europe, Asia, and Africa* (1782), on the other hand, was directed to imperial and commercial interests; its subtitle reads, "describing characters, customs, manners, laws, and produc-

[3] *A Voyage to Holland; or the Dutchman described* (1745), written by "a gentleman attending a late English Ambassador extraordinary at the Hague," contained both information of a diplomatic or political character and "observations on the manners and customs, nature and comical humours of the Dutch boors, or peasants." Aeneas Anderson, *A narrative of the British embassy to China, in the years 1792, 1793, and 1794; containing the various circumstances of the embassy, with accounts of the customs and manners of the Chinese; and a description of the country, towns, cities, etc.* (1795).

tions of nature and art: containing various remarks on the political and commercial interests of Great Britain; and delineating in particular a new system in the East Indies." Natural history was a central interest in the journal of Captain Cook's voyage, whose subtitle advertised "descriptions of several newly discovered countries in the southern hemisphere; and accounts of their soil and productions; and of many singularities in the structure, apparel, customs, manners, policy, manufactures, etc. of the inhabitants" (1774). But the vogue for foreign customs did not confine itself to serious reportage or what would now be called nonfiction.[4] Novelists also could book passage: *The disinterested nabob, a novel, interspersed with genuine description of India, its manners and customs* (1788); or the still more exotic *History of the customs, manners, and religion, of the moon. To which are annexed, several specimens of lunar poetry* (1782).

Often the culture was remote, but English readers also found the peculiarities of nearer nations worth the price. There are works on German, French, or Spanish customs,[5] as well as a number on the Irish, the Scots—especially the Highland Scots—and the Welsh. Hence: John Bush, *Hibernia curiosa. A letter from a gentleman in Dublin, to his friend at Dover in Kent. Giving a general view of the manners, customs, dispositions, etc. of the inhabitants in Ireland* (1769); similarly, *The Highlander delineated: or the character, customs and manners of the Highlanders: chiefly collected from the celebrated Scotch historians, George Buchanan, and Mr. Drummond of Hawthornden*, a book which appeared in the fateful year 1745.

Historical accounts followed similar patterns and are not always easy to distinguish clearly from other, overlapping genres. Histories of America often advertised an ethnographic interest, as in Richard Johnson's *History of north America. Containing a review of the customs and manners of the original inhabitants* (1795). William Winterbotham's *Historical, geographical and philosophical view of the Chinese Empire* (1798) comprehended, according to its subtitle, "a description of the fifteen provinces of China . . . ; natural history of China; government, religion, laws, manners and customs, literature, arts, sciences, manufactures etc." Elsewhere the context is clearly antiquarian, as

[4] John Foss combined the sensationalism of a captivity narrative with a picture of exotic female manners: *A Journal of the captivity and sufferings of John Foss; several years a prisoner at Algiers: together with some account of the treatment of Christian slaves when sick:—and observations of the manners and customs of the Algerines*, 2d ed. (1798).

[5] [John Andrews,] *An Account of the Character and Manners of the French; with occasional Observations on the English*, 2 vols. (London, 1770); Thomas Nugent, *Travels through Germany. Containing observations on customs, manners, religion, government, commerce, arts, and antiquities. With a particular account of the courts of Mecklenburg* (1768); Samuel Sharp, *Letters from Italy, describing the customs and manners of that country, in the years 1765 and 1766* (1767); Sir John Talbot Dillon, *Letters from an English traveller in Spain, in 1778, on the origin and progress of poetry in that Kingdom; with occasional reflections on manners and customs* (1781).

in Comerford's *History of Ireland* (1766), with its "dissertation on the laws, customs, and manners of the antient Irish"; or George Waldron's *History and description of the Isle of Man: viz. its antiquity, history, laws, trade, customs, religion and manners of the inhabitants* (2d ed. 1745).

Ethnography is generally the business of strangers. Where a culture is self-described, there is almost always a displacement of some kind—of class, of tribe, or of time. *The Cries of London* (1797) by Timothy Ticklecheek, a late-eighteenth-century version of an older genre, proclaims its intention to contrast city and country life for the instruction of children, by "displaying the manners, customs and characters of various people who traverse London streets with articles to sell." At the opposite end of the social scale, there is *A trip through the town* (1735?), which contained "observations of the customs and manners of the age." Archenholz's *A Picture of England: containing a description of the laws, customs, and manners of England,* a translation of a German work, reflects Englishness in the mirror of another nationality; so in its own way does Thomas O'Brien M'Mahon's *Candor and good nature of Englishmen, exemplified in their deliberate, cautious, and charitable way of characterising the customs, manners, constitution and religion of neighbouring nations* (1789).

Given this widespread interest in manners, apparent in so many contexts and genres, it is not surprising that the history of manners attracted a good deal of attention. In fact, the history of manners was widely greeted as an important new feature of eighteenth-century historiography.

In his journal of his tour to the Hebrides in 1773, Boswell recorded a conversation that gives a sense of the loosely defined, yet somehow widely assumed importance of this type of historical understanding. The exchange took place between himself, Samuel Johnson, and their host, the Scottish philosophical historian Lord Monboddo:

> Monboddo. "The history of manners is the most valuable. I never set a high value on any other history." Johnson. "Nor I; and therefore I esteem biography, as giving us what comes near to ourselves, what we can turn to use." Boswell. "But in the course of general history, we find manners. In wars, we see the dispositions of people, their degrees of humanity, and other particulars." Johnson. "Yes; but then you must take all the facts to get this, and it is but a little you get." Monboddo. "And it is that little which makes history valuable." Bravo! thought I; they agree like two brothers.[6]

Boswell, the anxious impresario of Johnson's meeting with Scotland, was much pleased by the success of this encounter. Clearly, it was the mutual agreeableness of the two literary eccentrics, not their actual agreement that he was

[6] Boswell, *Boswell's Journal of a Tour to the Hebrides with Samuel Johnson* (London: Heinemann, 1936), 55.

after. But the subject was well chosen; all three could find common ground in the idea of a history of manners, while actually moving off in quite different directions. Johnson drew the idea of manners in the direction of biography, one of his favorite literatures, and accepted only grudgingly Boswell's argument that all history, read appropriately, stands as a lesson in the history of manners. Meanwhile, Monboddo, first and last, kept to his insistence that manners constitute the true historical subject, or at least the truly valuable part of history.

The shared assumptions of this conversation are perhaps most revealing in the case of Lord Monboddo. He is principally known as the author of the six-volume speculative history of human communication, *The Origin and Progress of Language*. He was also a strident "ancient" who measured all languages and cultures against the standard of Greek.[7] Evidently, Monboddo's classicism, rigid though it seems, was able to incorporate a rather unclassical innovation in the idea of history. More importantly, his conversation with Boswell suggests that he regarded his own conjectural history of language as a contribution to the branch of historical studies that he considered uniquely valuable, the history of manners.

The conversation at Monboddo was echoed by Isaac D'Israeli, who flatly declared that "the history of manners has become the prime object of the researches of philosophers."[8] Yet this evidence of recognition needs to be weighed against the fact that Britain—though it fostered a whole school of northern Montesquieus—could claim no Voltaire. There was no one, that is, who could give the *histoire des moeurs* the coherence or prestige of a great literary performance. Setting aside the conjectural historians, like Ferguson or Millar, who will be discussed in the next chapter, we cannot point to a British work of high literary standard or wide circulation styling itself as a history of manners. Perhaps the closest we can come to Voltaire's model is Robert Henry's *History of Britain,* which seems to have been read especially for its histories of manners, arts, and letters. (See above, introduction.) But even Henry did not focus exclusively on manners, and though the work eventually had

[7] "When I first knew the Court of Sessions, he [Monboddo] was principally distinguished for his excessive admiration of the ancients, a passion for theatrical entertainments, and for his love of hunting and other manly exercises." See John Ramsay, *Scotland and Scotsmen in the Eighteenth Century*, ed. A. Allardyce, 2 vols. (Edinburgh, 1888), 1:351.

[8] Isaac D'Israeli, *Dissertation on Anecdotes* (London, 1793; rpt. New York: Garland, 1972), 6. D'Israeli goes on to stress the minuteness of research required and the value of private and contemporary sources. In much the same way, John Pinkerton confirms the inadequacy of traditional narratives from the point of view of this new interest in manners. Extolling the value of numismatics, Pinkerton writes that "the philosopher who writes, or peruses history, for that greatest of purposes, the knowledge of human manners, will learn more from medals than from the best histories." Pinkerton, *Letters of Literature* (London, 1785; rpt. New York: Garland, 1970), 336.

some real success, it had none of Voltaire's literary prestige and did not engender a school.[9]

Thus, despite the unanimous opinion of Boswell's friends on the importance of the history of manners, histories that formally define themselves in this way are fewer than might be expected, and they generally have an antiquarian rather than a literary character. It appears that in the absence of a definitive literary monument, interest in the history of manners was expressed in a miscellaneous collection of particular histories in which biographical, antiquarian, or anecdotal interests predominated. Considered in terms of genre, then, the history of manners, despite its acknowledged importance, lacked the solidity or coherence of conjectural history.

General History

I would like to begin the more detailed survey of the history of manners where Boswell would have us start, with general history. In this period, a number of historians filled out their narratives of national politics with specialist chapters devoted to manners, arts, and commerce. These thematic surveys exhibit on a small scale the sorts of materials that elsewhere receive a fuller and more detached treatment, in works on the history of private life, trade, women, the poor, law, or literature. In this way, the general histories stand as a guide to the conventional concerns of the history of manners.

Contemporaries identified Hume (along with Voltaire) as the historian who made a place for nonpolitical themes in his history.[10] In terms of simple bulk, of course, explicit discussion of manners remains a relatively small part of the *History;* what is more important, however, is that Hume made manners part of the framework of historical writing and gave prestige to the practice. "The chief use of history is, that it affords materials for disquisitions of this nature," Hume writes in his survey of arts, manners, and commerce at the time of the Commonwealth, "and it seems the duty of an historian to point out the proper inferences and conclusions" (6:140). On the other hand, it was still possible to complain that historians slighted such materials by relegating them to a special niche. "Mine are the subjects rejected by the historian to the end of each reign,

[9] A second conversation of Johnson's on the history of manners is useful here. The discussion (Apr. 29, 1778) was between Johnson and William Robertson, the historian. Johnson: " 'I have heard Henry's history of Great Britain well spoken of: I am told it is carried on in separate divisions, as the civil, the military, the religious history: I wish much to have one branch well done, and that is the history of manners, of common life.' Robertson: 'Henry should have applied his attention to that alone, which is enough for any man; and he might have found a great deal scattered in various books, had he read with that view.' " Boswell, *Life of Johnson* (1976 ed.), 980.

[10] See, for example, Vassall Holland's recommendation to Charles James Fox that he follow Hume's example and include dissertations on literature and manners (see above, chap. 3).

among the prodigies that distinguish it," wrote Richard Gough, a prominent antiquarian. "Yet is this detail not uninteresting? It is a picture of private, mixed with public life."[11]

William Russell offered a somewhat different model for integrating the history of manners into general history. His *History of Modern Europe* (1779) is a solid five-volume survey, written in the form of letters from a nobleman to his son.[12] Russell gives regular attention to social themes, but he also maintains a conventional division of historical subjects. Where the progress of society has affected the "national force," Russell writes at one point, he has dealt with the topic in the course of general history, leaving for separate discussion "such objects as cannot come within the line of general history; the progress of manners, of arts, and of polite literature."[13]

Russell's surveys of manners, arts, and letters touch on all of the standard topics of the history of manners—the position of women, for example, and the "polishing" effect of freer relations between the sexes, first in the age of the troubadour and later in that of the courtier. Similarly Russell comments on literary history, with the intercourse of manners, learning, and letters as a major theme.[14] Indeed, the equation of arts and manners is so easily made that many of his explanations seem no more than tautologies. ("The Romance, which had its rise in the manners of chivalry, and which rendered them still more romantic, fell into disrepute as soon as those manners began to decline" [2:212].) But the wide boundaries of these letters on nonpolitics give him room for easy surveys of large subjects—an overview of contemporary manners and letters in various parts of Europe, for example, or the progress of English letters after 1688.

For Russell, commerce also makes a major contribution to human happiness. "Politeness arises from the habits of social life, and the intercourse of men and of nations; it is therefore more likely to accompany commerce than learning," he writes; but he adds that manners are softened and polished by works of art

[11] Richard Gough, *Sepulchral Monuments in Great Britain* (1786), reviewed in *MR* 78 (1788): 277.

[12] William Russell (1741–1793) began as a bookseller's apprentice in Edinburgh. Later he moved to London, where he worked for Strahan as a corrector of press and as overseer of a printing house. His eventual success as a historian can be measured by the offer of 750 pounds from Cadell (a prestigious publisher) to write a history of England from the accession of George III to the end of the American war. The history was never written. (For Russell's career, see *DNB*.) Russell was also the author of a work—translated and "improved" from the French—on women: *Essay on the Character, Manners, and Genius of Women in Different Ages. Enlarged from the French of M. Thomas, by Mr. Russell*, 2 vols. (Edinburgh, 1773). Russell's additions to the work included passages from Ferguson, Millar, and other British authorities, as well as his own chapter, "Of the Progress of Society in Britain, and of the Character, Manners, and Talents of the British Women."

[13] [William Russell,] *History of Modern Europe*, 5 vols. (London, 1786), 2:201–2.

[14] Ibid., 2:208–9, 210–22, 4:272–92.

and sentiment and "dispose it to tenderness and social affection."[15] But inevitably the "softening" of morals also raises a note of alarm, suggesting effeminacy and loss of spirit. A "certain degree" of luxury is needed by the state, Russell concludes judiciously after a survey of English letters, but "philosophers have not yet ascertained where true refinement ends, and effeminacy or vicious luxury begins" (4:290–91).

The history of navigation also gives Russell (among others) a chance to narrate a more exotic story, the history of pirate-bands in the West Indies. These adventurous men, though engaged in a form of commerce, were as far removed as possible from its supposed polishing effects. Instead, the pirates seem to re-create the conditions of a primitive stage of society: "In a word, the Buccaneers, the most extraordinary set of men that ever appeared upon the face of the globe, but whose duration was transitory, subjected to their arms, without a regular system of government, without laws, without any permanent subordination, and even without revenue, cities and castles which have baffled the utmost efforts of national force; and if conquest, not plunder, had been their object, they might have made themselves masters of all Spanish America."[16]

For two generations after its publication, Russell's history remained popular as a textbook of European history.[17] Part of its attraction to students must have been its comprehensiveness, which was enhanced by the attention it paid to cultural and commercial themes. If so, there is a parallel with formal pedagogy, where the evidence is that classroom instruction took in a wider range of themes than the standard political narratives. The published lecture summaries of Priestley at Warrington or Wight at Glasgow, whether discussing the ancient or modern world, have liberal reference to commerce, navigation, festivals, law, and learning. Formal teaching of history was a new subject in the eighteenth century, and from the start it appears to have welcomed the "philosophic" spirit.[18]

Everyday Life: Creech, Ramsay, Strutt

Samuel Johnson's preference for biography "as giving us what comes near to ourselves, what we can turn to use" leads to another dimension of the history of manners—the history of everyday life. It would not be long, in fact, before

[15] Ibid., 2:205.

[16] Ibid., 5:42–43.

[17] On Russell's longevity as a textbook, see Peardon, *Transition in Historical Writing*, 65.

[18] For indications of the historical syllabus, see William Wight, *Heads of a Course of Lectures on the Study of History; given annually by William Wight DD., Professor of History in the University of Glasgow* (Glasgow, 1767); Alexander Fraser Tytler, *Plan and Outline of a Course of Lectures on Universal History, Ancient and Modern, delivered in the University of Edinburgh* (Edinburgh, 1782); Priestley, *Lectures on History.*

his own life, as minutely recorded by Boswell, would be welcomed precisely as this sort of anecdotal history of the times (see chapter 11), though the full extent of Boswell's efforts as a chronicler of ordinary days was not revealed until his massive diaries were uncovered in the twentieth century.

Scholars now appreciate more fully than they once did the peculiar gift and burden Scottishness was to men like Boswell. Like the Jewish writers of mid-twentieth-century New York and Chicago, eighteenth-century "North Britons" lived in watchful intimacy with the dominant society. Their self-consciousness in the face of England and its language meant that even those who (unlike Boswell) were content to stay at home saw themselves continually in the mirror of English comparisons.[19] Equally pervasive, as Scotland felt the effects of the Union, was the rapid pace of what today would be called "modernization." Further national traumas in 1715 and 1745 provided the Scots with historical markers, even when the transformations of their ways of life had little direct connection with great public events. Later and more locally, the building of Edinburgh's New Town had a similar effect on memories of everyday life.

The latter event was the pivot of the efforts of William Creech, a leading Edinburgh bookseller, to chart the changes of daily life in Edinburgh from 1763 to 1783. Creech's *Letters to Sir John Sinclair* (1783) is a compilation of particulars of social life presented without much order or connection. But few writers on manners could resist the philosophic note: "It is frequently difficult to assign a reason for the revolutions which take place in the circumstances and manners of a country, or to trace the causes that have occasioned a change; but, it is evident that the first step towards investigating the cause is to state the facts." Such efforts, he continues, if renewed from time to time, would be a practical instrument for reform and a "fund" of facts for the annalist, the philosopher, and the historian. And he also notes, "No history of the time could have given such detail."[20]

Many of Creech's comparisons involve the sorts of changes familiar in times of economic growth or sudden inflation—steep increases of land prices or rents; once fashionable districts now left to tradesmen while whole new precincts open up; major improvements in public conveniences, such as stage coaches or decent hotels. He has an easy appetite for statistics, whether the subject is tonnage at the docks of Leith or the annual sale of candles. He

[19] On Scottish linguistic self-consciousness, see Robert Crawford, *Devolving English Literature* (Oxford: Clarendon, 1992), and Crawford, ed., *The Scottish Invention of English Literature* (New York: Cambridge UP, 1998).

[20] [William Creech,] *Letters Addressed to Sir John Sinclair, respecting the mode of living, arts, commerce, literature, manners etc. of Edinburgh, in 1763, and since that period* (Edinburgh, 1793), 5–6, 30. The addressee of the letters, Sir John Sinclair, was the author of the multivolume statistical summary of Scotland. On Creech, see Barbara M. Benedict, " 'Service to the Public'; William Creech and Sentiment for Sale," in Dwyer and Sher, *Sociability and Society*, 119–46.

notes the demand for new trades or new manufactures (button makers, perfume makers, hairdressers, iron foundries, paper mills, starch manufactories), as well as the sharp rise in the "value of literary property," a matter of particular interest to the publisher-bookseller.

Creech delights in the details of carriages, mills, and domestic wages, but in the end these are only indices of change, and what impresses him most is the sheer rapidity and massiveness of what has taken place—unequalled, so he believes, in any city in Europe. As a result, "many features of the present time will probably appear prominent and striking, which, in the gradual progress of society, have passed altogether unnoticed, or have been but faintly perceived."[21] But there is a dark side to what often looks like an all too familiar boosterism. In Creech's second letter he turns to changes "which have a more immediate connection with Manners" (31), and it becomes evident that for Creech an interest in contemporary manners is inseparable from anxiety for contemporary morals. After another philosophical overture—the rise of nations from poverty and simplicity; their fall from opulence into sensuality and corruption—he chronicles a second set of the phenomena of the everyday, which is the obverse of the first: the decline of church attendance, looser supervision by masters over apprentices, rising wages of journeymen, a decline in clerical visitations, milder punishment for adultery, increases in crime and prostitution, the new sport of cockfighting, the popularity of theater no longer questioned, the building of a new jail.

This mix of philosophical pretension, moral anxiety, and curiosity about the rhythms and changes of daily life makes Creech's *Letters* a valuable miniature of eighteenth-century interest in the history of everyday life. The neat symmetry of optimism and pessimism in the first two sections is disturbed by the contents of a third, in which Creech appends an account of the "physical phenomena" of the period. Many of the events in this brief chronicle of volcanic eruptions, meteors, earthquakes, and other geological and meteorological disasters thankfully took place far from Edinburgh, and Creech leaves no explicit hypothesis about the connection between these physical events and his sense of history or morals. "I do not mean at present to draw any hypothesis or theory from what I have stated above," he concludes, "but merely to bring facts into one general view, and to induce others to make observations of the same kind."[22]

Creech's efforts were on a small scale; they were dwarfed by the work of another Scot, whose memorials can only be compared to Boswell's or, in the next century, Henry Cockburn's. John Ramsay of Ochtertyre (1736–1814) is mentioned by Lockhart as one of Scott's models for his antiquary Jonathan

[21] Creech, *Letters to Sinclair*, 6.

[22] Ibid., 52.

Oldbuck of Monkbarns.[23] More to the point, his vast memoir of Scotland in his day—a part of which was posthumously published as *Scotland and Scotsmen in the Eighteenth Century* (1888)—is a prime example of the kind of effort to hold on to local memory and tradition without which *Waverley* and its successors could never have been written. Unfortunately the proximity of Scott also makes it next to impossible now to feel the freshness of Ramsay's desire to capture what he calls "the antiquities of manners"; such is the power of Scott over the memory of his age and country that the antiquary has become the novelist's creation, rather than his progenitor.

Ramsay was educated as an advocate, but devoted himself to a combination of agricultural and antiquarian pursuits, both of which fed his memoir. According to its nineteenth-century editor, the manuscript was written in the last quarter of the eighteenth century and consists of ten bulky volumes derived from Ramsay's reading, recollections, and firsthand experience. Only parts of the work have been printed, but the way in which Ramsay himself divided his manuscripts is perhaps the clearest indication of his wide-ranging interests:

Language, Literature, and Biography (of Scotland) 3 vols.
Religion and Church Polity, and of their Influence on Society and the State. 2 vols.
Government, Clanship, and Law. 1 vol.
Prospects of Private Life. 3 vols.
Tracts on Forestry, Female Education, Superstitions, etc. 1 vol.

Understandably, the editor has given pride of place to its literary and biographical materials, such as the extensive portrait of Lord Kames, who was a neighbor; Ramsay himself, however, seems as much interested in the eccentricities of tenant farmers or the virtues of old-fashioned women as in literary notables. The memoir is infused with a vivid sense of a vanishing world and of the irreplaceable value of its living witnesses. "It will hardly be possible," writes Ramsay, "for the rising generation to form a just notion of the love and affection which subsisted between a powerful nobleman and his vassals and clients before the two last rebellions. Compared with it, modern patronage is cold and unavailing."[24] So far-reaching were the changes that it would not

[23] See Ramsay, *Scotland and Scotsmen*, introduction. On Ramsay, see Barbara L. H. Horn, ed., *Letters of John Ramsay of Ochtertyre* (Edinburgh: Scottish History Society, 1966). On the antiquary as a type, and some historical predecessors, see Stuart Piggott, "The Ancestors of Jonathan Oldbuck," in *Ruins in a Landscape* (Edinburgh: Edinburgh UP, 1976), 133–60, and *Ancient Britons and the Antiquarian Imagination: Ideas from the Renaissance to the Regency* (New York: Thames and Hudson, 1989).

[24] Ramsay, *Scotland and Scotsmen*, 2:46–47. It should be pointed out that his attitude toward this lost past, like Walter Scott's, is not merely nostalgic, and he goes on to state the negative: "On the other hand, they [the gentry] were not deficient in gratitude. Their veneration being boundless, they entered with violence into all their patron's friendships and resentments. This was, however, a most dangerous line of conduct."

be long before living memory no longer carried any genuine recollection of an earlier world of social manners. "At present there are hardly any chieftains who live with their clan upon the old footing of familiarity, or who profess general hospitality. And a few years more will remove every person who remembers their little courts, or has seen them in the field in all their state. Ere long it must be the province of the antiquary to describe the life and manners of a real Highlander" (2:387). But these are only the best-known and in that sense most banal examples of the changes Ramsay found in every part of life, and he drew on his own memories or patiently enquired from elders after any number of quieter alterations—especially the transformation of rural life in his part of Scotland. Without an extensive glossary or a fully annotated edition, most of us will never be able to take in the detail of what he has to tell us about changes in crops, foods, field patterns, tools, building materials, or even new articles of dress, social habits, and customs—all of them, like the "little court" of the Highlander, rapidly becoming the province of the antiquary.

Writing of the revival of letters in Scotland, Ramsay expresses his deep regret "that in a matter hardly eighty years old, it should already be next to impossible to trace a number of particulars respecting its rise and progress." Books and pamphlets, he goes on to say, can only supply a small part of what is wanted; "the most precious information would have been from the conversation of the aged. . . . Had I myself undertaken this work thirty years ago, I might have had much excellent information which is now irrecoverably lost."[25]

In this strongly expressed sense of the inadequacy of the written record, there is the hint of the paradoxes running through his own generous and even obsessive efforts at written recollection. In part, too, these deeply felt doubts point to the particular character of the memories that matter most to him, leading him "into paths little trodden by others."[26] Books and pamphlets were inadequate sources because so much of what Ramsay wanted to recall had taken place outside of public life: witness the revival of letters, which he stresses was not the result of official patronage, but the achievement of "a few private men," some of them quite obscure and not even acquainted with each other.

In his lengthy portrait of Lord Kames, Ramsay styles himself a "historian of private life." But this is not to say that he ignored the great events of the day; on the contrary, he saw the great political and military events of 1707,

[25] Ibid., 1:1–2. In these discussions the memories of the aged is a leitmotif: "And now of the husbandry which prevailed in this country at the time when it can first be traced by memory." Or, a few pages later: "Such were the labourers of the ground, and such their situation in former times, so far as we can collect from the conversations of the aged" (2:192, 204).

[26] Ibid., 1:3.

1715, and 1745 as both precipitants and markers of the social changes he chronicled. The change in manners was indirectly shaped by the public world, but this history possessed a texture of its own:

> The union of the kingdoms in the year 1707 produced great though not immediate revolutions in the sentiments and tastes of our ingenious contrymen. Indeed that memorable event hath led to consequences, good and bad, which were not foreseen by its able promoters or opponents. These, however, were the natural fruits of a free and constant intercourse between the Scots and the wealthy nation which had already attained to a high pitch of eminence in letters, arts, and arms.[27]

Ramsay was fully aware of the consistency and even inevitability of the transformations of Scottish life, and—as has been said so often of Scott—this is what gives his work a genuine historical sense, making it a true history of Scottish manners, not merely a loving collection of her antiquities.

In England, the history of private life had a narrower scope. Joseph Strutt was an engraver turned antiquarian and historian. In this he was unusual among antiquarians, whose formation was generally more learned and literary. But Strutt's works show how an artist's eye could be placed in service to a desire to recover the details of ordinary life in other ages. In 1774–75 he published *A Complete View of the Manners, Customs, Arms, Habits etc. of the Inhabitants of England;* later he published the *Chronicle of England* (1778–79), where he complains of the lack of attention to the manners and customs of the people. His own work, he explains, would be divided into three general parts: first, civil and military history, second, ecclesiastical history, and third, "the history of the manners, arts, habits, genius, etc. of the people." This material, Strutt continues, is further subdivided into ten chapters, "so that any particular subject may be easily referred to."[28] The arrangement seems an echo and a simplification of Robert Henry's plan, and indeed Henry's history is one of those Strutt frequently cites. Among the topics of his "dissertations" on government, laws, manners, and customs, we find the common themes of the history of manners, such as the ranks of men among the ancient Britons, their behavior toward the fair sex, their agriculture, diet, and so forth. But in keeping with his background as an engraver, Strutt also shows a distinctive interest in visual evidence, some of which is reproduced for his reader in handsome plates. Thus, by looking to early manuscript depictions and other sources, he draws what inferences he can about such matters as the clothing, armor, architecture, or agriculture of England before the Norman Conquest.

[27] Ibid.

[28] Joseph Strutt, *The Chronicle of England; or a compleat history, civil, military and ecclesiastical of the ancient Britons and Saxons*, 2 vols. (London, 1778), 1:iii–iv. On Strutt, see Peardon, *Transition in Historical Writing*, 157–60.

Strutt is at pains to stress the historical importance and accuracy of the plates, which he clearly expected to be a major attraction of his history. In part his emphasis on this dimension of his book is clearly a matter of professional pride, but more seems at stake than simply an opportunity to demonstrate his art or enhance the price of his book. Strutt evidently feels that, as against other forms of evidence or description, his engravings (taken from earlier depictions or from surviving artifacts) offer a gain in immediacy as well as accuracy. Regarding a plate, for instance, that reproduces an agricultural scene from an early manuscript, he writes that Saxon agriculture "will be far better understood, by being represented to the eye as given by the Saxons themselves, than by the most elaborate description."[29] The prominence given to the plates seems, in the final analysis, to speak to his own power of visualization, which is perhaps the force behind his conviction that he is capable of presenting something new and more immediate about those people he likes to call "our British and Saxon ancestors." "Thus much," he writes in his introduction, "the author hopes, will be thought new and interesting to the public; as it is presumed a view of the *very ideas of our ancestors* must give an additional pleasure in the perusal of their history" (1:iv; emphasis added).

Similar interests motivated Strutt's most popular work, the *Sports and Pastimes of the People of England* (1801), though here the indication of a general historical framework has all but disappeared. Instead the book opens with a blank assertion of the centrality of his subject. "In order to form a just estimation of the character of any particular people," he argues, "it is absolutely necessary to investigate the Sports and Pastimes most generally prevalent among them. War, policy, and other contingent circumstances, may effectually place men, at different times, in different points of view; but, when we follow them into their retirements, where no disguise is necessary, we are most likely to see them in their true state, and may best judge of their natural dispositions."[30]

It is amusing to see the confidence with which war and policy are reduced to "contingent circumstances." But Strutt's argument for the more enduring qualities of the private character is an adaptation of an argument frequently made by contemporary biographers, who distinguished the actor on the public stage, forced to wear various masks, and the true, unadorned private man, best seen when retired to his closet. Strutt's instincts, however, were for detailed description, not abstraction and argument. The book quickly settles into a re-

[29] Strutt, *The Chronicle of England*, 2:218.

[30] Joseph Strutt, *The Sports and Pastimes of the People of England* (London, 1830), xviii. This edition of 1830 was presented as a cheaper, popular edition, succeeding earlier folio editions of 1801 and 1810; all were illustrated with 140 engravings.

markable catalogue of English customs, with very little speculation or intellectual adornment, taking in everything from the hunting and hawking of aristocrats to the simplest games of rustic children.

Commerce: Adam Anderson

Adam Anderson was a historian of a very different type, and in many contexts it would seem very curious to pair his *Historical and Chronological Deduction of the Origin of Commerce* (1764) with the writings of Strutt or Ramsay. Anderson was a Scot who served as a chief clerk in the South Sea Company. He was also one of the trustees for the establishment of the colony of Georgia and was very well informed on British trade with the American colonies. His pioneering venture in economic history became a standard work, as witnessed by the fact that Adam Smith drew on it extensively for his *Wealth of Nations*. The book was republished by William Combe in 1801, who also brought its three huge volumes up to date with a fourth. Soon after, the work was extensively revised by David Macpherson, who also wrote the *History of European Commerce with India* (1812).[31]

Anderson's researches were held together by his conviction that the immense importance of British commerce had not yet been given proper historical recognition. "May it not therefore well merit our particular inquiry," he asks, "how, and from what causes and instruments; at what periods of time and from what various and respective places, or countries, such inestimable benefits have accrued to mankind."[32] He admits, however, that his account will suffer many deficiencies, owing to the ignorance of earlier times about the importance of commerce, as well as "what may justly be termed an unaccountably stupid contempt of Commercial History, testified even by some nations, who, nevertheless may be justly said to be indebted to commerce alone, not

[31] For Anderson's career, see the introduction by Joseph Dorfman to the 1967 reprint of the 1801 edition: *An Historical and Chronological Deduction of the Origin of Commerce from the earliest accounts, containing an history of the great commercial interests of the British Empire . . . revised, corrected, and continued to the present time* [continuation by William Combe], 4 vols. (London, 1801; rpt. New York: A. M. Kelley, 1967).

In his work on India, David Macpherson makes a similar case for the improper neglect of commercial history in relation to conventional historiography: "commercial history has occupied a good deal of my attention, ever since I have been convinced that mankind are much more deeply interested in contemplating the progress of industry, civilization, social order, comfortable subsistence, and happiness, which in every part of the world go hand-in-hand with well-directed commerce, than in studying the revolutions of empire, or the miseries brought upon the human race by the sanguinary exploits of conquerors." *History of European Commerce with India* (London, 1812), v–vi. On David Macpherson, see Peardon, *Transition in Historical Writing*, 261–62.

[32] Anderson, *Origin of Commerce*, 1:vii.

only for their present wealth, but, likewise, for their very existence, as a distinct and independent people" (1:xiv).

Anderson is careful to steer clear of "general history" except where commerce is affected; nonetheless, he takes a wide view of his subject, "as comprehending therein navigation, colonies, manufactures, fisheries, mines, agriculture, and money concerns." He also intersperses "some few notices or instances of the private or domestic customs, and usages of elder times" to indicate the "surprizing difference" in so many respects between earlier times and the present.[33] But he leaves little doubt that the largest and most relevant change from earlier times is the new appreciation by all classes of the importance of commerce and the new understanding of its operations.[34]

Anderson emphasizes the systematic quality of his own work in comparison to earlier discussions of commerce. In formal terms, however, his narrative framework is the simplest imaginable: a plain chronology that in the early books resembles a medieval chronicle. In fact, the work begins with the Flood and the Tower of Babel and dates events both by the age of the world and by years before Christ; later books carry this chronicle format, with greater and greater elaboration, into the medieval and then the modern centuries. The crudity of Anderson's narrative framework is worth noting as an adjunct to the novelty of his subject, since it puts the formal experimentation of a work like Henry's into some perspective.

In method much of the *Origin of Commerce* is clearly antiquarian. A good part of his early British material comes from the standard antiquarian sources, like Cotton or Rymer. Later, in volume 3, which deals with the eighteenth century, Anderson drew on wider resources, including his own experience with the South Sea Company and with colonial settlement in America. His account of the "Bubble" is very full, as is his information on Britain's trade with America.

His affinities with antiquarian scholarship are also evidenced in the enormous and elaborate index to the work, first alphabetical and then chronological. Other appended sections include an extract from a pamphlet on the sovereignty of the seas, a dissertation on the dignity of merchants, another "Of the various causes of the rise and increase of great and populous cities," and an elaborate survey of Europe in terms of trades, manufactures, and other aspects of economy. The history of commerce, like other histories of the time, had its philosophical appendices too.

[33] Ibid., 1:xvi.

[34] "Commerce is a mistress more eagerly courted by almost all nations in our age than in any preceding one: and it is highly probable, that, even before the conclusion of the present century, many new lights may be struck out for the further improvement of it: more especially as our nobility and landed gentry are, at length, clearly convinced, that the increase of our national commerce is in effect, but another phrase for expressing the advancement of the landed interest, wealth, and felicity of Great Britain and Ireland" (*Origin of Commerce*, 3:3).

The History of Women: William Alexander

"The progress of the female sex," wrote Lord Kames, "a capital branch of the history of man, comprehends great variety of matter, curious and interesting." As will be seen in the following chapter, the history of women occupied an important place in the thinking of conjectural historians and is especially prominent in Kames's *Sketches* and Millar's *Origin of the Distinction of Ranks*.[35] More broadly, gender was a pervasive theme in all considerations of manners, and the experiences of women found a place in biographies, memoirs, and histories of private life. But if the history of women was a well-established thematic in the history of manners, it was not yet a populated genre. With the exception of biography (including anthologies of female biography),[36] there are few eighteenth-century works specifically devoted to the history of women. It is indicative, however, that when the *Monthly Review* criticized William Alexander's *History of Women* (1779), it was for trivializing an important subject, not for aggrandizing a little one.[37]

William Alexander's *History,* the best-known of eighteenth-century histories of women, encapsulates many of the characteristic themes of eighteenth-century writing on manners. Alexander's subtitle—"giving an account of almost every interesting particular concerning that sex, among all nations,

[35] Lucy Aikin's verse epistles on the history of women should be mentioned here: *Epistles on Women, Exemplifying their Character and Condition in Various Ages and Nations* (1810). The work is intended as a defense of the female sex, but the author sets her poem in the familiar terms of the history of manners. "To mark the effect of various codes, institutions, and states of manners, on the virtue and happiness of man, and the concomitant and proportional elevation or depression of woman in the scale of existence, is the general plan of this work."

[36] The best example is George Ballard, *Memoirs of Several Ladies of Great Britain* (1752). On Ballard and his influence, see Margaret Ezell, *Writing Women's Literary History* (Baltimore: Johns Hopkins UP, 1993).

[37] See *MR* 61 (1779): 413. The reviewer writes, "The title of this work promises a great deal" and goes on to accuse the author of not being "sufficiently sensible of the difficulty of his undertaking." William Alexander, *The History of Women, from the earliest antiquity, to the present time*, 2 vols. (London, 1779). The work clearly enjoyed some popularity and went through several editions; a German translation appeared in 1780 and a French in 1791. I have used a reprint of the Philadelphia edition of 1796. Alexander was an Edinburgh physician and the author of two medical treatises as well as the *History.* On Alexander's career and the context of his history, see Jane Rendall's excellent introduction to the Thoemmes Press reprint (Bristol, 1995).

For other histories of women see William Russell's *Essay on the Character, Manners, and Genius of Women* (1773), a reworking of a French work, which has already been mentioned, as has Aikin's *Epistles*. Another derivative history is John Adams, *Woman. Sketches of the History, Genius, Disposition, accomplishments, Employments, Customs and Importance of the Fair Sex* (London, 1790). Adams cites Alexander, as well as a number of the conjectural historians, including Ferguson and Millar. His work is arranged for the most part in a more conventional historical sequence than Alexander's. Later chapters lose their straightforwardly historical character to become a miscellany of sentimental tales, essays, and advice.

ancient and modern"—indicates something of an antiquarian framework, but he evidently had a different audience in mind. In a book designed for women, Alexander remarks, it would be out of place to flourish "a long list of authors on the margin." Designed for the amusement and instruction of the fair sex, the history would be an antidote to novels and romances that mislead the understanding and corrupt the heart. In short, as occurs so often in genres devoted to the female reader, Alexander's history of women would in part serve the purposes of conduct literature, though it was not without lessons for men as well.[38]

Alexander gives an appropriately gendered version of the eighteenth century's faith in the fundamental sociability of human nature. Of all the influences that shape male manners, Alexander believes, nothing is more powerful than the company of women. Man, secluded from the company of women, is a rough and even a dangerous animal, but in each other's company both sexes improve. Men are transformed by a desire to please, while women, for their part, know that the art of pleasing is their pathway to greater influence.[39]

In the savage state, physical strength and courage are overwhelmingly important, and the weaker sex is condemned to slavish drudgery. Only later did women attain "consequence enough even to merit confinement" as in the harems of the East, much less to achieve "that exemption from labour and perpectual guardianship, by which, in Europe they are complimented and chained." The advance of humankind as it emerges from ignorance and brutality is marked "with great precision" by improvements in the condition of women. Indeed, if a country's history were silent on every other subject, the condition of women in that place would still enable us to judge "the barbarity, or culture of their manners."[40]

In short, the treatment of women is significant both as a cause and an index of the progress of society. Still, refinement of manners is far from uniform: chivalry, for instance, "for some time totally changed the sentiments and writings of mankind," only to give way to a reversal in a later age. On the other hand, while the "character and manners in Europe" went through such revolu-

[38] It is the habit of men, Alexander writes, "to teach [women] folly, and rail at them for having learned what we taught them" (*History of Women*, 1:xi).

[39] "Of all the various causes which tend to influence our conduct and form our manners, none operate so powerfully as the society of the other sex. If perpectually confined to their company, they infallibly stamp upon us effeminacy, and so other of the signatures of their nature; if constantly excluded from it, we contract a roughness of behaviour, and slovenliness of person" (ibid., 2:323).The widespread integration of the sexes in university dormitories across North America could be considered as only the most recent contribution of the Scottish Enlightenment to higher education.

[40] Ibid., 1:111. In another passage he writes: "In proportion as real politeness and elegance of manners advance," he wrote, "the interest and advantages of the fair sex not only advance also, but become more firmly and permanently established" (2:315).

tions, the East remained unchanged, fixed in the same state of patriarchy exhibited in the Bible.[41]

Like Joseph Strutt, Alexander holds that the most characteristic part of a society's history is bound up in its customs, and for this reason, he laments the scarcity of information on rituals and manners specific to women: "the manners and customs of a nation, besides being the most entertaining part of its history, serve also to characterise and distinguish it from all others, by pointing out the various pursuits to which the genius of its people are directed; the whims and caprices which climate, chance, or necessity has introduced; the force that the intellectual powers have exerted, in contriving or adopting ceremonies and customs agreeable to reason."[42]

As he ranges over a wide set of themes—customs of marriage and mourning, traditional beliefs in the inferiority of women, the horrors of witchcraft accusation, dress and ornament—Alexander does not hesitate to hold every reported practice up to rational examination and to assess every custom in terms of its origins and moral value. Even so, the condition of women exhibits too much variability to be explained by any one set of conditions. As a result, though Alexander has some pretensions to treat his subject systematically in the fashion of the conjectural historians, his real emphasis is on the variety of custom rather than on thoroughgoing comparison.

Literary History: Blackwell, D'Israeli, Warton

Surprisingly little attention has been given to the writing of literary history before the Romantics. As a consequence, literary scholars have had little to say about the interrelationship between histories of literature and other forms of historical writing in this period. Nonetheless, in the eighteenth century literary history became a prime vehicle for expressing certain kinds of historical concerns that were difficult to incorporate in the traditional historiographical modes. Notably, literary history offered opportunities for discussing the history of manners and the experience of everyday life. Equally, literary history opened windows on the history of opinion, a territory that was prized in theory, but otherwise difficult to explore in practice. (For more on literary history, see chapter 11 below.)

Thomas Blackwell's *An Enquiry into the Life and Writings of Homer* (1735) is an early and powerful example of the reciprocity between the study of manners and of literature. It has been pointed out that the *Enquiry* contains most of the elements of philosophical history.[43] The philosophical character of the

[41] Ibid., 1:xx–xxi.

[42] Ibid., 1:347.

[43] On Blackwell as philosophical historian, see Roger Emerson, "Conjectural History and Scottish Philosophers," *Historical Papers* (Canadian Historical Association, 1984), 76–79. More

work is certainly self-conscious, beginning with the nature of Blackwell's central question. Blackwell compares Homer to a comet whose seemingly irregular appearances have so far produced astonishment rather than careful questioning or calculation.[44] In this way, Blackwell signals his desire to look behind appearances and to think systematically—to see Homer as a problem as well as an event. To do so, Blackwell treats Homer's genius (in the eighteenth-century sense of unique character) as something necessary or determined. Only then can the "singular phenomenon" be scrutinized philosophically.

This is where the idea of manners makes an important contribution because Blackwell believes quite literally that manners maketh the man. Young minds, he says, receive a strong impression from the circumstances of the country in which they are raised, its constitution, the common manners of the inhabitants, their "ordinary way of living," as well as the manners of the times. Minds are stamped, too, by their education, social station, and profession—their "particular way of life":

> From these Accidents, Men in every country may be justly said to draw their Character, and derive their Manners. They make us *what we are,* in so far as they reach our Sentiments, and give us a peculiar Turn and Appearance: A Change in any one of *them* makes an Alteration upon *Us;* and taken together, we must consider them as Moulds that form us into those Habits and Dispositions, which sway our Conduct, and distinguish our Actions.[45]

Here is the element of necessity that Blackwell required to think philosophically about Homer. In combination with religion and language, these conditioning factors underwent a common evolution that he calls "a progression of manners."[46] Blackwell distinguishes three periods of Greek history. First there was a dark age before the Trojan War, a time of piracy, no fixed possessions, and frequent migrations. This insecurity pushed men in a second age to build walled cities, accept subordination, and begin the process of extending their commerce and refining their arts, all of which was brought to perfection in a third age of prosperous refinement. From the first two periods, Homer "drew his *Imagery* and *Manners,* learned his *Language,* and took his *Subject*" (13).

---

generally, see Howard Weinbrot, *Augustus Caesar in Augustan England* (Princeton: Princeton UP, 1978).

[44] *Enquiry into the Life and Writings of Homer* (London, 1736; rpt. Hildesheim: Olms, 1976), 4: "Here, My Lord, there seems to be occasion for a little Philosophy, to put us, if possible, upon the *Track* of this singular Phenomenon: It has shone for upwards of two thousand years in the Poetic world; and so dazzled Men's Eyes, that they have hitherto been more employed in gazing at it, than in enquiring *What formed it, or How came it there?*"

[45] Ibid., 12.

[46] Blackwell introduces the "progression of manners" (a fundamental element of philosophical history) as if speaking of a new concept: "There are some Things, *My Lord*, which, tho' they happen in all Ages, are yet very hard to describe. Few People are capable of observing it, and

In essentials the manners of the age of heroes differed little from those of Homer's own time, a point of great importance to Blackwell, given his view of literature as strict mimesis. The simple manners of primitive Greece were a gift to the poet because they left the play of human passions wide open to his inspection. The poet lived among the warriors, shepherds, and peasants of his poetry, and as a result his pictures of manners, characters, and events have all the force of truth—an advantage that later, more literary poets could not recapture. In short, Blackwell writes, it can be said of Homer and every great poet that "*what* he felt and saw, *that* he described; and that *Homer* had the good fortune to see and learn the *Grecian* Manners, at their true Pitch and happiest Temper for Verse."[47]

For many of Blackwell's successors, the poets of earlier times were especially valued as historians of the manners of rude nations. Robert Wood, for example, adopted this view in his remarkable examination of Homeric geography, history, and manners.[48] But Blackwell's purpose takes him in the opposite direction. His goal is not to contribute to the history of Greek manners, but to determine philosophically the necessity of Greece's greatest poet. Even so, the idea of the reciprocity of manners and arts, which Blackwell puts to such strict use, was widely shared in his time. As a result, the study of manners stood as a bridge linking two histories, enlarging the scope of both historical and literary understanding.

Thomas Blackwell was attracted to the study of manners as a way to make literary history more systematic; Isaac D'Israeli, on the other hand, valued the fragmentary, almost gossipy qualities of much literary history and literary biography. His *Dissertation on Anecdotes* (1793) plays with the ironies suggested by his title—a ponderous treatise on a flimsy subject—but he was perfectly sincere in suggesting that anecdotes are the key to literary history and even to history in general: "History itself derives some of it's most agreeable instructions from a skilful introduction of anecdotes. We should not now dwell with anxiety on a dull chronicle of the reigns of monarchs; a parish register might prove more interesting."[49]

Earlier I quoted his opinion that "the history of manners has become the prime object of the researches of philosophers." But even as D'Israeli magnified the importance of the subject, he insisted on the minuteness of its objects. The historian, he writes, "must assiduously arrange the minute anecdotes of the age he examines; he must oftener have recourse to the diaries of individu-

therefore Terms have not been contrived to express Perceptions which are taken from the widest Views of Human Affairs" (ibid., 13).

[47] Ibid., 33–35.

[48] *An Essay on the Original Genius and Writing of Homer* (1775).

[49] D'Israeli, *Dissertation on Anecdotes*, 4. D'Israeli's emphasis on "anxiety" and "interest" indicates the linkage between anecdotal history, everyday life, and the new assumptions about historical reading discussed in chapter 4.

als, than to the archives of a nation."[50] This diary-and-parish-register approach to history led to an emphasis on memoir and other forms of contemporary record. ("History instructs, but memoir delights.")[51] But most of all, it encouraged D'Israeli to a lifelong fascination with the records of literary history, which he pursued through a series of studies concerned with what he called "The Manners and Genius of the Literary Character." Here, among other things, he sketched the view that literary history gives access to the history of opinion and that writers "stand between the governers and the governed."[52]

D'Israeli saw a particular affinity between literary biography and the history of manners and cited (inevitably) the *Life of Johnson* as a prime example. But general literary history, which was still an emergent genre in this period, also showed the same affinity. This can be illustrated by a brief look at the most famous general literary history of the eighteenth century, Thomas Warton's *History of English Poetry*. Warton thought of his work as having the character of annals, but argued that a genuine historical account could not afford to be uniform or rigid.[53] In fact, the *History* combines its literary chronicle in a variety of mixes with elements of poetic anthology, précis, and critical essay. Historical surveys of reigns or periods combine with discussions of particular genres—romances, miracle plays, or classical translation—and for the later period especially, literary history is supplemented with chapters on the history of learning and ideas. In all of this, custom and manners provide a part of the glue necessary to hold together such a mix of different elements. "I make no apology for these seeming digressions," Warton remarks after a tour of the diversions of the Tudor court; "The manners and the poetry of a country are so nearly connected, that they mutually throw light on each other" (4:123).

This reciprocity gives breadth to Warton's literary chronicle, while also endowing it with an overall sense of movement and purpose. Since custom was

[50] Ibid., 6–7.

[51] Isaac D'Israeli, *Curiosities of Literature*, 2 vols. (London, 1791; rpt. New York: Garland, 1971), 2:293: "the minute detail of circumstances which is frequently found in writers of the History of their own times, is far more interesting than the elegant and general narratives of later, and probably of more philosophical Historians. It is in the artless recitals of memoir-writers, that the imagination is struck with a lively impression, and fastens on petty circumstances which must be passed over by the classical Historian."

[52] *An Essay on the Manners and Genius of the Literary Character* (London, 1795), 182. "What has been long meditated in the silence of the study, will one day resound in the awful voice of public opinion" (176).

[53] In his preface, Warton explains his reasons for rejecting the outline of a history of poetry proposed by Pope: "Like other ingenious systems, it sacrificed much useful intelligence to the observance of arrangement; and in place of that satisfaction which results from a clearness and a fulness of information, seemed only to substitute the merit of disposition and the praise of contrivance. The constraint imposed by a mechanical attention to this distribution appeared to me to destroy that free exertion of research with which such a history ought to be executed, and not easily reconcileable with that complication, variety, and extent of materials which it ought to comprehend." *History of English Poetry*, ed. W. C. Hazlitt, 4 vols. (London, 1871), 1:5.

acknowledged to be more variable than correct taste, curiosity about manners opened up a wider perspective on national literature than aesthetics alone could have allowed. In this way the canons of neoclassical criticism ceded some limited, but important ground to a more relativistic perspective that enabled works written in other epochs to be read in other terms. At the same time, the advance of manners provided Warton with the most comprehensive historical framework for his work as a whole. The refinement of manners, proceeding apace with the advance of learning, gives the history its progressive structure, though Warton shows a notable ambivalence about this schema when he writes that perhaps a leavening of superstition and romantic ingenuousness might offer a richer scope to the poetic imagination than pure reason. The age of Shakespeare, with its precious balance of reason and fantasy, possessed a poetic richness lost to the age of Pope.

For Warton, then, the effects of modern progress were not entirely happy for the poetic imagination. On the other hand, the contrast of modern refinement and ancient rudeness could be said to have created the very possibility of writing a history such as his. It was only natural, he argued, that an age of refinement would cultivate the study of the progress of society and look back with "conscious pleasure" at the steps that carried it from rudeness to elegance. The "manners, monuments, practices, and opinions" of earlier ages attract our attention because they form a striking contrast with the present day and exhibit human nature in new light.[54]

All this amounts to an idea of literary history shaped by the ambitions of a philosophical history of humankind:

> On these principles, to develop the dawning of genius, and to pursue the progress of our national poetry, from a rude origin and obscure beginnings, to its perfection in a polished age, must prove an interesting and instructive investigation. But a history of poetry, for another reason, yet on the same principles, must be more especially productive of entertainment and utility. I mean, as it is an art, whose object is human society: as it has the peculiar merit, in its operations on that object, of faithfully recording the features of the times, and of preserving the most picturesque and expressive representations of manners: and because the first monuments of composition in every nation are those of the poet, as it possesses the additional advantage of transmitting to posterity genuine delineations of life in its simplest stages.

This passage comes from the preface to Warton's history, and it has the kind of largeness and lack of specificity that suits its introductory purpose; its sense seems to be that Warton wants to connect the history of poetry to philosophic curiosity about the great story of human progress on two separable levels. Not only does the history of poetry pursue the same wide subject as philosophical history ("on these principles"), but, in complementary fashion ("for another

[54] Ibid., 1:3.

reason, yet on the same principles"), it also enriches the story with the vivid and expressive evidence preserved in its authentic record of "the features of the times." For Warton, in other words, the history of poetry contributes both to the history of manners, with its power to evoke the texture of other times, and to its more speculative and abstract counterpart, philosophical history. This doubled register is entirely characteristic of a period in which the most advanced speculations about history as well as a host of lesser forms of historical curiosity were tied together by the common currency of manners.

Pursuit of the history of manners has led, without any clear boundary, into a wide field of historical genres, including general history, memoir, and biography, as well as the histories of private life, women, and literature. In a number of these works it was not hard to discover gestures toward the more speculative and systematic histories to be considered in the next chapter. I have not, however, cited writers as diverse as Ramsay, Strutt, Anderson, Alexander, Blackwell, or Warton in order to examine their credentials for membership in a philosophical elite. Rather my aim has been to give some substance to the seemingly casual assertion (made at the height of an age we think of as dominated by neoclassical tastes) that of all possible histories the most interesting is the history of manners. It remains for the next chapter to consider the discontinuities as well as the continuities between the history of manners and "the history of man."

Seven

Conjectural History: A History of Manners and of Mind

THE MOST ambitious development in eighteenth-century historical writing was the genre known as "conjectural," "natural," or simply "philosophical" history.[1] Though contemporary usage was not consistent, I will use the term *philosophical history* to designate the broad thrust of eighteenth-century historiography toward a more systematic treatment of the social, while reserving *conjectural history* for that smaller group of works that in formal terms made the most radical break with classical tradition and dispensed with connected narrative altogether. By this definition, then, Hume's *History of England* is a philosophical history, but his *Natural History of Religion* is a conjectural one.

For the conjectural historian, history was not a political narrative governed by classical rhetorical prescriptions, but a moral science held together by the desire to investigate fundamental principles of human nature. The father of the genre was Montesquieu, but a considerable group of Scottish philosopher-historians soon created a body of speculative writing to rival the French. Works like Lord Kames's *Sketches of the History of Man,* Adam Ferguson's *Essay on the History of Civil Society,* or John Millar's *Origin of the Distinction of Ranks* acquired considerable prestige and ever since have been regarded as particularly characteristic of Scottish intellectual life in the Enlightenment.

The direction given to historical studies was not entirely new. The long development of historiography in the West could be written as a dialectic between systematizers and particularizers—between Polybius and Livy, Machiavelli and Guicciardini, or Bodin and de Thou. But in the eighteenth century the systematic impulse found new grounding in the Enlightenment aspiration to a science of the mind and new scope in the exploration of the structures of everyday life. These ambitions, as I have suggested, helped to differentiate the mature historiography of the eighteenth century from its classical and Renaissance predecessors, thus endowing the new classics of eighteenth-century Britain with a distinctive sense of achievement. Seldom, in fact, has a systematic

[1] "To this species of philosophical investigation, which has no appropriated name in our language, I shall take the liberty of giving the title of *Theoretical* or *Conjectural History;* an expression which coincides pretty nearly in its meaning with that of *Natural History* as employed by Mr. Hume, and with what some French writers have called *Histoire Raisonnee*." Dugald Stewart, "Account of the Life and Writings of Adam Smith," ed. I. S. Ross, in Smith, *Essays on Philosophical Subjects*, 293.

school been so prominent. The characteristic conjecturalist themes echo across the whole spectrum of historically minded genres and influenced the way contemporary audiences understood the entire framework of historical understanding. Histories of a more traditional character took up many of the themes developed more fully by the conjectural histories, while continuing to blend mimetic and didactic elements within the lineage of classical narrative.

The special prestige attached to these most philosophical of histories has encouraged scholars to consider conjecturalist works apart from other historical literatures of the time. Twentieth-century scholarship largely came to writers like Ferguson or Millar in search of the prehistory of the modern social sciences, Marxist and non-Marxist. In particular, much commentary has been shaped by the idea that the conjecturalists presented a materialist and progressive account of the development of civilization. Marx's acknowledgment of a debt to Ferguson pointed the way, and Smith's concept of four stages in the history of property—hunting, herding, agriculture, and commerce—has been identified as the core of a theory of historical progress characteristic of Scottish philosophical history as a whole.[2]

It is always a temptation in historical studies to seek out and canonize some key doctrine, which appears to be capable of giving a coherent identity to the thought of an earlier period—especially when that "key" doctrine corresponds to some presentist agenda. In my view, "the four stages theory" has served as just such a simplification, and even the recognition that stadialism itself can hardly be read in thoroughgoing materialist terms[3] has done little to modify the seemingly automatic identification of Enlightenment historical thought with the idea of the "four stages." In fact, as several judicious historians have pointed out,[4] the thematics of philosophical history were much wider than the questions of property and subsistence underlined by this theory. They ranged from Hume's discussion of slavery as a factor in the fertility of ancient popula-

[2] See especially R. L. Meek, *Social Science and the Ignoble Savage* (Cambridge: Cambridge UP, 1976); and A. S. Skinner, "Adam Smith: An Economic Interpretation of History," in *Essays on Adam Smith*, ed. A. S. Skinner and T. Wilson (Oxford: Oxford UP, 1975).

[3] Knud Haakonssen carefully reviews the materialist interpretation of Smith's stadial views and rejects the notion that Smith held human motivation to be ultimately economic in nature. He adds that it also cannot be the case that "situational factors which influence mankind as far as the maintenance and development of society are concerned" are strictly economic, since there are also "a large number of non-economic factors with determining influence." Haakonssen rightly points out that "certain broad, general conditions of an economic kind are necessary for certain broad, general kinds of social and political organization." He warns us, however, not to confuse taxonomy with explanation in thinking of the four stages. See *The Science of a Legislator: The Natural Jurisprudence of David Hume and Adam Smith* (Cambridge: Cambridge UP, 1981), 184–85, 188.

[4] For a wider view of the origins and purposes of conjecturalism, see especially Emerson, "Conjectural History." A similarly broad approach is outlined by David Allan, who points to the importance of understanding conjecturalism in the context of a "developing history of manners," in *Virtue, Learning, and the Scottish Enlightenment* (Edinburgh: Edinburgh UP, 1993), 161–69. See also the important work of Paul Wood on natural history, cited in the next note.

tions to Smith's analysis of curiosity about the stars, from Kames's speculations on the progress of sciences and morals to Millar's analysis of the "rank and condition of women in different ages." This range and diversity has been obscured, however, by the tendency to represent a single doctrine as an essential characteristic of this whole body of writing.

The general themes of this study suggest the value of considering conjectural history as one genre in a wider family of historical genres. In particular, I wish to explore conjectural history as a constituent part of the eighteenth century's broad critique of traditional political narrative, a critique that rejected history's conventional limitations in favor of a more inclusive conception that would give greater prominence to everyday and inward experience. In this light, the new conjecturalist genre can be seen as a systematization of the widespread discussion of manners outlined in the previous chapter. But although the speculative historians drew heavily on the materials of the history of manners, they were not content simply to represent common life in all its diversity of appearance. In their commitment to create a history that would be more systematic and farseeing, they built on a philosophical psychology of the human mind, as well as a comparative study of manners and customs. The reciprocities between these two methods of understanding provided the principal basis for a grand-narrative whose purpose was to represent the vast, undocumented history of human experience at every stage of social progress. Equally important, though not always equally explicit, is the underlying assumption that the entire "history of man" must be unified by fundamental and necessary principles. Whether the origin of these principles was to be sought in the workings of the human mind, divine purpose, or the methods of natural history,[5] the existence of some unifying principle or principles was a methodological necessity, without which it would be impossible to investigate the scattering of materials that came to hand. Even so, we should not mistake this desire for underlying principles for the idea that conjectural history was a unitary project founded on a single explanatory scheme.

A History "Interesting to All Mankind"

"The Human species is in every view an interesting subject," wrote Kames at the outset of his multivolume *Sketches of the History of Man,* a pioneering example of the genre, "and has been in every age the chief enquiry of philoso-

[5] Paul Wood points to the importance of natural history to the conjecturalist program in "The Natural History of Man in the Scottish Enlightenment," *History of Science* 27 (1989): 89–123, and "Hume, Reid, and the Science of the Mind," in *Hume and Hume's Connexions*, ed. M. A. Stewart and J. P. Wright (University Park: Pennsylvania State UP, 1994). The question is further reviewed in his introduction to Samuel Stanhope Smith, *An Essay on the Causes of Complexion and Figure in the Human Species* (Bristol: Thoemmes, 1995).

phers. . . . but there is still wanting a history of the species."[6] In this way, Kames indicates the extraordinary scope of his intended work—a scope that may in the end be the clearest feature distinguishing conjectural history from its humbler cousins among the various branches of the histories of manners. The sketches included in Kames's first book (man outside of society) closely resemble the themes already reviewed as part of the history of manners. There are chapters titled "Origin and progress of commerce," "Origin and progress of arts," "Progress of manners," "Progress of the female sex," and "Progress and effects of luxury." The second book (man in society) deals with a series of topics concerning forms of government, the progress of states, the sentiment of patriotism, finances, and the management of the poor. There is also a chapter on the character of life in great cities and one titled "Origin and progress of American nations"—that is, a description of Amerindian life, which for Kames as for so many others served as an essential laboratory of primitive custom. With the exception of the last three topics, these chapters obviously take us away from the typical concerns of the history of manners. Even so, Kames discusses government in a spirit already established by his first book; his subject is government as a human institution, not as the narrative of political actions. Finally, book 3 is concerned with the progress of reason, morality, law, and theology—themes related to the works of literary historians like Warton, though certainly wider in scope.

Clearly there are considerable continuities between the thematics of the history of manners and Kames's *Sketches,* but just as clearly there are large differences, especially in scope and method. Since Kames himself, with his loose and rambling style, does not discuss these questions of method in a helpful way, I will turn to a younger Scot whose lectures on philosophical history present some of its key assumptions in admirably concise form.

John Logan was an Edinburgh clergyman whose works include poetry, a tragedy called *Runnamede,* and the *Elements of the Philosophy of History* (1781). This last work was a version of public lectures he had given in Edinburgh, and we are told that the popularity of his performances encouraged him to contest the vacant chair of civil history in the university, a post that he lost to Alexander Fraser Tytler, the biographer of Lord Kames. Logan did not live to publish the intended second part of his work, and the printed fragment was never widely known. Nonetheless, in its brevity and sharpness of outline—the product of lecture notes that are only partially fleshed out by illustration—the *Elements* still makes a valuable introduction to the presuppositions of conjectural history.

Logan put forward a strong argument for a distinctively modern understanding of history. Since the Renaissance, he writes, the moderns began to imitate

[6] Henry Home, Lord Kames, *Sketches of the History of Man*, 2d ed., 4 vols. (Edinburgh, 1778; rpt. Hildesheim: Olms, 1968), 1:1.

ancient writings, and many arts were improved. History in particular benefited from the wider frame of experience open to modern observers. "Thrice within the limits of authentic record, we behold mankind running the career of policy, from rudeness to refinement. A field now opens for cultivating a part of Philosophy little known to the ancients, the Theory of Man as a political being, and the History of Civil Society."[7]

Others in this period would make a parallel argument that contact with other lands had now opened up to Europeans what Burke would call "the great map of mankind"; but whether the expanded scope was seen primarily in anthropological or historical terms, the fundamental claim was much the same. The moderns had open to them a body of experience much greater than anything the ancients possessed, and they could proceed to a deeper understanding of society under the flag of a Baconian program of empirical discovery and systematic arrangement. "To common minds every thing appears particular," writes Logan. "A Philosopher sees in the great, and observes a whole" (10).

In these preliminary lectures, Logan offers his audience three fundamental principles for seeing history "whole":

> **1.** Physical and Moral Causes concur in forming the character of nations. (13)
>
> **2.** The arrangements and improvements which take place in human affairs result not from the efforts of individuals but from a movement of the whole society. (14)
>
> **3.** Similar situations produce similar appearances; and where the state of society is the same, nations will resemble one another. . . . Man is one animal; and where the same situations occur, human nature is the same. (16)

Given these general principles, for Logan the conclusion was clear: "Hence the foundation of every thing is in nature; Politics is a science; and there is a system in human affairs" (16).

Logan's formulations all work in the direction of establishing a more systematic science of history built on several principles of unity in social life. These unities are traced (1) to the operation of intertwined physical and moral causes, (2) to the collective character of institutions, and (3) to the regularities of human nature. To these generalizations, a fourth can be added, which is the principle of progress. "It is peculiar to the human race," Logan states, "that the species improves as well as the individual. Hence a noble field presents itself to the philosophical Historian, to trace the rise and progress of Society, and the history of Civilization" (18).

Logan's emphasis on the collective, social basis of historical understanding can be traced back to Hume's distinction between the philosophical understanding that is possible in respect to the regularities of collective experience and the merely contingent knowledge we possess when events are guided by

[7] John Logan, *Elements of the Philosophy of History. Part First* (Edinburgh, 1781), 3–4. Subsequent citations appear in the text.

the quirkiness of individual will. Logan was far more flamboyant, however, in his antagonism to the individualistic assumptions of traditional narratives. Historians, he argued, have often been ignorant of the regularities of human nature, and as a result history has often degenerated into "the panegyric of single men." Historians record the names of lawgivers, but forget the people, as though institutions could be planned out on paper: "No constitution is formed by a concert: no Government is copied from a plan. Sociability and policy are natural to mankind. In the progress of society, instincts turn into arts, and original principles are converted into actual establishments" (14–15).

Ten years later, much the same argument would take on a more pointedly ideological form in Burke's critique of misguided revolutionary rationalism. Like Burke, Logan recognized that societies cannot be understood primarily in terms of their formal constitutional outlines. Rather, public institutions are the expressions of customs and beliefs that, being more deeply held, are not so exposed to willful interference:

> Rising, in this manner, from Society, all human improvements appear in their proper place, not as separate and detached articles, but as the various, though regular phenomena of one great system. Poetry, Philosophy, the Fine Arts, national manners and customs, result from the situation and spirit of a people.
>
> All that Legislators, Patriots, Philosophers, Statesmen, and Kings can do, is to give a direction to that stream which is for ever flowing. (16)

This criticism of the classical myth of the heroic founder was one of the shibboleths of the philosophical approach to history.[8] In Logan's mind, it marked an epoch-making change in the methods of history. From now on, not only would history encompass a much broader social framework, but its truths would also be relevant to the lives of a far wider readership:

> It is this that renders History, in its proper form, interesting to all mankind, as its object is not merely to delineate the projects of Princes, or the intrigues of Statesmen; but to give a picture of society and represent the character and spirit of nations.[9]

"The Capacities of the Human Mind"

Logan's formulation of the philosophic spirit was echoed by Dugald Stewart, who as the Minervan owl of the Scottish Enlightenment was perhaps the most authoritative commentator on its principles. Reviewing the progress of philosophy since the Renaissance, Stewart writes:

[8] For Millar's treatment of the topic, see below.

[9] Logan, *Elements*, 16. It is worth noting that Logan's assertion that history "in its proper form" would interest all mankind parallels the claim by biographers that their genre was more relevant to readers because of its concern for common life.

> That the capacities of the human mind have been in all ages the same, and that the diversity of phenomena exhibited by our species is the result merely of the different circumstances in which men are placed, has been long received as an incontrovertible logical maxim. . . . And yet, till about the time of Montesquieu, it was by no means so generally recognised by the learned as to have a sensible influence on the fashionable tone of thinking over Europe. The application of this fundamental and leading idea to the natural or *theoretical history* of society in all its various aspects;—to the history of languages, of the arts, of the sciences, of laws, of government, of manners, and of religion,—is the peculiar glory of the latter half of the eighteenth century, and forms a characteristical feature in its philosophy, which even the imagination of Bacon was unable to foresee.[10]

Stewart's summary is a reminder of the breadth of the themes that philosophical historians looked to investigate and to unify. Languages, arts, sciences, religion, government, manners—all of these go to make up human experience, and their history in all stages of society is the proper study of the "theoretical" historian. Mind, not property, is the connecting principle here. Hence the prominence given by a number of philosophical histories to literary history and the history of the arts; hence also the interest in the natural history of religious belief as well as in the progress of science.

Stewart's "leading idea" derived from a famous passage of the *Treatise* in which Hume argued for the centrality of knowledge of the human mind to an understanding of all the sciences. "Even *Mathematics, Natural Philosophy, and Natural Religion,*" Hume concludes, "are in some measure dependent on the science of MAN."[11] Hume's investigation of the natural history of religion is evidently a working out of this central principle; so, too, is Adam Smith's early "History of Astronomy." Smith never wrote the ambitious work he had projected, which would have been "a sort of Philosophical History of all the different branches of Literature, of Philosophy, Poetry and Eloquence,"[12] nor can we simply take the "Astronomy" as directly representative of Smith's more mature ambitions. Nonetheless, the "Astronomy" survives as a brilliant early example of the methods of theoretical history, as well as a reminder of the important place that histories of knowledge occupied in the conjectural scheme.

Smith's purpose was not to write a technical history of astronomical theory leading up to Newton; that would have constituted a decidedly unphilosophic

[10] Dugald Stewart, *Dissertation: Exhibiting the Progress of Metaphysical, Ethical, and Political Philosophy, Since the Revival of Letters in Europe*, in *Collected Works*, ed. W. Hamilton, 11 vols. (Edinburgh, 1854), 1:69–70.

[11] Hume, *A Treatise of Human Nature*, ed. L. A. Selby-Bigge (Oxford: Clarendon, 1968), xix.

[12] Smith to Duc de La Rochefoucauld, November 1785, in *Correspondence of Adam Smith*, ed. E. C. Mossner and I. S. Ross (Indianapolis: Liberty, 1987), 286–87. On Hume's importance to Smith's interest in science, see the general introduction by D. D. Raphael and A. S. Skinner to Adam Smith, *Essays on Philosophical Subjects*, 15–21.

history of astronomy. The "Essay" must be viewed, his first editors wrote, not as a history of Isaac Newton's astronomy, "but chiefly as an additional illustration of those Principles in the Human Mind which Mr. Smith has pointed out to be the universal motives of Philosophical Researches."[13] His thesis is that philosophical enquiry is above all a search for imaginative coherence, whose central principles must be understood in relation to the sentiments that direct all forms of discovery—surprise, wonder, and admiration. Nature seems to present us with events that are solitary and incoherent, thus disturbing the easy movement of the imagination; the philosophical mind tries to overcome these obstacles to its native tranquillity by finding the underlying principles of order. Surprise leads to wonder and eventually to admiration:

> Philosophy, by representing the invisible chains which bind together all these disjointed objects, endeavours to introduce order into this chaos of jarring and discordant appearances, to allay this tumult of the imagination, and to restore it, when it surveys the great revolutions of the universe, to that tone of tranquillity and composure, which is both most agreeable to itself, and most suitable to its nature. Philosophy, therefore, may be regarded as one of those arts which addresses themselves to the imagination. (45–46)

Following these principles, Smith pursues the phases of theorizing about the heavens in terms of the imaginative construction of systems of order, rather than as successive discoveries of the rules actually governing the cosmos. This avoidance of the conventional language of discovery is, of course, consistent with his thesis, but it also allows him, in a wonderful concluding passage, to express the triumph of Newtonianism as the loss of his own philosophic distance in the face of a construct so complete and satisfying to the imagination. No wonder, then, Smith writes, that mankind in general have come to accept Newton's theories "not as an attempt to connect in imagination the phaenomena of the Heavens, but as the greatest discovery that ever was made by man, the discovery of an immense chain of the most important and sublime truths" (105).

For a twentieth-century historian brought up on the theories of Thomas Kuhn, what Smith's essay lacks in surprise it makes up in admiration. Smith himself, however, came to regard the imaginative unity of his own historical construct with some suspicion. But if, as he thought, the essay was too narrowly drawn, the very purity of its intellectual grounds is valuable to the present context. By comparison, although their essential procedures are much the same, other philosophic histories of sciences or literatures often seem plodding and unself-conscious.

Kames's history of theology, for example, in *Sketches of the History of Man,* book 3, takes as the necessary starting point for a history of conceptions of the

[13] Smith, *Essays on Philosophical Subjects*, 105.

divinity an analysis of the principles of human nature leading to belief and devotion. "We have thus traced with wary steps, the gradual progress of theology through many stages," Kames writes, "corresponding to the gradual openings and improvements of the human mind."[14] Thus the progress of natural religion, like that of astronomy, reflects the needs of human nature and forms a part of the history of the human mind. And if Kames's history lacks the sheer brilliance of Smith's "Astronomy" (or Hume's *Natural History of Religion*), one reason is that Kames could not take the same pleasure in overthrowing common knowledge. Kames was in some respects an unconventional Christian, but he was a devout believer in Providence, and in its largest dimensions the entire plan and method of *Sketches* is shaped by a theodicy. Though the work is often rambling and idiosyncratic, it is held together by a conviction that every part of God's design manifests a necessary order. The result, from a methodological standpoint, is reminiscent of the functionalist assumptions of mid-twentieth-century sociology; in both, there is a strong presumption that every social arrangement is laid out upon a structure of necessity. The consequence is that every empirical discovery about social practices, no matter how fragmentary or exotic, ultimately serves only to strengthen the pattern of coherence. As a result, Kames's history of "the gradual openings of the human mind with respect to Deity"[15] has nothing of the skeptical energy that animates Hume's speculation on the natural history of religion.

Adam Ferguson

The best-known of all conjectural histories is Adam Ferguson's *Essay on the History of Civil Society,* which brings together a philosophical portrait of human nature, an anthropology of "rude nations," and a moralist's preoccupation with the weaknesses of contemporary society.

Ferguson begins with a substantial first section titled "General Characteristics of Human Nature" in which he covers much of the common ground of Enlightenment moral philosophy. But Ferguson does not see himself as an abstract philosopher who favors theoretical over empirical methods. On the contrary, he carries on a running polemic against those who make insupportable pronouncements on such topics as the state of nature, or generalize from the extraordinary circumstances of a "wild man" caught in the woods. For Ferguson, there is no prehistory of human nature, no purer state for the philo-

[14] Kames, *History of Man*, 4:244. On Kames's life and intellectual career, see Ian Simpson Ross, *Lord Kames and the Scotland of His Day* (Oxford: Clarendon, 1972). On his legal thought, see David Lieberman, *The Province of Legislation Determined: Legal Theory in Eighteenth-Century Britain* (Cambridge: Cambridge UP, 1989).

[15] Kames, *History of Man*, 4:246.

sophic speculator to recover. Human nature is essentially unchanged, and human experience, though not uniform, is unified by its "general characteristics"—sociability, communicativeness, sympathy, and so on—which are everywhere evident in the contemporary world, as well as in history.

But above all Ferguson emphasizes the active, restless quality of human nature, which makes humans from the very first creatures destined "to invent and contrive." The result is that the progress of the species is itself a natural principle of human nature, so that it is wrong to say that man "has quitted the state of his nature" as civilization advances. The savage in the forest takes the first steps, "which led nations more advanced, from the architecture of the cottage to that of the palace, and conducted the human mind from the perceptions of sense, to the conclusions of science."[16]

The active, striving side of humanity is often directed to survival in the struggle for existence, but the fullest display of our human capacities comes in response to social, not material challenges; the stimulus is not simple necessity, but human sympathy. On first observation, Ferguson writes, we are likely to conclude that subsistence is the main "spring" of human actions. But attention to material needs will not give us the real story of human history. "What comes from a fellow-creature is received with peculiar attention. . . . The bosom kindles in company, while the point of interest in view has nothing to inflame."[17] The philosopher who attributes human motives to mere profit and loss, Ferguson concludes, is no better than the foreigner who thought that Othello was enraged over the loss of his handkerchief.

Property remains a crucial factor in Ferguson's view of human progress, but the material basis of subsistence cannot be separated from Ferguson's picture of the human mind. The restless inventiveness that is characteristic of humankind lifts us out of savagery, inventing property and with it new types of subsistence, new forms of subordination, and new arts. None of this is fully intentional, but the process is nonetheless a product of human desire and imagination.[18] As a result, it would be more accurate to say that it is not property as such that transforms the social world, but the *idea* of property, the new habits and appetites, the previously unfelt attention to interest and futurity

[16] Ferguson, *History of Civil Society*, 14. On Ferguson, in addition to Oz-Salzberger's excellent introduction, see especially David Kettler, *The Social and Political Thought of Adam Ferguson* (Columbus: Ohio State UP, 1965); and Duncan Forbes's introduction to his edition of the text (Edinburgh: Edinburgh UP, 1966).

[17] Ferguson, *History of Civil Society*, 36.

[18] "Mankind, in following the present sense of their minds, in striving to remove inconveniences, or to gain apparent and contiguous advantages, arrive at ends which even their imagination could not anticipate. . . . He who first said, 'I will appropriate this field: I will leave it to my heirs'; did not perceive, that he was laying the foundation of civil laws and political establishments" (ibid., 119).

that come with the new institution. The difference between "savage" and "barbaric" society, for example, hinges on the absence or presence of property, but Ferguson characterizes the change in more than simple material terms, calling barbaric societies those "under the *Impression* of Property and Interest" (emphasis added).

Commercial society brings still greater opportunities for the display of human powers—a greater diversity of occupations, interests, customs. Here Ferguson devotes some attention to the familiar topics of the history of manners—the histories of arts and literature, the difference between ancient and modern manners, the effects of chivalry on the position of women, the manners of polished societies. But Ferguson is more wary of the apparent success of commercial societies than most conjecturalist writers, and he points with some alarm at the separation of the arts and professions into distinct specialties. As in manufacture, the resulting specialization brings an increase of power, but especially in the arenas of political and military service, it threatens a loss of public spirit.

In all this there is no possible goal, no imaginable end to the process of striving and self-revision. Since active exertion is an essential principle of human nature, the only alternative is a "relaxation" of national spirit, a subject that dominates the final two sections of the book, which deal with the linked topics of decline and luxury. In these sections of the *Essay,* Ferguson's commitment to a classical republican program of civic virtue is particularly clear; his wide philosophical portrait of human nature in all stages of life as active, striving, and restless takes on a narrower, historically more definite shape as a eulogy of the self-denying virtues of a Cato or Brutus.

Within this framework of progress and decline, the discussion of manners is an important part of Ferguson's thought, both moral and historical. For Ferguson, as for other conjectural historians, the similarity of manners of widely separated societies was a foundation stone of the comparative method. If polished societies could abandon their pretended superiority, they would find in the manners of "rude nations" their clearest access to their own beginnings. Thus the Romans might have found an image of their own ancestors in the Germanic tribes, and modern Britons can study "the features of our own progenitors" in the present condition of the Indians of North America. Ferguson projects this insight into an imagined future: if ever "any American tribe escape the poison which is administered by our traders of Europe, it may be from the relations of the present times, and the descriptions which are now given by travellers, that such a people, in after ages, may best collect the accounts of their origin."[19]

[19] Ibid., 80.

Ferguson's methods, however, do not always call for a simple comparison of like stages of progress. When he examines the differences between ancient and modern manners, contrasting the fierceness and public spirit of the ancients with the politeness and compassion of modern customs, the explanations are genetic rather than stadial. The contrast of ancient and modern manners is particularly marked in war. In modern nations, we make a distinction between the state and its subjects, and we are "accustomed to think of the individual with compassion, seldom of the public with zeal."[20] The rules of war have been softened; politeness mingles with the sword. The ancient Greeks and Romans, by contrast, made no distinction between the enemy state and the enemy people. They warred against their opponents by destroying the people and ruining the land. Battles were conducted with desperation, since "an enemy, when disarmed, was, for the most part, either sold in the market, or killed, that he might never return to strengthen his party" (184).

This stark contrast poses several problems to any simple stadial scheme. In the first place, Ferguson recognizes that in his initial account of progress the Greeks must be called barbaric, and for much of their history the Romans too, if by this we mean a people not far advanced in commerce, "profuse of their own lives," and vehement in their attachments and enmities. Only the greatness of ancient literature—especially of their historians—has allowed the moderns to accept their manner of life. To drive the point home, Ferguson indulges in a rare bit of fancy, imagining the negative description of the Greeks that would be given by a traveler such as "we sometimes send abroad to inspect the manners of mankind."[21] And yet, of course, by their "activity of mind," their abilities, and their spirit, the Greeks have acquired the first rank among nations.

An equal and opposite difficulty awaits in assessing the character of modern nations, whose manners acquired much of their characteristic softness while these nations lived in a condition every bit as barbaric as the Greeks. In short, if the ancients became illustrious without ever becoming truly civil, the moderns were chivalric long before their commerce made them polite. Thus we have the problem of explaining the origins of opposite ideas of honor "among nations equally rude, equally addicted to war, and equally fond of military glory."[22] Clearly, the stadial scheme gives little help here, and for an explanation Ferguson turns to evidence of the continuity of European manners—specifically to romance and popular tradition, which show that the chivalric system is deeply ingrained among European nations. And reaching still further back, he argues that even in the forests of Germany a kind of devotion was paid to the female sex, while Christianity made its contribution by preaching

[20] Ibid., 190.
[21] Ibid., 185.
[22] Ibid., 191.

a doctrine of meekness. In short, "the foundations of what is now held to be the law of war, and of nations, was laid in the manners of Europe, together with the sentiments which are expressed in the tales of chivalry, and of gallantry."[23]

As a man of science, Ferguson was not committed to any single scheme of analysis, and he seems unconcerned with the evident tensions between stadial and genetic explanations. But as a moralist, Ferguson was deeply troubled by the problem of corruption of manners and national decline. He emphasizes repeatedly that there is nothing inevitable about this process and that commerce and corruption are by no means identical.[24] Nonetheless he feared the tendency of commercial society to dissolve into dispersed and alienated fragments. It is clear, too, that he regards the tradition of European manners as lacking the passionate interest in the public realm that might be the strongest defense against the worst effects of commerce. Thus, though he does not say so explicitly, Ferguson seems to feel that the combined effect of these two systems of manners—commercial and (for want of a better term) chivalric—pose particular dangers to the societies of modern Europe.

Like Machiavelli, his great predecessor in this strain of political moralism, Ferguson believed that national vitality is a matter of spirit as much as of law. But the eighteenth century was more aware than the sixteenth of the social force of private will. Even Ferguson, who more than any of his contemporaries followed Machiavelli in asserting the primacy of public values over private ones, could not set aside his own century's knowledge of the ways in which the social impinged on and even constituted the political sphere:

> Men, in fact, while they pursue in society different objects or separate views, procure a wide distribution of power, and by a species of chance, arrive at a posture for civil engagements, more favourable to human nature than what human wisdom could ever calmly devise.
>
> If the strength of a nation, in the mean time, consists in men on whom it may rely, and who are fortunately or wisely combined for its preservation, it follows, that manners are as important as either numbers or wealth; and that corruption is to be accounted a principal cause of national declension and ruin.[25]

[23] Ibid. Burke made much the same point when he said in a famous passage in the *Reflections* that European manners had been formed by two principles, "the spirit of a gentleman and the spirit of religion." *Reflections on the Revolution in France*, ed. J. Pocock (Indianapolis: Hackett, 1987), 69.

[24] "It is, however, well known from the history of mankind, that corruption of this, or of any other degree, is not peculiar to nations in their decline, or in the result of signal prosperity, and great advances in the arts of commerce." He goes on to say that in small-scale societies, the bonds of common purpose are very strong; nonetheless even savage or barbaric nations can fall into this kind of weakness (*History of Civil Society*, 229).

[25] Ibid., 225.

Here, political economy and civic moralism seem to stand side by side without any real resolution or rapprochement. Both, however, are characteristic of Ferguson, and both are linked to his general view of the striving, passionate quality that defines the best of human nature. It would be too crude an opposition to say that in Ferguson the civic moralist attempted to remedy what the civil historian had discovered. But certainly some of the vividness that lifts the *Essay* above most conjecturalist works is owing to the way in which it combines these two different discourses of manners.

John Millar

John Millar was professor of civil law at Glasgow, where he was regarded as the leading Whig intellectual.[26] Francis Jeffrey affectionately described his gifts as a teacher, particularly his way of abandoning the formalities and privileges of the lectern to draw his students into respectful debate. His influence as a writer was also considerable, and in our own time—if we except Hume and Smith themselves—Millar probably has the highest reputation among all the Scottish philosophical historians as an original social analyst.

One reason for the high esteem in which Millar is now regarded is that it is comparatively easy to induct him into the honors of modern sociology. Unlike Ferguson, he does not find it necessary to begin with a general investigation of human nature, nor is he preoccupied with moral problems of decline and corruption. Instead much of the *Origin of the Distinction of Ranks* (1771) seems to the modern reader an austerely secular analysis of inequality and domination in which economic relationships are certainly the dominant (though not exclusive) interest. "The first attention of a people is directed to the acquisition of the mere necessaries of life," Millar writes, "and to the exercise of those occupations which are most immediately requisite for subsistence." Success in gaining the necessities only leads to "a gradual increase of their wants," and thus to a renewed effort to supply their expanded material needs.[27] In this way attention shifts from mere subsistence to more refined tastes, and society becomes more polished as a result. In Millar, too, it is clear that the four-stage development of society is not a peripheral notion, as it was for Kames, but a central tool of analysis. He is consistently interested in

[26] On Millar's life, see W. C. Lehmann, *John Millar of Glasgow* (Cambridge: Cambridge UP, 1960). A brief summary is offered by J. V. Price in his edition of *The Origin of the Distinction of Ranks* (Bristol: Thoemmes, 1990), which reprints the 4th edition (Edinburgh, 1806); also included is John Craig's "Account of the Life and Writings of the Author" (1806). On Millar's debt to Smith, see Knud Haakonssen, *Natural Law and Moral Philosophy: From Grotius to the Scottish Enlightenment* (Cambridge: Cambridge UP, 1996), chap. 5.

[27] Millar, *Distinction of Ranks*, 99.

economic relations, and in separated passages it would be easy to give the sense that he was committed to a kind of economic determinism. Millar wrote, however, at a time when there was no pressure to choose between materialist and cultural explanations. For this reason, his investigations typically unify rather than separate questions of manners and matters of economy. Primitive societies are indeed governed by narrow material necessities, but "polished" nations have won a wider freedom and form a more complex unity. Their situation is expressed in repeated phrases like "the advancement of commerce and the arts," or "the advancement of a people in the arts of life," which bring together the material and moral situation of a society (295, 220).

The Origins of the Distinction of Ranks belongs to the eighteenth century's gathering critique of the established historiographical tradition and needs to be read in that context. Like other works in the conjecturalist genre, the book presents its opposition to the older convention in terms that are (implicitly at least) both formal and thematic. Such works argue, in other words, that their deployment of a nontraditional historiographical form is required by their concern for a set of historical conditions that the dominant tradition has excluded from consideration. "The following Inquiry," writes Millar, "is intended to illustrate the natural history of mankind in several important articles. This is attempted, by pointing out the more obvious and common improvements which gradually arise in the state of society, and by showing the influence of these upon the manners, the laws, and the government of a people."[28]

This sets out the scope of the "Inquiry" in its most general terms as an investigation of social conditions, manners, and institutions. Because the object of historical study here is essentially a new one, it cannot be defined in a single, conventional phrase. Instead it is laid out in a series of overlapping descriptions that simultaneously refer to the thematics of his study and a view of historical change that is inseparable from these interests. Millar's subject is *gradual* change in the "state of society," or more concretely, progress in its manners, laws, and government. Put positively, then, his "Inquiry" is defined by its focus on the experiences of common life ("the more obvious and common improvements") considered as elements of a slow, but progressive change. As is so often the case, however, the identity of the new genre can only be completed by way of a contrast to the conventions of traditional historical writing, to which his "Inquiry" stands fully opposed:

> With regard to the facts made use of in the following discourse, the reader, who is conversant in history, will readily perceive the difficulty of obtaining proper materials for speculations of this nature. Historians of reputation have commonly overlooked the transactions of early ages, as not deserving to be remembered; and even in the

[28] Ibid., 11–12.

> history of later and more cultivated periods, they have been more solicitous to give an exact account of battles, and public negotiations, than of the interior police and government of a country.[29]

Conventional historiography, then, with its exclusive attention to matters of state and its contemptuous ignorance of the ordinary organization of the social realm, is of no help even in supplying the information required by the deeper researches of the conjectural historian. The paradoxical consequence, as Millar goes on to say, is that his best evidence has been furnished by what would typically be considered a less reliable source. Travellers, not historians, have been his best informants, Millar writes. And though he freely acknowledges the weakness of such evidence when authors are taken one by one, he strongly defends their reliability when their descriptions are compared across different nations or ages.

Millar's concern with "interior police and government" is evident in the subject matter and organization of his book. Reflecting, in part, the natural law tradition from which his teaching of law derived,[30] the *Distinction of Ranks* is as much concerned with the domestic and social dimension of power as with those that are public and political. Millar begins with an extended discussion of "the rank and condition of women in different ages" and then moves on to the power of fathers over children. Only then does he extend his comparative history of relationships of power and subordination to public forms of authority—that of a chief over his tribe (chap. 3) and of a sovereign over his subordinates (chap. 4). In his fifth chapter, Millar considers the effects of progress in the arts and in polished manners on government—the situation of contemporary Europe—and then returns in his final chapter to yet another form of private power, the authority of a master over his servants, a chapter that becomes also an investigation of the forces increasing or decreasing the independence of the people in modern, commercial societies.

In all this, Millar wants to incorporate the widest series of relationships of power, ranging from the most private to the most public. Politics, it is clear, are hardly forgotten, but Millar analyzes public authority as building upon and extending the most pervasive private forms of domination and dependency—the power of men over women, of fathers over children, of masters over servants. Though a traditional concern for the law, these domestic and civil concerns had no place, of course, in classical narratives. As a result, to pursue his

[29] Ibid., 12.

[30] See Haakonssen, *Natural Law;* and for the wider legal background, Peter Stein, *Legal Evolution* (Cambridge: Cambridge UP, 1980). Critics have also pointed out, however, that the thematics of the natural law tradition were so widely diffused in eighteenth-century moral sciences that it becomes difficult to pin down more specific questions of influence. On this point, see Pauline Westerman, "Hume and the Natural Lawyers: A Change of Landscape," in Stewart and Wright, *Hume and Hume's Connexions*, 83–104.

comparative history of "interior police and government," Millar has to look well outside of the historiographical canon—not only to the abundant literature of travel and ethnography, but (like other philosophic historians) to antiquities, law, and the poets of primitive ages. A particularly striking feature of Millar's work is his many references to the Hebrew Bible, which he treats as a descriptive ethnography of pastoral ages.

A useful, self-contained example of Millar's procedures is his discussion of the decline of servitude in Europe, an achievement that he considers a distinguishing mark of European culture as well as economy.[31] In primitive ages, to be a servant was almost universally the same thing as to be a slave, but in later times, under the influence of "opulence and civilized manners," conditions changed, leading to the gradual loosening of the bonds of agricultural servitude, the rise in the price and efficiency of agricultural labor, the development of artisanal skills, and the increasing independence of labor.[32] These topics form the core of his discussion, but Millar goes on to devote several more pages to "other circumstances . . . which, in a subordinate manner, have, perhaps contributed something to this remarkable change in European manners" (272). These "circumstances" are the moral teachings of Christianity, the influence of the clergy, and the role of civil government, all of which are treated skeptically, though not dismissed. Millar concludes that in most of Europe slavery has gradually declined and disappeared "from the natural progress of manners, and without any express interposition of the legislature" (278).

Millar's view of the decline of servitude echoes similar discussions in both Hume and Smith of the causes of the eclipse of the feudal nobility.[33] In fact, explanations of historical change that emphasized the primacy of slow changes in manners were a key feature of what was becoming an increasingly self-conscious program of historical studies. As we saw in Logan's lectures, conjectural historians were hostile to the idea that society might be understood by reference to willed changes instituted by great originating figures. This ancient tradition of political argument is best exemplified in modern times by Machiavelli's admiration for the founders of constitutions; but despite the favor with which Machiavelli was often read as a notable precursor of the philosophical approach, the new philosophical historians overthrew his central political myth in favor of a new gradualist vision of history proceeding under a regime of

[31] "By what happy concurrence of events has the practice of slavery been so generally abolished in Europe? By what powerful motives were our forefathers induced to deviate from the maxims of other nations, and to abandon a custom so general retained in other parts of the world?" (Millar, *Distinction of Ranks*, 261).

[32] The phrase is quoted from the heading for section 2: "*The usual effects of opulence and civilized manners, with regard to the treatment of Servants*" (ibid., 250).

[33] See especially his discussion of the way in which in a commercial society money comes to undermine traditional dependency (ibid., 234). This analysis closely follows the discussion in Hume and Smith on the decline of the feudal aristocracy; on which see chapter 11 below.

manners. To Millar, the sorts of changes that might be produced by the individual will of the legislator seemed slight when compared to the slower rhythms and half-conscious movements of custom and habit.[34] Thus, in the new philosophical understanding of historical change, Hume and Burke, not Machiavelli, would come to occupy the central position.

Let me turn finally to the place of the history of manners in Millar's understanding of conjectural history. "Those who have examined the manners and customs of nations have had chiefly two objects in view," he declares at the opening of the *Distinction of Ranks*. Millar points first toward those who seek a practical application and employ their knowledge to select the kinds of institutions and ways of governing that seem most worthy of being adopted. His own purpose, however, is a more theoretical and speculative one: his aim is "to investigate the causes of different usages" and to "contemplate the amazing diversity to be found in the laws of different countries, and even of the same country at different periods."[35]

This distinction between more practical and more speculative forms of the history of "manners and customs" is a useful one, especially when placed alongside the passage quoted earlier in which Millar defines his work against the deficiencies of traditional historiography. In simple terms, his program envisages a triangular pattern of historical genres, each defined by its rivalries and reciprocities with the other two. On one flank, Millar presents his claim for conjectural history in competition with classical narrative and its assumption of the primacy of public action and the individual will. In this regard, Millar's terms ("historians of reputation") are a little more circumspect than John Logan's ("vulgar historians"), but it is clear that this rivalry is for both a defining feature of the new genre. This is also the significance of his invitation to an informed and complicit reader ("the reader who is conversant in history") to share his dismay with the limitations of conventional historians who have overlooked the sorts of materials required for his enquiry.

Millar indicates considerably more common ground with respect to the history of manners, but here too he leaves some distance. As already indicated, his opening lines speak of two classes of writers who have "examined the manners and customs of nations": those seeking a practical understanding and those wanting to investigate the causes of the different usages of mankind. By linking the history of manners to the higher, more analytic program of conjecturalism, Millar implicitly answers the objection that works of the latter sort are overly abstract and lack the solidity of real history. Thus his gesture

[34] For Millar's attack on the classical idea of the founders, see ibid., 6–8.

[35] Ibid., 1. The passage reads, "To investigate the causes of different usages has been likewise esteemed an useful as well as an entertaining speculation. When we contemplate the amazing diversity to be found in the laws of different countries, and even of the same country at different periods, our curiosity is naturally excited to enquire in what manner mankind have been led to embrace such different rules of conduct."

to the history of manners is collaborative—in this sense quite different from the dismissal handed to conventional historians. Even so, in distinguishing between the two forms of enquiry into customs, one practical, the other theoretical, Millar establishes a firm sense of hierarchy in the investigations of the "state of society."

This same distance is also registered by the more miscellaneous writers I have grouped under the history of manners, through gestures of a reciprocal character. In works like Blackwell's *Homer,* Alexander's *Women,* or Warton's *History of English Poetry,* we frequently encounter brief speculations on the origins or diversity of customs that would not be out of place in the more systematic and far-reaching enquiries of Kames or Ferguson. Short of adopting Robert Henry's taxing device of multiple narratives, historians of everyday life, commerce, women, or literary tradition were largely left without the guidance provided by classical conventions of narrative. For these historians, it seems reasonable to speculate, the more philosophical enquiry into the "causes of different usages" spoken of by Millar served as an alternative point of reference. Hence their many gestures toward the higher, more theoretical genre, gestures that both acknowledge and attempt to bridge the gap between the two kinds of enquiry into manners and customs.

CONTINUITIES

Eight

James Mackintosh: The Historian as Reader

JAMES MACKINTOSH was one of those men of early promise who spend the latter half of a long life in the inescapable company of disappointed ambitions. He had broken into public attention with the *Vindiciae Gallicae*, the strongest of many Whig defenses of the French Revolution against Burke's attack. Before long, however, the radicalization of the Revolution forced a change of position. Mackintosh recanted his support for France and sought a kind of absolution from Burke himself. This public apostasy clouded his political prospects, and a subsequent appointment as recorder of Bombay failed to make his fortune. His return to England, after seven years service in India, was followed by a parliamentary career, which, though respectable, lacked brilliance. Parallel frustrations checked Mackintosh's literary ambitions. His writings on politics and philosophy advanced his reputation, but his steadiest ambition came to focus on writing the history of English liberty as secured by the Revolution of 1688. He published a short, popular history of England and numbers of essays on historical and literary themes, as well as a *Dissertation* on the history of moral philosophy in the eighteenth century, but Mackintosh's long-promised and laboriously prepared history of the revolution appeared only as a posthumous fragment.[1]

[1] See the *History of England*, 3 vols. (London, 1830–32), and *History of the Revolution in England in 1688, prefaced by a notice of the Life, Writings and Speeches of Sir James Mackintosh*, ed. William B. Wallace (London, 1834). Mackintosh deserved a better custodian than Wallace, whose prefatory life seems curiously insulting to the memory of the man nominally being honored. Many of the works were brought together as *The Miscellaneous Works of the Rt. Honourable Sir James Mackintosh*, ed. Robert Mackintosh, 3 vols. (London, 1846). I cite the one-volume edition (London, 1851).

On Mackintosh's life, the chief source is the *Memoirs*. There is a good narrative account in Patrick O'Leary, *Sir James Mackintosh: The Whig Cicero* (Aberdeen: Aberdeen UP, 1989). The most complete study of Mackintosh's political ideas remains Jane Rendall, "The Political Ideas and Activities of Sir James Mackintosh (1765–1832)," Ph.D. diss., London University, 1972, a study that unfortunately remains unpublished. See also Lionel McKenzie, "The French Revolution and English Parliamentary Reform: James Mackintosh and the *Vindiciae Gallicae*," *Eighteenth-Century Studies* 14 (1981): 264–82; as well as James T. Boulton, "James Mackintosh: *Vindiciae Gallicae*," *Renaissance and Modern Studies* 21 (1977): 106–18. On Mackintosh's ideas in the context of Scottish understandings of politics and natural law, see the acute study by Haakonssen, *Natural Law*, chap. 8. For an overview of English political thought, with useful discussions of Mackintosh, see H. T. Dickinson, *Liberty and Property: Political Ideology in Eighteenth-Century Britain* (Methuen: London, 1977).

The role for which Mackintosh had prepared himself—to be the Whig successor to David Hume—fell to a younger member of the *Edinburgh Review* circle, Thomas Babington Macaulay, who repaid his predecessor with a generous tribute. Writing from India, where like Mackintosh himself, but with greater success, he had gone to make his fortune, Macaulay saluted the history as the last testament of a departed elder. "All the little peculiar cadences of that voice from which scholars and statesmen loved to receive the lessons of a serene and benevolent wisdom are in our ears."[2] By stressing the note of personal tribute, Macaulay opened the way for a humane, but consciously optimistic assessment of Mackintosh's achievement as a historian.[3] "We have no hesitation in pronouncing this Fragment decidedly the best history now extant of the reign of James the Second" (2:289). Macaulay admitted that, as might have been expected from a "Scottish *feelosopher*," Mackintosh was inclined to mix too much "disquisition" in his narrative. Yet he was surprised by the discovery that "Sir James could tell a story as well as Voltaire or Hume" (2:289). In its best sections, the work could be compared to the best of modern histories. "We find in it the diligence, the accuracy, and the judgment of Hallam, united to the vivacity and the colouring of Southey. A history of England, written throughout in this manner, would be the most fascinating book in the language. It would be more in request at the circulating libraries than the last novel."[4]

Behind this tribute, with its characteristic ambition to broaden (and perhaps regender) history's audience, the shape of Macaulay's own ambitions as a historian is clearly visible. Less evident, though not entirely hidden, is Macaulay's judgment that Mackintosh, however worthy as an ancestor, could not be a troublesome competitor in the race for historical honors. Mackintosh himself would not have disagreed with this assessment of his achievements, and his journal is full of melancholy self-recrimination, mixed with schemes for

[2] Macaulay, "Sir James Mackintosh" (first published in 1835), in *Critical, Historical, and Miscellaneous Essays*, 3 vols. (New York: Albert Cogswell, 1859), 2:83.

[3] A second rhetorical strategy is the comparison that immediately follows to "another celebrated Fragment," Charles James Fox's history of James II. This allows Macaulay to place Mackintosh in the select circle of statesman-historians: those who "had one eminent qualification for writing history: they had spoken history, acted history, lived history" (*Miscellaneous Essays*, 2:84). Further, it allowed the essayist to demonstrate a kind of nice discrimination within the Whig Parnassus by admitting that Mackintosh was as superior to Fox in historical writing as he was inferior in parliamentary debate: "Mr. Fox wrote debates. Sir James Mackintosh spoke essays" (2:85).

[4] Ibid., 2:90. In this essay, as elsewhere, Macaulay expresses the view that the historian's imagination is primarily involved in selection and arrangement ("The triumph of his skill is to select such parts as may produce the effect of the whole, to bring out strongly all the characteristic features, and to throw the light and shade in such a manner as may heighten the effect"). It is interesting to see Macaulay putting his metonymic principle to work in the very moment of articulating it.

self-reform and revivals of his historiographical ambitions. An entry for late October 1810, written from India, is characteristic: "23rd—I have just been caressing poor little Tartar [a favorite terrier], whom, as Robin's playmate, I consider as my almost single friend. 24th.—The forty-fifth year of a life of indolence is this day closed."[5] In March of the following year, he wrote: "23rd.—It is now about twenty years since I published my answer to Burke. It was not a brilliant dawn, but it promised a better day; we are now in the afternoon" (2:295).

Unlike Macaulay, Mackintosh never could make the final choice for authorship over public life, a hesitation that his friends charitably offered for his failure to produce the great works expected of him. Certainly his journals offer many evidences of his historiographical ambitions, as well as hints why they were never properly realized. Homesick and isolated in Bombay, he thought about the advantages of returning home on an American ship: "in one of them, I might go to take a glance at American juries, elections, etc, which are much in my line. . . . If I write the 'History of England,' the sight of America would be useful. I suspect after all, that I have a better chance of being an historian than a lawgiver; and perhaps the first is the most suitable to my character, and the most conducive to my happiness, but I shall always have a hankering after the last" (2:84).

In the end it was a British merchant ship that carried him home, and on shipboard he turned his attention once again to beginning his history. The circumstances occasioned a wry comparison to the author of the *Decline and Fall:*

> If ever it should turn out to be good for anything, it will be rather curious to recollect where it may be said to have been begun. It was under circumstances more inauspicious and vulgar than that which was projected amidst the ruins of the capitol. But a cabin nine feet square in a merchant ship, manned by Mahommedan sailors, on the coast of Malabar, is, if not a convenient, at least a characteristic place, for beginning the history of a maritime and commercial empire. (2:154)

After Mackintosh's return to England, a place was found for him in Parliament, where he spoke up for Ireland, Poland, and Canada, as well as for legal and electoral reforms. But he never moved into the indisputable front ranks of his party, and increasingly he became one of those figures recognized as an elder without ever having occupied the trust of leadership. Even so, public business continued to occupy him, as well as a variety of literary interests. It was not for nothing that his friend Mme. de Staël urged that if he were ever to complete his history, it might be necessary to imitate Gibbon more closely and seclude himself on Lake Geneva (2:329).

In the meantime, the idea of a history of England drew him on, and from time to time there were energetic spurts of travel and manuscript hunting. "I

[5] Mackintosh, *Memoirs*, 2:62; subsequent citations appear in the text.

try this place for a fortnight more," he wrote in the autumn of 1812, during a visit to the Wedgewoods—to whom he was connected by marriage—"after which, if I am able, I am to go to Wimpole in Cambridgeshire, the seat of the Earl of Hardwicke, who is to communicate to me papers of the greatest importance to my history of England during the reign of George the Second. With the same object I afterwards, for a few days, go to the Earl of Chichester's in Sussex, and return to town about February, to begin my labours as an historian, and perhaps a little as a lawyer—those as a member of parliament not commencing till the beginning of June" (2:259–60).

Mackintosh pursued his researches seriously and in the next year reported his gratitude that the prince had "granted me access to a very valuable collection of papers, which he has lately procured." The papers had come from the deposed Stuarts; their chief attraction was in "innumerable letters to and from the exiled family, from 1701 to 1749, which are particularly curious, and abound with unexpected proofs of the very wide diffusion of Jacobitism at a period when it was generally supposed to be extinct. I go to the library at Carlton House four hours of three days in the week to make extracts from them."[6]

The apparent end of the Napoleonic wars in 1814 reopened travel to France for the first time since the Peace of Amiens. The result was his Edinburgh essay "On the State of France in 1815" and the opportunity for much research in the documents of the Foreign Office. I have "already made discoveries of the utmost importance," he wrote, "and I have no doubt of entirely resolving the historical problem of the plans of counter-revolution formed by the Tories from 1710 to 1714."[7] These notes and others went into the impressive collection of manuscript abstracts that now lie in the British Library as a reminder of the extent of Mackintosh's researches toward the posthumously published fragment, the *History of the Revolution in England in 1688* (1834).[8] The real beneficiary of his labors, however, was Macaulay, who had the use of his predecessor's papers in preparing his great history.

The Historian as "Novellophagist"

Mackintosh's early writing for the *Monthly Review* and his later essays for the *Edinburgh* reflect his growing authority on a variety of historical, political, and literary subjects, including the French Revolution, early Hanoverian Brit-

[6] Ibid., 2:265–66, and also 267. Access to the papers was later withdrawn.

[7] Ibid., 2:313–14. For the essay on France (originally published in *ER*, Nov. 1814) see *Miscellaneous Works*, 630–639.

[8] There is considerable pathos in Robert Mackintosh's gesture to his father's remains: "It may give an idea of the anxiety of his preparations for a faithful narrative, to state that his collection of Ms. authorities amounted to fifty volumes. Such it now remains, serving at least to mark the broad and deep foundations, from which only the majestic proportions of the intended superstructure can now be ascertained."

ain, and the history of philosophy. Complementing this public chronicle of opinion, Mackintosh's journals contain an informal and sometimes intimate record of reading and reflection, the richest parts of which were written in India, where the lonely and unpopular magistrate found companionship primarily in his books. Temporary separation from his wife, who had returned to England when she found Bombay life insupportable, added to his painful isolation, so the journals were kept in small notebooks suitable for sending home as an extended letter. This double purpose gives these parts of the journal an added dimension. Unfortunately, her replies were as sparse as his were copious, and his rather ponderous efforts at intimacy often spill over into sheer self-pity. Much of this material—to the modern reader the most interesting—was excised by Mackintosh's son Robert when he published a life of his father largely based on his letters and journals. Expurgated or otherwise, the journals have an obvious biographical value, but more than that, the detailed record of responses to books and ideas we find in these pages helps to define the climate of reception in which history was read and thought about in the early part of the century. As a result it is tempting to reverse the obvious judgment on Mackintosh's literary career and say that although as a writer of history he may in the end have proved a failure, as a reader he deserves a good deal of appreciation.

I will discuss Mackintosh's views of history and literary history shortly. I want to begin, however, by going back to the novel, a genre that is almost entirely absent from his public writings and whose prominence in the journal is accordingly all the more striking.

Mackintosh certainly makes no secret of his love for fiction, or—more unusually—of the seriousness with which he takes the novel's claims to moral value. In chapter 4 I reviewed the extended passage from the shipboard journal of 1811 on the moral effect of fiction, which Mackintosh ends by equating the pathetic powers of history and fiction. In fact, this argument for the moral powers of fiction seems to have been a long-standing preoccupation, since a small fragment of a manuscript journal that has been dated to May 1804 records an earlier discussion of the same theme. It is worth quoting not only as a reminder of Mackintosh's commitment to the moral power of the novel, but also as a vignette of shipboard literary conversation:

> In several discussions which arose this forenoon but especially in one on the moral effect of Novels Mrs. A. showed a superiority over Mrs. G. at which Tyler was surprised. My position was that fictitious narrative in all its forms, Epic poem, tale, tragedy, Romance, Novel was one of the grand instruments employed in the moral education of mankind—because it is only delightful when it interests and to interest is to excite sympathy for the heroes of the fiction, that is in other words to teach men the habit of feeling for others. The objectors had I thought looked only to the imperfections and faults of this mode of discipline which however all modes of moral discipline have. It is more imperfect than real life because sympathy in real life is

followed by active benevolence—and it is always mixed with the Vices of the age the country and the writer. To take the strongest Case Tom Jones teaches all the greatest virtues though mixed most unnecessarily and blameably with some vices—and it is my opinion that the world is better for Tom Jones though not by a great deal so much better as it might have been made by such a Genius for comic fiction as that of Fielding.

Mrs. G. persisted to the last in considering this as a mere Question for a Governess whether she ought to allow her Girls [to] subscribe to the Circulating Library—Mrs. A who set out with these notions rose to the level of the Question and only warned Kitty not to mistake my meaning as if I recommended the study of novels to Young Ladies.[9]

Female audiences and female authors were never far from the question of fiction, and in the "essay on fiction" in the 1811 journal (see chapter 4) he stressed the fact that the novel marked the first epoch of literature in which women played the dominant role. At other times, his journals also record his pleasure in the works of Richardson, Inchbald, Burney, Edgeworth, and others. "To soothe before court," he wrote in Bombay, "and to refresh after it, I indulged myself in reading a novel of Charlotte Smith's, called the 'Old Manor House.' . . . It interested me beyond its reputation, and, I was going to have said, beyond its power; I have seldom felt greater anxiety about the issue of events, which are improbable enough."[10]

Among his favorites was Jane Austen, as emerges from the report of a much later conversation, as recorded by a friend near the end of his life:

> Something recalled to his mind the traits of character which are so delicately touched in Miss Austen's novels. "There was genius in the sketching out that new kind of novel." He was vexed for the credit of the "Edinburgh Review," that it had left her unnoticed; the "Quarterly" had done her more justice. It was impossible for a foreigner to understand fully the merit of her works. Madame de Stael, to whom he had recommended one of her novels, found no interest in it, and, in her note to him in reply, said it was "*vulgaire*," and yet he said nothing could be more true than what he wrote in answer,—"*there is no book which that word would suit so little*." "Every village could furnish matter for a novel to Miss Austen. She did not need the common materials for a novel—strong passion, or strong incident." Novels generally, he thinks, are the source of much fine feeling.[11]

[9] Mackintosh journals: BL Add mss. 52436A (1804) 2v–3v.

[10] Mackintosh, *Memoirs*, 2:105. At various times we hear a good deal of *Clarissa* and *Grandison*, about Edgeworth's tales and the expectations for her new novel, as well as references to Defoe's *Plague Year*, *The Man of Feeling*, or the novels of Mme. de Staël. But there was less serious fare as well. He records his reading in Barbauld's collection of English novelists and approves her admiration of Inchbald and Burney. Also "she informs me that Mrs Haywood was the authoress of "Betsy Thoughtless," one of the favourites of my youth" (*Memoirs*, 2:105).

[11] The conversation this records took place in 1830. See Mackintosh, *Memoirs*, 2:472.

Equally telling is a brief lament of about the same period dropped into a letter to his sister-in-law—another valued female friend who seems to have been more sympathetic to his literary tastes and foibles than her censorious sister. Writing in the library of the House of Commons in March 1831, Mackintosh notes regretfully the effect of the reform politics of the day on his favorite reading: "The frosts of Reform and the tempest of Revolution," he wrote, "have killed the whole spring crop of novels. Nothing readable has appeared. I mean readable even by so voracious a *novellophagist* as I am" (2:481).

The Whig historian as confessed "novellophagist." This was not the usual image of the learned politician who (as Macaulay says) "spoke essays" when he rose in the Commons.[12] But Mackintosh's love of fiction is remarkably unapologetic, and it seems evident that he recognized the ways in which being a confirmed "novellophagist" was attached to the most serious side of his mind: his moral concerns, his confessed "passion for literary history,"[13] and the sentimentalism that runs equally through his interest in history and fiction.

Reading Histories

Mackintosh was unusually open in the way in which he embraced the importance of the novel, but the journal and the published reviews show just as clearly that when Mackintosh read history he looked for many of the same satisfactions as he found in fiction. Even more than the abstract arguments of his "essay" on fiction, Mackintosh's responses to particular works of history, biography, and memoir indicate ways in which the reading habits associated with literary sentimentalism transformed the climate of reception for historical writing.

Mackintosh's journals are particularly helpful as a guide to the changes that overtook Hume's reputation as a historian. Mackintosh knew Hume's philosophical writings well and had read the *Essays* many times. Nonetheless, he rated Hume's history as certainly the best of his many works and probably the greatest history yet written. This evaluation was, to a large extent, a tribute to Hume's affective powers. "No other narrative seems to unite, in the same degree, the two qualities of being instructive and affecting. No historian approached him in the union of the talent of painting pathetic scenes with that

[12] See above n. 3. Mackintosh had a prodigious memory and the academic's love of quotation; Coleridge claimed a sign hung over Mackintosh's forehead, saying "Warehouse to let," and Hazlitt, with a little less venom, but no obvious liking, called him "an Encyclopedia of knowledge." *Complete Works of William Hazlitt*, ed. P. P. Howe, 21 vols. (London: J. M. Dent, 1930–34), 11:102.

[13] See below, n. 48.

of exhibiting comprehensive views of human affairs."[14] Mackintosh's encomium repeats the familiar pattern (discussed in the introduction) of describing history in terms of a union of instructive and mimetic functions. But Mackintosh also amends the traditional formula, changing its emphasis considerably. History, always characterized as both instructive and truthful, is now understood to be "instructive and affecting." None of this, however, is spoken with any air of conscious innovation; to the common sense of this early-nineteenth-century reader, it seems, history had become philosophy teaching by sympathetic example.

Hume's narrative, Mackintosh goes on to say, is always fluent and adapted to its subject: "in common events, short and clear; in great actions, rapid and animated; in affecting incidents, circumstantial and picturesque."[15] No wonder then that in his journal-essay on fiction when Mackintosh looked to history for a counterpart to the death of Clarissa, he found it in Hume's Mary Stuart.

For all his admiration of Hume, Mackintosh had criticisms to make as well. He found Hume's character too cold and too skeptical fully to appreciate the English tradition of political freedom; he seemed, wrote Mackintosh, "only to be occasionally sensible of the value of liberty."[16] This criticism of Hume's politics echoes the oldest accusations against his work, but in Mackintosh it is joined to the view that Hume's characteristic attitude of rational detachment also tended to limit his capacity for historical understanding. Too often, Mackintosh thought, he used his intelligence to fill the place that belonged to the investigation of evidence. In part, this failure was simply a matter of laziness—a charge that was to become common in nineteenth-century criticisms of

[14] Mackintosh, *Memoirs*, 2:168: "His greatest work, and that which naturally claims most attention, was his 'History of England,' which, notwithstanding great defects, will probably be at last placed at the head of historical compositions." The passage comes from a sketch of Hume's life and character that was part of the gallery of portraits he composed on his voyage home.

[15] Ibid., 2:169. It should be added that Mackintosh found Mary, for obvious reasons, a figure that engaged the heart. While supervising a trial in India of an Armenian woman accused of attempting to murder her mother-in-law, he wrote, "During the trial of Dustergool, my mind was full of Mary, Queen of Scots, in whose history I had just read, for the thousandth time, efforts more successful than those of the Armenian Mary [who was on trial before him] by a vicious and beautiful wife, to murder a bad husband." But Mackintosh went on to criticize Robertson, whose account he had been reading, for romanticizing the Scottish queen: "As soon as Mary goes into England, Robertson is tempted, by the interest of his story, into constant partiality to her. Her abilities are exaggerated to make her story more romantic; she was a weak girl of elegant accomplishments" (2:114–16).

[16] Ibid., 2:170: "The more sublime sentiments of morals were, indeed, somewhat alien from the pacific and indulgent genius of his philosophy, which led him not to expect much from men, and to be more compassionate to their weakness, than severe in reprobating their faults. . . . Upon the whole, his moral standard, was not so high as that of history ought to be; he too much doubted the purity of the highest public virtue, and he undervalued those domestic duties of which the appearance is the most easily assumed by the hypocrite, and of which the real excellence has been most hidden by fanatical exaggeration."

Hume, reflecting new standards of documentary research. But Mackintosh also thought he detected a more fundamental limitation, and he believed that the same habits of skeptical abstraction that checked Hume's enthusiasm for liberty also limited his narrative powers. Hume's sensibility was at its best when it was a question of excusing human weakness, as in the portrayal of the unfortunate queen of Scotland. But Mackintosh wanted a deeper, more imaginative engagement than this display of sympathy for virtue in distress. Hume "was too habitually a speculator and too little of an antiquary, to have a great power of throwing back his mind into former ages, and of clothing his persons and events in their moral dress; his personages are too modern and argumentative—if we must not say too rational" (2:169).

This was a prophetic critique—one attached to a larger vision of history that we will find more fully articulated in his later writing. In calling for a historian who would also be an antiquary, for a researcher who would not tire of the documents, for a writer capable of "throwing back his mind" into the past, Mackintosh points to an idea of history that reinterpreted the traditional obligation to mimesis as consisting above all in a power of evocation. The result was a shift in the norms of historical distance that affected every genre of historical writing and every aspect of historiographical practice in the early nineteenth century. Clearly this shift built on earlier experiments with immediacy; nonetheless the result was an altered climate of reception (evident even in Mackintosh) that made an appreciative reading of Hume and his Enlightenment contemporaries more and more difficult. In the process, the real continuities linking the sensibilities of Hume or Kames to the early essays of Macaulay or Carlyle were lost sight of by those who saw themselves as giving history new emotional depth and power. In fact, historians and literary critics ever since have tended to reproduce the successor generation's sense of its own innovation, and have paid too little heed to those, like James Mackintosh, who might have guided us to a sense of a more gradual and nuanced evolution.[17]

Mackintosh's comments on Robertson and Gibbon, though not as suggestive as his reading of Hume, proceed from much the same view of historiographical narrative. Robertson's dignity of style he found at first stiff and prim, though "as we advance, his singular power of interesting narrative prevails over every defect" (2:110). But Gibbon, the third of the triumvirate, was no favorite. "He might have been cut out of a corner of Burke's mind without his missing it," Mackintosh is reported to have said.[18] He found Gibbon cold and stately, penetrating in intellect, but unsympathetic in imagination and literary manner. This view was summed up in a review of Gibbon's *Miscellaneous Works*, published in the *Monthly* in 1796, in which Mackintosh acknowledged the

[17] On romantic themes in historiography, see Bann, *Romanticism*. Bann is not concerned, however, with the questions of continuity and discontinuity that I am discussing here.

[18] Green, *Extracts from Diary*, 139–40 (June 13, 1799).

superiority of Gibbon's scholarship, but preferred Robertson for the simplicity of his narrative and his power of "picturesque and pathetic description."[19] Even in his autobiography, Mackintosh complained, Gibbon could not forgo the dignity of the historian. The book was all emotional reserve and philosophic generality, with none of the closeness he expected of self-portraiture. "Occupied too constantly in general views, he gives us but few specimens, in any part of his writings, of that minute narrative which alone is painting."[20]

As we have seen before, *painting* was a key word in the vocabulary of historical criticism, one that served as a shorthand for just those aspects of historiographical narrative that differentiated contemporary taste from its neoclassical roots. It suggests a historiographical equivalent of the picturesque, an aestheticization of narrative experience that transforms reading into a kind of historical spectatorship. To achieve this effect, as Kames and Priestley had written long before, it was crucial that narrative provide the sort of concrete detail that would give presence to the scene. Mackintosh saw the absence of this needed degree of specification (or historical presence) as a general weakness of Gibbon's writing, but he found it especially wanting in a work of autobiography. Gibbon's habit of generality and emotional reserve stands as a barrier to everything we most want to know: "We wish to be admitted into his closet; to see him in an undress; to follow him through the business of ordinary life; and, after having admired the writer, at length to know the man."[21] Instead, even in a genre that promises the opposite, Gibbon offers only distance. He "will not admit us to his familiar acquaintance. . . . he is like those Monarchs of the East who never exhibit themselves to their people, except on occasions of ceremony, and in all the splendour of royalty" (439). Mackintosh ascribed this reserve to excessive decorum, which bars us from knowing "the heart and soul of the writer." In the end, only Gibbon's correspondence—which Mackintosh pronounced a real gift to the public—gives us what we are after: the "free and unreserved communication of the sentiments of such a mind" (441).

There is something characteristic in this path from history to biography to letters. Mackintosh understood, of course, the differences in style and approach required by each genre.[22] Even so, it is also evident that in his reading he

[19] *MR* 20 (1796): 77–84, 307–16, 437–51."Inferior probably to Mr. Gibbon in the vigour of his powers, unequal to him perhaps in comprehension of intellect and variety of knowledge, the Scottish historian has far surpassed him in simplicity and perspicuity of narration, in picturesque and pathetic description, in the sober use of figurative language. . . . He adorns more chastely in addressing the imagination, he narrates more clearly for the understanding, and he describes more affectingly for the heart" (308).

[20] Ibid., 438: "He is described as by an historian, instead of being painted by himself."

[21] Ibid., 438–39.

[22] In his review of Gibbon, he praises Hume's corresponding flexibility of style: Hume "understood so perfectly the art of varying his manner from perspicuous discussion in metaphysics, to pathetic description in history, and to elegant vivacity in familiar correspondence" (ibid., 314).

looked for a meeting of minds or hearts that would ultimately make differences of genre—those separating history from autobiography or even history from fiction—seem much less important.

Biography and Memoir

Biography offers a wide middle ground between history and fiction, and for someone of Mackintosh's sensibilities, it was a particularly attractive genre. Once again the journal provides the best evidence of Mackintosh's reading. Not long after outlining his essay on fiction, he recorded at some length his reaction to the life of Lord Nelson by Macarthur and Clarke.[23] Though he was severely critical of the biography, Mackintosh was much moved by the story of Nelson's life, and he took the time for a lengthy sketch of the great commander's character—"before he was surrounded by that blaze of glory, which makes examination impossible."

The formula is a little disingenuous, since Mackintosh soon makes it clear that he had other reasons for focusing on Nelson's character in the early stages of life. Nelson was born, Mackintosh writes, "with a quick good sense, an affectionate heart, and a high spirit; he was susceptible of the enthusiasm either of the tender or the proud feelings; he was easily melted or inflamed." It went without saying that the hero of Trafalgar was fearless. But he was also in "the highest degree simple and frank." This gave him an instinctive understanding of the sailors he later commanded.[24] And when he was thrust into Mediterranean service, the challenge expanded both his skills and his character. "Scarcely emerged from his retreat at his father's parsonage, he began to negotiate with generals, ambassadors, and princes." His mind became exalted with images of glory and service to his country, kindling "that fierce flame of enthusiasm which converted his whole soul into genius."

Everything in Nelson marked the hero. But for James Mackintosh, at least, the deepest emotions stirred by Nelson's biography did not come from the brilliance of his victories or the heroism of his death. Mackintosh's reading was colored most of all by pathos, not tragedy. "Why is it not possible to wipe

[23] Stanier Clarke and John McArthur, *Life of Admiral Lord Nelson*, 2 vols. (London, 1809). For what follows, see Mackintosh journals, BL Add mss. 52438 B 171v–179v; *Memoirs*, 2:137–40. Robert Mackintosh (henceforth RJM) printed almost all of the entry, with one or two significant omissions. He has also interpolated one passage into the main body of the sketch to give it more unity.

[24] Mackintosh argued that these "qualities of his heart" had not been mentioned simply for the sake of praise: "however singular it may sound, I will venture to affirm that they formed no small part of the genius of Nelson: they secured attachment and confidence and they revealed to him the feelings of other men—that great secret in the art of command, which reason alone can never disclose."

out from history the scenes in the bay of Naples? I read over the passage which respects them three or four times, in hopes of discovering a vindication; but alas! it is impossible." Mackintosh could find no way to vindicate Nelson's arbitrary and authoritarian conduct as commander in Naples, though it is clear that everything in his sketch responded to that desire. "It might be thought affectation," he wrote, "but it is true, that I have read them [the pages on the Bay of Naples] with no small pain." From this moment, Mackintosh goes on, "the charm of the kind and honest Horatio Nelson is gone. His correspondence with his poor wife becomes cold and rare. She, the companion of his poverty and obscurity, entirely loses him, at the moment when he became the most celebrated man in Europe. His excellent father, notwithstanding the virtues and the glory of his son, seems nobly to have joined his injured wife."

The story, of course, had its bad angel as well as its good one: "that ferocious strumpet Lady Hamilton."[25] Mackintosh was much taken by the discovery that Sir William Hamilton had once intended to leave Naples, and this "might-have-been" led to another outburst of regret: "if some accursed suggestion had not kept him at Naples, Nelson's Character would have been privately and publicly spotless."[26]

Sentimental outbursts of this sort are familiar in the fiction of the latter part of the eighteenth century, where they express overflowing feelings and provide appropriate cues to the reader. Mackintosh's responses were all that a writer of such fictions could have wished:

> What excites the most bitter regret is that he who was seduced into barbarity and public as well as private perfidy had a soul full of honour and humanity, that he was the same who never punished a Seaman, and whose nerves were convulsed at seeing him punished, that he was the very same whom the Sailors called "Nel, mild as a lamb and bold as a lion."
>
> I have relieved my nerves by crying at the thought. I can again calmly Reason.[27]

(Once again, Robert Mackintosh, illustrating the changing temper of the next generation, saw fit to protect his father's reputation by quietly dropping the final sentence.)

Biographical narrative clearly exercised real fascination for Mackintosh, but he read letters and memoirs, the unmediated materials of life histories, with perhaps even stronger engagement.

His response to reading Mme. de Sévigné was characteristic. Sévigné was a seventeenth-century French noblewoman of great charm and good education. Widowed early, she devoted her life to her daughter, to whom most of her

[25] Mackintosh journals, BL Add mss. 52438 B 178r. RJM edited this strong phrase out.

[26] Ibid., 172r–v; largely edited out by RJM.

[27] Ibid., 178v–179r, and (except for the last sentence, which RJM excised) *Memoirs*, 2:139.

letters were addressed. These, collected after her death, became famous for their natural, picturesque style and the intimate picture they unfolded of the life of the nobility at court and in social and domestic relations. With their combination of historical interest and literary talent, of anecdotal charms and the intimacies of a feminine milieu, Sévigné's letters were perfectly calculated to attract a sensibility like Mackintosh's:

> The talent of painting and the power of interesting must always depend on sensibility and imagination. But to describe Madame de Sévigné's Genius in these general terms will give you a very vague notion of it. . . . She confined her whole sensibility and fancy to the description of the ordinary feelings, passions, and occurrences of human life. . . . she paints life as it strikes a human being who takes a part in it, not as it is seen by an Author who looks at it in order to describe it. . . . We have such letters of eminent statesmen which give us the real picture of political Events. Mme. de Sévigné's letters are the secret history of common life. By concentrating her whole feelings and fancy upon it she has given the most lively interest to a life without a single remarkable occurrence.[28]

This is a valuable summary. Traditional historiography, as Mackintosh implies, had no access to the eventless and private world of "the ordinary feelings, passions, and occurrences of human life." Hence the enormous attraction of all those parahistoriographical genres that might provide such a history by other means. For Mackintosh, though, letters held a special fascination, since (as Richardson and Carte had both argued long before) they conveyed the actuality of experience in a way no third-person narrative could. In this sense, the letters of a woman like Sévigné constituted not so much the "secret history" as the private archive of common life.[29]

In what sense could common life have a history at all? The answer Mackintosh gave was the same he would have given for any novel more concerned with character and sentiment than with plot. If Mme. de Sévigné's uneventful life had been without passion, he wrote, it could not have been made interesting. But she had a passion for her daughter "of which the letters are the history." This daughter, Grignan, is the true subject of the letters: "She is the heroine of the domestic Epic. It could not have existed without her. The repetitions, the importunities, the incoherencies, the fond triflings of affection, are no doubt tiresome to those who read to have their understanding instructed or

[28] Mackintosh journals, BL Add. mss. 52440, 95r. See also the much edited version in *Memoirs*, 2:217–22.

[29] To call a history "secret" is, of course, to make it more valuable. But unlike the "secret histories" of an earlier day (also associated with female authorship) Sévigné's letters were not devoted to the scandals of well-known people. On secret histories, see Annabel Patterson, *Censorship and Interpretation: The Condition of Writing and Reading in Early Modern England* (Madison: U of Wisconsin P, 1984).

their fancy amused. Such readers should keep aloof from what is delightful only as a symptom of affection and which can only be enjoyed by the heart."[30]

Mackintosh pitched his intense interest in this "domestic Epic" against a contrary reputation that saw the letters as vignettes of the court of Louis XIV. For him, the backdrop of an illustrious age added only a secondary interest: "I was not quite charmed and bewitched till the middle of the collection, when there are fewer anecdotes of the great and famous. I felt that the fascination grew as I became a member of the Sévigné family. It arose from the history of the immortal mother and the adored Daughter and it increased as I knew them in more minute detail, just as my tears in the dying chamber of Clarissa depend on my having so often drunk tea with her in those early volumes, which are so audaciously called dull by the profane vulgar."[31]

Julie-Jeanne de Lespinasse (1732–1776) was a woman of a later time and a very different temper. Mackintosh described her passionate love letters as brandy to Sévigné's wine. She was a remarkable woman who, though without fortune or beauty, made her salon a gathering point for the leading writers of Paris. D'Alembert was a close friend, and among her other intimates were Condorcet and (one of Mackintosh's heroes) Turgot. But the deep attraction of her letters lay in her passionate pursuit of the love of the count Guibert and in the suffering that led to her death. "Torn in pieces by affection for the memory of Mora [her former lover] and unrequited love for Guibert, by passion, disappointment, humiliation, shame, and remorse, Mlle. de l'Espinasse was [taken by] a disorder in the orifice of the Stomach. She had no quiet in the day and no sleep in the night, but from great quantities of Opium. A smile from Guibert gave her more enjoyment than the constant friendship of the best men of her age. Her frail body was at last destroyed by this dreadful conflict of passions."[32]

Mackintosh showed some signs of confusion over his own passion for this book, the record of an obsessive love affair that he knew very well could be written off as sordid and immoral.[33] But in the end his defense of its value is powerful and direct:

> The letters are in my opinion the truest picture of deep passion ever traced by a human being. When I was young, Rousseau moved my heart to the bottom; very lately I was most powerfully affected by Goethe. But how much more eloquent is

[30] Mackintosh journals, BL Add mss. 52440, 95v–96r.

[31] Ibid., 98v; *Memoirs*, 2:221.

[32] Mackintosh journals, BL Add mss. 52440, 84v–85v. RJM gives an edited transcript in *Memoirs*, 2:207–10.

[33] The entry begins: "I could not tear myself from the letters of Mlle de L'Espinasse. It is easy to represent or rather it is natural to think that it would [?] be ridiculous to feel so deep an Interest in such a book that if it were only to justify myself I must give some account of the reflexions which this singular book has occasioned and of the feelings which it has awakened" (Mackintosh journals, BL Add. mss. 52440, 83v). RJM proved his father's point by excising this passage.

Love. These letters speak of nothing else. They contain few anecdotes and not many reflections; But they abound in strokes of nature. The poor writer's heart beats through every sentence.[34]

As a compressed history of his own sensibility this is very striking. So is a rather tortured follow-up in which Mackintosh both discloses and reaffirms the conventional double-standard in sexual morality. "If they had been written by a Man this merit would have ensured them universal admiration. They contain nothing which in our Sex would not be thought pardonable. But for a woman to make love ardently to a Man in love with another, through all the forms of caressing and reproaching for three years, to make the last sacrifices to him and allude to these sacrifices is such an outrage upon our Sentiments that it is difficult for us to consider it dispassionately."[35]

This was difficult ground, and Mackintosh soon abandoned it for the easier defense that Lespinasse should only be judged by the moral standards of eighteenth-century Paris. Even so, the revelation of his own character was not to be rescinded. "The energy and sensibility of Mlle. de l'Espinasse attract me irresistibly," he told his wife. "You may disapprove the particular effect, but you have no interest in wishing the attraction of these qualities to be abated."[36]

What Mackintosh achieved by this flattering gesture to his wife we can't know. Only the day before he had ended the discussion by saying, "More of this tomorrow, if I dare, but I dread your ferocious prudery."[37]

Literary History

Mackintosh's comments on Sévigné, Lespinasse, and others suggest the importance of literary history as a sphere in which his sensibilities and his historical interests might meet. Here, as in biography, a sympathetic imagination could explore past experience more freely than was yet possible in works governed by the decorum of "authentic history."

Mackintosh's interest in literary history found public expression at an early date in his reviews of Roscoe and Gibbon written for the *Monthly*, but its real fruit comes in a small cluster of articles published between 1813 and 1816 in the *Edinburgh Review*.[38] Not as numerous as his contributions on politics and

[34] Ibid., 85r; *Memoirs*, 2:208–9.

[35] Mackintosh journals, BL Add mss. 52440, 85r (also excised).

[36] Ibid., 85v.

[37] Ibid. Several times he suggests a resemblance between his wife and his eighteenth-century Parisian heroine.

[38] In reviewing Roscoe's *Life of Lorenzo de' Medici* (1795), Mackintosh wrote: "The account of the House of Medici is scarcely interesting till, under Cosimo, the history of that family becomes the history of literature. . . . There is perhaps nothing more interesting in literary annals,

history, this group included reviews of the poetry of Rogers (1813), of Mme. de Staël's writings on suicide and on Germany (1813), and of Godwin's lives of Milton's nephews (1815). In these writings Mackintosh made a general argument for the importance of literary history, while also establishing the outlines of a specifically English literary tradition.

Before coming to these essays, I want to call attention to a passage in Mackintosh's review of Dugald Stewart's *General View of the Progress of Metaphysical, Ethical, and Political Philosophy* (1816). This does not seem the most obvious place to look for thoughts on literary history, but Mackintosh begins with a lengthy quotation from Bacon's *Advancement of Learning*, which (as interpreted by Mackintosh) has the effect of claiming Bacon as the prophet of a distinctly contemporary idea of literary history. Bacon had written that history encompassed four parts: natural, civil, ecclesiastical, and literary. Histories of the first three had been written, Bacon wrote, but the last was entirely neglected. No one had traced the state of learning as it advanced from age to age, "without which the world seemeth to me to be as the statue of Polyphemus with his eye out; that part being wanting which doth most show the spirit and life of the person."[39]

Bacon's reference here is clearly to the history of learning more than it is to "literature" in the distinctive sense the word later acquired.[40] Mackintosh, however, seizes on Bacon's complaint as evidence of his characteristic inventiveness and foresight. It shows him as the progenitor of "modes of thinking which were to prevail in distant generations."[41] With Stewart, he believed that Bacon's call for a literary history anticipated some of the "questions most arduous in a history of philosophy;—'the causes of literary revolutions; the study of contemporary writers, not merely as the most authentic sources of information, but as enabling the historian to preserve in his own description the peculiar colour of every age, and to recall its literary genius from the dead.' "[42]

Mackintosh's explication evidences a good deal of anachronism. His concern for "the causes of literary revolutions" and especially the value he places on the evocative possibilities of literary history ("the peculiar colour of every

---

than the discovery of antient manuscripts by those learned men who were patronized by Cosimo de' Medici." *MR* 20 (1796): 430.

[39] "On the Philosophical Genius of Lord Bacon and Mr. Locke," in Mackintosh, *Miscellaneous Works*, 147. The essay first appeared as a review of Dugald Stewart in *ER* 27 (1816).

[40] As, indeed, Mackintosh later acknowledges. On the modern signification of *literature*, see especially Timothy Reiss, *The Meaning of Literature* (Ithaca: Cornell UP, 1992).

[41] Mackintosh is at pains to stress the poetical side of Bacon's intellect. "This wide ranging intellect was illuminated by the brightest Fancy that ever contented itself with the office of only ministering to Reason." Bacon's style showed the same gift. "No man ever united a more poetical style to a less poetical philosophy." Cf. *Miscellaneous Works*, 147–48.

[42] Ibid., 152.

age") belong to his own time more than to Bacon's. But his eagerness to promote the value of literary history, together with his faith in Bacon's genius, combined irresistibly to suggest the idea of Bacon as a prophet of new directions in historical writing. (For more on this evolution, see chapter 9 below.)[43] Bacon's outline, he wrote, "has the uncommon distinction of being at once original and complete. In this province, Bacon had no forerunner; and the most successful follower will be he, who most faithfully observes his precepts."[44]

This discussion of Bacon indicates something of Mackintosh's feeling for the general importance of literary history as a branch of study, but in an earlier essay on the poetry of Samuel Rogers, published in 1813, he had already outlined a particular view of the evolution of English literary history. The occasion seems in many ways an odd one for this sort of sketch. Not only was Rogers a contemporary (and a friend), therefore not a writer whose life and letters could be made into an instrument for recovering the "peculiar colour" of earlier times, but he was also a writer of rather old-fashioned virtues whose poetry hardly exemplified the changes in literary sensibility that Mackintosh wanted to discuss. For a good part of the review, however, Samuel Rogers hardly seems to matter, as Mackintosh sets out a brief philosophical history surveying the outlines of English poetic traditions. This historical excursus takes up a little more than half the essay.[45]

It seems unlikely, Mackintosh wrote, echoing Hume's essay "Of the Rise and Progress of the Arts and Sciences," that a history of the arts could be understood under terms of general laws. Such a consideration is possible for "the more robust faculties of the human mind," but taste is affected by factors too various and minute. The task would be as subtle and hopeless "as to account for one summer being more warm and genial than another." Yet letters do follow a history of sorts because they "depend on some of the most conspicuous, as well as powerful agents in the moral world." These arise from "revolutions of popular sentiments," which are connected in turn to the manners of the refined and the passions of the multitudes. Changes in religion or government, alternations of war or tranquillity have their effect; "indeed every conceivable

[43] Shortly after this passage, Mackintosh offers a qualification: "It is obvious, that Bacon had the history of science more in view than that of literature . . . he seems, from his language, more to have contemplated the history of that philosophy which discovers the foundation of the sciences in the human understanding, and which becomes peculiarly connected with the practical sciences of morals and politics—because, like them, it has human nature for its object. It is that which is most immediately affected by the events and passions of the world; and on it depends the colour and fashion of all other researches." This passage does not appear in the edited version in *Miscellaneous Works*. See "Stewart's Introduction to the Encyclopaedia," *ER* 27 (1816): 190. It is not easy to understand the earlier passage in light of this, more sober reflection of Baconian ideas on the history of philosophy. The apparent shift of direction reveals, perhaps, Mackintosh's own enthusiasm for literary history of a more contemporary stamp than Bacon's work could actually authorize.

[44] *Miscellaneous Works*, 152.

[45] "Review of Rogers' Poems" (originally in *ER*, 1813) in *Miscellaneous Works*, 512–20.

modification of the state of a community, show themselves in the tone of its poetry, and leave long and deep traces on every part of its literature."[46]

Mackintosh's founding assumptions, as I have noted, were the same as Hume's, but he moved much more quickly to their historicist implications. In Mackintosh's reworking of Hume, it is precisely the subtlety of taste in the "elegant arts"—its weatherlike quality of mutability, its resistance to general laws—that finally makes poetry so deeply expressive of the course of social change. "Geometry is the same, not only at London and Paris, but in the extremes of Athens and Samarcand: but the state of the general feeling in England, at this moment, requires a different poetry from that which delighted our ancestors in the time of Luther or Alfred."[47]

The differences between Mackintosh and his philosophical mentor were not, it is clear, so much a matter of principle as of situation and intention. Hume's essay sets out the lines of a general investigation, while Mackintosh reviews the same principles for the purposes of characterizing a particular national literature. Behind the difference of purpose stands a new literary politics shaped by the intensification of national feeling that came with the French Revolution and the wars that ensued. Mackintosh himself was hardly a narrow nationalist: a Scot who was knowledgeable about both French and German literature, he ranked among the most cosmopolitan intellectuals of his day. Nonetheless, among the important motives of his self-declared "passion for literary history" was a desire to identify the lines of a national tradition underlying and unifying the vicissitudes of taste.[48]

English literature in the eighteenth century, Mackintosh writes, showed very clearly "the state of the country." This was a time of security and tranquillity. It was exempt from popular enthusiasms and undisturbed by the sort of extraordinary events that excite the imagination. Poetry subsided into a "calm, argumentative, moral, and directly useful character." Under the influence of French correctness, it was "neither the most poetical nor the most national part of our literary annals." It was also, Mackintosh remarks tellingly, "the golden age of authentic history."[49]

Around the midcentury, "great though quiet changes" began to appear in both letters and politics. But it was also at this time, when the neoclassical

[46] Ibid., 512–13.

[47] Ibid., 513.

[48] Mackintosh's journals contain many expressions of his love of "literary history." In 1812, he expressed his pleasure in reading Scott's life of Dryden, "as I have a passion for literary history, and the highest admiration for Dryden" (*Memoirs*, 2:196–97). Earlier, on reading Laharpe's letters, he remarked: "You know my passion for literary history and anecdotes; the book, therefore, pleases me. He gives the Grand Duke an account of new publications and representations, much as I do here of what I read, but with not quite such careless honesty, still with much good nature" (2:38–39).

[49] *Miscellaneous Works*, 513.

taste was about to be swept away, that this school of poetry found its critic in Samuel Johnson. "A school of poetry," Mackintosh remarked, "must have prevailed long enough, to be probably on the verge of downfal [*sic*], before its practice is embodied in a correspondent system of criticism."[50] (Elsewhere, it is worth noting, Mackintosh would make the same point about constitutions; in both spheres, practice precedes precept, and codification is largely retrospective.)

For Mackintosh, echoing the founders of Enlightenment philosophical history, the "natural progress of society" is mirrored in a comparable evolution of literature: "the songs which are the effusion of feeling of a rude tribe, are gradually polished into a form of poetry still retaining the marks of the national opinions, sentiments, and manners, from which it originally sprung."[51] In the literary history of England, the poetry of the Elizabethan period, though mixed with classical pedantry, still retained this "national" feeling, which was continued in the drama of Shakespeare and the Jacobeans. The Restoration, however, introduced a new, imported classicism, which all but obliterated the distinctiveness of English literature. Nonetheless, when the neoclassical taste began to weary English ears, it was only natural that literature turned to a cultivation of an indigenous poetry.[52]

For Mackintosh the dynamics of literary history are in part internal to the history of taste, but it is clear that he was struck by the more than coincidental relationship between the poetic and political revolutions that took place in his time. "As the condition and character of the former age had produced an argumentative, didactic, sententious, prudential, and satirical poetry; so the approaches to a new order (or rather at first disorder) in political society were attended by correspondent movements in the poetical world. Bolder speculations began to prevail."[53] I do not have the space to reproduce in detail his characterization of this new speculative boldness, which occupies the next several pages, though—given the fact that his editor, Francis Jeffrey, is so often cited for his negative judgment on Wordsworth—it is worth noting that Mackintosh's valuation of the early Romantics is generally positive. More importantly, Mackintosh explicitly separates the issue of critical judgment from that of historical understanding, and he makes it clear that even those who do not share his appreciation of their work should benefit from his historical approach. "It is sufficient," he writes, "to have proved the reality, and in part perhaps to have explained the origin, of a literary revolution."

It is only at this point that Mackintosh turns at last from literary history to criticism and begins to speak directly about the poetry of Rogers, and, after so

[50] Ibid.

[51] Ibid., 514.

[52] "The poetry which once grew in the bosoms of a people, is always capable of being revived by a skilful hand" (ibid., 515).

[53] Ibid.

long an introduction, it has to be anticlimactic to hear that Rogers's work, though always popular, stood at an equal distance from both literary epochs. In light of this critical appraisal, one could argue that the elaborate historical prologue was nothing more than a disconnected academic exercise, or even an evasion of the central task of the reviewer. But the essay on Rogers, despite the apparent disjuncture between its two halves—perhaps even because of it—seems to me more interesting than that. No doubt the zeal with which Mackintosh pursues his narrative of English literary history reflects an enthusiasm for the subject that is independent of his admiration for the author of the "Pleasures of Memory." But it is clear, too, that his admiration for Rogers has much to do with the poet's calm independence of the changes in literary fashion that overtook his generation. In the end, the essay manages the still unusual task of historicizing a contemporary figure while paying its respects to the ways in which individual temperament and talent as well as the "revolutions of popular sentiments" enter into the making of literary history.

In the essay on Rogers, Mackintosh had a subject that seemed to resist incorporation into a scheme of literary history. In reviewing Mme. de Staël, on the other hand, he confronted a writer whose enthusiasm for literary history outran even his own.[54] Indeed, Staël's friendship in these years, as well as the force of her personality, must surely have given an extra impetus to his interest in the subject.[55] Staël wanted to capture the essential spirit of the German nation in all its individuality, and she looked especially to German literature as an expression of the nation. This romantic vision differed from Mackintosh's own sense of history, which remained rooted in both the ideas and sensibilities of Hume and Burke. Even so, Mackintosh felt the force of Staël's personality, and he came as close in this essay as he ever would to embracing romantic ideals.

Both the subject and the author, wrote Mackintosh, gave the book unusual interest. Already famous as the author of the romantic novel *Corinne*, Staël had now "thrown off the aid of fiction" for an even more dazzling work mixing poetry and philosophy. The book was indeed a masterpiece of "the talent for painting nations"[56]—a phrase that (remembering the special meaning given to *historical painting*) indicates the evocative power Mackintosh looked for in her work and perhaps, more generally, in works in this genre.[57] Staël's portrait

[54] Mackintosh's review of Staël's *De L'Allemagne* (originally *ER*, 1813), in *Miscellaneous Works*, 521–35.

[55] Staël called Mackintosh her English Cicerone. He was flattered by her attentions, and wrote: "She treats me as the person she most delights to honour; I am generally ordered with her to dinner, as one orders beans and bacon" (quoted by O'Leary, *Sir James Mackintosh*, 111).

[56] *Miscellaneous Works*, 526.

[57] It is worth noting Mackintosh's appreciation of as well as strictures on Staël's style. "Very often in poetry, and sometimes in eloquence, it is the office of words, not so much to denote a succession of separate ideas, as, like musical sounds, to inspire a series of emotions, or to produce

of Germany was divided into four parts: manners; literature and the arts; philosophy and morals; religion and enthusiasm. But the most interesting to Mackintosh was certainly the review of German literature, where Staël built on Auguste Wilhelm Schlegel's famous distinction between classic and romantic spirits in literature, the former being identified now with France, the latter with Germany. Here was a country long distinguished among European nations for its lack of a national literature, a country where scholarship and speculation seemed to have supplied the place of imaginative works. Very late, "a great revolution" began, which in a short space of time gave Germany its own literature—perhaps the "most characteristic" of any nation. This special color was in part a reflection of the historical position of German letters in an age of enlightenment, in part a reflection of national spirit. The result was best expressed by comparison to France. "In the dramatic art, the most national part of literature, the French are distinguished in whatever relates to the action, the intrigue, and the interest of events: but the Germans surpass them in representing the impressions of the heart, and the secret storms of the strong passions" (523).

This contrast hinges on an opposition between outward and inward life, a polarity of action and spirit, which Staël carries into a series of further contrasts that directed her views of national literatures, including ancient and modern, Latin and Teutonic, classical and gothic. Mackintosh, for his part, was inclined to be less categorical, and he thought her terms somewhat overstated. (Staël, indeed, teased him about his anxiety to see both sides of every question.) In particular, he wanted to give more weight than she had done to the influence of history and less to national character alone.[58] Nonetheless, he admired her greatly for the brilliance of her insights and the evocative power of her writing. She was a "philosophical traveller," he writes, who had demonstrated the rare gift of being able "to recall what a nation has been, to sympathise with their present sentiments and passions and to trace the workings of national character in amusements, in habits, in institutions, and opinions."[59] Above all, Mackin-

a durable tone of sentiment. . . . A series of words may, in this manner, be very expressive, where few of them singly convey a precise meaning: and men of greater intellect than susceptibility, in such passages as those of Mad. de Stael—where eloquence is employed chiefly to inspire feeling—unjustly charge their own defects to that deep moral and poetical sensibility with which they are unable to sympathise" (ibid., 534). Even so, Mackintosh complained of the excessive brilliance of the prose. "The natural power of interesting scenes or events over the heart, is somewhat disturbed by too uniform a colour of sentiment, and by the constant pursuit of uncommon reflections or ingenious turns. The eye is dazzled by unvaried brilliancy. We long for the grateful vicissitude of repose" (534).

[58] Ibid., 525.

[59] Ibid., 524: The genius of "the philosophical and poetical traveller," he writes, "is founded in the power of catching, by a rapid glance, the physiognomy of man and of nature. It is, in one of its parts, an expansion of that sagacity which seizes the character of an individual. . . . The application of this intuitive power to the varied mass called a "nation," is one of the most rare efforts of

tosh praised Staël for possessing in almost unique measure the synthesizing power of imagination. In her writing on Germany she had been able to paint a national portrait that somehow managed to combine the vivacity of first impressions with the accuracy of careful examination. She had succeeded, he wrote, in "placing a nation, strongly individualised by every mark of its mind and disposition, in the midst of ancient monuments, clothed in its own apparel, engaged in its ordinary occupations and pastimes amidst its native scenes, like a grand historical painting, with appropriate drapery, and with the accompaniment of architecture and landscape, which illustrate and characterise, as well as adorn" (524).

For all his evident admiration, however, it seems clear that Mackintosh's praises reflect Staël's understanding of literary history more than his own. His effort in the essay on Rogers to trace the fluctuations of English poetic style seems to belong to a different (though not, of course, unrelated) idea of what literary history might accomplish and how it should pursue its goals.

Sismondi's *History of France*

Most of Mackintosh's scattering of reviews on historical subjects reflect his researches into the materials of British history and his reputation as a man knowledgeable about European politics. He wrote on Wraxall's memoirs (1815), on the papers of James II (1816), on the memoirs of Sir George Mackenzie (1821), and on the disputed authorship of the *Eikon Basilike* (1826). There were also essays on Spain (1813), Poland (1822), and Denmark (1826). Against these pieces, which treat matters of national politics or documentary research, only his essay on Sismondi's *History of France* (1821) stands apart as a wider statement of his views on history. In this appreciation of a major contemporary historian who was also a friend, Mackintosh took the opportunity to voice convictions about history's affective powers that hitherto we have only seen in his journals.

Mackintosh met Sismondi through the friendship of Mme. de Staël. Though Staël reserved her highest praises for Schlegel (also a member of Staël's entourage), Mackintosh noted that he had found more to talk about with the Swiss historian. In fact, in their outlook on history and politics, they shared much common ground, and they continued their occasional contacts over the years in a friendship reinforced by the marriage of Sismondi to Catherine Mackintosh's sister.

---

the human intellect. The mind and the eye must co-operate with electrical rapidity, to recall what a nation has been, to sympathise with their present sentiments and passions and to trace the workings of national character in amusements, in habits, in institutions, and opinions."

Mackintosh opens his review by declaring that the history of France is "one of the most important chasms in the literature of Europe."[60] This verdict on the weakness of French historiography reminds us how far the second half of the eighteenth century had reversed the earlier consensus on the inferiority of the English in this field of literature. Ironically, however, it came on the eve of a Romantically inspired revival of French historical writing.

Mackintosh wanted to make two points about this weakness in French literature, one of which connected history to political freedom, the other to the character of historical knowledge. Like other Whigs, Mackintosh saw British history in particular as a progress toward the achievement of liberty, but he also shared the widespread conviction that historical writing itself would not flourish except in an atmosphere of liberty.[61] A second cause of this weakness was that in recent times the popular writers of France lacked the "habits of research" essential to history. Ingenious speculation, he insists, is a poor substitute for close investigation, nor can history be written in a spirit of satire. It is not the historian's business "to sneer or laugh at men, or to lower human nature. It is by maintaining the dignity of man, and the importance of his pursuits, that history creates a fellow-feeling with his passions, and a delight in contemplating his character and actions" (491).

In offering these observations Mackintosh probably had Voltaire in mind, but, like the remarks on Hume discussed earlier, they indicate a change in the norms of historical distance that would affect the reputation of all the historians of the previous century. It was not simply that a new standard of historical research was being erected that eighteenth-century narratives could rarely meet;[62] in the earnestness with which Mackintosh presses his views, the familiar eighteenth-century idea of historical sympathy ("fellow feelings") takes on a new solemnity. History written in this spirit—the spirit of a "serious and deep interest in the affairs of men"—calls the reader to a close engagement with the dramas of the past that is very unlike the speculative and skeptical spirit of eighteenth-century narratives. In Mackintosh, this modification of the prevailing norms of historical distance is coupled with a sense of the particular evocativeness of the original sources. Echoing Sismondi himself, he insists that the history of remote ages must be drawn from "original writers," and he adds that it has been a particular weakness of English history that, until very recently, almost every modern historian has taken the basis of his narrative from his predecessors.

[60] Mackintosh, "Sismondi's *History of France*," *ER* 35 (1821): 488–509. The quotation is on 488–89.

[61] France had produced its outstanding historians in the "irregular liberty" maintained by religious and civil conflict. But after Louis XIV succeeded in establishing a "polished and peaceable despotism," history dwindled and disappeared (ibid., 490).

[62] It is notable that in his *History of the Revolution in England in 1688*, Mackintosh very seldom cites Hume's account, either in support or in criticism.

Mackintosh's commitment to the value of the "authentic sources" also had a practical expression. In 1821, the same year as his review of Sismondi, he had been appointed to the Commission on Public Records, and both in the commission and in Parliament he was pressing for the government to take a hand in publishing important documents of English history.[63] It is no coincidence, then, that Mackintosh couples his criticism of English historiography with the hope that "when Government have done their duty by making public the ample materials under their control, we may hope to see our ancient history illustrated from authentic sources."[64]

Mackintosh's views (and behind them Sismondi's) on the importance of writing history on the basis of the "authentic sources" will sound familiar to academically trained historians today. We have been raised up professionally on a textbook history of historiography in which, with almost unquestioned dogmatism, the birth of modern historical practice has been tied to Ranke's supposed discovery of the importance of original documents, as announced in the preface to the *History of the Latin and Teutonic Nations* of 1824.[65] But whatever Ranke meant by the famous phrase about writing history "as it really was," Mackintosh gives the clearest testimony that his contemporaries had reasons that went well beyond factual accuracy for valuing original sources. Authenticity of another kind was at least as much his concern:

> But it is not to accuracy only that the consultation of original authorities is essential. The delight with which we peruse the history of ages long passed, depends chiefly on its lively and picturesque representation of men, manners, and events. But these are only to be found in the dramatic narrative of the eyewitness or the contemporary, who had always seen the manners which he paints, and had generally felt some degree of the passions which actuated his heroes. The spirit of these original narratives evaporates when they are poured from compilation to compilation. If a modern historian can recover this charm, it is only when he either borrows directly from the first sources, or when frequent and familiar contemplation of them has kindled his imagination, and enabled him to *antiquate* his feelings, so as to become for a moment the contemporary of those ages of which he is the historian. (492)

[63] See Rendall, "Political Ideas and Activities," 313–14; and Peardon, *Transition*, 284–310. For the subsequent history, see Philippa Levine, *The Amateur and the Professional: Antiquarians, Historians, and Archaeologists in Victorian England, 1838–1886* (Cambridge: Cambridge UP, 1986), especially chap 5.

[64] Mackintosh, "Sismondi's *History of France*," 492.

[65] Note that Sismondi himself attributes the idea of writing history from the original sources to his teacher, Johann Muller. In a passage from his introduction quoted in Mackintosh's review, Sismondi writes: "My work was begun and completed from the originals, according to the advice which I formerly received from the great historian John de Muller" (ibid., 491).

The works of a modern historian who lacks this insight ("a mere modern thinker"), Mackintosh concludes, will always be "uninteresting" because the writer cannot "paint, or even conceive, the feelings from which these events arose."

Mackintosh's stance here is easily labeled "romantic." Certainly it would be easy to find parallel passages in Thierry's *Letters on History*, a near contemporary work that can be taken as a manifesto of romantic narrative. Yet the terms of Mackintosh's discussion are entirely familiar. His stress on "lively and picturesque" writing, on historical painting, and on "dramatic narrative" can easily be traced back to the discussions of Kames and others of the middle of the past century. Perhaps the most characteristically novel element is the expressivism of the last sentence—the sense that events arise out of an inward dimension of feeling to which they must be traced back as the ground of understanding—but even here the centrality of that typically sentimentalist word "uninteresting" builds a direct bridge to earlier views.

This continuity with eighteenth-century views is again apparent in the succeeding paragraphs, in which Mackintosh restates his old argument (familiar from his shipboard journals of 1804 and 1811) that the moral force of narrative comes from its power to evoke sympathy:

> It is on the sympathy which History excites that its moral effect depends. The moral improvement to be derived from all narrative, whether it be historical or what is called fictitious, is in proportion to the degree in which it exercises and thereby strengthens the social feelings and moral principles of the reader. In both cases it excites emotions similar to those inspired by the men and actions which surround us in the world. Our habits of moral feeling are formed by life;—and they are strengthened by the pictures of life. In the perusal of History or Fiction, as in actual experience, we become better by learning to sympathize with misfortune, and to feel indignation against baseness.[66]

History does not teach effectively by offering explicit lessons, Mackintosh continues; its general adages are already known to every child. Rather the historian can improve his readers only by interesting them in the events he recounts. "The narrative of events which have occurred, or which may probably occur, is thus one of the most important parts of the moral education of mankind."

Only the greater density and directness of the argument distinguish this late restatement from the journal entries of 1804 and 1811. Here at last history does not enter the discussion as an adjunct to the moral powers of fiction; rather the Kamesian argument about reading as vicarious moral exercise is made with full reference to history from the start. Otherwise, Mackintosh's position on

[66] Ibid., 492–93.

the moral powers of literature seems just what it had been ten years earlier, or even seventeen. It is worth noting, however, that although he presents his ideas with full confidence, he no longer attaches a claim to having discovered a new philosophical argument, a bit of historical blindness that was so curious a part of the journal essay of 1811.

The Persistence of Sentiment

In October 1808 James Mackintosh, writing from India, addressed a warm and grateful letter to a valued female correspondent, Mrs. John Taylor of Norwich.[67] In it he reflected on the sensibilities of their generation and the ways in which they had been deflected by the French Revolution. Like other writings from this period of his life, the letter is written with an openness of feeling that makes it hard to pass over. As a result, the letter seems to offer an appropriate summary glimpse at Mackintosh's character and sensibility. Always eager for news from his literary and political friends in his eastern exile, Mackintosh gave a special warmth to his thanks. "I know the value of your letters," he wrote. "They rouse my mind on subjects which interest us in common—friends, children, literature, and life. Their moral tone cheers and braces me. I ought to be made permanently better by contemplating a mind like yours. . . . your character is so happily constituted, that even the misfortunes of those who are dear to you, by exciting the activity of your affection, almost heal the wound which they would otherwise have inflicted." Such kindness, he went on to say, produces a natural gladness that "is the balm appointed to be poured into the wounds of sympathy."[68]

This letter is marked by a tone that often characterizes Mackintosh's private self. Like the journal, but on a much smaller scale, it displays a world of feeling that, as his friend Sidney Smith observed, would not have been expected from his public personality.[69] And as in the journal too, the letter makes the expression of those feelings an invitation to a similar response from his correspondent, a woman he admires and from whom he asks in return a kind of sentimental acknowledgment.

In a sentimental novel of the previous century, the tone of this letter and the range of its topics—children, friendship, the uplifting of affections in the face of misfortune—would instantly have marked the correspondent as a "man of

[67] Susannah Taylor (1775–1823) had been well known as a friend of French liberty and a literary woman of strong character, known to her friends as "Mme. Roland." She was a very close friend of Anna Barbauld and much visited by other literary friends, like Mrs. Opie and Henry Crabbe Robinson. She was the wife of John Taylor, the Unitarian hymn writer and founder of the literary family of the Taylors of Norwich. See *DNB*, 55:444–45 (1898).

[68] Letter to Mrs. John Taylor, Norwich, October 10, 1808, in Mackintosh, *Memoirs*, 1:439–40.

[69] Mackintosh, *Memoirs*, 2:504.

feeling." But Mackintosh also shows a combination of self-knowledge and historical understanding that clearly reflects the upheavals of the 1790s, when his own prominence among the friends of the Revolution forced a public recantation. Writing nearly two decades after the outbreak of the Revolution, he knew both that he was a man of sentiment and that sentiment was no longer in fashion:

> Nothing short of your letter could have betrayed me into this strain. It would now, I believe, be ridiculed under the name of sentiment. The dreadful disappointment of the French Revolution, and the reaction of the general mind produced by it, have made many things unpopular besides liberty. Coarseness and barbarity seem to be eagerly sought, in order to be as far as possible from the refinement and humanity which were fashionable before the Revolution. Cruelty and perfidy are praised as vigour; the fall of governments is ascribed to their benevolence instead of their feebleness; . . . the beneficence of individuals is laughed at as hypocritical or visionary; that of men in authority is condemned as a prelude to anarchy. Eloquence is rejected as the talent of demagogues; and all observations on the feelings which are the finer springs of action, especially if they be written or spoken with sensibility, are sneered at as sentiment. (1:439–40)

Perhaps the French Revolution had put an end to the age of "sensibility," but Mackintosh's words do not indicate any change of heart, nor any fear that Mrs. Taylor might find his feelings risible. On the contrary, the sense is that, though the world has turned away from sensibility, the two correspondents have not, and that this will make their sympathy all the closer. The real change made by the Revolution, then, does not seem to be the extinction of feeling. Rather, the letter seems to say, the Revolution had forced sentiment out of public life, confirming the need for sensibility to shelter itself in quieter, more private communications and in a life of reading.[70]

[70] On the fiction of this period and the decline of sensibility, see Nicola Watson, *Revolution and the Form of the British Novel, 1790–1825: Intercepted Letters, Interrupted Seductions* (Oxford: Clarendon, 1994), as well as Jones, *Radical Sensibility.*

Nine

Burke, Mackintosh, and the Idea of Tradition

In tracing the career of James Mackintosh as a reader and a reviewer of history, I have reserved one important theme for separate consideration. This is the question of Mackintosh's understanding of Burke's concept of tradition. Mackintosh's prominence among critics of Burke's *Reflections* and his later public renunciation of sympathy for the French Revolution make him a key witness to Burke's influence on British historical thought. In the movement from his early defense of the French Revolution, the *Vindiciae* of 1791, to his later writings on law, freedom of the press, and English history, Mackintosh illuminates the process by which Burke's powerful sense of the continuities of British life became a usable framework for historical understanding.

Burke is generally regarded as the fountainhead in Britain of a modern, secularized idea of tradition. Unfortunately, Burke's memorable evocations of tradition in the *Reflections* form part of a furious war of ideas, a circumstance that makes it difficult to distinguish Burke's concept of tradition considered as a view of historical process from the ideological position that manifests itself as traditionalism. In contrast, James Mackintosh always remained a friend to reform, albeit by the later 1790s a cautious and chastened one. The contrast between Burke's counterrevolutionary politics and Mackintosh's reformism—helped by the calmer terms in which Mackintosh spoke—gives us room to introduce a degree of separation between tradition considered as a historical concept and the ideological causes in which it was employed. For a historiographical study this opening is important, since the Burkean idea of tradition as respect for mediated and gradual change far outlasted the radical conflicts of the 1790s, to become one of the major frameworks of British historical writing in the nineteenth century and beyond.

Mackintosh provided his ideas on historical change with a philosophical and political genealogy that links his conception of tradition with the views of his Enlightenment mentors. Following Mackintosh's lead, this chapter will trace some of the affinities between the Burkean idea of tradition and the historical outlook of Burke's Scottish contemporaries, especially Hume and Smith. In the course of it, I hope to show that the Humean idea of history and the Burkean concept of tradition drew on a number of common assumptions about historical change and, in some senses, functioned as similar frameworks for expanding the scope of historical narrative. Above all, Burkean tradition, like Humean philosophical history and Smithian political economy, entailed the revelation of the limits of political action and thus the need for historians to reconceptualize historical change within a broad narrative of social experience.

Important differences remain, but I want to suggest that from a historiographical point of view the most salient distinctions between Humean and Burkean narratives are registered in a dimension of these texts untouched by the usual focus on the politics of progress or tradition. Hume's desire to enlarge his countrymen's capacity for detachment with respect to the revolutions of the previous century was founded on his confidence in the achievements of postrevolutionary Britain, just as his philosophical skepticism rested on an acceptance of the groundwork of custom in the affairs of common life. Burke, on the other hand, wrote from what he saw as the brink of a threatened loss of that stability of manners on which Hume generally believed his polite and commercial society could rely. These differences express themselves in a notable shift of historical distance. As a result, in the writings of Burke and his followers the distanciation cultivated by Hume gave way to an anxious insistence on the affective power of historical presence.

To write history in the framework of tradition means, of course, to take the long view. Paradoxically, however, the long view of history may well be the path to the sort of presentism that Butterfield stigmatized as the "whig interpretation," by which historical continuities are invoked in order to authorize a current creed. This, to use a more recent vocabulary than Butterfield's, amounts to marshaling history for the purposes of memory, and its stylistic signature is a rhetoric of immediacy designed to heighten history's prescriptive force. Thus, in the name of respect for a current of change that runs deep and slow, historical narrative is foreshortened in ways that endow particular aspects of past experience with a special power to shape both the present and the future.

It is crucial, of course, that this historiography of presence took shape at a time when acute national and ideological conflict brought questions of loyalty and identity to the forefront. In the revolutionary and Napoleonic era, writers working in many genres came to see politics as a battle for public opinion, which all sides agreed in seeing as the foundation of political power. In this context, the emerging idea of tradition brought a reassuring emphasis on the fundamental stability of the collective experience over long periods of time. Tradition, to adopt a phrase of James Mackintosh's, stood for "the embodied experience of mankind."[1] Genuine and fruitful change, therefore, would not only be gradual, it would also be mediated by persistent social habits that lay well beneath the surface of ordinary politics and almost beyond the reach of conscious interference. Thus, as an integrative notion, tradition not only con-

[1] "But we shall see that it is necessary for man to be governed, not by his own transient and hasty opinion upon the tendency of every particular action, but by those fixed and unalterable rules, which are the joint result of the impartial judgment, the natural feelings, and the embodied experience of mankind" (Mackintosh, *Miscellaneous Works*, 173).

nected a selective vision of the past to a putatively shared present, but it also assimilated disparate moments and experiences under the banner of a common national experience. Reframed appropriately, remote events could be brought forward as emblems of later destinies, while the manners of earlier ages—loosened from universalizing schemes of eighteenth-century historical anthropology—might acquire new significance as evidences of persisting national characteristics. Most striking of all, perhaps, was the way that the concept of tradition found a home in literary history, enabling critics to reconceive the writings of poets and recluses as a narrative of national opinion. I will come back to this subject in the next chapter.

Ironically, the word *tradition* that we apply so freely to Burke does not appear in his work in the secular sense we now give it, nor is it to be found in other writings of his time. Rather, in the historical writings of this era the word generally refers to knowledge passed down orally, which accordingly is weaker or less precise than what is written down.[2] Given this shift of usage, we have to accept a degree of conscious anachronism in speaking of a Burkean concept of tradition. Perhaps, however, the very fact that the eighteenth century lacked a single, accepted term to encompass this emergent idea helps account for the profusion of images that makes Burke's appeal to tradition both so lively and so difficult to reduce to any brief definition.

Burke's literary executors pointed to his sense of the continuities of history as the distinctive sign of the capaciousness of his mind. "In general, men see

[2] Thomas Sheridan's dictionary defines *tradition* as "The act or practice of delivering accounts from mouth to mouth without written memorials; any thing delivered orally from age to age." "Traditional. Delivered by tradition, descending by oral communication; observant of traditions, or idle rites." "Traditionally. By transmission from age to age; from tradition without evidence of written memorials." "Traditionary. Delivered by tradition" (*General Dictionary of English*, 1780).

The reader of Hume's *History* frequently encounters *tradition* in this sense of weak or unreliable testimony. On the opening page of the work, we find a warning against ingenious speculation on early ages, since "the history of past events is immediately lost or disfigured, when intrusted to memory and oral tradition" (*History of England*, 1:3). Instances of this usage could be multiplied indefinitely. Even so, the prime context for discussion of tradition in the eighteenth century remained the Reformation debate between the Protestant doctrine of the sole authority of Scripture and the Catholic insistence that scriptural truth needed to be interpreted in the light of tradition.

On oral tradition in this period, see Nicholas Hudson, " 'Oral Tradition': The Evolution of an Eighteenth-Century Concept," in *Tradition in Transition: Women Writers, Marginal Texts, and the Eighteenth-Century Canon*, ed. Alvaro Ribeiro and James Basker (Oxford: Clarendon, 1996). On Christian understandings of tradition, the most comprehensive work is Yves Congar, *Tradition and Traditions: An Historical and a Theological Essay*, trans. Michael Naseby and Thomas Rainborough (New York: Macmillan, 1967). See also Jaroslav Pelikan, *The Christian Tradition: A History of the Development of Doctrine*, 4 vols. (Chicago: U of Chicago P, 1971), as well as Pelikan's brief work *The Vindication of Tradition* (New Haven: Yale UP, 1984). And in a Jewish context, see Gershon Scholem, "Revelation and Tradition as Religious Categories in Judaism," in *The Messianic Idea in Judaism* (New York: Schocken, 1971); and Yosef Yerushalmi, *Zakhor: Jewish History and Jewish Memory* (Seattle: U of Washington P, 1982). The most comprehensive study of the concept of tradition remains Edward Shils, *Tradition* (Chicago: U of Chicago P, 1981).

that side only, which is nearest to them, in the order of things, by which they are surrounded, and in which they are carried along; but the clear and penetrating sight of his mind comprehended in one view all the parts of the immense whole, which varying from moment to moment, yet continuing through centuries essentially the same, extends around and above to every civilized people in every age, and unites and incorporates the present with the generations which are past." Presented in this way, Burke's understanding of tradition becomes the fruit of the sort of panoptic vision that the eighteenth century associated with both the philosophic spirit and the ideal of disinterested service.[3] Implicitly, in fact, his capacity to comprehend history "in one view" seems an intimation of a kind of all-seeing vision reserved to God alone.

Burke was certainly farsighted, but he was hardly calm or detached. In the late works belonging to his counterrevolutionary crusade, he often reads like an inspired paranoid whose time had come. His purpose was always thoroughly polemical. Again and again he turned to images expressive of propertied inheritance, the continuity of generations, and organic growth in order to enforce a contrast between the impatient, speculative arrogance of the revolutionists and the reverent caution of Britons who approach their constitution in the spirit of men acting "in the presence of canonized forefathers." This attitude of respect, Burke insisted, had long been a part of English life, and it gave the present generation of Englishmen a special duty in relation to their inherited institutions. "This idea of a liberal descent inspires us with a sense of habitual native dignity," Burke wrote. "By this means our liberty becomes a noble freedom. It carries an imposing and majestic aspect. It has a pedigree and illustrating ancestors. It has its bearings, and its ensigns armorial."[4]

The reader who approaches such passages looking to understand tradition as a historical process of transmission will find the *Reflections* a frustrating text. Burke is more concerned to urge his readers to revere what is traditional than to define tradition as such. Mortmain, entail, natural growth, partnership, contract, the succession of generations—any of these ways of figuring continuity might have been made the basis for a description of the way tradition functions, but mixed together in the urgency of his arguments, the rapid play of metaphor creates the sense of something largely resistant to definition, yet pervasively present in our world.

This combination of hazy outline and enlarged presence is entirely characteristic. In Burke, tradition is not a thing in itself, but a manner of experiencing the world. Like sympathy or sublimity, tradition is best understood as a sentimental construction. Accordingly, we understand tradition not so much by

[3] *Three Memorials on French Affairs. Written in the Years 1791, 1792 and 1793. By the Late Right Hon. Edmund Burke* (London, 1797), xxix–xxx. On panoptic vision, see Barrell, *English Literature in History*, chap. 1.

[4] Burke, *Reflections on the Revolution*, 30.

direct inspection as by the way it is registered in the eyes of spectators; and if this spectatorial technique blurs the outlines a good deal, it also endows the sense of tradition with a suggestiveness that greatly widens its application. At the same time, this way of construing our relationship to tradition mediates between its ideological and historiographical meanings, surrounding the historical past with an aura of reverence that enraged Burke's rationalist opponents and continues to defy simple definition.

Characteristically, Burke's understanding of tradition is most fully expressed in passages where he names what he fears most to lose. "Nothing is more certain," he writes in a famous passage, "than that our manners, our civilization, and all the good things which are connected with manners and with civilization, have, in this European world of ours, depended for ages upon two principles; and were indeed the result of both combined; I mean the spirit of a gentleman, and the spirit of religion."[5] Enlarged in this way, tradition is far from being limited to the constitution or other formal institutions of government or law. It enters, rather, into the whole texture of social life, and is best expressed in the continuities of manners and opinions that, for Burke as for his Scottish contemporaries, constituted the most fundamental level of historical experience.

For historiography, the question of how we locate this idea of tradition in the history of historical writing is a matter of some significance: the Burkean concept of tradition together with the Scottish idea of historical progress have rightly been described as constituting "the warp and woof" of nineteenth-century Whig historiography.[6] But behind this apt characterization of nineteenth-century historical writing stands an assumption about the previous century that needs reexamination, namely the view that Burke's concept of tradition and the Scottish analysis of social development belong to essentially separate strands of eighteenth-century thought. Schemes of historical progress, it is widely assumed, built on the relatively cosmopolitan outlook of Scottish political economy and philosophical history, while the Burkean idea of tradition was rooted in respect for precedent enshrined in the common law and the myth of an immemorial ancient constitution—in short, in an earlier form of traditionalism.[7]

This view of the Burkean concept of tradition as heir to an older, native traditionalism seems far too selective to do justice to Burke's thought. It aligns Burke's historical outlook with an antiquated conception of English history that had ceased to be compelling, as witnessed, for instance, in Hume's utter rejection of ancient constitutionalism. In fact, the effect of viewing Burke

[5] Ibid., 69.

[6] Burrow, *A Liberal Descent*, 22.

[7] See Pocock's influential essay "Burke and the Ancient Constitution: A Problem in the History of Ideas," in *Politics, Language and Time*, 202–32.

against the background of seventeenth-century ideas of an immemorial constitution would be to isolate him from the most interesting problems of historical writing in his own day, in which the discoveries of political economy and the philosophical history of manners, not the myth of the ancient constitution, posed the crucial challenges. Inevitably, the consequence is a simplification of Burke's views that makes it difficult to grasp how the Burkean concept of tradition could become so powerful an influence on later historiography.

The historiographical issues explored in this book suggest ways to bring Scottish ideas of progress and the Burkean concept of tradition into common focus. If we think of tradition as a framework for historical narrative rather than simply as an ideological stance, Burke's concept of tradition seems in many respects to continue the impetus of eighteenth-century historiography toward a reframing of history in social and sentimental terms. As a historiographical concept, tradition meant more than a simple appeal to national feeling and ancient ways; it also implied a concept of historical writing that would require historians to evoke a more profound, but less easily defined social process that worked beneath the surface of ordinary politics, just as it lay beyond the direct reach of legislative will.

In responding to the challenges posed by this expanded conception of the historical, writers could draw on much of the most interesting historical thinking of the eighteenth century. The slow growth of institutions, the partnership of generations past and future, the half-conscious wisdom of time-tested ways of life, these familiar Burkean themes gave new prominence to areas of collective experience that were already the focus of eighteenth-century works on political economy, conjectural history, and history of manners. In fact, as we will see in some detail, the idea that the most profound changes in history depended on silent revolutions in manners and customs, not on the will of individual actors, was already fundamental to the work of Hume, Smith, Kames, and others. But there are also crucial differences to be noted, which I earlier characterized as amounting to a transformation of historical distance. The affective presence Burke brought to the idea of tradition endowed certain forms of enduring social habit with a new *prescriptive* power. Thus, as the history of manners was reworked as a history framed by tradition, history acquired a new ideological task that shaped any number of historical narratives in the following century.

James Mackintosh: The *Vindiciae* and the *Discourse*

To appreciate the force of Mackintosh's later espousal of Burkean principles we have to begin with a brief look at his *Vindiciae*, the important early work that marked him out as Burke's most effective antagonist among Whig publicists. Here Mackintosh argued that freedom must be asserted on the basis of rights based in reason and justice, not lawyerlike discussions of precedent. The latter only disgraces liberty, he protests, "with the fantastic honour of a pedigree."[8] Mackintosh attacks the "mysterious nonsense" spoken by Coke, Blackstone, and Burke as a cloak for political fraud and speaks with contempt of this "Gothic transfer of *genealogy* to truth and justice." The champions of freedom, he laments, "have abandoned the strong hold of right for precedent, which, when the most favourable, is, as might be expected from the ages which furnish it, feeble, fluctuating, partial, and equivocal" (305–6).

In fact, the equivocal nature of discussions of precedent was well illustrated in this debate, which centered on the interpretation of the Revolution of 1688 and its relations to that of 1789. Burke had pictured the transfer of the crown from James to William and Mary as a revolution undertaken to preserve principles of legitimacy. The English event could not, therefore, be used to justify the violent overthrow of monarchy in France a century later. The irony of this position (which Mackintosh saw and exploited) was that it put Burke, as the great advocate of precedent, in the position of arguing that 1688 set no precedents. For his part, Mackintosh had to admit that in their formal pronouncements the Whigs of 1688 had done their best to preserve the language of legitimacy, but he argued that the evidence of their actions spoke otherwise.[9] Though the movers of the revolution did not entirely understand what they had put in progress, the revolution was a truly revolutionary event.[10] As such, it ruptured the continuities of English history and nullified most of the precedents of an earlier time.[11]

With respect to issues of historical continuity, this position contained ironies of its own, since in nullifying earlier precedents the revolution set in motion a train of new ones—especially, as Mackintosh insisted, if we look not so much

[8] *Vindiciae Gallicae* (London, 1791), 304: "The system of lawyers is indeed widely different. They can only appeal to usage, precedents, authorities, and statutes. They display their elaborate frivolity, their perfidious friendship, in disgracing freedom with the fantastic honour of a pedigree."

Later he writes: "It is not because we *have* been free, but because we have a right to be free, that we ought to demand freedom. . . . Let us hear no more of this ignoble and ignominious pedigree of freedom. Let us hear no more of her Saxon, Danish, or Norman ancestors" (306).

[9] Mackintosh speaks of a "repugnance between the conduct and the language of the Revolutionists" (ibid., 298).

[10] "Our ancestors at the Revolution, it is true, were far from feeling the full force of these sublime truths," Mackintosh wrote in a strain that bears some resemblance to the way in which the common lawyers he derided spoke of the Great Charter; "nor was the Public mind of Europe, in the seventeenth century, sufficiently enlightened and matured for the grand enterprizes of legislation" (ibid., 309).

[11] Mackintosh had earlier made this same argument that the revolution represented a radical break in English history in an anonymously published pamphlet on the issue of the Regency: *Arguments Concerning the Constitutional Right of Parliament to Appoint a Regency* (London, 1788).

at its direct effect on English government but on "its indirect influence on the progress of human opinion."[12] England became an asylum for freedom of thought, and in consequence a new body of ideas arose that silently produced a "*moral* revolution" of the widest significance. "From this progress of opinion arose the American Revolution, and from this, most unquestionably the delivery of France" (329–30).

By the end of the decade in which this was written, Mackintosh had publicly retracted his defense of the French Revolution and espoused a gradualist vision that owed much to Burke's influence. But if these changes had tempered his optimism about the melioration of the social order by a great and silent moral revolution, he was not any less interested in the "progress of opinion," an idea that always remained at the center of his understanding of history.

Mackintosh's public renunciation of the French Revolution came in a set of public lectures on law that he gave at Lincoln's Inn in 1799 and 1800. The text of these lectures, unfortunately, was never published, except for an outline or preliminary sketch that appeared as the *Discourse on the Study of the Law of Nature and of Nations* (1800). In this short work Mackintosh briefly outlines a theory of gradual historical change that is both comprehensive and succinct, though in reading it we are always aware that what we have is only the prospectus for a course of lectures in which these ideas were to be dealt with at much greater length. Two circumstances help to give an additional dimension to the text. First, as suits a work of scholarship as well as of consolidation, the *Discourse* provides a body of citations to the authors from whom Mackintosh drew support for his own ideas, and they were evidently intended to establish a kind of intellectual genealogy for his arguments. Second, among Mackintosh's auditors was William Hazlitt, who left a vivid, if jaundiced portrait of the speaker and the occasion in *Spirit of the Age*.[13]

Hazlitt, who remained attached to the ideals of the Revolution, resented what he saw as a public demonstration of Mackintosh's political apostasy,

[12] Mackintosh, *Vindiciae Gallicae*, 328.

[13] Additional sense of the context of the occasion can be gleaned from two brief references in Adam Ferguson's correspondence. Writing to Sir John Macpherson in July 1799, he asked: "Do you know Mr McIntosh whose project to give Lectures on the Law of Nature and Nations has been Announced in a preliminary Discourse? . . . The specimen I have seen inclines me to think he is one of the greatest Moralists this Island has produced and I consider the publick Character as involved in his success." In September, he wrote again: "I have heard very favourable accounts of Mr McIntoshs performances at Lincoln's Inn. As I judge only from his pamphlet his Tone tho' perhaps more harmonious is in unison with mine. . . . He will probably procure the moral Philosophy that Popularity in England which I wished for but have been unable to Obtain. His taking his ground in the Law is not so apt to allarm the Universities and the Church as if he had called his Object Moral Philosophy which those Authorities sometimes mention among the Corruptions of the Times." *The Correspondence of Adam Ferguson*, ed. Vincenzo Merolle, 2 vols. (London: Pickering, 1995), 2:456–57.

aggravated by unfairness to William Godwin, formerly a friend and political ally. But even in his ironic and largely hostile report, Hazlitt attests to the sensation produced by the lectures:

> The havoc was amazing the desolation was complete. As to our visionary sceptics and Utopian philosophers, they stood no chance with our lecturer. . . . Poor Godwin, who had come, in the *bonhomie* and candour of his nature, to hear what new light had broken in upon his old friend, was obliged to quit the field, and slunk away after an exulting taunt thrown out at "such fanciful chimeras as a golden mountain or a perfect man."[14]

In cold print the *Discourse* makes a more sober impression than Hazlitt suggests, but it is clear that Mackintosh had embraced a new politics, central to which was a firm commitment to a principle of gradualism and a consequent renunciation of any attempt to force the pace of historical change. Outlining his thoughts on the constitution, Mackintosh writes:

> Such a body of political laws must in all countries arise out of the character and situation of a people; they must grow with its progress, be adapted to its peculiarities, change with its changes, and be incorporated into its habits. Human wisdom cannot form such a constitution by one act, for human wisdom cannot create the materials of which it is composed. The attempt, always ineffectual, to change by violence the ancient habits of men, and the established order of society, so as to fit them for an absolutely new scheme of government, flows from the most presumptuous ignorance, requires the support of the most ferocious tyranny, and leads to consequences which its authors can never foresee; generally, indeed, to institutions the most opposite to those of which they profess to seek the establishment. But human wisdom indefatigably employed for remedying abuses, and in seizing favourable opportunities of improving that order of society which arises from causes over which we have little control, after the reforms and amendments of a series of ages, has sometimes, though very rarely, shown itself capable of building up a free constitution, which is "the growth of time and nature, rather than the work of human invention[.]" Such a constitution can only be formed by the wise imitation of "*the great innovator* TIME,"—"which, indeed, innovateth greatly, but quietly, and by degrees scarce to be perceived."[15]

Mackintosh evidently sees the political constitution as something much like the character of an individual. It is "incorporated" in the habits of the people

[14] Hazlitt, *Complete Works*, 11:98.

[15] *Discourse on the Law of Nature and of Nations*, 3d ed. (London, 1800), 53–55; see Mackintosh, *Miscellaneous Works*, 178. The footnotes have been omitted here for later discussion. The text printed in *Miscellaneous Works* derives from an earlier edition and varies in small ways that are mostly unimportant; it does not, however, include the interesting footnote to Bishop Shipley, discussed below.

and is really inseparable from their social being. In this light, the constitution belongs not so much to the state as to the society, of which it is a fundamental expression. For Mackintosh, as heir to the historical sociologies of the Scottish Enlightenment, this embeddedness of the constitution in the structures of the social world also means that the fundamental laws are a product of history and must change with the changing circumstances of society. At the same time, he embraces the idea that recognizing the historicity of constitutions means accepting a doctrine of gradualism, combined with the most severe limitations on the possibilities of direct political action. Reform cannot ignore "the ancient habits of men," or if it does will produce "consequences which its authors can never foresee." Even so, Mackintosh is careful to distinguish the caution born of this recognition of unforeseen consequences from simple conservatism or passivity. Under the right circumstances and given sufficient time, there exists a real, though always restricted possibility for human wisdom to work toward the improvement of society.

Mackintosh's commitment to gradualism stands on his conviction that the social order is irreducibly complex, an assumption that emerges clearly in the description of the English constitution that follows immediately after. "I shall attempt to exhibit this most complicated machine, as our history and our laws show it in action; and not as some celebrated writers have most imperfectly represented it, who have torn out a few of its more simple springs, and, putting them together, miscall them the British constitution."[16] The reference here is to Montesquieu, a writer whom he refers to several times with deep respect mixed, as here, with criticism. Against the great French writer's too simple ideas on mixed government, Mackintosh insists on the need for "patient and minute investigation of the practice of the government in all its parts, and through its whole history." To this effort, "a lawyer without a philosophical spirit" would be wholly inadequate, but still more so "a philosopher without practical, legal, and historical knowledge."[17]

The great source of error in all these discussions, Mackintosh writes, is "the attempt to give an air of system, of simplicity, and of rigorous demonstration, to subjects which do not admit them. The only means by which this could be done was by referring to a few simple causes, what, in truth, arose from immense and intricate combinations, and successions of causes."[18] The result is a theoretical simplicity that has no application to human affairs. "The causes which the politician has to consider are, above all others, multiplied, compli-

[16] Mackintosh, *Discourse*, 56; *Miscellaneous Works*, 179.

[17] Mackintosh, *Discourse*, 56–57; *Miscellaneous Works*, 179. Note Mackintosh's statement, "No experienced philosophical British statesman has yet devoted his leisure to a delineation of the constitution, which such a statesman alone can practically and perfectly know." Evidently he did not consider Burke's writings as having accomplished this task.

[18] Mackintosh, *Discourse*, 57–8; *Miscellaneous Works*, 179.

cated, minute, subtile, and, if I may so speak, evanescent, perpetually changing their form, and varying their combinations; losing their nature, while they keep their name; exhibiting the most different consequences in the endless diversity of men and nations on whom they operate."[19]

But for all his insistence on the complexity of society as an object of study, Mackintosh holds out the hope that historical change can be studied in a systematic way. These things can in fact be brought under theoretic study, he writes, but only by "a theory formed on the most extensive views, of the most comprehensive and flexible principles, so as to embrace all their varieties, and to fit all their rapid transmigrations; a theory, of which the most fundamental maxim is distrust in itself, and deference for practical prudence."[20] Only Aristotle and Bacon—the two "greatest philosophers who have ever appeared in the world"—have observed this maxim.

Mackintosh's Genealogy of Tradition

Aristotle and Bacon are only the most prominent of Mackintosh's many references to earlier writers. Hazlitt, whose own writing goes to the opposite extreme of informal allusiveness and unattributed quotation, was clearly irked by the lecturer's academic formality, and he draws a satiric picture of Mackintosh as a sort of political apothecary, provided with a nostrum for every social ailment:

> he seemed to stand with his back to the drawers in a metaphysical dispensary, and to take out of them whatever ingredients suited his purpose. . . . The writings of Burke, Hume, Berkeley, Paley, Lord Bacon, Jeremy Taylor, Grotius, Puffendorf, Cicero, Aristotle, Tacitus, Livy, Sully, Machiavel, Guicciardini, Thuanus, lay open beside him, and he could instantly lay his hand upon the passage, and quote them chapter and verse to the clearing up of all difficulties, and the silencing of all oppugners.[21]

For Hazlitt, this display of learning made the lectures, for all their brilliance, nothing more than a "kind of philosophical centos"—a learned patchwork lacking originality. But behind the constant production of authorities, a more sympathetic ear than Hazlitt's might have detected other reasons for Mackintosh's strategy of citation.

Mackintosh's references serve a number of political as well as scholarly purposes. A disparaging remark on those who think that a constitution must be a written document is a clear reference to Paine, just as an encomium to

[19] Mackintosh, *Discourse*, 58; *Miscellaneous Works*, 179.

[20] Mackintosh, *Discourse*, 58–59; *Miscellaneous Works*, 180.

[21] Hazlitt, *Complete Works*, 11:99.

both Burke and Fox—"whose name I here join, as they will be joined in fame by posterity"[22]—reasserts the old unity of the Whig party. But nowhere in this text is the importance of citation so clear as in the central passage on change and the constitution I have quoted.[23]

One note identifies Bacon as the source of the quotation on time: "the great Innovator, Time, which, indeed, innovateth greatly, but quietly, but by degrees scarcely to be perceived." A second note identifies the statement that the constitution is "the growth of time and nature, rather than the work of human invention." The sentiment seems redolent of Burke, but in fact Mackintosh takes it from "the beautiful account of the English constitution" of the liberal churchman, Bishop Shipley.[24]

The most elaborate footnote to this brief passage on constitutional change joins three seemingly very different authorities in support of the idea that any attempt to "change by violence the ancient habits of men" is foolish and will likely produce consequences opposite to those first intended. Let me take these in reverse order. Matthew Hale's "Considerations Touching the Amendment or Alteration of Laws" is an important discussion of change and continuity in law by one of the great lawyers of the seventeenth century.[25] This is as close

[22] Mackintosh, *Discourse*, 52n; *Miscellaneous Works*, 177.

[23] For what follows, see Mackintosh, *Discourse*, 54n–55n. The two paragraphs of text (quoted above) are amplified by four footnotes, which for the sake of convenience I will reproduce here as a single block:

> See an admirable passage on this subject in Dr Smith's *Theory of Moral Sentiments*, vol ii, p. 101–112 in which the true doctrine of reformation [i.e., reform] is laid down with singular ability by that eloquent and philosophical writer. See also Mr Burke's speech on economical reform; and Sir M. Hale on the amendment of laws, in the collection of my learned and most excellent friend, Mr. Hargrave, p. 248.
>
> "Pour former un gouvernement modéré, il faut combiner les puissances, les régler, les tempérer, les faire agir; . . . donner pur ainsi dire un lest à l'une, pour la mettre en état de resister à une autre; c'est un chef-d'oeuvre de législation que le hasard fait rarement, et que rarement on laisse faire à la prudence. . . . Montesquieu, *De l'Esprit des Loix*, liv.v.c.14."
>
> I quote this passage from Bishop Shipley's beautiful account of the English constitution. (Shipley's Works, vol ii p.112), one of the finest parts of a writer, whose works I cannot help considering as the purest and most faultless model of composition that the present age can boast.

Bacon, Essay xxiv, *Of Innovation.*

[24] Jonathan Shipley, bishop of St. Asaph (1714–1788), had been a good friend of Burke's, as well as of Benjamin Franklin, whose *Autobiography* was partly written in Shipley house. Sir William Jones, another famous associate, became the bishop's son-in-law. What all three men had in common was a warm sympathy for the American cause as well as strong reformist leanings. In Shipley's case, in fact, his outspoken politics had cost him preferment in the church, but clearly had won him James Mackintosh's admiration.

In his reading diary, Thomas Green reports reading Bishop Shipley on Mackintosh's recommendation (*Extracts from Diary*, 164).

[25] The "Considerations" had been published in 1787 as part of an important collection of law writings, Francis Hargraves's *Law Tracts* (1787). Hale, who had survived the convulsions of the

as Mackintosh comes to invoking the common-law tradition, often thought to be decisive for Burkean ideas of tradition. Nothing in this reference, however, indicates that Mackintosh saw Hale as anything other than a spokesman for moderately paced reform.

The second citation, a reference to Burke's "Speech on the Economical Reform" (Feb. 11, 1780), may be more pointed. This great speech against wasteful and corrupt government was a high moment of Burke's reformist energies and was sometimes quoted against Burke by his critics when he accepted a government pension. Mackintosh's feelings toward Burke at this point were certainly positive, but his choice of this speech rather than the *Reflections* may represent an appeal from the old Burke to the young.[26]

Of the three references in this note, the longest and most admiring is to Adam Smith's *Theory of Moral Sentiments*, "in which the true doctrine of reformation is laid down with singular ability by that eloquent and philosophical writer." Mackintosh cites an extended discussion of political reform that Smith added to the work in its sixth and last edition (1790). Smith's message of cautious gradualism corresponds very closely to Mackintosh's views a decade later. The pages are justly famous:

> The man of system . . . is apt to be very wise in his own conceit; and is often so enamoured with the supposed beauty of his own ideal plan of government, that he cannot suffer the smallest deviation from any part of it. He goes on to establish it completely and in all its parts, without any regard either to the great interests, or to the strongest prejudices which may oppose it. He seems to imagine that he can arrange the different members of a great society with as much ease as the hand arranges the different pieces upon a chess-board. He does not consider that the pieces upon the chess-board have no other principle of motion besides that which the hand impresses upon them; but that, in the great chess-board of human society, every single piece has a principle of motion of its own, altogether different from that which the legislature might chuse to impress upon it. If those two principles coincide and act

---

Civil War and Commonwealth, spoke for a moderate position in which the dangers of innovation were balanced against the need for change. The effect of his writings was to shift emphasis away from Coke's faith in the immemorial character of the common law toward a more conscious program of legislative reform. The continuity that English law possessed Hale liked to express by a comparison to the Argonauts, who, in the course of a lengthy voyage were forced to replace almost every timber in their vessel, which nonetheless remained the same ship.

On Hale's career and his view of the law, see Charles Gray's introduction to his edition of Hale's *The History of the Common Law of England* (Chicago: U of Chicago P, 1971), as well as Alan Cromartie, *Sir Matthew Hale (1609–1676): Law, Religion, and Natural Philosophy* (Cambridge: Cambridge UP, 1995).

[26] It is curious that Mackintosh quotes the *Reflections* elsewhere in this work, but not by name. The "Speech on the Economical Reform" was an effort to reduce the costs of government and limit the scope of patronage, thereby protecting the independence of Parliament against the influence of the Crown. For the background to Burke's reform efforts, see Stanley Ayling, *Edmund Burke: His Life and Opinions* (London: Cassell, 1988), chap. 9.

> in the same direction, the game of human society will go on easily and harmoniously, and is very likely to be happy and successful. If they are opposite or different, the game will go on miserably, and the society must be at all times in the highest degree of disorder.[27]

Like Hale and Burke, with whom he is associated in this note, Smith carefully balances the dangers and potentials of reform. But the most distinctive feature of these pages from *Moral Sentiments* is the way in which Smith ties the gradualist message to a corresponding recognition of the limitations of the political will. Smith, it is evident, was hardly a rigid opponent of state action, as some of his later admirers have thought. But his view of the possibilities for practical reform was firmly grounded in a recognition of the autonomy and complexity of the social process. For his part, Mackintosh had come to a very similar recognition, as the entire tenor of the *Discourse on the Law of Nature and of Nations* makes clear, and we can assume that this combination of gradualism and complexity was what he had in mind in calling Smith's work the "true view of reformation." Indeed, when we consider Mackintosh's appeal for a theory of society that would avoid the simplistic habits of earlier analysts, it seems very likely that—though Aristotle and Bacon may have been the remoter ancestors of this new philosophy—its nearest model was Smith's "science of the legislator."[28]

"Domestic and Gradual Revolutions"

On one level, Mackintosh's citation to Smith was simply good strategy for a man in his politically awkward circumstances. His recruitment of Smith at the head of a family of authorities that included not only Burke himself, but Aristotle, Bacon, Hale, Shipley, Hume, and others, raises his discussion of a slowly evolving British social constitution high above mere partisan debate, thus providing his views on reform with what Burke would call a "liberal descent." But this construction of a partly Scottish genealogy for his own ideas also finds real support in the major writings of the Scottish Enlightenment, in which a key theme is the problem of understanding slow, pervasive, and unforeseen social change. Indeed, though we do not generally think of the Scottish Enlightenment in relation to ideas of tradition, the linkage of historical gradualism and social complexity is so characteristic that explanations taking this form were an identifying feature of the rhetoric of scientific explanation in this period.

[27] Smith, *Theory of Moral Sentiments*, VI.ii.2.17.

[28] On Smith's "science of the legislator," see Donald Winch, *Riches and Poverty: An Intellectual History of Political Economy in Britain, 1750–1834* (Cambridge: Cambridge UP, 1996), pt. 1; as well as Haakonssen, *Science of a Legislator*, chap. 4 .

A useful opening example can be taken from Lord Kames, who sketched so many of the themes of the social discourse of the Scottish Enlightenment. In his pioneering treatise on legal history, *Historical Law-Tracts* (1758), Lord Kames makes the following observation on the gradual substitution of publicly enforced penal codes for habits of private revenge:

> A Revolution so contradictory to the strongest propensity of human nature, could not by any power, or by any artifice, be instantaneous. It behoved to be gradual, and, in fact, the progressive Steps tending to its completion, were slow, and, taken singly, almost imperceptible; as will appear from the following history.[29]

Similarly, what we might call scientific gradualism is essential to Adam Ferguson's vision of the progressive character of human nature. "Natural productions are generally formed by degrees," Ferguson writes in the opening sentence of the *Essay on the History of Civil Society* (1767). "This progress in the case of man is continued to a greater extent than in that of any other animal. Not only the individual advances from infancy to manhood, but the species itself from rudeness to civilization."[30] Ferguson's argument for the progressive character of human nature rests on another favorite theme of eighteenth-century Scottish thought that is related to the idea of tradition: the idea that habit, customs, and manners form a kind of second nature that shapes human life.[31] The connection between individual habit and social evolution is made most explicitly in his later lectures, published as the *Principles of Moral and Political Science* (1792). Man's progressive nature means more, he stresses, than a susceptibility to changes that come from external causes; it means that human beings, like other progressive things, undergo changes that "proceed from a principle of advancement in the subject itself."[32] This internal principle of progress, however, requires a matching mechanism that can explain how society is able to retain the work accomplished by its progressive energies. Ferguson finds his explanation in the idea of habit, which serves him in much the same way that the association of ideas functioned in philosophical psycholo-

[29] Kames, *Historical Law-Tracts* (Edinburgh, 1761), 19–20.

[30] Ferguson, *History of Civil Society*, 7. It is worth noting that this passage was quoted extensively in the favorable notice of Ferguson carried by the *Annual Register* of 1767; Burke was the editor of the periodical and quite possibly the author of the review.

[31] "He is, withal, in a very high degree susceptible of habits; and can, by forbearance or exercise, so far weaken, confirm, or even diversify his talents, and his dispositions, as to appear, in a great measure, the arbiter of his own rank in nature, and the author of all the varieties which are exhibited in the actual history of his species" (*History of Civil Society*, 16–17).

[32] *Principles of Moral and Political Science*, 2 vols. (Edinburgh, 1792), 1:190. See also his statement that "to advance, we may again repeat, is the state of nature relative to him" (1:199). Ferguson also warns against understanding progress as a series of statically conceived stages. Every stage, like the whole, is a matter of continued change; "the distinctive character of any progressive being is to be taken . . . from an accumulative view of its movement throughout" (1:192).

gies of the period. He also links habit to the effects of experience (another key element of what becomes the Burkean vocabulary) and makes it responsible for the regularity and predictability of the social order.

Man, says Ferguson, makes "a trial of different practices" and learns what most suits his needs and situation. But every new situation does not throw the individual back on the first lessons of experience; habit ensures that similar responses will naturally follow similar situations.[33] Indeed, if such were not the case, human life would be "a scene of inextricable confusion" in which it would be impossible to exercise prudence or foresight. The result would be much the same as if physical laws ceased to apply in the natural world.

Habit, then, is a principle of order, essential to the stability of both social institutions and social understanding. But Ferguson is anxious to deny that his emphasis on habit amounted to a denial of free will. Rather, accenting the positive, he asks us to rejoice "in a circumstance, which appears to give fixed possession of the attainments we may have made."[34] And though he recognizes that the force of habit might preserve evil dispositions as well as good ones, he argues that it is "the tendency of experience to detect every false opinion, and, by this means, to narrow the scope of aberration and mistake." Experience, in short, leads to progress, but only because, through habit, there is a natural incorporation of the lessons of experience into further courses of action. Thus, for Ferguson, man's "bias to retain the form he has once adopted" proves to be a principle at once of progress and tradition.

Ferguson distinguishes between history, which is engaged with particulars, and science, which investigates the "general order" that connects particular facts together.[35] Hume makes a similar distinction, but ties it more carefully to the idea that there are certain types of events and certain classes of causation that are most open to general or philosophical explanation. In his essay "Of the Rise and Progress of the Arts and Sciences," Hume argues that the "domestic and the gradual revolutions of a state must be a more proper subject of reasoning and observation, than the foreign and the violent, which are commonly produced by single persons, and are more influenced by whim, folly, or caprice, than by general passions and interests."[36] To make his point more

[33] Ibid., 1:232–33. "The measures, which his experience in former times has led him to employ, recur to his mind on every subsequent occasion of the same kind; and, even if he . . . should have forgot the grounds of his former proceeding, mere habit will lead him to repeat the same choice, and to perform the same action. This bias to retain the form he has once adopted, though without any original propensity, is with him nearly of the same effect with the instinct of other animals" (1:233).

[34] Ibid., 1:234.

[35] Ibid., 1:272.

[36] Hume, *Essays*, 112. Though there will always be room for dispute over particular cases, Hume writes, the underlying principle is clear: "What depends upon a few persons is, in a great measure, to be ascribed to chance, or secret and unknown causes: What arises from a great number, may often be accounted for by determinate and known causes" (112).

concrete, Hume cites the case of the "depression of the lords, and the rise of the commons" in England, which, so he says, is more easily accounted for than the vicissitudes that led to the loss of Spanish power and the rise of the French after the death of Charles V.

This historical example proved compelling, and for both Hume and Smith it became a showcase of the philosophical method. "Of the Rise and Progress of the Arts and Sciences" appeared in the *Essays, Moral and Political* in 1742;[37] by 1759, when Hume published the two volumes of his *History* on the Tudors, the "depression of the lords, and the rise of the commons" had grown into a full-scale historical argument, and still later Adam Smith gave it even more elaboration in book 3 of *The Wealth of Nations* (1776). By their manner of presenting the case, both Hume and Smith indicate that they regard their explanation of the decay of feudal dependency as a prime demonstration of the added depth and complexity their philosophical method could bring to the study of history.

In appendix 3, with which he concludes his volumes on the Tudors, Hume observes that the evidence shows that the nobility of England, while preserving many of their ancient customs, had acquired a new taste for luxuries, which had fundamentally altered their position in society. Much more than the actions of any monarch, this change of manners was the fundamental reason for "the great revolution, which happened about this period in the English constitution."[38] Hume's reasoning is that expensive commodities dissipated the fortunes of the great aristocrats and diverted their spending from supporting bands of retainers to consuming expensive commodities. This change benefited merchants and artisans, people whose livelihood made them largely independent of the barons. Thus, "instead of that unlimited ascendant, which he was wont to assume over those who were maintained at his board . . . [the lord] retained only that moderate influence, which customers have over tradesmen, and which can never be dangerous to civil government" (4:384). At the same time, Hume continues, the aristocratic landholders, now having more need for money than for men, enclosed their fields and took other measures that reduced the number of their dependents—men who "formerly were always at their call in every attempt to subvert the government, or oppose a neighbouring baron." In the long run, the consequence of these changes was to promote the power of the commons, "yet in the interval between the fall of the nobles and the rise of this order, the sovereign took advantage of the present situation, and assumed an authority almost absolute" (4:384).

[37] See Eugene Miller, introduction to Hume, *Essays*, xiii n.

[38] Hume, *History of England*, 4:384. As always, I cite the Liberty Press edition, which reprints the edition of 1778, the first after Hume's death. The chief difference between the 1759 edition and this lies in the separation of this section as appendix 3.

Hume's argument here depends upon the same distinction between general and particular phenomena advanced long before in the *Essays*. In opening, he contrasts the "peculiar causes" associated with the situation and character of the king to the change in manners, whose influence was general and enduring. Similarly, in closing, Hume gives special weight to his explanation by contrasting it to more customary historical views, however authoritative. "Whatever may be commonly imagined, from the authority of lord Bacon, and from that of Harrington, and later authors, the laws of Henry VII contributed very little" toward these important changes; the "change of manners," he reiterates, "was the chief cause of the secret revolution of government" (4:385). Hume does not hide his satisfaction in being able to trump such famous writers and reveal unsuspected complexities overlooked by more conventional views of history. But it is important to note that the confidence with which he unlocked this "secret" has less to do with the weight of his empirical evidence than with a prior philosophical commitment to certain kinds of explanation. The "manners of the age" was a general cause that inherently possessed more explanatory power than anything bound up in the action of kings. This is not yet the prescriptive notion of tradition that emerges among the Burkeans under the impact of counterrevolutionary ideology.[39] Rather it is a prescription for writing history in an explanatory framework established by "the domestic and the gradual revolutions of a state."

Presumably it was Hume's influence that started Adam Smith thinking about the problem of the decline of the feudal nobility, though on another level one could say that the entire history of the Highlands in the eighteenth century was a standing provocation to examine the issue. The passages devoted to it in Smith's jurisprudence lectures of 1762–63 still read like a rather inelegant abridgement of Hume's history,[40] but in *The Wealth of Nations* he put his own stamp on the discussion. Here he sets out the economic logic of Hume's argument with great force, while also giving the analysis an extra edge by adding a sharp note of moral contempt for the shortsighted selfishness of the aristocrats. ("All for ourselves, and nothing for other people, seems, in every age of the world, to have been the vile maxim of the masters of mankind.")[41] Most

[39] I do not mean, of course, that there is no element of political prescription in Hume's *History*. On Hume's conservatism and on the later prescriptive uses of Hume's historiographical work, see Laurence Bongie, *David Hume: Prophet of the Counter-Revolution* (Oxford: Clarendon, 1965).

[40] See Smith, *Lectures on Jurisprudence*, ed. R. L. Meek, D. D. Raphael, and P. G. Stein (Indianapolis: Liberty, 1982). The decline of nobiliar power is rehearsed several times. For the lectures of 1762–63 *(LJa)* see pp. 261–65; and for a treatment in the 1766 lecture report *(LJb)* see pp. 59–60.

[41] Smith, *An Inquiry into the Nature and Causes of the Wealth of Nations*, ed. R. H. Campbell and A. S. Skinner, 2 vols. (Indianapolis: Liberty, 1981), III.iv.10 (subsequent citations are given in the text).

of all, Smith gives the historical example a new thrust. Where Hume had set up the shallow judgments of earlier historians as his foil, Smith puts the blindness of the historical actors themselves, thus establishing the decline of the baronage as one of the great historical examples of the operation of unintended consequences:

> A revolution of the greatest importance to the publick happiness, was in this manner brought about by two different orders of people, who had not the least intention to serve the publick. . . . Neither of them had either knowledge or foresight of that great revolution which the folly of the one, and the industry of the other, was gradually bringing about. (III.iv.17)

This idea of unintended consequences was perhaps latent in Hume's treatment, and certainly Hume expressed comparable views in other parts of the *History.* But in Smith this emphasis on the blindness of the historical agents has a different resonance because it links this important historical example to the widest themes of his political economy, namely the operation of self-love and the power of the division of labor. In turn, the division of labor is central to Smith's understanding of the complexity of social processes—a condition that severely limits the Legislator's options for intervening in the workings of a social and economic order that Smith conceives as largely self-regulating.

Every reader of *The Wealth of Nations* remembers Smith's description of the manufacture of pins as a case study of the complex elaboration of tasks brought about by the division of labor. Unfortunately, as Smith himself half recognized, the example is almost too striking, and it tends to swallow up the larger principle it is meant to illustrate. It is important, therefore, to pay attention to the context of the discussion. "The effects of the division of labour," Smith writes, "*in the general business of society* will be more easily understood, by considering in what manner it operates in some particular manufactures" (I.i.2; emphasis added). In fact, he continues, it is commonly thought that the division of labor has been carried furthest in relation to rather trivial items. This, however, is a mistake that occurs because observers misunderstand the scale of the problem. In trivial manufactures all stages and occupations can be gathered together under a single roof, and "placed at once under the view of the spectator." In contrast, great manufactures supplying far more important needs employ so many people that we can seldom see at a single glance more than one branch of the work. As a result, "the division is not near so obvious, and has accordingly been much less observed."[42]

Evidently, to observe the most general effects of the division of labor would require a spectator capable of a wider kind of survey. In fact, for reasons

[42] *Wealth of Nations*, I.i.2. On this point, see David Levy, "The Partial Spectator in the *Wealth of Nations:* A Robust Utilitarianism," *European Journal of the History of Economic Thought* 2 (1995): 299–326.

that are at least in part rhetorical, Smith directs us to look for evidence where we least expect to find it: not in the mills or factories, which were the most obvious symbols of commercial productivity, but in the clothing, furniture, or housing of the common people. Here, more than in the celebrated description of the manufacture of pins, we get the full sense of the way in which the division of labor operates to create an enormously elaborated system of social interdependence that is barely visible to ordinary observation just because it is so broadly ramified:

> Observe the accommodation of the most common artificer or day-labourer in a civilized and thriving country, and you will perceive that the number of people of whose industry a part, though but a small part, has been employed in procuring him this accommodation, exceeds all computation. (I.i.11)

The example is well chosen for its ability to surprise, allowing Smith to extend his argument over two pages in which he relishes the opportunity to elaborate on the wide variety of skills and trades that provide the ordinary goods used by working people. When we think of all this, he concludes,

> we shall be sensible that without the assistance and cooperation of many thousands, the very meanest person in a civilized country could not be provided, even according to, what we very falsely imagine, the easy and simple manner in which he is commonly accommodated. (I.i.11)

Smith's premise that his description has to do with a "civilized and thriving country" is an important one, since it grounds the operations of the division of labor in a progressive historical scheme. In a less commercial society, much of the material side of a peasant's life would simply be homemade. By same token, the effective limitation on the operation of the division of labor lies in the extent of markets and transport, which means that the principle is carried furthest in the most industrious and thriving societies.[43] In short, if from a purely economic point of view the division of labor stands as the prime explanation of the growing productive power of labor, from a still more general perspective it can be taken as an index of an interdependence and complexity extending to every realm of social life. Even philosophy has become subject to a subdivision of tasks that makes its workers more effective (I.i.9).

But though the division of labor increases with social complexity, its fundamental principles rest in instincts of human nature that are observable at every stage of development. The division of labor, Smith writes, "from which so

[43] Without access to extensive markets, the worker would be unable to exchange the surplus of his labor for his various necessities and therefore would have no incentive to specialist work. For this reason many trades can only be carried on in large towns or where there is easy access to transport (I.iii.1).

many advantages are derived, is not originally the effect of any human wisdom, which foresees and intends that general opulence to which it gives occasion." Rather, it is "the very slow and gradual consequence" of the human instinct to "truck, barter and exchange one thing for another" (I.ii.1). The division of labor, in other words, can be considered a prime instance of the operation of those "general passions and interests" that in their impersonal operation account most clearly for what Hume had called the "domestic and gradual revolutions of a state."

Burke and the History of Manners

The overpowering rhetoric of Burke's ideological traditionalism in the *Reflections* has often led observers—his own contemporaries as well as later historians—to draw a sharp divide between Burke's nostalgic chivalry and the commercial interests of his Scottish contemporaries. "In the school of Mr. Burke, trade and manufactures are words that sound meanly," wrote one pamphleteer. "Early education, natural taste, and peculiar sublimity of imagination, have made, I presume, the detail and the exactness of commerce, disgusting to Mr. Burke; and have furnished his mind with those grand and obscure ideas, that associate with the lofty manners of chivalry and the Gothic gloom of a darker age. Hence probably . . . we are to explain his strong preference of the feudal relicts of our constitution, and his dread of the progress of commerce, as leading to innovation and change."[44]

Burke gave many hostages to this sort of view of his prejudices, but he also made strong claims to the contrary.[45] When provoked to review his record

[44] [James Currie,] *A Letter, Commercial and Political, addressed to the right Honorable William Pitt: in which the Real Interests of Britain in the Present Crisis Are Considered, and Some Observations Are Offered on the General State of Europe*. By Jasper Wilson, Esq. (London, 1793), 32. Currie was a Scottish doctor, transplanted to Liverpool, who later found literary fame as the biographer of Burns. The pamphlet is an attack on paper credit, but a strong defense of the commercial interest, which Currie thought was being undermined by Pitt's manipulations of credit. For Currie, commerce was inseparable from British manners and British liberty. The references to Burke's early education hints at the common hostility to Burke's Irish and Catholic connections.

[45] The conflict between these two images of Burke has been discussed by a number of historians. For a fine assessment of the tensions in Burke's political economy, see Winch, *Riches and Poverty*, especially chaps. 5 and 7. See also John Pocock, "The Political Economy of Burke's Analysis of the French Revolution," in *Virtue, Commerce, and History*, 193–212. As Pocock acknowledges, his reading of the *Reflections* here sharply contrasts with his earlier interpretation (in "Burke and the Ancient Constitution") of the *Reflections* as a text that "should be understood in the context of a tradition of common-law thought in the age of Sir Edward Coke" (193). Pocock refuses to discuss the evident tensions between these two interpretations; nonetheless he insists that the earlier common-law thesis remains correct (193–94).

of public service by an attack on his pension, Burke made a particular point of his diligent and precocious study of political economy; it had occupied him, he said, "from my early youth to near the end of my service in parliament, even before . . . it had employed the thoughts of speculative men in other parts of Europe." In what was presumably a reference to Adam Smith, he added, "Great and learned men thought my studies were not wholly thrown away, and deigned to communicate with me now and then on some particulars of their immortal works."[46] Later, near the end of his life, Burke repeated the claim in still stronger terms in his interview with Mackintosh. After giving much praise to Smith, Mackintosh reported, Burke said that Smith "was the only man who, without communication, thought on these topics exactly as he did."[47]

Burke's enthusiasm for the philosophical history of manners is as easy to document as his interest in political economy.[48] When William Robertson sent him a copy of his *History of America*, Burke replied in the most glowing terms, giving special emphasis to the book's study of manners:

> The part which I read with the greatest pleasure is the discussion on the manners and characters of the inhabitants of that new world. I have always thought with you, that we possess, at this time, very great advantages towards the knowledge of human nature. We need no longer go to history to have it in all its periods and stages. History, from its comparative youth, is but a poor instructor. When the Egyptians called the Greeks children in antiquities, we may well call them children; and so we may call all those nations which were able to trace the progress of society only within their own limits. But now the great map of mankind is unravelled at once, and there is no state or gradation of barbarism, and no mode of refinement, which we have not, at the same instant, under our view.[49]

[46] "A Letter To A Noble Lord" in *Further Reflections on the French Revolution*, ed. Daniel Ritchie (Indianapolis: Liberty, 1992), 295.

[47] Robert Bisset, *Life of Edmund Burke*, 2 vols. (London, 1800), 2:429. On Burke and Smith, see D. Bryant, *Edmund Burke and His Literary Friends* (St. Louis: Washington UP, 1939), 247–49; and Winch, *Riches and Poverty*, chap. 5.

[48] The favorable reviews that the *Annual Register* under Burke's editorship gave to Ferguson and Robertson among others add weight to the case for his receptiveness to philosophical history. We do not know with certainty that Burke was the author of these reviews, but there is a strong presumption that he was. Copeland, who studied the issue with care, concludes that Burke wrote all of the reviews that appeared to 1766 and that it is somewhat less probable that he wrote the twenty-seven that appeared from 1766 to 1773. However, Copeland also argues that there are a half dozen reviews in the latter group for which there is strong evidence of Burke's authorship: this includes the review of Ferguson's *History of Civil Society* (1767), a review that extracts passages most consonant with Burke's sense of gradualism. See Thomas Copeland, *Our Eminent Friend Edmund Burke* (New Haven: Yale UP, 1949), 118–45.

[49] Burke to William Robertson, June 9, 1777, in *Correspondence of Edmund Burke*, ed. Thomas Copeland, 10 vols. (Cambridge: Cambridge UP, 1958–78), 5:350–51.

Burke went on to compliment the historian on having made noble use of the advantages the times had given him: "You have employed philosophy to judge of manners, and from manners you have drawn new resources for philosophy."[50]

Burke's enthusiasm for Robertson's writings reflected his own interest in the history and political economy of the Americas. Two decades before, he had cooperated with his "cousin" William Burke in publishing (and perhaps also in writing) *The Account of European Settlement* (1757), a comparative study of the geography, history, and commerce of the various European colonies. Another work of the same period that had much to say about what Burke in his letter to Robertson calls "the humble scenes of political economy" was Burke's uncompleted history of medieval England, the *Essay Towards an Abridgement of English History.* Begun on fairly ambitious lines and then abandoned for reasons that have never been clear, the *Abridgement* incorporated considerable descriptions of the history of manners, including chapters on the religion of the Druids and the manners of the Saxons.[51]

Both of these early works have real value as sources for Burke's sense of history. But the most compelling and most mature expression of Burke's interest in the history of manners, if we except the *Reflections* itself, comes in Burke's writings and speeches on India. Burke, who was passionately engaged with attempts to reform English rule, made himself as knowledgeable as possible on Indian history and civilization. As he said in his important speech on Fox's India Bill (1783), he had "thought himself obliged, by research of years, to wind himself into the inmost recesses and labyrinths of the Indian detail."[52] When, very largely as a result of his efforts, Warren Hastings's conduct was examined and condemned by the Commons, Burke brought all his extensive studies to bear in the great "Speech on Opening" (1788) that initiated the

[50] We should note, too, Burke's use of the now standard trope that sets a more genuine history that encompasses everyday matters against a narrowly conceived history concerned only with military and political affairs: "I am heartily sorry we are now supplying you with that kind of dignity and concern, which is purchased to History at the expense of Mankind. I had rather by far that Dr. Robertson's pen were only employed in delineating the humble Scenes of political economy, and not the great Events of a civil war. However, if our Statesmen had read the book of human nature instead of the Journals of the House of Commons, and history instead of Acts of Parliament, we should not by the latter have furnished out so ample a page in the former" (ibid., 351).

[51] Only a few pages were published in Burke's lifetime; the text was published in 1811 under the title *Essay Towards an Abridgement of the English History.* See also the useful extracts in *Selected Writings and Speeches*, ed. Peter Stanlis (Chicago: Regnery, 1962), 64–87. On Burke's views of medieval England, see Smith, *The Gothic Bequest*, 85–90.

[52] "Speech on Fox's India Bill," December 1, 1783, in *Writings and Speeches of Edmund Burke*, ed. Paul Langford, 9 vols. (Oxford: Clarendon, 1981), 5:382. On Burke's view of India, in addition to P. J. Marshall's invaluable introductions to vols. 5 and 6 of *Writings and Speeches*, see Frederick Whelan, *Edmund Burke and India: Political Morality and Empire* (Pittsburgh: U of Pittsburgh P, 1996).

prosecution in the Lords—though perhaps only a man in the grip of an obsession would have lectured the British peerage for four successive days on Indian history and customs.

In both the *Reflections* and the "Speech on Opening" the history of manners served Burke as the framework for conceptualizing grand narratives of the widest possible scope. But as steeped in history as both works are, neither is in any formal sense a historical narrative. Indeed, since both works privileged historical memory over even loosely conceived historical narrative, it is important to underline the fact that Burke adapted other genres to present his vision of history. Though the pretext of letter writing or the actuality of speechmaking were certainly strained by the outsized uses Burke gave them, nonetheless the tone and structure of these genres permitted the sort of immediate appeal to an audience that suited his sentimental construction of tradition. Given the decorum associated with history in the eighteenth century, it would have been harder to incorporate such blatant presencing effects as the famous (or infamous) paean to Marie Antoinette in a formal historical narrative.

In sheer volume as well as in brilliance, Burke's outpourings on India easily match those on France. Indeed, the huge "Speech on Opening" bears about the same relation to ordinary speechmaking that the *Reflections* bears to ordinary letter writing. But there are more substantial reasons to make the comparison, since in fundamental ways his stance in both campaigns was much the same. In India as later in France, Burke imagined himself as the defender of an ancient and aristocratic system of manners against the rapacity of a class of self-interested new men without deep roots or settled interests. But of course there were also obvious political differences. On India, as formerly on America, Burke's views were decidedly for reform; here for the last time, in fact, he stood with Fox and Sheridan before the French Revolution shattered their party and divided them personally. Geographically, too, the situations of France and India were wholly different. Burke was acutely aware of the remoteness of India from the mind of Britain. This meant that overwhelming distances stood in the way of both the historical explanations and the sympathetic identification that English opinion needed if it was to remedy the evils that the East India Company had done to the ancien régime of India.

Recent critics have tended to emphasize rhetorics either of presence or distance in Burke's India speeches, as though these were mutually exclusive strategies.[53] In fact, Burke needed both of these to accomplish his purpose, since the urgency of reform would only be felt if he could make India real to his

[53] Suleri insists on Burke's sense of the difficulty of representing India and therefore on a distanciating rhetoric, while Musslewhite argues for a picturesque proximativeness. See Sara Suleri, *The Rhetoric of English India* (Chicago: U of Chicago P, 1992); and David Musselwhite, "The Trial of Warren Hastings," in *Literature, Politics, and Theory*, ed. Francis Barker et al. (London: Methuen, 1986).

audience as a land that had long preexisted English conquest and that was now suffering terribly by it. He approached this complicated task by mixing the language of manners and of sentiment within the framework of eighteenth-century ethnography and philosophical history. Empire in India, Burke insisted, had not given Britain dominion over some remote and savage place. This was an ancient civilization, older than Britain—"a people for all ages civilized and cultivated; cultivated by all the arts of polished life, whilst we were yet in the woods."[54] India was a vast land, "diversified by manners, by religion, by hereditary employment," a variety of custom that made the rulers' task all the more "critical and delicate." Searching for a stabilizing comparison, Burke found one in the Holy Roman Empire, with its multitude of states, large and small. But the analogy, as he knew, was just a makeshift. He had offered it, he told the Commons in 1783,

> not for an exact resemblance, but as a sort of a middle term, by which India might be approximated to our understandings, and if possible to our feelings; in order to awaken something of sympathy for the unfortunate natives, of which I am afraid we are not perfectly susceptible, whilst we look at this very remote object through a false and cloudy medium. (5:390)

These were the terms used in the "Speech on Fox's India Bill" of 1783; in the longer, more stately "Speech on Opening," Burke presented a substantial review of the main stages of Indian history, which we might think of as replacing the historical shorthand of the comparison to Germany. The terms of this history drew directly from the kind of narrative he had admired in Robertson, as is made clear by a contemporary account of the trial:

> He then went into a general view of the history of Hindostan, and of its particular history as affected by English enterprize and English rapine. He enumerated and described the various ranks of English society in India, and carried them through their several gradations. . . . He passed from this to the Indian character, and drew the picture of a Banyan [i.e. an Indian servant of a European master] in the most forcible and glowing colour. He next went into a short but admirably drawn history of the people, religion, manners, and revolutions of the Gentoo tribes—their division into casts—their local religion and prejudices—the irruption and change made by the Mahometan—the revolution accomplished by the Tartar Tamerlane, and the slow but more portentous consequences of the English inroad. In the course of his speech he worked up the passions of the Court in so powerful a manner, when he described the sufferings of the native Hindoos under the government of Mr. Hastings, that the Court repeatedly called out HEAR! HEAR![55]

[54] Burke, *Writings and Speeches*, 5:390; subsequent citations appear in the text.
[55] *The Trial of Warren Hastings, Esq. Late Governor General of Bengal* (London, 1788), 3.

It is clear that, as in the earlier speech on Fox's India Bill, Burke aimed to establish both sympathetic understanding and historical comprehension. His audience on this first day could not have known, however, how much further Burke intended to take them along this path, as the relatively distanced observations of the opening survey of manners and civilization gave way on the third day to passages that registered the details of the most dreadful crimes. "In this part of his speech," the same contemporary account reports, "Mr. Burke's descriptions were more vivid—more harrowing—and more horrific—than human utterance on either fact or fancy, perhaps, ever formed before. The agitation of most people was very apparent—and Mrs. Sheridan was so overcome, that she fainted."[56]

Burke always stresses the vastness of India (both spatially and temporally) and hence the magnitude of the responsibilities faced by its British governors. In the earlier speech Burke had used the language of law to make the point: it was painful to him, he said, to hear members introducing the ordinary terminology of the law, as though they were managing a suit concerned with simple municipal issues (5:381–82). Similarly, in the later speech, Burke again found it important to insist that the issue of India stood well above the ordinary level of legal proceedings. In fact, a distinction of this kind would be crucial to the outcome of the trial, since much would depend on whether the evidence against Hastings was examined under the stricter rules of common law, or the more forgiving standards of the now antiquated process of impeachment. But for Burke, who was addressing public opinion as well as the Lords, the stakes were finally moral and historical rather than merely procedural. He conceded that impeachment had not been used for two generations and that the times were such that "antiquity [had] lost all its effect and reverence on the minds of men" (6:272). Nonetheless, he urged the case for reviving what he called "the oldest process known to the Constitution" very largely on the basis of tradition. In doing so, however, his concern was at least as much for the precedents that would be set as for those that were being followed—a reminder that tradition is always a prescription addressed to posterity as well as a look back to the past.[57] To allow impeachment to fall into disuse, he insisted, would be to deprive later generations of an essential part of English government. "[T]his is the cement which binds it all together," he argued. "This is the individuating principle that makes England what England is" (6:272–73).

Burke's appeal to tradition so enlarged the temporal dimension of the case that he was able to convince himself that the very identity of Britain was at stake. At the same time, he also argued that this identity was already trans-

[56] Ibid., 7–8n.

[57] In fact, Burke concluded that they would have "recommended this proceeding to posterity, even if it had not been supported by the example of our ancestors" (*Writings and Speeches*, 6:273).

formed spatially by the extension of British dominion to India, a change that gave the Lords a "boundless object" for their jurisdiction. Significantly, Burke expressed the moral enlargement attendant on this physical expansion in the familiar terms of the philosophical historian. "It is not from this Country or the other, from this district or the other, that relief is applied for, but from whole tribes of suffering nations, various descriptions of men, differing in language, in manners and in rights, men separated by every means from you" (6:277).

If Burke could invoke manners to enlarge the moral dimensions of the trial, Warren Hastings was able to marshal the same observations on diversity of language, manners, and rights to argue against the simple application of English standards of behavior to Asian conditions (6:346n). In fact, this sort of relativizing of morals and manners was one of the attractions of the anthropological perspective. For Burke, however, the need to counter Hastings's argument stood as a further provocation to his own discussion of the manners of India. Stigmatizing Hastings's plea as amounting to a system of "Geographical morality" (6:346, 361), he went on to insist that every Indian code of law, Moslem or Hindu, made it clear that, far from being the place of arbitrary rule Hastings depicted, this was a civilization characterized by the strictest forms of legality. Nor was it a matter of law alone; Burke took every opportunity to reinforce the point that the traditional order of India was upheld by its codes of manners and customs—especially its principles of aristocratic order, its reverence for the female sex, its religious institutions, its unshakable faith in the rules of caste. Conversely, in the catalogue of English crimes, perhaps the worst cruelties were those that violated these ancient codes, especially the deliberate manipulation of caste to threaten high-born Indians with defilement, perhaps the ultimate weapon in a war of manners (6:302–5).

Much more could be said on the question of aristocratic virtue in distress as a central theme of Burke's portrait of Indian manners. But I want to conclude with a dimension of Burke's study of manners that is more likely to be overlooked. The issue before the Lords was the personal guilt or innocence of Warren Hastings, but Burke chose to open on a much wider plane. He began, in fact, with a brief study of the ways that the history and political economy of the East India Company favored not just casual but systematic misrule. Burke's strategy was to depict the company as an inversion of the usual structures of political and economic governance. It was, he charged, a "State in the disguise of a Merchant." And yet if its outward form was mercantile, "the principal, inward, real part of the Company is entirely political" (6:283–84). The consequence was that these outward forms—especially the long apprenticeship that they implied—had broken down, and instead of acquiring experience under the careful watch of older men, immature youths were entrusted with excessive powers.

A further peculiarity of this commercial polity was that it was "a Commonwealth without a people" (6:285). The British had not come to India as a nation, but simply as a cadre of officials. The company formed "a Kingdom of Magistrates" united by a strong bond of common interest, while feeling themselves equally separated "both from the Country that sent them out and from the Country in which they are" (6:286). The result was a sense of mutual dependence and loyalty—an esprit du corps—that protected abuses from the scrutiny of outsiders.

Burke accused the Company of taking young men with the title and pay of a junior or senior merchant and no knowledge of the law and giving them enormous judicial responsibilities. Worse yet, these men had been sent over to India too early to have grown up fully in the ways of their own country, hence too soon to have been socialized in its political culture. "We know too," says Burke, in a passage that gives his century's attention to manners the characteristic accents of his own creed,

> that, in the habits of civilized life, in a cultivated society, there is imbibed by men a good deal of solid practice of government, of the true maxims of State, and every thing that enables a man to serve his country. But these men are sent over to exercise functions at which a Statesman here would tremble, without any study, without any of that sort of experience which forms men gradually and insensibly to great affairs. (6:289)

One could not ask for a better summary of Burke's characteristic idea of tradition—or, more precisely, of his stress on individual experience and everyday sociality as the groundwork of the grander, historical dimensions of tradition. Too young, too inexperienced, too foreign, the immature servants of the company are forced to rely upon the guidance of their native servants, or *banyans*. For Burke, the depredations of this class of people and their perverse rule over their white, English masters emblematizes the whole structure of misrule in English India. "They serve an apprenticeship of servitude to qualify them for the trade of tyranny. They are pawns without whom an European can do nothing" (6:292).

Tradition and Prolepsis

The substantial common ground that Burke shared with his Scottish contemporaries points to the ways in which Burkean understanding of history continued and complicated the central themes of eighteenth-century historical thought, creating yet another version of the formal and conceptual problems raised when history's object of study became enlarged and socially mediated. But Burke's invocation of tradition not only stands as confirmation of this eighteenth-century expansion, it also served many nineteenth-century historians as a crucial means of solving some of the problems of narrative that ensued.

We have already seen in other contexts that the problem of constructing a narrative on the wide horizon of eighteenth-century social thought provoked a variety of experiments with both the forms and the thematics of historical narration. In similar ways, the emergent idea of tradition offered its own possibilities for reconstituting historical narrative in the light of new questions and new audiences. First, the thematics of tradition offered a useful way of grouping a variety of disparate social experiences so that they became relevant to a narration of national development. In this, tradition very much resembles "public opinion," another assimilative category that becomes ubiquitous in this period. (See chapter 11.) Second, the long view associated with tradition redrew the time-horizon of historical narrative, with considerable consequences for the ways narrative was constructed. Surprisingly, perhaps, the result was not an increased stress on historical distance, but rather a desire to bring elements of remoter times forward and make them bridges to the present moment.

To follow these large changes into the great body of nineteenth-century historiography is well beyond the scope of this book and has been done beautifully elsewhere.[58] Anticipations of this sort of reconfiguration, however, can be clearly seen in another of Mackintosh's early works, the "Defense of Jean Peltier" (1803), to which I will now turn.

Peltier was an exiled French royalist publicist who was charged (in an interval of peace) with libeling Napoleon and inciting his assassination. The case, though not so grand an occasion as the Hastings impeachment, brought Mackintosh a good deal of attention and an opportunity of his own to survey history for the special purposes of a political trial. For Mackintosh, however, the organizing concept was not manners, but the related idea of opinion—another legacy of Humean philosophical history that acquired new urgency in the ideological and national contests of the 1790s.

In strict legalities, there was little doubt of the guilt of Jean Peltier, but Mackintosh vastly enlarged the scope of the trial by turning his defense into an impassioned plea for preserving the liberty of the press. Francis Horner, reviewing the "Defense" in the *Edinburgh Review*, wrote admiringly, "those principles have never been illustrated with such force of historical painting, such extent of philosophical reflection, and such warmth of oratorical diction."[59] Horner was perhaps forgetting the *Areopagitica*. But, in contrast to

[58] See especially John Burrow's study of nineteenth-century historical writing, *A Liberal Descent*.

[59] *Edinburgh Review* 2 (1803): 478. The editors of the new collection of Horner's papers stress the motives of political ambition that may have motivated Horner's praises. (See Kenneth Bourne and William Banks Taylor, eds., *The Horner Papers: Selections from the Letters and Miscellaneous Writings of Francis Horner, M.P., 1795–1817* [Edinburgh: Edinburgh UP, 1994], 17, 210.)

Milton, Mackintosh was less concerned to argue for the liberty of the press than to present Britain as the particular homeland of such freedoms and its last asylum in postrevolutionary Europe. This thematization of press freedom as the salient feature of English history is what makes his speech an invocation of tradition. In this case, however, the tradition defended is not Burke's spirit of the gentleman and the church, but rather the idea of liberty of opinion, as protected by the sturdy independence of English juries.[60] In short, though it has its mix of Burkean nostalgia, Mackintosh's representation of an English tradition of liberty was fundamentally whiggish and progressive.

Despite the evident nationalism of his central arguments, Mackintosh was a man of cosmopolitan sympathies, and some of the most interesting passages in the speech salute the now vanished possibilities for freedom of discussion in the middling and smaller states of the old Europe. "These Governments," he writes, "were in many respects one of the most interesting parts of the antient system of Europe" (85). Exempted themselves from a desire for domination and free to cultivate literature and reason, they were "the impartial spectators and judges" of the contests of the larger powers. Their position made them peculiarly qualified to be "the organs of that public opinion which converted Europe into a great republic."[61] Now, however, these refuges of opinion have disappeared, along with "those antient principles," which had protected them from more aggressive states. Britain was now the only protector of free discussion. "Every other monument of European liberty has perished.—That ancient fabric which has been gradually reared by the wisdom and virtue of

But Brougham's response both to the speech and to Horner's review deserves attention: "As to Peltier, still more of the *con amore*, but, by God, the speech deserved much, and I don't see why a review should be devoid of passions" (*Horner Papers*, 299). In the same collection, see also Horner's comments on Mackintosh in a letter to J. A. Murray of the same period, where Horner acknowledges Mackintosh's debt to Burke while defending his independence and importance (301).

[60] Mackintosh stresses the role of juries, among other "securities" established by "our ancestors" against the wide powers of government. Juries, he writes, were "popular in their origin, popular in their feelings, popular in their very prejudices, taken from the mass of the people, and immediately returning to that mass again." [James Mackintosh,] *The Trial of John Peltier, Esq. for a libel against Napoleon Buonaparte, First Consul of the French Republic* (London, 1803), 90–91; subsequent citations are given in the text.

[61] Ibid., 85–86. Mackintosh carries Smith's idea of spectatorship to the international stage. "If acts of internal tyranny were perpetrated, they resounded from a thousand presses throughout all civilized countries. Princes on whose will there were no legal checks, thus found a moral restraint which the most powerful of them could not brave with absolute impunity. They acted before a vast audience, to whose applause or condemnation they could not be utterly indifferent. The very constitution of human nature, the unalterable laws of the mind of man, against which all rebellion is fruitless, subjected the proudest tyrants to this controul. No elevation of power, no depravity, however consummate . . . can render man wholly independent of the praise or blame of his fellow men" (86).

our fathers still stands—It stands, thanks be to God! solid and entire—but it stands alone and it stands amidst ruins" (89).

Mackintosh's language here is resonant of both Smith and Burke (with anticipations of Tocqueville), but the central preoccupation with opinion is very much his own. In the *Vindiciae*, speaking in the rationalist and optimistic tones of his early politics, he had presented the English Revolution as an event less significant for its immediate political consequences than as a powerful first step in a revolution of opinion. A dozen years later in the very different circumstances surrounding the Peltier trial, he joined his concern for free opinion to the need to maintain the loyalty of the whole English people, including its more popular elements.[62] Mackintosh emphasized the crucial importance of public spirit, which he called "the chief defensive principle of a state" (99). In comparison to the *Vindiciae*, this was a way of thinking about opinion that was avowedly less rationalist. But Mackintosh could convince himself that, for Britons at least, public spirit and the free expression of public opinion amounted to much the same thing. "Of all the stimulants which rouse it [i.e., public spirit] into action," Mackintosh warned, "the most powerful among us is certainly the Press; and it cannot be restrained or weakened without imminent danger, that the national spirit may languish and that the people may act with less zeal and affection for their country in the hour of its danger."[63]

Mackintosh's thematization of freedom of the press as capturing the essential character of English historical experience is carried forward on several levels. In addressing the jury he called upon the ancient ways of English justice as created by those "who slowly built up the fabric of our laws."[64] In proclaiming his own populist political credo, he insisted that his principles were "genuine old English principles" (100), even if they had been abused by fanatics in the present day. He touched on some of the familiar themes of Whig historical myth, notably that Britain as a great commercial nation had no interests on the continent but those of peace and justice. But most of all, in pursuing his theme of the growth of free opinion, he offered the jury a brief history of

[62] Mackintosh emphasizes the need "not to forget the political rights which are not uniformly with-held from the lowest classes" and the need to appeal to them in the name of the interests of the state. "Whoever were unwarily and rashly to abolish or narrow these privileges (which it must be owned are liable to great abuse, and to very specious objections) might perhaps discover, too late, that he had been dismantling his country" (ibid., 99).

[63] Ibid., 99–100. Public spirit, Mackintosh writes, depends less on the advantages of a free government, which are prized by "calm reason, than upon those part [*sic*] of it which delight the imagination, and flatter the just and natural pride of mankind" (99).

[64] Ibid., 89. The accused was grateful, Mackintosh proclaimed, that "we still continue to meet together, after the manner of our fathers, to administer justice in this her ancient sanctuary" (83). The contrast, of course, was to the course of justice in Peltier's homeland.

the past three centuries as a rehearsal for the present contest between British freedom and French despotism. The proleptic strategy—and the power it gives to memory—is fully explicit:

> I cannot conclude without bringing before you the sentiments and examples of our ancestors in some of those awful and perilous situations by which Divine Providence has in former ages tried the virtue of the English nation. We are fallen upon times in which it behoves us to strengthen our spirits by the contemplation of great examples of constancy. Let us seek for them in the annals of our forefathers. (148)

The central figure here is Elizabeth—a rather unlikely reading, given Mackintosh's admiration of Hume, who had offended many patriotic Britons by comparing Elizabeth's personal rule to the powers of an oriental despot.[65] For Mackintosh, however, Elizabeth's reign opened the modern history of England, especially in its relations to the state-system of Europe, and stood as the first of several eras in which English freedom of opinion was pitted against continental oppression. Opposing her stood Philip II, who as the leader of Catholic Europe exercised "formidable power over opinion" and pursued dreams of universal domination (149). Elizabeth's only really effectual ally in the defense of European liberties was the spirit of her people, and it was her genius—Mackintosh calls it "a sort of prophetic instinct"—to see how powerful an instrument the press could be in rousing their support.[66] In a subsequent period, the "great conspirator" against civil and religious liberty was Louis XIV, but the English people were betrayed by their Stuart monarchs, and it was left to the Dutch government to uphold the existence of a free press.[67] Only with the revolution did the British return to "the feelings and principles of their ancestors" (157). Finally, in the course of the eighteenth century, the spread of newspapers brought a great change in the state of political discussion on both domestic and foreign politics. The multiplication of these channels of popular information produced what Mackintosh calls "a gradual revolution" in government. "By increasing the number of those who exercise some sort of judgment

[65] For the sense of injury that Hume's portrait of Elizabeth's reign produced, see William Belsham, "On the Reign and Character of Queen Elizabeth," in *Essays, Philosophical, Historical, and Literary*, 2 vols. (London, 1799), 2:1–48.

[66] *Trial of John Peltier*, 152: "when I consider that this mode of rousing a national spirit was then absolutely unexampled, that she could have no assurance of its efficacy from the precedents of former times, I am disposed to regard her having recourse to it as one of the most sagacious experiments, one of the greatest discoveries of political genius, one of the most striking anticipations of future experience, that we find in history. I mention it to you, to justify the opinion that I have ventured to state, of the close connexion of our national spirit with our press, and even our periodical press."

[67] Ibid., 156: the Dutch government was "then charged with the defence of a free press against the oppressor of Europe, as a sacred trust for the benefit of all generations. They felt the sacredness of the deposit, they felt the dignity of the station in which they were placed."

on public affairs, it has created a substantial democracy, infinitely more important than those democratical forms which have been the subject of so much contest" (161).

Mackintosh left for India soon after the Peltier case, and his checkered career as a historian makes it difficult to pursue these questions into work that is formally historiographical: it was not until 1830 that he published the semi-popular survey called *The History of England*, where a number of the themes adumbrated in the Peltier speech reappeared, though tempered by other elements present in a more complex narrative. In the same year as the Peltier trial, however, the Scottish anti-Jacobin writer Robert Bisset published a history that exhibits both the thematics and poetics of national tradition with particular clarity. As it happens, the author was an admirer of Mackintosh's, as well as the author of an early and sympathetic biography of Edmund Burke.

Bisset turned his hand to many forms of writing, all of them vehicles for his anti-Jacobin political ideas. In addition to his biography of Burke (1799; 2d ed. 1800), he wrote and edited a literary and political magazine modeled on the *Anti-Jacobin Review*. His *Sketch of Democracy* (1796) is a polemical historical essay, attacking the "speculative" ideas of ancient and modern democrats in the name of a Burkean dogma of "experience." He also published several novels, all with political themes. Though history was at the center of all his literary activity, his multivolumed *History of the Reign of George III* (1803) was his only venture into formal historiography.

Bisset prefaced his *George III* with a long introductory book, which he called a "A view of the progressive improvement of England, in prosperity and strength to the accession of His Majesty." Here British history is marshaled in the same unabashedly proleptic manner already familiar in Mackintosh's speech in defense of Peltier—though the resulting foreshortening seems much cruder in the context of a formal history. Thematically, too, there are some differences, since for Bisset the "progressive improvement of England" is mostly a question of commerce and national prestige. Bisset's primary theme is, in fact, social and imperial: an anticipated future of commercial prosperity and naval dominance guides this narrative, not liberty of the press or the ancient constitution. From the remotest epochs of British history, in fact, the commercial destiny of Britain is the standard by which every event is ultimately evaluated. Even the Roman conquest figures primarily as the discovery of Britain's potential resources. "From her civilized subduers," he writes, "Britain first learned the power which she possessed, and which, inspired by liberty and enlightened by knowledge, she has since carried to so unparalleled an extent."[68]

[68] Robert Bisset, *The History of the Reign of George III. To the Termination of the Late War. To which is prefixed, A View of the Progressive Improvement of England in Prosperity and Strength; to the Accession of his Majesty*, 6 vols. (London, 1803), 1:3.

Rather than entering into the detail of Bisset's "view," let me simply take note of a series of marginal glosses drawn from the early pages. Though no history should be judged on such material, these brief advertisements for Britain's commercial and imperial destiny convey a quick sense of the direction in which Bisset steers his narrative: "Saxons begin to understand the importance of naval force and of commerce (8); "Alfred discerns that the security and aggrandizement of England must arise from her navy" (11); "Contest with the maritime depredators beneficial to England" (13); "Edward III in Flanders discovers the importance of manufactures and commerce" (17); "Wars of Lancaster and York interrupt the progressive advancement of England, internal and external" (20); "In England the middle class preserves liberty" (24); "Henry VII. Improvements under him. He reduces the feudal aristocracy, and encourages navigation and nautical discovery (25–26); "Political security, the principle of English interference in foreign affairs" (40).

It would be easy to make fun of such blatant foreshortening of England's early history. My point, however, is not the crudity with which Bisset fashioned a history to match the commercial and imperial present—which after all was the principal task of nineteenth-century historiography—but rather to underscore the fact that his Burkean faith consistently led him to collapse the distances separating his early-nineteenth-century reader from otherwise remote chapters of national history.

The point is best made contrastively by taking one last look back to the philosophical historians of the previous generation. The likely model for Bisset's "view" was William Robertson, who had used a similar device to open his *History of Scotland* (1759) and his *Charles V* (1769). (The "View of the Progress of Society" that introduces the latter is, of course, one of the great set-pieces of Enlightenment philosophical history; the earlier "Review of the Scottish History previous to the death of James V" keeps closer to traditional patterns of national narrative, but serves the same function as its more famous successor.) In making use of the opening "view," Bisset, like Robertson, signaled his desire to accommodate tasks that could not easily be reconciled within the structure of a single narrative. And in both writers the consequence was to give the thematics of "progressive improvement" a saliency that would not have been possible if the same elements had to be woven through long passages of conventional narrative.

Robertson's "Review of the Scottish History" bears an obvious resemblance to Bisset's later summary, but the points of similarity only make the difference all the more striking. The *History of Scotland* presents a history framed by an idea of difference, and nowhere more so than in its introductory "Review." In stark contrast to Bisset's continual assimilation of earlier history to later themes, Robertson's predominant message concerns the remoteness and even unknowability of the medieval past. "The first ages of the Scottish history are dark and fabulous," Robertson writes at the start of his "Review." "Nations, as well as men, arrive at maturity by degrees, and the events, which happened during their infancy or early youth, cannot be recollected, and deserve not to be remembered."[69]

Of the four epochs into which he divides Scottish history, Robertson explains that the main body of his work will deal only with the last, the beginnings of Scotland's modern history, for which information was abundant. Similarly, he did not extend the introductory "Review" to the whole course of Scottish history prior to that time, but summarized only the relatively well-lit third period (1286–1542). Even here, however, Robertson stressed the obstacles to understanding, which arose not only from paucity of information, but from the peculiar stamp of Scottish history. Indeed, it is very striking that Robertson consistently accepts *English* institutions and developments as normative, not those of his native country, thus rendering the history of medieval Scotland doubly a history of difference.

For all that, Robertson's assumptions about Scottish history were certainly as progressive as Bisset's, and the book ends with a paean to the effects of the Union in bringing Scotland into a prosperous modernity.[70] The history Robertson recounts, however, concerns the preceding epoch—the time before the time of progress, though preparatory to it. For the moderate and polished modern Scot, that time was now over, and the progress made in the present century offered a vantage from which earlier struggles could be resolved into their due proportion and appropriate distance.

Time and Custom

Hume shared Robertson's perspectives and admired his elegant *History*, and certainly he would have found Bisset's foreshortening crude and propagandistic. Nonetheless, in a remarkable passage from the *Treatise*, Hume outlined the psychological mechanisms at work in such a writing of tradition. "Time and custom," he wrote, "give authority to all forms of government, and all succession of princes; and that power which was at first founded only on injus-

[69] William Robertson, *The History of Scotland*, 2 vols. (London, 1761), 1:1.

[70] Witness Robertson's summary of the effects of the Union: "At length the Union having incorporated the two nations, and rendered them one people, the distinctions which had subsisted for many ages gradually wear away; peculiarities disappear; the same manners prevail in both parts of the island; the same authors are read and admired; the same entertainments are frequented by the elegant and polite; and the same standard of taste and of purity in language, is established. And the Scots, after being placed during a whole century, in a situation no less fatal to the liberty than to the taste and genius of the nation, were at once put in possession of privileges more valuable than those which their ancestors had formerly enjoyed; and every obstruction that had retarded their pursuit, or prevented their acquisition of literary fame, was entirely removed" (ibid., 2:306–7).

tice and violence, becomes in time legal and obligatory. Nor does the mind rest there; but returning back upon its footsteps, transfers to its predecessors and ancestors that right, which it naturally ascribes to their posterity, as being related together, and united in the imagination."[71]

This passage gives us the opportunity once again to observe how differently Hume and Burke situated themselves in relation to what both recognized as the power of tradition. Where Burke fashioned his rhetoric to cooperate with the workings of "time and custom," Hume studied tradition as a phenomenon of the imagination—a kind of necessary illusion that is foundational for government. According to Hume, tradition is the consequence of an activity of mind, which is drawn to regularity in social life as in nature. This desire for relatedness makes us read the sequences of history in both directions, not only from past to present, but (however illogical it may seem) from present to past. Contrary to conventional wisdom, in other words, which casts tradition simply as the past imposing itself on the present, Hume recognized that the power of tradition also shows itself in proleptic readings of history in which the present models the past.

Hume's insight helps to explain the paradox that taking the long view of history—which is what we do when we write history in the framework of tradition—so often leads to presentism. The consequence, as I said earlier, may be the sort of fallacy Butterfield stigmatized as the "whig interpretation," by which historical continuities are invoked in order to authorize a current creed. But Hume's insight into the proleptic imagination has implications far beyond the kind of simple reductiveness so evident in Bisset. Many Europeans of this period were engaged by a desire to recover a new, more immediate relationship to their past. (Tradition, of course, was one name for this altered relationship.) The index of this desire, registered in all genres of historical representation, was a characteristic shift of historical distance, and it soon made the histories of the eighteenth century seem remote and unreadable to the audiences of the new century.

[71] Hume, *Treatise of Human Nature*, 566.

LITERARY HISTORY, MEMOIR, AND THE IDEA OF COMMEMORATION IN EARLY-NINETEENTH-CENTURY BRITAIN

Ten

"The Comedy of Middle Life": Francis Jeffrey and Literary History

FOR TWO and a half decades Francis Jeffrey directed the *Edinburgh Review*, which he made the most influential periodical of the age. Though Jeffrey contributed an astonishing number of essays to the review and wrote on a broad range of subjects, scholars have focused almost exclusively on his literary criticism, especially his hostility to Wordsworth and the Lake poets.[1] In a study of the climate of reception for historical writing, however, there are good reasons to go back to Jeffrey, since on history as on other topics, he played no small part in forming the standards of public judgment in whose name he wrote.[2] But Jeffrey's writings are much more than an index of educated opinion in the first part of the nineteenth century; he and his circle of reviewers played a key role in transmitting and adapting the historical interests of their Enlightenment mentors to a new generation of readers.

We will lose much of the value of Jeffrey's views on history, however, if we pay attention only to what he called "regular history." His writing covered a wide territory, indicative of what Bagehot would later call the "general, diversified, omnipresent information of the North." With respect to questions of historical reception, this breadth of interest is invaluable since it gives us ample

[1] The most engaging introduction to Jeffrey and his circle remains Henry Cockburn's *Memorials of His Time* (Edinburgh, 1856; rpt. Edinburgh: James Thin, 1988), as well as his *Life of Lord Jeffrey, With a Selection from his Correspondence*, 2 vols. (Edinburgh, 1852). Modern scholarship on the Edinburgh reviewers begins with John Clive, *Scotch Reviewers: The Edinburgh Review, 1802–1815* (London: Faber, 1957). See also Bianca Maria Fontana, *Rethinking the Politics of Commercial Society: The Edinburgh Review, 1802–1832* (Cambridge: Cambridge UP, 1985). On the intellectual milieu of the reviewers, see J. W. Burrow, Stephan Collini, and Donald Winch, *That Noble Science of Politics: A Study in Nineteenth-Century Intellectual History* (Cambridge: Cambridge UP, 1983), chap. 1. For his criticism, in addition to the work of Bate cited in n. 3 below, see James Greig, *Francis Jeffrey of the "Edinburgh Review"* (Edinburgh: Oliver and Boyd, 1948); and Peter Morgan, *Literary Critics and Reviewers in Early Nineteenth-Century Britain* (Beckenham, Kent: Croom Helm, 1983). Morgan has collected some of Jeffrey's important literary essays as *Jeffrey's Criticism* (Edinburgh: Scottish Academic P, 1983). On the importance of periodicals in the formation of reading publics in this period, see especially Jon Klancher, *The Making of English Reading Audiences, 1790–1832* (Madison: U of Wisconsin P, 1987).

[2] On Jeffrey as a Humean spokesman for educated opinion, see David Bromwich's comparison between Jeffrey and Hazlitt, in *A Choice of Inheritance: Self and Community from Edmund Burke to Robert Frost* (Cambridge: Harvard UP, 1989), 10–12. The comparison is a useful one, though too obviously tinged with advocacy for a certain style of romantic individualism.

opportunities to see history not as an isolated literature, but as a family of genres occupying a key location—though a contested one—in a whole culture of letters.

Jeffrey's essays on literature are generally arranged under the single category of "criticism," where, as I have already remarked, attention has been directed especially to his views on Wordsworth and the Lake poets. A good part of Jeffrey's literary writing, however, might be better seen as contributions to literary history, an emergent genre that, much like the novel, both complemented and rivaled "regular" history.[3] Jeffrey's writings on both kinds of history—the histories of the literary as well as of the political nation—should be read together for what they can tell us about the possibilities of historical narrative in this period.

The intrinsic interest of Jeffrey's ideas is, quite obviously, enhanced by the importance of the role he created for himself as editor of the *Edinburgh Review.* But the journal's success was owed to something more than simply his own individual talents, or those of the small circle of gifted and self-confident young friends grouped around him. Their achievements, as well as many of the principle themes of their writings, reflected their position as inheritors of the outlook and energies of the Scottish Enlightenment. Jeffrey's own life is particularly interesting in this respect, since he stands as a link between the generation of Dugald Stewart and that of Carlyle and Macaulay, both of whose early work owed a great deal to Jeffrey's interest and support. For anyone interested in the history of historical thought in Britain, there is surely something remarkable about a man who could count himself friend and patron to two sensibilities so different and yet so characteristic of the following generation.

Jeffrey's success as an editor owed much to a network of friendships that combined sentimental and intellectual attachment in a high degree. "Edinburgh had never contained such a concentration of young men as now inspired it," wrote Jeffrey's friend and biographer Henry Cockburn, "of whose presence the Review was only one of the results."[4] This network, it seems, was made possible both by the scale of life in the Scottish capital and by the consciousness shared among the members of this circle of forwarding and adapting a singular heritage of Scottish speculation. Cockburn, whose *Memorials* are the affectionate chronicle of this generation, depicts Jeffrey's circle of young Whig lawyers as "doomed youths" who—excluded from preferment in Tory-dominated Edinburgh—congregated in the Outer House of the law courts (149).

Ironically, considering Edinburgh's reputation for enlightenment, Cockburn explains the intellectual distinctiveness of his peers by the repressive anti-intellectualism of the city in his youth. His elders spoke of little else but the

[3] On Jeffrey's views on literary influence and hence literary history, see the acute discussion in Bate, *Burden of the Past*, 99–103.

[4] Cockburn, *Memorials of His Time*, 176; subsequent citations are given in the text.

French Revolution, which they made their justification for discouraging any sort of intellectual independence or speculation. Of Adam Smith, he adds by way of characterizing the times, his father's generation knew nothing, "except that he had recently been a Commissioner of Customs, and had written a sensible book" (45–46).

The principal enlightener of the younger generation in Edinburgh was Dugald Stewart, whose teaching Cockburn describes in heartfelt terms, making it clear that it shaped their moral and intellectual ambitions. It was because of Stewart and his links to the generation of Hume and Smith that Cockburn could proudly contrast the narrowness of mind of his father's circle to the eagerness of his own generation for contact with the works of the Enlightenment: "The young, by which I mean the liberal young of Edinburgh, lived upon [Smith]. With Hume, Robertson, Millar, Montesquieu, Ferguson, and De Lolme, he supplied them with most of their mental food" (46).

In looking back from the vantage of the 1820s, Cockburn was well aware that he saw the companions of his youth with a special affection that was enhanced by the dispersal of their gifted circle. The departure of Francis Horner, Sydney Smith, Henry Brougham, John Allen, and others left their group "thinned by emigration"—its key members, as he puts it in another place, "devoured by hungry London" (176, 181). But what Cockburn seems unwilling to recognize is that the same centrifugal energies that propelled his friends' careers beyond Scotland also played their part in the parallel dispersal of Scottish opinion through the pages of Britain's most influential review. Through twenty-seven years of Jeffrey's editorship and beyond, the "liberal young" of Edinburgh became some of the foremost opinion-makers of Britain.

Decentering the Political Narrative

Jeffrey outlined his views on the limitations of "regular" history in his essay of 1808 on Charles James Fox's posthumous *History of the Early Part of the Reign of James the Second*, a work that I mentioned in an earlier chapter because of Fox's insistence on the absolute primacy of narrative in historical composition (see chapter 3). In reviewing the work of this hero of the Whig party, Jeffrey had the delicate job of separating Fox's politics from his historiography, so that he could praise Fox as a champion of a beleaguered British liberty while also condemning his misguidedly narrow view of historical composition. In fact, Jeffrey's stance on both the political and historiographical issues raised by Fox's narrative can be traced to much the same fundamental commitment. Jeffrey, one of the foremost opinion-makers of his day, believed that in politics power ultimately rests with "public opinion," which in modern times he generally identified with the views of an enlightened middle class. By extension, history's most important function was to give an account of the character and experience of those social groups most actively engaged in shaping general opinion. Unfortunately, however, Fox's commitment to purity of narrative had narrowed the scope of his history, reducing its value as a history of opinion.

On the political front, Jeffrey welcomed Fox's posthumous history in the hope that this account of an English revolution by a famous Whig politician might encourage a revival of the discussion of liberty in Britain. Until the French Revolution, he writes, the growth of wealth and education in the lower and middling orders had been working to extend the power of "public opinion, which is in all countries the great operating check upon authority."[5] Unfortunately, revolutionary excesses in France had done incalculable harm to the interests of "practical liberty," and now, long after the threat of Jacobinism—always exaggerated—had clearly receded, the apologists of power still used it as a shield.

But while drawing strength from Fox's politics, Jeffrey remained sharply critical of the narrow limits Fox had imposed on himself as a writer of history. For Jeffrey, the question of narrative went well beyond superficial considerations of style or even of structure. Since Fox had forbidden himself to follow Hume's example in the use of appendices, one particular limitation was that he had found no way to take notice of contemporary literature, though "nothing could serve so well to illustrate [the] true state and condition [of the times] as a correct estimate and description of the great authors they produced" (1:526). I will return later in this chapter to the view of literary history suggested by this remark; for the moment it is important to see how far-reaching Jeffrey's objection really was. For Jeffrey, in fact, Fox's exclusionary principle of narrative raised questions about the fundamental issue of what makes the historical process intelligible at all. All "permanent and important occurrences in the internal history of a country" are the result of changes in the "general character" of its people—changes from which kings and ministers take their cue. "To trace the causes and the modes of its variation, is therefore to describe the true sources of events; and merely to narrate the occurrences to which it gave rise, is to recite a history of actions without intelligible motives, and of effects without assignable causes."[6]

Jeffrey's confidently expressed views on social change are, of course, the legacy of Montesquieu, Hume, Smith, Ferguson, and Millar—the writers that Cockburn said provided the "mental food" of his generation. So complete, in

[5] Jeffrey, *Contributions to the Edinburgh Review*, 2d ed., 3 vols. (London, 1846), 1:521; subsequent citations are given in the text.

[6] Ibid., 1:527. Jeffrey's view on the scope of historical composition remained consistent. His last substantial contribution to the *Review*—an admiring and nostalgic essay of 1835 on Mackintosh—once again upheld the idea of a broad, philosophic history against the "singular notion that history should consist of narrative only" (3:671–73).

fact, was his absorption of their views that he could scarcely entertain any other basis for understanding society, and he rejected Fox's fussy classicism with a sort of calculated impatience. In the process, Jeffrey was unusually explicit about the consequences of the Enlightenment critique of social knowledge for history's traditional focus on politics. He freely acknowledged that political events themselves play their part in the formation of the character of a people, but he denied that politics is the leading agent in this process, as traditional historical narrative would imply. It is undoubtedly true, he writes, "that political events operate in their turn on that national character by which they are previously moulded and controuled: but they are very far, indeed, from being the chief agent in its formation; and the history of those very events is necessarily imperfect, as well as uninstructive, if the consideration of those other agents is omitted" (1:527).

In short, Jeffrey's response to Fox stands as a kind of summary of the process of the recentering of historical narrative that I have been tracing (though generally in less self-conscious or explicit texts); and it is worth noting that he concludes his discussion of the insufficiency of politics with remarks that anticipate the central principle of Carlyle's eccentric brand of historicism, the idea that history is "the essence of innumerable biographies." Rather than politics, Jeffrey writes, the forces shaping the character of the nation consist of "everything which affects the character of individuals:—manners, education, prevailing occupations, religion, taste, and, above all, the distribution of wealth, and the state of prejudice and opinions" (1:527).

Jeffrey had a particular fondness for historical memoirs and other parahistoriographical genres because, much more than "regular history," they offered direct access to "the state of prejudice and opinions." As he wrote many years later, private diaries, letter collections, and the like are "the true key to the cipher in which public annals are almost necessarily written."[7] Indeed, Jeffrey seldom comments on historical memoirs without speaking of his enjoyment of the genre and advocating its value as a corrective to conventional history. His criticism of conventional historiography takes larger and smaller forms; sometimes its terms seem primarily empirical, sometimes primarily moral. But in one way or another the issue remains that "regular" history lacks access to everyday life and hence to the most fundamental experiences of society. In fact, much of his most interesting commentary on the problems of historical representation arises from consideration of memoirs and other parahistoriographical genres.

[7] Review of *Memoirs of Lady Fanshawe* (first published in *ER*, 1829), in ibid., 1:464. Jeffrey adds, in the sort of language of resurrection that is more often associated with Godwin or Carlyle, "and their disclosure, after long intervals of time, is almost as good as the revocation of their writers from the dead—to abide our interrogatories, and to act over again, before us, in the very dress and accents of the time, a portion of the scenes which they once guided or adorned" (1:465).

A case in point is the review of Lucy Hutchinson that appeared in the same year as the essay on Fox. Jeffrey greeted the first publication of this seventeenth-century memoir with an enthusiasm he could not feel for Fox's narrative, and he took the chance to restate his criticisms of "regular history" in positive terms. "By far the most important part of history," writes Jeffrey, "is that which makes us acquainted with the character, dispositions, and opinions of the great and efficient population by whose motion or consent all things are ultimately governed. After a nation has attained to any degree of intelligence, every other principle of action becomes subordinate."[8]

This broadly "philosophical" observation frames Jeffrey's reading of Hutchinson in a manner that differs substantially from the sentimental reading promoted by the work's editor, Julius Hutchinson. (See chapter 3 above.) Like Julius Hutchinson, Jeffrey valued the memoir for the access it gave to private life, including the private lives of women—a group, as he remarks, so often absent from general histories (1:439). For him, however, the memoir's real importance resided in the portrait it supplied of the English gentry, who in the largely rural, agricultural world of the seventeenth century constituted "the truly governing part of society." Country gentlemen were then "all in all in England; and the nation at large derived from them its habits, prejudices, and opinions."[9] Their manners had not yet been Europeanized, but still retained the national peculiarities that "united and endeared them" to the rest of their countrymen, including a certain religious seriousness that later was turned to caricature by the courtly wits of the Restoration. "There is nothing, in short, more curious and instructive," writes Jeffrey,

> than the glimpses which we here catch of the old hospitable and orderly life of the country gentlemen of England, in those days when the national character was so high and so peculiar—when civilization had produced all its effects but that of corruption—and when serious studies and dignified pursuits had not yet been abandoned to a paltry and effeminate derision. (1:438)

I will return to the scheme of national history hinted at here—the rustic sincerities of old England done away with by the courtly, frivolous, and French-dominated culture of the Restoration—in discussing Jeffrey's views on literary history. For the present, I want only to observe the shifts of tone that take us from the austere historical sociology of the opening remarks to this celebration of a specifically English national character in which Burkean accents predominate, though echoes of Ferguson or Millar remain. "England

[8] Jeffrey, *Contributions to Edinburgh Review*, 1:436. The review of Hutchinson first appeared in the *ER* in 1808.

[9] Ibid., 1:436. Jeffrey refers to the "rustic aristocracy" and the "country gentlemen." The terms point to the lesser aristocracy or gentry, rather than the peerage and larger landholders.

should be proud, we think," Jeffrey writes at the end of the piece, "of having given birth to Mrs. Hutchinson and her husband; and chiefly because their characters are truly and peculiarly English; according to the standard of those times in which national characters were most distinguishable" (1:462).

Jeffrey returned to his "philosophic" mode in an essay of 1812 on English government ("Leckie") whose central theme is the power and importance of public opinion.[10] The essay generalizes the concerns of the Hutchinson review, making the connection between class and opinion a key question for both politics and history. The proper flow of opinion, Jeffrey now argued, virtually defined the proper functioning of government in the present age, while arbitrary blockages to public opinion explained the breakdown of effective government in the past, most spectacularly in 1649 and 1789.

The fundamental role Jeffrey assigns to opinion rests on the historical assumption sketched in the earlier essay and here restated in still more general terms, namely that "actual power" in society belongs to "the predominant mass of physical and intellectual force in every community."[11] This axiom of politics combines Hume's idea that all governments, even despotic ones, are effectively based on consent with the Harringtonian view that power follows the "balance of property."[12] The effect was to give the often vague idea of opinion a real historical concreteness by tying it to the views of those groups that we might now call hegemonic and that Jeffrey calls "the efficient force of the nation" or "the efficient body of the people." Jeffrey took it as a certainty that the class enjoying this hegemonic position would ultimately be able to impel the government "in the direction of its interests and inclinations." As a result, the fundamental question of politics for him—as famously for Macaulay at the time of the Reform Bill—came down to the choice whether political and constitutional arrangements would work to facilitate or to obstruct this neces-

[10] On the history of the concept of opinion, and especially "public opinion," see J. A. W. Gunn, *Beyond Liberty and Property* (Kingston: McGill Queen's UP, 1983), chap. 7. Gunn stresses that the aphorism that opinion rules the world was already an old one in the eighteenth century. See also, by the same author, "Opinion in Eighteenth-Century Thought: What Did the Concept Purport to Explain?" *Utilitas* 5 (1993): 17–33.

[11] Jeffrey, *Contributions to Edinburgh Review*, 3:157. The review of Gould Francis Leckie, *Essay on the Practice of the British Government*, was first published in *ER*, 1812. Jeffrey made the same point in still more universal language in 1814. Summing up the lessons to be understood in the new Europe that will follow Napoleon's overthrow, he writes that "public opinion had tacitly acquired a commanding and uncontrollable power in every enlightened community; and that to render its operation in any degree safe, or consistent with any regular plan of administration, it was absolutely necessary to contrive some means for bringing it to act directly on the machine of government, and for bringing it regularly and openly to bear on the public counsels of the country" (*Contributions to Edinburgh Review*, 3:215; the essay was first published in April 1814).

[12] See John Pocock, "Machiavelli, Harrington, and English Political Ideologies in the Eighteenth Century," in *Politics, Language, and Time*, 104–7.

sary process.[13] Both the English and French Revolutions provided clear illustrations of what can happen when this truth is ignored too long.[14]

As a framework for history, Jeffrey's argument on power and opinion combined elements of the older "philosophical" approach with the newer and narrower focus on national concerns. His ideal picture of modern government rests on a familiar historical sociology, which contrasts the narrow confinement of primitive societies with the wide diffusion of property and the free flow of intelligence in commercial civilization—a stage of historical development for which modern Britain is clearly the model.[15] In between these extremes stand traditional regimes such as those of Stuart England or Bourbon France. But even in these authoritarian societies, he argues, there were always "channels" by which the views of the people should have reached their governors—the "channel of the press, for example, and of general literature—provincial magistracies and assemblies . . . —even the ordinary courts of law—the stage—the pulpit—and all the innumerable occasions of considerable assemblages for deliberation on local interests, election to local offices, or for mere solemnity and usage of festivity" (3:160). From a historiographical point of view, of course, such "channels" would have strategic importance for any history of opinion, such as that which Jeffrey adumbrates in these essays.

Jeffrey's essay of 1812 on Leckie built on his earlier discussion of the importance of understanding the opinions of the "truly governing part of society," though without reference to the formal historiographical concerns that had been central to his discussions of Fox and of Hutchinson. To put this another way, the essay makes the case more strongly than ever for seeing the history of opinion as a central issue for historical understanding, but fails to raise the question (which had been present in the earlier essays) of how the history of opinion is to be discovered or narrated. For a discussion of these issues, we need to turn to Jeffrey's review of Pepys, published in 1825.

It is no accident that Pepys's *Memoirs*, like Lucy Hutchinson's *Life*, provoked such a discussion; its genre as well as its historical period brought Jeffrey back to the critique of "regular" history provoked by the exaggerated purism of Charles James Fox. Under the running head "gross defects of regular

[13] "The great point, then," he writes in summary, "is to ensure a free, an authoritative, and an uninterrupted communication between the ostensible administrators of the national power and its actual constituents and depositories; and the chief distinction between a good and a bad government consists in the degree in which it affords the means of such a communication" (*Contributions to Edinburgh Review*, 3:162–63). On this argument, see Gunn, *Beyond Liberty and Property*, 294–97.

[14] See the essay on Mme. de Staël's posthumous history of the French Revolution for a restatement of his views on opinion, including a direct citation of Hume. The essay is also occasion for a discussion of the merits and shortfalls of contemporary history.

[15] See his description of "a nation abounding in independent wealth, very generally given to reading and reflection, and knit together in all its parts by a thousand means of communication and ties of mutual interest and sympathy" (*Contributions to Edinburgh Review*, 3:172).

history," Jeffrey argues that without the "minute details" that history customarily rejects as beneath its dignity, there can be no life or meaning to historical narrative:

> It is not in the grand tragedy, or rather the epic fictions, of History, that we learn the true condition of former ages—the real character of past generations, or even the actual effects that were produced on society or individuals at the time, by the great events that are there so solemnly recorded. If we have not some remnants or some infusion of the Comedy of middle life, we neither have any idea of the state and colour of the general existence, nor any just understanding of the transactions about which we are reading. (3:478)

Once again Jeffrey's words echo a rumble of complaint that had been present in British writing on history for a half century and more. History, it had been said many times, is bound up with the pomp of public life and seems deaf to the lesser circumstances of private existence. "Every one feels," Jeffrey writes, as if summing up the accepted common sense of his readership, "how necessary this information is, if we wish to understand what antiquity really was, and what manner of men existed in former generations" (3:477). But, as we have seen in earlier essays, Jeffrey gives the missing something of history a more distinct social location than had generally been true in the writers of the previous century. His "Comedy of middle life" refers simultaneously to a middling rank of people, remote from the pomp of power, and to the mixture of private activities that make up the decorum of their ordinary lives. History as tragedy or as epic, on the other hand, can only be an aristocratic fiction: it ignores "the real character" of the past and is incapable of reproducing "the state and colour of general existence."

Jeffrey's social message is somewhat softened by being coded in the language of a literary convention. Even so, it is evident that he comes close to calling for a history that could serve Britain's middle classes by giving them their own mirror on the past. Of course, he was too sophisticated a reader of history to think that "the colour of general existence" remained constant in all periods and circumstances. The country gentlemen that were "all in all" to Lucy Hutchinson's England had long since given way to other groups with better claims to constitute the "efficient force of the nation." (That, in fact, was part of the memoir's evocative charm.) But in a scheme of history predicated on both tradition and improvement—the wider diffusion of both property and "intelligence" that had enlarged the operations of opinion—the idea of succession posed no problem, and the sturdy rustic virtues of seventeenth-century British gentlemen could figure as a legacy handed down for the benefit of those very different classes who claimed the same title in the present. For Jeffrey, then, it is clear that "regular" history was hardly a sufficient guide to the past; the historical imagination needed other, parahistoriographical genres to capture the specific coloration of social life in earlier times. If we want to imagine how it would have been to live among the Greeks, he continues, we need something else beside their famous historians: the anecdotes of Plutarch, the incidental passages of the Platonic dialogues, and the details of private orations serve us better.[16] Similarly, for "personal knowledge" of the Romans, the historians will not greatly help. We need to look to the letters of Cicero, to Pliny and Seneca, to biographies and anecdotes of the empire, or the books of the civil law. For the Middle Ages, the romances embody the details of aristocratic life, while the memorialists and chroniclers offer "so many individual pictures and redundant particularities" that we have a full picture of the manners and character "and even the daily life and conversation, of the predominating classes of society." Even the lives of serfs and vassals can be traced in scattered passages of such works or in ancient ballads or legends.

Jeffrey's argument is clear and hardly needs elaboration, though I want to underline his continued attention to rank and his conviction that social life is often best revealed by the incidental detail of works written for other purposes. Still more to the point here is the brief review of English literary history that follows. Not surprisingly, he attributes our knowledge of the "ordinary life" of England in earlier centuries above all to Shakespeare, but adds the interesting point that this knowledge has been "reinforced and supported by the infinite quantity of obscure and insignificant matter which the industry of his commentators has brought back to light for his elucidation—and which the matchless charm of his popularity has again rendered both interesting and familiar."

For more recent times as well, Jeffrey continues, the best picture of manners and habits is not conveyed by any "public histories,"

> but by the writers of farces and comedies, polite essays, libels, and satires—by collections of private letters, like those of Gray, Swift, Arbuthnot, and Lord Orford—by private memoirs or journals, such as those of Mrs. Lucy Hutchinson, Swift's Journal to Stella, and Doddington's Diary—and, in still later times, by the best of our gay and satirical novels—by caricature prints—by the better newspapers and magazines,—and by various minute accounts (in the manner of Boswell's Life of Johnson) of the private life and conversation of distinguished individuals. (3:479)

This passage is not merely a summary of Jeffrey's argument about sources for understanding everyday life, it is also a brief sketch of much of what interested Jeffrey and his contributors in recent literary history. Among his own essays, for example, we find major reviews of both Swift and Hutchinson, along with others dealing with private memoirs, correspondence, and novels,

[16] This discussion is worth noting as an example of the way Jeffrey, in common with many others in his times, so often combines an appeal to the recuperative powers of the imagination with the philosophical quest for underlying structures of explanation: "for all that enables us to imagine what sort of thing it would have been to have lived among them, or even what effects were produced on the society of Athens or Sparta by the battles of Marathon or Salamis" (ibid., 3:478).

both in Britain and in its continental neighbors. But before we examine the ways in which Jeffrey worked out a view of both national literature and national character in these essays, I would like to explore what his contemporaries understood by literary history. This will require a considerable digression, but a wider background of this sort is indispensable if we are to see how Jeffrey's literary interests compared with the received views of his time. In particular, it seems important to ask whether (and how widely) Jeffrey's idea that history can be illuminated by literary works was matched by the reciprocal realization that literature should be understood in a framework of history.

Literary History as the History of Learning and Letters

The history of literary history in late-eighteenth- and early-nineteenth-century Britain presents us initially with a perplexing appearance. On the one hand it is clear that contemporary writers used the term *literary history* without apology or special explanation, an indication that the idea was relatively unproblematic for them. On the other hand, when we look for significant literary histories in this period, we have a good deal of trouble identifying texts that stand, in modern terms at least, as unquestioned representatives of this type of writing. Thomas Warton's great *History of English Poetry* (1774–81), now often seen as defining the genre, appears to have had no immediate successors, just as it had no major predecessor. This discrepancy suggests that modern conceptions of literary history may not match those of 1800 and that the genre of literary histories as we now know it was still in formation.

In 1765, Thomas Warton wrote to Thomas Percy that he was at work on his history, "which has never yet been done at *large* and in *form*."[17] Warton's claims to authority are evident, yet the publication of his history—however important in the long view—does not seem to have given immediate shape, as large works sometimes do, to a recognizable genre.[18] Like history itself, literary history continued to encompass a variety of narrative and nonnarrative forms. Ritson's fierce attacks on Warton's scholarship, for example, took the form of antiquarian commentary, not a rewriting of Warton's narrative. William Hayley wrote lengthy poems on both history and epic poetry, continuing an old tradition of verse chronicles of the history of letters, while Clara Reeve's *Progress*

[17] Thomas Warton to Thomas Percy, June 5, 1765, *The Correspondence of Thomas Warton*, ed. D. Fairer (Athens: U of Georgia P, 1995), 189.

[18] It is clearly the assumption of Wellek's pioneering study that the "rise" of English literary history culminated in Warton's *History*, the advent of which marks the beginnings of a stable and well-defined genre. Surprisingly, despite many good specialized studies, Wellek's work still remains almost alone as an attempt to assemble a comprehensive narrative of English literary history before the Romantic generation. See Rene Wellek, *The Rise of English Literary History* (Chapel Hill: U of North Carolina P, 1941).

of Romance is shaped as a dialogue and is prefatory to a tale.[19] Isaac D'Israeli's favorite vehicles for his studies were the anecdote and the miscellany. "To seise the dispositions of the Literary Character," he wrote, "I looked therefore into Literary History, and my collections exceeded my hopes."[20] But undoubtedly the most popular type of literary history was biography, probably because it possessed the least formal and most flexible approach to narrative. In the life-and-letters format pioneered by Mason in his *Life of Gray* (1774), it became possible to write a compelling biography of a great poet in whose quiet and scholarly existence the largest outward event was the move across a street separating one Cambridge college from another. Still more remarkable was the *Life of Johnson* (1791), in which, as contemporaries remarked, Boswell created a great biography out of the incidental conversation of a private man.

In contemporary usage, then, the term *literary history* incorporated a considerable range. At its homeliest, as D'Israeli will testify, literary history referred to anecdotes of the lives of men of letters—though D'Israeli also demonstrates that anecdotal history could be the vehicle for serious studies. At its grandest, literary history was said to form a central part of the history of the human mind, the ideal subject of philosophical history. A. F. Tytler, the biographer of Lord Kames, uses the term in this sense when he writes, "As the progress of the Human Mind forms a capital object in the Study of History, the State of the Arts and Science, the Religion, Laws, Government, and Manners of Nations, are material parts, even in an elementary work of this nature. The History of Literature is a most important article in this study."[21]

Most contemporary usage, however, rests somewhere closer to the middle of this spectrum and connotes a well-defined chapter of general history concerned with the history of arts and letters—a subject comparable, perhaps, to ecclesiastical history, though one (as its proponents always insist) much less written upon. A listing of works published by C. and H. Baldwin, for example, advertises Henry Steuart's translation and commentary on Sallust as "chiefly designed to illustrate the Civil, and in particular, the Literary History of the Age of Augustus."[22] Robert Henry's much-advertised "new plan" is the fullest working out of such a view of literary history. In his *History of Great Britain* (1771–93), the fourth chapter of every book consists of a history of learning and the fifth of a history of the arts. Taken as a whole, the arrangement of Henry's work makes it plain that literary history is to be seen as a division of

[19] See Hayley's *An Essay on History, in Three Epistles to Edward Gibbon*, 2d ed. (1781), and his *Essay on Epic Poetry* (1782); as well as Clara Reeve, *The Progress of Romance* (London, 1785; rpt. New York: Garland, 1970).

[20] Isaac D'Israeli, *An Essay on the Manners and Genius of the Literary Character* (London, 1795; rpt. New York: Garland, 1970), iv.

[21] A. F. Tytler, *Elements of General History, Ancient and Modern* (Edinburgh, 1801), preface.

[22] This comes from an end paper of Anne Hamilton's *Epics of the Ton*. On Steuart's *Sallust*, see above, chapter 3.

general history, equivalent to the history of manners, of commerce, or of civil and military affairs. Henry's view of literary history, though pursued with unrivaled thoroughness, was certainly not a new one. As we saw in James Mackintosh, the idea was generally regarded as going back to Bacon's *Advancement of Learning*, though we also saw that Mackintosh could invoke Bacon's authority to legitimate a much wider, more expressive view of letters than Bacon himself intended.

One of those who acknowledged Bacon's inspiration was Charles Philpot, author of *An Introduction to the Literary History of the Fourteenth and Fifteenth Centuries* (1798). This rather obscure work gives us a useful look into the ways in which literary history was understood near the end of the century. Philpot's subject was the "revival of learning," a favorite topic for literary history that had been projected by a number of British authors, including Thomas Gray, William Robertson, and both Wartons.[23] Before embarking on his own, relatively unambitious undertaking—"a cursory, yet not indistinct, review of the revival of literature"—Philpot outlines two wider views of what such a history might be. The largest plan he takes from Samuel Johnson, who had told Boswell that a history of the revival of learning would "contain an account of *whatever* contributed to the restoration of literature, such as controversies, printing, the destruction of the Greek empire, the encouragement of great men, with the lives of the most eminent patrons and professors *of all kinds* of learning in *different* countries."[24]

To Philpot, however, Johnson's idea seemed too ambitious for any ordinary scholar, as also was Bacon's "noble outline of a general history of learning." Accordingly, Philpot turned to his third view, which he considered a more practical, though less comprehensive plan. His purpose, he wrote, was to "arrange the striking parts of literary history on its revival, record and illustrate those material causes by which its progress was obviously affected, exhibit those pre-eminent characters, whether of patrons or scholars, who most filled the public eye, and connect the literary with the political and general history of the period."[25]

Philpot's outline indicates clearly that in its ideal form literary history would take on very large historical dimensions, and even in the more modest scope

[23] See, for instance, William Roscoe's preface to his *Life* of Pope Leo X (1st ed. 1805), where Roscoe recounts a conversation with Joseph Warton in 1797: "By him I was informed that it had been the intention of himself, his brother, and several of their literary friends, to give a history of the revival of letters, not only in Italy, but in the principal countries of Europe, and that the history of English poetry by Mr. Thomas Warton was only a part of this great design." See Roscoe, *The Life and Pontificate of Leo the Tenth*, 2 vols. (London, 1846), 1:xi.

[24] Charles Philpot, *An Introduction to the Literary History of the Fourteenth and Fifteenth Centuries* (London, 1798; rpt. New York,: Garland, 1970), v. The work is sometimes attributed to John Logan.

[25] Ibid., preface.

he settled for in his own work, what the age called "general history" features prominently in his outline. Thus Philpot includes a chapter outlining political events that influenced the revival, such as the Arab conquests and the Crusades, and gives some account of chivalry, the civil and canon law, patronage, and the establishment of the universities. What distinguishes Philpot's work from Warton's, in other words, is not the breadth of his historical framework, which is essentially that of Enlightenment philosophical history, but the lack of detail or depth in his literary commentary.

Philpot stresses that in undertaking this work he had few models to turn to, especially in England. The nearest approach to the ideal of literary history set out by Bacon and Johnson is the "noble" work of Tiraboschi, but English writing had been sparse compared to that of the continent. Gibbon is mentioned as someone who might have done wonders, had war and politics not "monopolized such a prodigality of talents"; otherwise only Warton and Roscoe stand as exceptions to the "disgraceful sterility" of English efforts.[26]

After Warton, Roscoe is, indeed, the obvious figure on whom a history of English literary history might turn.[27] His *Life of Lorenzo* (1795) was greeted as a major contribution to Italian literary as well as political history, made all the more remarkable, as everyone commented, by being the work of a Liverpool banker who had never visited the country.[28] When compared to a work like Philpot's, Roscoe's *Lorenzo* distinguishes itself by the strength of its literary and biographical scholarship. Drawing on distinguished continental prede-

[26] Ibid., ix.

[27] On Roscoe as a "cultural historian," see Francis Haskell, *History and Its Images: Art and the Interpretation of the Past* (New Haven: Yale UP, 1993), 209–14. See also Henry Roscoe, *The Life of William Roscoe, by his son Henry Roscoe*, 2 vols. (Boston, 1833); and George Chandler, *William Roscoe of Liverpool* (London: Batsford, 1953).

[28] The book sold well and was generously received by scholars and cognoscenti in Italy as well as in England. Walpole, for instance, applauded it by quoting Roscoe's own praises for Tenhove's earlier work: "the most engaging work that has, perhaps, ever appeared on a subject of literary history, is written by a native of one country, in the language of another, on the affairs of a third" (quoted in Roscoe, *Life of William Roscoe*, 1:117–18). It is not clear whether Walpole intended any comment on Liverpool English.

I should note that Roscoe's identification of himself as "literary historian" is consistent. For instance, in an apologia that he suppressed before publication, he wrote: "With this publication, to which I have been reluctantly impelled, by the just defence of myself and my writings, I take a final and a grateful leave of the public in the character of a literary historian" (see ibid., 1:254). Similarly, he professed his pleasure in the commendation of Abate Andres, "a critic, who, since the death of Tiraboschi of Modena, is, perhaps, the best literary historian in Italy" (1:143).

Despite Roscoe's profession that he would cease his activity as a literary historian, he did in fact go on to publish other works in this area, though in the vein of commentary, not narrative. See "On the Origin and Vicissitudes of Literature, Science, and Art, and their Influence on the Present State of Society. A Discourse delivered on the opening of the Liverpool Royal Institution; 25 November, 1817," *Pamphleteer* 11 (1818): 507–36.

cessors,[29] Roscoe provided English readers with an account of Italian humanism, especially as it was displayed in the work of men like Angelo Poliziano, who were closely associated with the Medici. Roscoe was also able to publish a considerable appendix of Lorenzo's poetry, transcribed by his friend William Clarke from manuscripts in the Laurenziana, as well as an assortment of letters, addresses, and other documents.

In short, considered as a literary history, the *Life of Lorenzo* is far from Philpot's rather simple application of the framework of philosophical history to the matter of literature. Even so, within the limitations of biography Roscoe retained many of the concerns of general historians. He regarded his second Medicean study, the *Life and Pontificate of Leo the Tenth* (1805) as linked to the first, and he confessed his attraction to the opportunity that such a continuation provided to speak to some of the greatest events of modern history. "I was desirous of embracing," he confessed, "as far as my subject would allow, the history of the principal events in Europe, from the downfall of Constantinople to the accession of Charles V; and thus of connecting, although by a link of very inferior workmanship, the golden histories of Gibbon and of Robertson."[30]

Some Contexts of Literary History: Anti-Jacobinism, Sentimentalism, Medievalism

Eighteenth-century traditions of literary history as the history of learning and letters did not simply disappear in the early nineteenth century, as Roscoe's biographies clearly show. Even so, a number of new preoccupations, all in some way connected to the impact of the French Revolution on British literary sensibilities, intervened to make the older forms of literary history less attractive to Jeffrey and his readers. The ideas and activities of four writers—Thomas MacDonald, Thomas Mathias, William Godwin, and Walter Scott—offer an opportunity to sketch some of the ideas and practices that changed the context of literary history in this time. These include the anti-Jacobin emphasis on the vital connection between literature and national character; sentimentalist interest in literature as a place of evocation, especially in relation to the Middle Ages; and the role of periodical reviewing as a new arena for literary history.

As a useful point of departure, we can return to Jeffrey's preoccupation with the power of opinion, and behind that, to Hume's philosophical adage that "though men be much governed by interest; yet even interest itself, and all

[29] As biographer of Lorenzo, Roscoe could draw on the important works of Tenhove and especially Fabroni.

[30] *Life of William Roscoe*, 1:238. Henry Roscoe takes the quotation from "an unpublished tract." On Roscoe's sense of the two works as a sequence, see also, in the same work, 1:232.

human affairs, are entirely governed by *opinion*."[31] Hume's *History* does, in fact, pay a good deal of attention to the operation of opinion; nonetheless, the philosophic tone of this maxim, its air of calmly producing a surprising truth, tells its own story. In contrast, the French Revolution transformed this detached philosophic insight into a matter of the deepest ideological contention. "When ancient opinions and rules of life are taken away, the loss cannot possibly be estimated," wrote Edmund Burke, summarizing the effects of the Revolution in a famous passage on the loss of chivalry. "From that moment we have no compass to govern us; nor can we know distinctly to what port we steer."[32]

British observers saw the dramatic events in France as a revolution of opinion, and both sides were prepared to join in a bitter struggle to capture public opinion in their own country. The ensuing propaganda war made the private mind a matter for intense public scrutiny. "The security of every state must ultimately depend on the opinions and principles of private men," wrote Thomas MacDonald; "The rest is form."[33] As much anti-Jacobin writing implicitly recognized, this stress on opinion meant that future security depended on a dimension of social life that was extraordinarily difficult to police, especially in a time of ideological contest. Hence the bitterness and the anxiety that marked the conflict, and especially the tense attention both sides gave to writing as an instrument for shaping opinion:

> The formation of opinions is therefore the first movement of general good or evil: and opinion is formed in private society. No laws or rules of government will ever controul it. Even reason is possessed of no absolute or exclusive sovereignty over it. The mind of the majority is only to be reached by the influence of respect, or the force of habit. (2–3)

Following Burke's lead, anti-Jacobin writers also found a kind of comfort in this reference of public safety to the fundamentals of private life, the domain of "habit," "respect," and the slow-to-change instincts of the people. Certainly, MacDonald had no doubt that for Britain the best safeguard lay in national character and especially in the domestic virtues that he thought especially characterized the British nation. Nonetheless, national character was not unassailable, and he feared especially the corrupting powers of literary mercenaries who promote atheism, "political metaphysics," and confusion of social ranks. Touching a historical note that will have an interesting echo in Jeffrey's writing

[31] Hume, *Essays*, 51.

[32] Burke, *Reflections on the Revolution*, 68–69. For Burke, opinion and manners are closely linked. Immediately after, he speaks in the same tones of "the spirit of our old manners and opinions" (69). So, too, he defines chivalry as a "mixed system of opinion and sentiment" (67).

[33] Thomas MacDonald, *Thoughts on the Public Duties of Private Life, with Reference to Present Circumstances and Opinions* (Edinburgh, 1795), 2–3. Macdonald states at the outset of his polemical pamphlet: "The private conduct of every individual is at present of immediate importance to the country" (1).

on literature, MacDonald adds that the present danger to the national character runs much deeper than the "temporary intoxication" that affected the court of Charles II in its reaction to Puritanism.[34]

The case for seeing literature as the central battleground for shaping opinion was made still more urgently by Thomas Mathias, author of the annotated satirical poem *The Pursuits of Literature* (1st ed. 1794). "Government and Literature are now more than ever intimately connected," argues Mathias, in summary of the purpose of his book. "The history of the last thirty years proves it beyond a controversy."[35] The truth is, however, that nothing is ever beyond controversy in Mathias's compulsively reiterated attack on Jacobinism. In fact, as much as the content of the book, the near-hysterical tone of much of the writing gives us the sense of what is at stake in this satirist's war of words:

> When I have read and thought deeply on the accumulated horrors, and all the gradations of wickedness and misery, through which the modern systematic philosophy of Europe has conducted her illuminated votaries, to the confines of political death and mental darkness, my mind for a space feels a convulsion, and suffers the nature of an insurrection.[36]

Following in Burke's footsteps, Mathias traces the convulsions in France to the false doctrines of the philosophes—a view that, as I have already indicated, establishes the French Revolution as perhaps the most mighty event in the history of opinion.[37] With the stakes so high, Mathias called for the most urgent response, unrestrained by delicacy or fear. Our weapons, he writes, "must be instruments of war, able to break down the strongholds of anarchy, impiety and rebellion, and mighty to vindicate the powers of legitimate authority."[38] The fierce instrument he holds up is nothing less than satire, and with it he means to appeal beyond the law itself, to "perhaps a still higher tribunal, that of public opinion, character, and reputation."[39] Later he proclaims: "Wherever the freedom of the press exists, (and WITH US may that freedom be perpet-

[34] Ibid., 14. "The national character," he wrote, "is not invulnerable; and the minds of the best and most moral people on earth may be changed by the gradual introduction of foreign fashions" (13–14).

[35] [Thomas Mathias,] *The Pursuits of Literature. A Satirical Poem in four dialogues*, 5th ed. (London, 1798), v. This is from the "Introductory Letter" written for the fifth edition, when the four dialogues were first collected together. The individual dialogues were published from 1794 to 1797.

[36] Ibid., xiv–xv.

[37] It is of some interest that the first essay Jeffrey wrote for the *Review* took up exactly this theme and argued, though in much more moderate terms, that the ideas of the philosophes bore considerable responsibility for the Revolution, even though these authors themselves often had no idea of producing such an outcome. See Jeffrey's review of Mounier, *De l'influence des philosophes*, *ER* 1 (1802):1–18.

[38] Mathias, *The Pursuits of Literature*, 4.

[39] Ibid., 4–5.

ual!) I must assert *that* LITERATURE, *well or ill conducted,* IS THE GREAT ENGINE *by which, I am fully persuaded, all* civilized *states must ultimately be supported or overthrown.*"[40]

Some of the heaviest fire of the anti-Jacobins was directed at Rousseau and his followers, whose sentimentalism, it was said, threatened the moral life of the nation with the corruptions of unbridled egotism. Despite these attacks, however, the sentimentalist's interest in evoking past experience often seems[41] to cooperate rather than clash with the anti-Jacobin preoccupation with national character—particularly when the subject was the remoter periods of national history. In terms of genre, too, sentimentalism held special attractions for writers of literary biography, who were drawn to understanding the inward dimensions of an individual life, or—more ambitiously—to seeing the single life as a way of evoking the character of experience in another time.

To hostile reviewers, the dangerous attractions of sentimental biography were very much on view in Godwin's *Life of Chaucer* (1803). The first of two major experiments in literary biography, Godwin's *Chaucer* was written as a kind of conspectus of late medieval English life, as seen from the vantage of the poet's work and experience.[42] (See chapter 5 above.) As the story of a great poet-courtier, Chaucer's life might have offered some comparison with Roscoe's study of Lorenzo, but Godwin possessed neither Roscoe's biographical documentation nor his literary scholarship. As a result, his work lacks the specific documentary linkages that draw together the life and times of the hero in more conventional biographies. Instead, Godwin relies on sentimental evocation to lend unity to his picture of the poet's world.

Today, the *Life of Chaucer* could perhaps be called a microhistory. From a wide variety of contemporary sources, Godwin offers a survey of the life and manners of the fourteenth century as a sort of conjectural representation of the "state of England, as Chaucer saw it"—a procedure that Walter Scott, writing in the *Edinburgh Review*, scornfully describes as "hooking in the description and history of every thing that existed upon the face of the earth at the same time with Chaucer."[43] Scott, in the company of most other reviewers, hated

[40] Ibid., 119–20.

[41] See especially Marilyn Butler's pioneering study of this conflict, *Jane Austen and the War of Ideas* (Oxford: Clarendon, 1987).

[42] A later experiment in literary biography was Godwin's study of Milton's nephews, *The Lives of Edward and John Philips* (London, 1815).

[43] Scott, *Periodical Criticism of Sir Walter Scott*, 5 vols. (Edinburgh, 1835), 1:60. Anticipating this review, Jeffrey wrote that "as he [Scott] understands the subjects, and hates the author, I have a notion he will make a good article of it" (Cockburn, *Life of Lord Jeffrey*, 2:86). Horner, writing to Jeffrey, calls this review "amusing enough, after Scott's coarse manner," but thinks Scott goes too far (*The Horner Papers*, 322). For this and other, mostly hostile, reviews, see Kenneth Graham, ed., *William Godwin Reviewed: A Reception History, 1783–1834* (New York: AMS, forthcoming). I am very grateful to Prof. Graham for the chance to consult his valuable work before its publication.

Godwin's politics. He was scathing about the amateurishness of Godwin's literary scholarship and merciless in attacking a procedure that emphasized not so much "what Chaucer did actually *do*, as of what he and all his contemporaries *might, could, would, or should have done*."[44]

Godwin may indeed have added few facts to what was known of the poet's life, as Scott and other critics complained. But whatever its failures of scholarship, Godwin's *Chaucer*—like Dobson's *Petrarca* or Berington's *Abelard* before it—demonstrates the powerful attractions of literary biography as a kind of sentimental history of the times. Godwin's aspiration is to offer the reader an imaginative entry into the experience of a remote past. "It was my purpose to produce a work of a new species," he writes. Unlike the cold antiquarian, he wants to "rescue for a moment the illustrious dead from the jaws of the grave, to make them pass in review before me, to question their spirits and record their answers. I wished to make myself their master of ceremonies, to introduce my reader to their familiar speech, and to enable him to feel for the instant as if he had lived with Chaucer."[45]

Godwin's language here foreshadows the resurrectionary images that would be a notable feature of his "utopian" essay on commemoration, the "Essay on Sepulchres," published in 1809. (See chapter 12 below.) Indeed, I know of no better statement than this of the powerful desire for historical evocation that had such influence upon both historical and fictional writing in this period. And notwithstanding Scott's view of Godwin's failures, it seems fair to say that the readers Godwin hoped to engage in imagining Chaucer's world were also those who, eleven years later, made *Waverley* a best-seller.

We do not need to wait for Scott's emergence as a novelist, however, to appreciate what the two adversaries had in common. In 1805 Scott published a review of a new translation of Froissart that makes an interesting comparison with his attack on Godwin:

> Whoever has taken up the chronicle of Froissart, must have been dull indeed if he did not find himself transported back to the days of Cressy and Poitiers. In truth, his history has less the air of a narrative than of a dramatic representation. The figures live and move before us; we not only know what they did, but learn the mode and process of the action, and the very words with which it was accompanied. This sort of colloquial history is of all others the most interesting.[46]

Scott's hostility to Godwin was certainly fueled by Tory patriotism as well as pride in his superior antiquarian expertise. But on prime questions of historical understanding—especially on the increasingly central aspiration to evoke the past through the study of its literature—there seems little difference between them.

[44] Scott, *Periodical Criticism*, 2:64.

[45] Godwin, *Life of Chaucer*, 1:xi.

[46] Scott, *Periodical Criticism*, 3:113.

Scott's activities as an editor and critic have been rather neglected, but for the "rise" of literary history, he is a figure of the greatest interest. Perhaps better than anyone else, Scott united many of the different motives, entrepreneurial as well as intellectual, that come together to give weight to the production of literary history in this period. He was a serious antiquarian, a champion of local traditions, an editor and popularizer of early verse, a translator of German poetry, a "medievalist," a student of Scottish philosophical history. All of these interests, combined with his immense energy and his financial stake in the printshop of his friend John Ballantyne, made Scott an industrious and enterprising student of literary history.

Scott's correspondence records a number of ambitious publishing projects, all aimed at keeping Ballantyne busy and profitable. One that excited Scott greatly was an edition of the British poets in one hundred volumes, but it was eventually rejected as impractical. "As for the British Poets," he told Ellis, "my plan was greatly too liberal to stand the least chance of being adopted by the trade at large, as I wished them to begin with Chaucer."[47] A second suggestion, one that came from Ellis, was to print a corpus of English historians or chroniclers. Scott rejected the idea, however, saying that the existing editions were too incorrect to be used, and whoever undertook the project would need ready access to the manuscript collections of Oxford and Cambridge.[48] In the event, Scott gave his energies to what in one letter he refers to as "My grand edition of Dryden's Works,"[49] including an extensive life of the poet. Later, this project was followed by an equally important edition of Swift. On a smaller scale, he wrote extended essays on chivalry (1818), drama (1819), and romance (1824) for the supplement to the *Encyclopedia Britannica;* he also wrote a series of lives of novelists, which were issued as prefaces to republication of their works, though the purpose of these introductory pieces was more critical than historical. In addition to these literary tasks, Scott also produced several editions of historical materials, including a number of historical memoirs (genuine and spurious) and an important collection of pamphlets.

Scott was also an active reviewer, first for the *Edinburgh* and then for the *Quarterly*, the rival journal he helped to found in 1809.[50] Scott's literary jour-

[47] *The Letters of Sir Walter Scott*, ed. Herbert Grierson, 12 vols. (London: Constable, 1932), 1:259.

[48] Scott, letter to George Ellis, about September 5, 1805, *Letters*, 1:258–59; in another letter, written in late October or early November, Scott speaks of his hesitation "whether to undertake much of it myself. What I can, I certainly will do; but I should feel particularly delighted if you would join forces with me, when I think we might do the business to purpose. Do, Lord love you, think of this *grande opus*" (1:266).

[49] Scott, *Letters*, 1:303.

[50] Scott's literary reviews for Jeffrey (with year of publication) were *Amadis of Gaul* translated by Southey and Rose (1803), George Ellis's *Specimens of the Early English Poets* (1804), Godwin's *Chaucer* (1804), Chatterton's *Works* (1804), Todd's edition of Spenser (1805), W. Herbert's

nalism has particular interest here, not only because it brought Scott and Jeffrey together for a time, but also because it has to do with the formation of a crucial literary forum that helped to redefine the terms of literary history for the early nineteenth century. Like Jeffrey, Scott played a part in giving literary reviewing a historical horizon—a horizon that helped to endow the attractively miscellaneous and gentlemanly activity of reviewing with a sense of serious and even concerted purpose. This orientation to history, though never fully explicit or carefully defined, connected together a number of convictions that were central to the literary-political culture of the period, notably a sense of the evocative power of literary texts, a commitment to the importance of national character, and a view of the progression of English literary history from the Elizabethans to the Romantics.

Scott's early reviewing is marked by a sensitivity to the formal requirements of literary history taken as a genre and to the history of work in this vein. Scott had roots in the tradition of literary antiquarianism, and his essays make frequent reference to his predecessors in this field, especially to Percy, Warton, Pinkerton, Ritson, and his friend George Ellis.[51] But Scott's vision of literary history goes beyond the sorts of miscellaneous researches that often characterized antiquarian work. Reviewing Ellis's *Specimens of the Early English Poets* in 1804, he remarks that a "distinct and connected history of our poetry" had long been wanted. It was a task, he wrote, "to which Johnson was unequal, through ignorance of our poetical antiquities, and in which Warton had failed, perhaps, because he was too deeply enamoured of them." Scott thought that Warton exhibited a total neglect of plan or system; in consequence, his *History of English Poetry* remains "an immense common-place book of *memoirs to serve for such an history*."[52]

Scott's criticism of Warton—several times repeated[53]—is an important corrective to the modern assumption that Warton's *History* marked the emergence of literary history in Britain. It indicates, too, Scott's belief that literary history could be held up to standards of narrative coherence similar to those customarily applied to general history; Warton's failure to meet those standards relegates his work to a less prestigious subgenre. Formal concerns are also evident

translations of poetry in various European languages (1806), Ellis and Ritson's collections of metrical romances (1806).

[51] See, for instance, Scott, *Periodical Criticism*, 1:21–22, 25–26.

[52] Ibid., 1:4–5.

[53] See, for example, his review of Ellis and Ritson on metrical romance (1806): "Whenever he has occasion to mention a tale of chivalry, in his *History of English Poetry*, it seems to operate like a spell, and he feels it impossible to proceed with the more immediate subject of his disquisition, until he has paced through the whole enchanted maze, and introduced his reader into all its labyrinths. Of the great variety of strange and anomalous digressions, with which that work abounds, and which, separately considered, possess infinite merit and curiosity, a large proportion arose solely from his attachment to this romantic lore" (ibid., 1:19).

in Scott's praises for Ellis's chapter on private life in the Middle Ages. The point of the compliment is that Ellis had found an orderly manner in which to bring historical concerns into the fabric of his literary narrative—a procedure that is the precise mirror image of the brief surveys of arts and letters incorporated into so many general histories.[54]

Like Jeffrey, Scott argues for literature as the best historical record of private life and inward feeling. Since antiquaries have begun to study medieval verse, he writes in a review of works by Ellis and Ritson on metrical romance, more "insight" has been gained into the language and character of feudal Britain than was ever produced by laborious research in monastic records. The romances give us an "intimate knowledge" of past times; they tell us what "our ancestors" thought, the language they used, "their sentiments, manners, and habits." "From the romance we learn what they were; from history, what they did; and were we to be deprived of one of these two kinds of information, it might well be made a question, which is most useful or interesting?"[55]

Scott's continual deployment of the language of sentiment, culminating in this division between a history of feeling and a history of doing, reminds us of how much literary history in this form was nourished by sentimentalist assumptions. Nor can we miss the Burkean strain—itself closely related to sensibility—in this reverent evocation of ancestral temperament. At the same time, both sentimental and patriotic themes were complemented by a philosophical note that was an equal part of Scott's inheritance and an inevitable accompaniment to any discussion of the connection of poetry and manners.[56]

Here, too, national character proves to be a preoccupation. Thus Scott begins his review of Ellis's *Specimens of the Early English Poets* by connecting the history of poetry to the history of language, a platform that offers him opportunity to argue for the unique interest of English. Disclaiming any national partiality, however, he asserts that his judgment is built on purely philological ground. The particular circumstances of the formation of English meant that the "language of Locke and of Shakespeare" alone bridges the two great lan-

[54] "The serenades, the amusements, the food, the fashions, the manners of the period, are all illustrated by quotations from the authors who have referred to them; and, with the singular advantage of never losing sight of his main subject, Mr Ellis has brought together much information on collateral points of interest and curiosity" (ibid., 1:13). A similar point can be made about his criticism of Todd's edition of Spenser (*ER*, 1805). Here Scott vigorously objects to the editor's use of a mix of narrative and quoted correspondence in making up his life of the poet. The letters of Spenser, he insists, should have been published as a separate appendix, not only because of the documentary value of the letters, but because of the "confused and inelegant effect [of] this medley of narrative and quotation. The biographer should always study to give his work the appearance of continuity. . . . the text ought to be expressed historically, and in the language of the author himself" (*Periodical Criticism*, 1:82–83).

[55] *Periodical Criticism*, 1:18.

[56] For Scott's debt to philosophical history, see Garside, "Scott and Philosophical Historians"; and Ferris, *Achievement of Literary Authority.*

guage families of Europe, the Latin and Teutonic. It is interesting to observe, writes Scott, that for a long time, the Teutonic language spoken by the "vanquished Anglo-Saxons" continued a separate existence from that of the Norman conquerors. "It is still more interesting to observe how, after having long flowed each in its separate channel, they at length united and formed a middle dialect, which . . . at length superseded the individual speech of both, and became the apt record of poetry and philosophy."[57] These views on language and nation building evidently stayed with Scott, since fifteen years later they reappear as the framework of the plot of *Ivanhoe* (1819).

I have confined my comments thus far to Scott's early reviews, where as Jeffrey's favorite medievalist, he popularized a historical view of early literature. A hint in his 1803 review of Southey's *Amadis of Gaul* suggests the possibility that the concerns of the medievalist might widen into a still larger historical vision: "The popular romance always preserves, to a certain degree, the manners of the age in which it was written. The novels of Fielding and Richardson are even already become valuable, as a record of the English manners of the last generation. How much, then, should we prize the volumes which describe those of the era of the victors of Cressy and Poitiers!"[58]

With respect to the Middle Ages, observations on the reciprocal value of literature and manners had become a commonplace. Scott, however, was evidently ready to extend the same notion to the literature of later ages, where criticism, not history, still held sway.[59] In Warton, for example, the recurrent stress on manners serves as a way of resolving the tension between assumptions about art that remained largely classical and his evident fascination with the unrefined productions of a "gothic" taste. In this manner, medieval romances, with their "rude" or "incorrect" taste, might be rescued for modern appreciation by a sense of history.[60] A much more thoroughgoing historicism would be required, however, if more recent literary schools were to come under the same forms of judgment. Scott's seemingly offhand suggestion that Fielding and Richardson illuminated the manners of their own time gives evidence of a new historical distance on the literature of more recent and more polished ages. This distance, and the enlargement of the scope of literary-historical thinking that went with it, can be taken as one of the principal achievements of Scott's generation, which in the midst of much self-conscious medievalizing also directed itself to more recent scenes of literary history.

[57] *Periodical Criticism*, 1:3.

[58] Ibid., 2:38.

[59] See Philpot's remarks on the need to limit his history to the revival of learning and not pursue it into later periods: "Literature had then passed its dawn, the proper subject of historical and critical consideration, and was advancing fast to its meridian splendour" (*Literary History*, iv).

[60] On the way in which Warton combined classical assumptions and an interest in the Gothic, see Levine, *Humanism and History*, 195–204.

In a longer study of Scott's contributions to literary history, we would want to pursue this theme in relation to his editions of Dryden and Swift. I would like to return, however, to Francis Jeffrey, whose key position in British criticism, as well as the wide range of his commentary, provides rich material for exploring the directions that literary history took among the heirs of the Scottish enquiry.

Francis Jeffrey and the Epochs of National Literature

Francis Jeffrey's writings on literature and history exhibit a double movement. First, it is evident that Jeffrey looked to literature as an avenue for understanding some crucial dimensions of the history of modern Britain—dimensions that had become especially important, as I have emphasized, as a consequence of displacements in the position of political narrative. As a useful shorthand, we might call this view "literature as history." This way of understanding the relationship between history and literature stands in evident continuity with earlier Scottish efforts to find a way of conceptualizing a history of the social. It assumes a definition of literature that is broadly inclusive and one that is closely allied to that catch-all of eighteenth-century social thought, arts and manners. This understanding of literary history seems to have been present in Jeffrey's writing from early on, but a second, balancing position only develops in the course of his evolution as a critic. In Jeffrey's early critical writings reference to history is muted or subordinate, but by the second decade of the century he had produced a narrative of the evolution of British literature (in the more restrictive sense of "works of imagination") that serves to make sense of his own critical positions. This second movement might be labeled as "the history of national literature." It assumes the narrower definition of *literature* that is becoming dominant in this period and stands, therefore, much closer to the modern sense of literary history.

In Jeffrey's scattered periodical writings, it is the reciprocity of these two movements that truly justifies speaking of his critical and historical reviewing as engaging with the literary history of the nation. For the sake of clarity, however, it is useful to separate these two movements. Accordingly, I will begin with the latter, more restricted sense of "the history of national (imaginative) literature" and then turn to the historical uses of literature.

Jeffrey's lifelong polemic against the Lake school, which has so monopolized the attention of modern critics as a gauge of his criticism, is also our best guide to the development of his historical understanding. Jeffrey's opening salvo against the Lake poets comes in a review of Southey's *Thalaba* published in the first volume of the *Review* (1802). Here Jeffrey confidently—even extravagantly—took his stand for taste against history:

> Poetry has this much, at least, in common with religion, that its standards were fixed long ago, by certain inspired writers, whose authority it is no longer lawful to call in question; and that many profess to be entirely devoted to it, who have no *good works* to produce in support of their pretensions.[61]

The "catholic poetical church," he goes on to say, has done few miracles since its first ages and has been more prolific of doctors than of saints. And like the Christian Church, it, too, has produced its heresies and reformations, including that promoted by the "sect" to which Southey belongs.

It is characteristic of Jeffrey that he takes a kind of prankish joy in seeing how far he can push this already overextended metaphor. In implicit comparison to the Protestant Reformation, he points to the (alleged) German origins of romanticism (not, of course, his term) and also to the influence of its "great apostle of Geneva." He is even willing to speak of his own critical duties as requiring him to discharge his "inquisitorial office conscientiously." This ironic distancing is worth noting since Jeffrey's criticism is often misunderstood by those who fail to appreciate his tone, as though the harassed young Scottish lawyer who began the *Review* almost on a whim literally imagined himself as having the powers of the Inquisition. Clearly, Jeffrey meant to undercut the dull solemnities attendant on a defense of poesy, while combating the earnest babble characteristic (as he saw it) of both the manifestos and the verse of the Lake poets.

At the heart of Jeffrey's polemic is his unhappiness at what he calls their "affectation of great simplicity and familiarity of language."[62] He writes mockingly that the Lake poets disdain to make use of poetic phraseology, saying there is "too much *art* in this, for that great love of nature with which they are all inspired." To make matters worse, through a kind of literary sentimentalization of the poor, these poets choose to take the language of the lowest orders as their model.[63] In Wordsworth's phrase (quoted from the "Preface" of 1798) they seek "to adapt to the uses of poetry, the ordinary language of conversation among the middling and lower orders of the people."[64]

[61] Jeffrey, review of Southey's *Thalaba*, in *ER* 1 (1802): 63.

[62] Ibid., 1:64.

[63] Not only is the language of the "higher and more cultivated orders" superior in its associations, but he is even prepared to argue that the different classes of society have distinct passions as well as different idioms. "The poor and vulgar may interest us, in poetry, by their *situation;* but never, we apprehend, by any sentiments that are peculiar to their condition, and still less by any language that is characteristic of it" (ibid., 1:66).

[64] In fact, by the preface of 1800 Wordsworth himself had retreated from his earlier position regarding the language of the lower orders, and he speaks more broadly of wanting to deal with "incidents and situations from common life . . . in a selection of language really used by men." We can only speculate whether Jeffrey held to the earlier wording with its emphasis on social class simply because of the polemic advantage it gave him, or because the contrasting condition

Jeffrey evidently saw this sort of talk as a simultaneous attack on the power of educated speech and on the rigorousness of conscious art. In his view, their pronouncements gave evidence of a kind of literary and political nihilism, "a splenetic and idle discontent with the existing institutions of society."[65] This charge—which has obvious parallels in anti-Jacobin propaganda—goes with an allegation that the Lake poets were afflicted by a love of abstract system that led them to devalue real experience and real achievement. Thus, in a summary passage, Jeffrey writes that the style of "our modern poets" is "the unhappy fruit of a system that would teach us to undervalue that vigilance and labour which sustained the loftiness of Milton, and gave energy and direction to the point and fine propriety of Pope" (69).

This tirade against the Jacobinism of the "modern poets" unwittingly demonstrates the fragility of the antihistorical stance Jeffrey adopted in this review of Southey as a defense of poetry's ancien régime. In fact, though he continued to cherish Milton, he soon came to see Pope's "fine propriety" with other eyes: so much so that, while he never reconciled himself to Wordsworth, he came to set a much higher value on the poetry of the new century than on that of the century before. Accordingly, many of Jeffrey's literary essays, beginning with the first decade of the century, involved his attempt to gauge the power and direction of the contemporary revolution in poetic feeling, without withdrawing the fundamentals of his position on poetic language.

Jeffrey's position in regard to the great literary revolution of his age is curiously reminiscent of those English anti-Jacobins (including Wordsworth and Southey) who spent many years struggling with the guilt or contradictions entailed in their swing from pro- to antirevolutionary fervor. Certainly, Jeffrey had a great deal of trouble putting aside his quarrel with the Lake school. Not only did he renew it in a series of subsequent reviews of Wordsworth and Southey, but he seems almost incapable of speaking about the work of other poets without enlisting their virtues in his cause. He closes a review of Burns (1809), for example, by pointing to the contrast between his real and their affected simplicity,[66] while Crabbe's portraits of ordinary life inevitably provoke a lengthy comparison to the "fantastic and unheard of beings" of the opposing school.[67] And similar, if briefer comments in essays on Campbell,

---

of the social orders played so large a part in his own thinking. See Wordsworth, "Preface to the Second Edition of *Lyrical Ballads*" (1800), in *Selected Poems and Prefaces*, ed. Jack Stillinger (Boston: Houghton Mifflin, 1965), 446.

[65] Jeffrey on Southey, *ER*, 1:71.

[66] "He [Burns] has copied the spoken language of passion and affectation, with infinitely more fidelity than they have ever done. . . . But he has not rejected the helps of elevated language and habitual associations; nor debased his composition by an affectation of babyish interjections" (Jeffrey, *Contributions to Edinburgh Review*, 2:175).

[67] In a review of 1808, Jeffrey praises Crabbe for showing us the common people of England "pretty much as they are," while Wordsworth and his brethren "invent for themselves certain

Scott, Byron, and Keats show his continued preoccupation with justifying the same set of judgments.[68] The cumulative effect was to create an alternative canon of contemporary verse that allowed Jeffrey to celebrate the richness of the Romantic sensibility while marginalizing the Wordsworthian dogmas he continued to despise.

The Lake school did not, of course, provide Jeffrey with an automatic historical framework. If anything, as we have seen, the initial impetus led him to an ahistorical defense of the standards of the "universal poetical church." But the depth of Wordsworth's challenge to traditional ideas of poetic language and the obsessiveness of Jeffrey's own response produced an answer that proved much deeper and more systematic than it might otherwise have been. In the present context, too, it matters especially that Jeffrey's continued worrying of the question meant that, although he came to be something of a champion of an Elizabethan and Jacobean revival, his view of English poetry would never be focused on remote ages or earlier masters. On the contrary, Jeffrey's interest in literary history cannot in the end be separated from his critical reflections on the taste of his own age.

In 1811 Jeffrey took the opportunity of a new edition of the works of the Jacobean playwright John Ford to set out a complete sketch of the development of the national literature. The essay is a celebration of the greatness of the age of Elizabeth and James I, an era that "indeed, has always appeared to us by far the brightest in the history of English literature—or indeed of human intellect and capacity" (2:38). Many of the writers Jeffrey brings forward in proof might not now be assigned to the history of literature. Bacon, Hooker, Taylor, Barrow, Napier, Cudworth: these names suggest the older concept of a history of learning and letters.[69] But we soon see that it is not so much the learning of these men he wants to celebrate as their richness of language and power of expression—a power so conspicuous that there is more genuine poetry in their prose "than all the odes and the epics that have since been produced in Europe" (2:41). More than a Baconian history of learning, in fact, what Jeffrey proposes is a Burkean celebration of native genius. "They are the works of Giants, in short—and Giants of one nation and family;—and their characteristics are, great force, boldness, and originality; together with a certain raciness of En-

whimsical and unheard-of beings, to whom they impute some fantastical combination of feelings" (ibid., 2:277–78).

[68] Reviewing Campbell's *Gertrude of Wyoming* in 1809 he writes: "We rejoice once more to see a polished and pathetic poem—in the old style of English pathos and poetry. . . Without supposing that this taste has been in any great degree vitiated, or even imposed upon, by the babyism or the antiquarianism which have lately been versified for its improvement, we may be allowed to suspect, that it has been somewhat dazzled by the splendour, and bustle, and variety of the most popular of our recent poems" (ibid., 2:176).

[69] The same view of literary history is suggested by Jeffrey's speculations whether the Reformation was the cause or effect of the brilliance of this time.

glish peculiarity, which distinguishes them from all those performances that have since been produced amoung ourselves, upon a more vague and general idea of European excellence" (2:39–40).

Jeffrey's characterization of subsequent periods follows from this celebration of native genius. In the fanatical atmosphere of the period of the Civil War, poetry lost its ease and drama was suppressed. The Restoration, in turn, brought a polite, French taste that "reduced us to a province of the great republic of Europe." Jeffrey's discussion, though necessarily brief, is not simplistic, and he concedes the attractions of the new courtly style:

> It was a witty, and a grand, and a splendid style. It showed more scholarship and art, than the luxuriant negligence of the old English school; and was not only free from many of its hazards and some of its faults, but possessed merits of its own, of a character more likely to please those who had then the power of conferring celebrity. . . . It came upon us with the air and the pretension of being the style of cultivated Europe, and a true copy of the style of polished antiquity. (2:40–41)

Some consideration then follows of the qualities of Dryden, Addison, Pope, and Swift, along with a discussion of those who, beginning with Thomson and culminating in Cowper, gradually "made some steps back to the force and animation of our original poetry" (2:46).

Eight years earlier Jeffrey had described Cowper as a poet who had overcome a century of fastidious taste and "reclaimed the natural liberty of invention, and walked abroad in the open field of observation as freely as those by whom it was originally trodden."[70] In light of the later essay it is clear that this earlier characterization was only incipiently historical, having more to do with general ideas of originality and imitation than with plotting the evolution of national taste. In 1811, however, Jeffrey sets Cowper much more precisely in a narrative of national literature: he is the poet who first really threw off "French criticism and artificial refinement," leading a return to the freedom that had belonged to "the old school of English literature" (2:47–48). As such, Cowper also stands as father to the most recent generation of poets, all of whom—including the Lake poets—have thrown off the influence of Pope and Addison for "the native beauties of their great predecessors."

[70] Ibid., 1:411. The passage comes from a review of Hayley's *Life and Posthumous Writings of William Cowper*, first published in *ER*, 1803. The passage begins: "The great merit of this writer appears to consist in the boldness and originality of his composition, and in the fortunate audacity with which he has carried the dominion of poetry into regions that had been considered as inaccessible to her ambition. The gradual refinement of taste had, for nearly a century, been weakening the force of original genius. Our poets had become timid and fastidious, and circumscribed themselves both in the choice and the management of their subjects, by the observance of a limited number of models, who were thought to have exhausted all the legitimate resources of the art. Cowper was one of the first who crossed this enchanted circle" (411–12).

As always, Jeffrey cannot enter this territory without rejoining his quarrel with Wordsworth. But though he is unrelenting in his fundamental views, Jeffrey softens his estimation of the Lake poets in a manner that seems to be the direct result of setting his criticism in the framework of history:

> But we have said enough elsewhere of the faults of those authors; and shall only add, at present, that, notwithstanding all these faults, there is a fertility and a force, a warmth of feeling and an exaltation of imagination about them, which classes them, in our estimation, with a much higher order of poets than the followers of Dryden and Addison; and justifies an anxiety for their fame, in all the admirers of Milton and Shakespeare. (2:48–49)

Jeffrey's new scheme of literary history—first fully set out in this essay on Ford in 1811 and then repeated in various ways in other places—evidently enlarges the framework of his earlier criticism, so that his likes and quarrels are set within a broader understanding of literary development. Criticism, then, is folded into literary history, but history, which gives criticism space to reflect upon itself, serves larger purposes too, which have to do with nationality and tradition.

Jeffrey presents his outline of literary history with little fanfare. The unmistakable energy of the essay comes, in fact, from Jeffrey's advocacy of Jacobean poetry, not from his historical approach. If, however, we press the question a little further and ask why Jacobean literature needs this sort of advocacy, we come to an important point regarding the context of literary history. Foreigners, says Jeffrey, say that our national taste has been corrupted by our idolatry of Shakespeare. Accordingly, before discussing the works of Ford, it is necessary to establish that there was a distinct national school in Shakespeare's time and that it was superseded by the imposition of a foreign standard at the time of the Restoration:

> Our love of Shakespeare, therefore, is not a *monomania* . . . but is merely the natural love which all men bear to those forms of excellence that are commmodated to their peculiar character, temperament, and situation; and which will always return, and assert its power over their affections, long after authority has lost its reverence, fashions been antiquated, and artificial tastes passed away. In endeavouring, therefore, to bespeak some share of favour for such of his contemporaries as had fallen out of notice, during the prevalence of an imported literature, we conceive that we are only enlarging that foundation of native genius on which alone any lasting superstructure can be raised, and invigorating that deep-rooted stock upon which all the perennial blossoms of literature must still be engrafted. (2:50)

This is a justification of literary study not so much from history as from tradition. Its xenophobia, its organic metaphors, its assumptions about what is genuine and therefore long-lasting, its manner of authorizing change in the name of continuity, all these clearly tell us that we are in the world of Burkean traditionalism as it has found a home in literary history. Without question the great flowering of literary history in the nineteenth century owed much to the currents of national sentiment and especially to the idea that the elusive, but all-important traits of custom and habit that gave a nation its character were best expressed in its imaginative literature.

Historical Distance and Literary Tradition

Earlier, in a discussion of Hume, I suggested that historical distance is neither simple nor invariable, but rather is the complex effect of interplays between recuperative and distanciating movements. A similar tension is displayed in Jeffrey's literary history, where the sense of proximity cultivated by tradition is offset by impulses to a more detached historical and critical standpoint. As an essayist and reviewer, of course, he was particularly free to develop a variety of approaches, unconstrained by the formal unities of narrative.

Jeffrey's reconfiguration of English literary history as a story of rupture and recovery entailed significant complexities of explanation as well as emplotment. A narrative written along these lines would need to comprehend not only the interruption of an earlier tradition, but also its recovered vitality in recent times; and since these explanations were, at least in part, extraliterary—the imposition of foreign taste by a victorious Stuart court, the spreading excitements of the revolutionary era just now fading—this schema called for an alignment of the literary history of the nation with larger movements in the history of opinion. But above all this revision of literary history provided the critic-historian with a mirror in which to see recent and contemporary literature in a more distanced perspective than he had been capable of (or desired to be capable of) at an earlier stage.

These considerations emerge most clearly in Jeffrey's review of Scott's edition of Swift (1816), an essay that is really the mirror image of the concerns of the earlier essay on Ford. The opening sentences make the newfound historical distance on the Augustans the key marker of fundamental changes in contemporary taste: "By far the most considerable change which has taken place in the world of letters, in our days," Jeffrey begins, "is that by which the wits of Queen Anne's time have been gradually brought down from the supremacy which they had enjoyed, without competition, for the best part of a century."[71] Thus Jeffrey's first interest in reviewing Scott's edition has less to do with Augustan literature as such than with the recent revolution in literary criticism that has been revealed by this reversal. If, in the end, both epochs are opened up

[71] Review of *Works of Jonathan Swift*, ed. W. Scott (first published *ER*, 1816), in *Contributions to Edinburgh Review*, 1:158.

to examination, it is the more recent one that seems most in need of historical explanation.

I will not rehearse Jeffrey's judgment on the weaknesses of the Augustans—weaknesses that make their eventual fall in reputation appear natural—nor follow in any detail this second survey of the history of English literature. Let me simply quote its conclusion:

> This brings us down almost to the present times—in which the revolution in our literature has been accelerated and confirmed by the concurrence of many causes. The agitations of the French Revolution, and the discussions as well as the hopes to which it gave occasion—the genius of Edmund Burke, and some others of his land of genius—the impression of the new literature of Germany, evidently the original of our lake school of poetry, and of many innovations in our drama—the rise or revival of a more evangelical spirit, in the body of the people—and the vast extension of our political and commercial relations, which have not only familiarized all ranks of people with distant countries, and great undertakings, but have brought knowledge and enterprise home, not merely to the imagination, but to the actual experience of almost every individual. (1:167)

There is an obvious continuity between such passages and the sorts of explanations earlier historians like Robertson or Philpot regularly offered for the rise of chivalry or the revival of learning. But even in so short a sketch, it is evident that the air of mechanical explanation that generally adheres to the historical sociologies of the Enlightenment has given way to something subtler and more comprehensively historical. Here the object of study is not the manners of a remote age, but a deep change in everyday life and feelings in the writer's own lifetime. This historicization of the present seems to make it harder to draw any easy boundary between events and ideas, or between politics and imagination, all of which seem equally at stake in any explanation Jeffrey might be able to offer for this fundamental shift in the history of national opinion.

More could be said to fill in the details of Jeffrey's schematization of English literary history, but I want now to turn briefly to Jeffrey's aesthetic and philosophical interests, which brought another dimension to his writings on history and literature.[72] Once again the best starting point is his continuing preoccupation with explaining the climate of contemporary poetry.

In his review of Scott's *Lady of the Lake* (1810), Jeffrey undertook an elaborate consideration of Scott's popularity and its implications for the problematic relationship that now existed between elite and popular audiences. Generaliz-

[72] It is indicative that when Jeffrey republished his essays as *Contributions to the Edinburgh Review,* he gave pride of place to his 1811 essay on the associationalist theory of aesthetics. The essay was first published in 1811 as a review of Archibald Alison's *Essays on the Nature and Principles of Taste*, then enlarged and republished as the article "Beauty" for the supplement to the *Encyclopaedia Britannica* (1824).

ing the problem further, Jeffrey examined the phenomenon of Scott's success in terms of the struggles of what he calls "after-poets" to find originality in the wake of the influence and advantages of great ancestral voices.[73] Only Scott had found a way to overcome this challenge without sacrificing popularity; for the others, it had meant cultivating a narrower audience and a more limited, sometimes less natural, poetic range:

> In this way we think that modern poetry has both been enriched with more exquisite pictures, and deeper and more sustained strains of pathetic, than were known to the less elaborate artists of antiquity; at the same time that it has been defaced with more affectation, and loaded with far more intricacy.[74]

A similar conjectural history introduces Jeffrey's appreciation of Byron's *Corsair* (1814). Here, too, originality and the deeper range of emotions cultivated in modern poetry are central considerations. Poetry's origins, writes Jeffrey, lie in "rude ages" characterized by violent passions, but as civilization advances, men grow ashamed of this violence and attempt to subdue or conceal their emotions. Strong feeling is proscribed and is replaced by ceremonious politeness. In consequence, "poetry becomes first pompous and stately—then affectedly refined and ingenious—and finally gay, witty, discursive and familiar."[75]

But another stage of civilization and of poetry awaits. When the dangers of "intemperate vehemence" disappear from the upper ranks of society, the restraints on strong emotions are eased. Men grow impatient with the joyless elegancies of fashion, and they seek out again strong and natural feelings. "This is the stage of society in which fanaticism has its second birth, and political enthusiasm its first true development—when plans of visionary reform, and schemes of boundless ambition are conceived, and almost realized by the energy with which they are pursued—the era of revolutions and projects—of vast performances, and infinite expectations."[76]

Poetry, too, "reflects and partakes" in this transformation; indeed it is axiomatic for Jeffrey that poetry, in its combination of universality and imaginative power, is a uniquely sensitive reflector of the social world—hence a mirror held up to history as well as nature. In this new era of feeling, poetry becomes "more enthusiastic, authoritative and impassioned." Searching for stronger emotions, it inevitably returns to some of the themes and characters of its earlier ages, and it does not disdain "in pursuit of her new idol of strong emotion, to descend to the very lowest condition of society, and to stir up the most

[73] See Bate, *Burden of the Past*, 99–103.

[74] Review of Scott, *The Lady of the Lake* (first published *ER*, 1810), in *Contributions to Edinburgh Review*, 2:244–45.

[75] Review of Byron's *The Corsair* (first published *ER*, 1814), in *Jeffrey's Criticism*, 76–78.

[76] Ibid., 78.

revolting dregs of utter wretchedness and depravity."[77] It is a simple fact, writes Jeffrey, not only that the poets of the last twenty years have dealt with much more powerful sensations, but also that they have made use of subjects that would have been rejected by the fastidiousness of an earlier age "more recently escaped from barbarity."

But Jeffrey does not want us to think that because poets in this "late stage of civilization" have reached back to the scenes of ruder, more passionate times, their work shares in any genuine sense the feeling of the earliest poets:

> It is chiefly by these portraitures of the interior of human nature that the poetry of the present day is distinguished from all that preceded it and the difference is perhaps most conspicuous when the persons and subjects are borrowed from the poetry of an earlier age. Not only is all this anatomy of the feelings superadded to the primitive legend of exploits, but in many cases feelings are imputed to the agents, of which persons in their condition were certainly incapable, and which no description could have made intelligible to their contemporaries—while, in others, the want of feeling, probably exaggerated beyond nature also, is dwelt upon, and made to produce great effect as a trait of singular atrocity.[78]

This contrast between ancient and modern temperaments was a favorite of Romantic criticism, which set the unself-conscious wholeness of primitive life against the divided and complex interiority of the modern personality.[79] But Jeffrey offers no hint of the corresponding notion that primitive emotions directed to new ends might be reintegrative for the moderns. (Indeed, this myth is part of what worries him about Byron's "morbid exaltation of character"[80] or Wordsworth's attraction to solitaries, rustics, and children.) In this sense, Jeffrey's anatomy of modernity's pervasive Byronism employs the Romantic myth of the primitive even while seeking a kind of distance from it that allows him to treat it with considerable historical detachment.

The epochs of feeling that Jeffrey traces in this conjectural history of Byronism have recognizable parallels in the narrative of opinion or of national tradition, but the frameworks of interpretation remain distinct. In respect to tradition, for example, Dryden's neoclassicism or his unacceptable obscenity are understood as specific signs of the way that foreign mores have distorted taste and corrupted morals. The dilemmas of the "after-poet," on the other hand, or the persistent human desire for strong feeling belong to a history that draws

[77] Ibid.

[78] Ibid., 81.

[79] The *locus classicus* of this contrast of ancient and modern sensibilities is, of course, Schiller's *On Naive and Sentimental Poetry.* Jeffrey, like Mackintosh, probably felt the influence of these ideas primarily through the writings of Staël, who popularized the views of the Schlegels. See Jeffrey's long and admiring report on Staël's *De La Litterature considere dans ses rapports avec les institutions sociales*, in *Contributions to Edinburgh Review,* 1:79–135.

[80] Review of *Childe Harold* (*ER*, 1816), in *Contributions to Edinburgh Review*, 2:437.

on the universal qualities of poetry, rather than its historical and national particularities. These struggles and desires belong to a natural history of poetry, one that is written against the grid of the history of civilization or of the human mind, not that of the British nation.

Poetry, History, and the Historical Canon

As an occasional reviewer, Jeffrey was under no pressure to establish a single, consistent doctrine. On the contrary, the strength of his writing lies in its wide-ranging inventiveness and informality. For this reason, it is not possible to define a strict position that resolves the various tensions in his conception of literary history—between, for example, a regulative conception aiming to fix membership in the "catholic poetical church" and a more tolerant historicism open to new schools and tastes. Nor, in his role of universal critic, does he seem interested in defining the choice between a literary history clearly focused on the evolution of certain specific genres or, on the other hand, one broadly reflective of other histories.

Our best opportunity for one final look at these balances comes in his review of a major anthology, Thomas Campbell's *Specimens of the British Poets* (1819)—a work that took up the idea projected by Scott of a comprehensive collection of British verse. In this essay, Jeffrey revives the comparison of poetry and the church, but this time from a latitudinarian, not a High Church perspective. Poets, Jeffrey writes, are frequently sectarian in their tastes, apt "to invent articles of faith, the slightest violation of which effaces the merit of all other virtues."[81] Campbell, however, had avoided this danger; indeed, Jeffrey argues that a wide survey of this kind, like "familiar intercourse with men of different habits," might itself be a strong instrument of education working to dispel narrow prejudices. In this light, Jeffrey places Campbell's work as an honorable successor to Percy's *Reliques*, Warton's *History*, Johnson's *Lives*, and the many commentators on Shakespeare, all of whom he honors for helping the nation to recover "from that strange and ungrateful forgetfulness of our older poets, which began with the Restoration, and continued almost unbroken till after the middle of the last century" (2:9). This clear assertion of a constructive role for literary history is new in Jeffrey's writing and is especially interesting if it is taken as a retrospect on his own essays earlier in that decade on Ford and Swift.

Nothing is more delightful, writes Jeffrey, than to trace the progress of poetry, this "highest and most intellectual of the arts." Colored as it is by the manners as well as the wisdom of the times, it gives us "a brief chronicle and abstract of all that was once interesting to the generations which have gone

[81] Review of Thomas Campbell, *Specimens of the British Poets* (*ER*, 1819), in ibid., 2:6.

by" (2:10). It is evident, however, that the historical interest of poetry lies as much in its openness to feeling and to everyday experience as to the refinements of the intellect.

> Conversant as poetry necessarily is with all that touches human feelings, concerns, and occupations, its character must have been impressed by every change in the moral and political condition of society, and must even retain the lighter traces of their successive follies, amusements, and pursuits; while, in the course of ages, the very multiplication and increasing business of the people have forced it through a progress not wholly dissimilar to that which the same causes have produced on the agriculture and landscape of the country. (2:10–11)

Here the speculative note of philosophical history mixes with the broad social concerns of the history of opinion, as well as with the celebratory purposes of tradition. It is the latter, however, that rounds out the description, as Jeffrey paints a picture of national progress rendered in metaphors of a changing landscape. After the "dreary wastes" of earliest times and the "vast forests and chases" of feudal England came "woodland hamlets, and goodly mansions, and parks rich with waste fertility," culminating in the "crowded cities, and road-side villas, and brick-walled gardens, and turnip fields, and canals, and artificial ruins, and ornamented farms and cottages trellised over with exotic plants!" (2:11).

This is certainly a picture of progress, but it is not without ambivalence. The successive transformations of the English landscape represent the evolution of English letters as a set of pervasive and perhaps irresistible changes. Most important, for those who would see themselves as the new makeweights of public opinion (and therefore members of the class that Jeffrey had earlier called the "truly governing part of society"), it offers a flattering picture of a spacious inheritance that descends from earlier days. Thus change, however radical, becomes acceptable when it is part of a celebration of a rich ancestral legacy. At the same time, countering this story of progressive cultivation, Jeffrey's lightly ironic tone also plays over the reduced landscapes of the present, so that the horizons of contemporary Britain—crowded, suburbanized, and artificial—stand as an oblique comment on the diminished world of the "after-poets."

In another way, too, Jeffrey's response to Campbell's anthology displays an ambivalent mix of progress and diminution—or, to put it in other terms, of awareness of transience and historical distance. Of the 250 authors represented in the anthology, Jeffrey observes, not 30 now enjoy popularity. And though such works as Campbell's may help, as an act of piety, to preserve some fragments, the sheer "superfluity and abundance of our treasures" dictates that much will be cast aside and never be revived.

When we see how much the past two hundred years have done to the ranks of British poets, Jeffrey laments, "we cannot help being dismayed at the prospect which lies before the writers of the present day." Extrapolating from the prolific production of his own times, Jeffrey could only predict a vast multiplication of the problem, spurred on by the extension of "wealth, population, and education":

> Now if this goes on for a hundred years longer, what a task will await the poetical readers of 1919! Our living poets will then be nearly as old as Pope and Swift are at present—but there will stand between them and that generation nearly ten times as much fresh and fashionable poetry as is now interposed between us and those writers:—and if Scott and Byron and Campbell have already cast Pope and Swift a good deal into the shade, in what form and dimensions are they themselves likely to be presented to the eyes of our great grandchildren? The thought, we own, is a little appaling;—and we confess we see nothing better to imagine than that they may find a comfortable place in some new collection of specimens—the centenary of the present publication. (2:15)

This is the furthest extension of Jeffrey's capacity for finding historical distance on the present, and it is telling that it is his own whiggish faith in progress, carried to its logical end, that brings him to this brink. It is worth noting, too, the place of genre in underscoring these perplexities of progress. As Jeffrey pointed out, Campbell's *Specimens* belongs to a genre that had been instrumental in extending the sense of English literary history. But an anthology, if carried out in the ecumenical spirit Jeffrey recommended, necessarily confronted the considerable tensions inherent in forming a historical canon. Scott had earlier failed in his effort to convince the publishers to undertake a hundred volumes of British verse; how many volumes might be needed a century later?

In the face of such tensions, Jeffrey's only recourse was, at least negatively, to call upon the all-transcending power of Shakespeare: "We have no Shakespeare, alas! to shed never-setting light on his contemporaries!—and if we continue to write and rhyme at the present rate for 200 years longer, there must be some new art of *short-hand reading* invented—or all reading will be given up in despair" (2:15).

Eleven

"The Living Character of Bygone Ages": Memoir and the Historicization of Everyday Life

In pursuing Francis Jeffrey's engagement with literary history and literary tradition, we have had more than one glimpse of the nineteenth century's fascination with one of its favorite narrative genres, the historical memoir. As Jeffrey wrote in reviewing the memoirs of Lady Fanshawe (a work that, he admitted, in most respects failed to live up to his expectations), "it still gives us a peep at a scene of surpassing interest from a new quarter; and at all events adds one other item to the great and growing store of those contemporary notices which are every day familiarizing us more and more with the living character of by-gone ages; and without which we begin, at last, to be sensible, that we can neither enter into their spirit, nor even understand their public transactions."[1] So appealing was the genre, in fact, that one reviewer complained of misrepresentation when a new life of Bolingbroke was given what he called "the attractive title of '*Memoirs*.' "[2]

Jeffrey's words do not suggest that memoirs are a substitute for a traditional narrative of "public transactions," but rather that these more informal accounts capture an inner spirit that is essential to understanding the external events that are the usual preoccupation of historians. To one degree or another, of course, all forms of primary document ("contemporary notices") held this sort of attraction, but it is not surprising that an age that saw itself as addicted to the pleasures of biography gave special prominence to historical memoirs. Among the many advantages of the genre were its lack of formality, the opportunities it offered to satisfy curiosity about the textures of everyday life, and the space it gave to female authorship and female biography. All this made for a path that—to quote Jeffrey again—avoided the "gross defects of regular history," while also keeping clear of the seductions of fiction.

[1] Jeffrey, *Contributions to Edinburgh Review*, 1:464. The review of the *Memoirs of Lady Fanshawe* appeared in *ER* in October 1829.

[2] The reviewer was J. W. Croker. Since the author had done nothing to search out "more secret or particular information," he objected, "an essay on the life and writings" would have been truer and more modest. See Croker's review of *Memoirs of Lord Bolingbroke*, by George Wingrove Cooke, *Quarterly Review* 54 (1835): 368.

The closeness of memoir to everyday life, however, also meant that it was hard, even for those who loved the genre, to shake the accusation that they were indulging in intrusive or illicit curiosity. We see this in the twists and turns of another of Jeffrey's declarations:

> We have a great indulgence, we confess, for the taste, or curiosity, or whatever it may be called, that gives its value to such publications . . . and are inclined to think the desire of knowing, pretty minutely, the manner and habits of former times,—of understanding in all their details, the character and ordinary way of life and conversation of our forefathers—a very liberal and laudable desire; and by no means to be confounded with that hankering after contemporary slander, with which this age is so miserably infested, and so justly reproached.[3]

Clearly, the effective difference between "liberal" curiosity and simple prying had everything to do with distance, a distance that the philosophical postures adopted in Jeffrey's own reviewing, as well as the scholarly efforts of editors and publishers, did much to establish.

One considerable field of memoir reading belonged to the history of France before and during the Revolution. Another, as Jeffrey's enthusiasm for Lucy Hutchinson reminds us, was the English seventeenth century, the period of Britain's own domestic upheavals. In fact, when we read the firsthand accounts we most associate with the seventeenth century, we often forget how much is owed to the biographical interests of the early nineteenth: Hutchinson's *Life* was first published in 1806, Evelyn's diary in 1818, Pepys's in 1825, Dorothy Osborne's letters in 1836. Nor was this interest in retrieving the everyday quality of earlier times confined to a period now sufficiently remote to allow for a kind of romantic distanciation. More recent and less exotic times were also beginning to attract the same interest, as was demonstrated by the appeal of John Wilson Croker's edition of Boswell's *Life of Johnson* (1831). This extensively annotated republication carried the *Life* well beyond its original biographical interest and endowed it with a new meaning as the preeminent *historical* account of the daily life of literary London in the eighteenth century. "It is not speaking with exaggeration," wrote Carlyle, "but with measured sobriety, to say that this Book of Boswell's will give us more real insight into the *History of England* during those days than twenty other Books, falsely entitled 'Histories,' which take to themselves that special aim."[4]

The publication or republication of memoirs of earlier times constituted a characteristic effort to appropriate biography to wider historiographical purposes, ones for which history proper still possessed insufficient formal or technical resources. In this respect, it would not be unreasonable to compare

[3] See Jeffrey's review of Pepys (*ER*, 1825), in *Contributions to Edinburgh Review*, 1:476.

[4] Thomas Carlyle, "Boswell's Life of Johnson," in *The Works of Thomas Carlyle*, 30 vols. (New York: Scribner, 1904), 28:80.

the efforts of an editor to decode Pepys's private ciphers to the mixture of historical imagination and antiquarian knowledge that produced the Waverley novels. For the purposes of this chapter, however, the comparison I would like to draw is not to Scott's fictions, already so well discussed by so many students of this period, but to a further, complementary example of memoir, Henry Cockburn's *Memorials of His Time*.[5] Cockburn, who was Jeffrey's friend and biographer, casts his recollections less as a traditional autobiography than as a sketch for a social history of the present. As a collective portrait of the social and intellectual life of early-nineteenth-century Edinburgh, the book in effect projects the experience of reading Evelyn or Boswell onto the curiosity of future generations.

The Perils of Biography: Wordsworth and Croker

Hutchinson, Evelyn, Pepys, Croker's Boswell, Cockburn's *Memorials*—these publications speak clearly to the appetite for biographical memoirs that characterized this period and the way in which that appetite could be directed to historical purposes. I want to begin, however, not with the indisputable presence of this interest in biography, but with the resistances that it provoked, especially the fear (already noted in Jeffrey) that an indiscriminate taste for private revelation had corrupted the taste of the age.

"A life which is worth reading," Mackintosh once declared to John Wilson Croker, "ought never to have been written."[6] This rueful witticism expresses the chagrin of a failed autobiographer, but it also expresses a widely felt anxiety about the dangers to privacy inherent in the rage for biography. Many others might be quoted to illustrate this point, but I will restrict myself to just two, William Wordsworth and John Wilson Croker. Ironically, the former was the supreme autobiographical poet of his age, the latter was Boswell's editor.

Wordsworth's "Letter to a Friend of Robert Burns" (1816) is many things: a defense of Burns's character, a plea for tolerance of his private failings, a sermon on the moral value of poetry and hence the need to attend to a poet's works rather than his life, a chance to even the score with Francis Jeffrey by championing a brother poet against the complacencies of the *Edinburgh Review*. But in its broadest aspect, the "Letter" is a polemic on the dangers to national character posed by the public's appetite for intrusive biography, a danger all the more insidious because it threatened the private character of Englishmen:

[5] Cockburn's *Memorials of His Time* was not published until 1856, but he began collecting the materials in 1821 and completed the work by 1830. See below, note 35.

[6] Mackintosh's aphorism is quoted by John Wilson Croker in his review of the *Life of W. Wilberforce*, *Quarterly Review* 62 (1838): 216.

> The life of Johnson by Boswell had broken through the preexisting delicacies, and afforded the British public an opportunity of acquiring experience, which before it had happily wanted; nevertheless, at the time when the ill-selected medley of Burns' correspondence first appeared, little progress had been made (nor is it likely that, by the mass of mankind, much ever will be made) in determining what portion of these confidential communications escapes the pen in courteous, yet often innocent, compliance—to gratify the several tastes of correspondents.[7]

Biography, Wordsworth insisted, is not an indiscriminate or disinterested inquiry, like science. In biography as much as in fiction, we seek truth "only for obviously justifying purposes, moral or intellectual."[8] Wordsworth did not deny that the truth in question might be unpleasant, but to trace the life of an "afflicted pilgrim" was justified only so far as the story of the journey will be edifying for others. Since Boswell, however, another spirit had imposed itself—a spirit that, if allowed to prevail, threatened the health of English society in fundamental ways. Like the anti-Jacobin polemicists of an earlier decade, Wordsworth rested his case on a conviction that enormous public consequences rested on maintaining the quality of private life. Wise men, he argued, "respect, as one of the noblest characteristics of Englishmen, that jealousy of familiar approach, which, while it contributes to the maintenance of private dignity, is one of the most efficacious guardians of rational public freedom."[9]

Curiously, though Boswell was alleged to be the initiator of this intrusive and corrupting style of biography, Boswell's most significant early-nineteenth-century editor, John Wilson Croker, shared many of Wordsworth's doubts. Indeed, Croker would excuse his decision to reedit the work by saying that, though the original decision to publish the *Life* could be questioned, once published, the work was best presented accompanied by proper historical materials. Croker considered himself an expert on biography, and he reviewed the state of the art on a number of occasions, including a review of Mackintosh's life. "The most remarkable feature, we think, in the literature of the present day is the great and increasing proportion which biography, and particularly *autobiography*, appears to bear to the general mass of publications."[10] But in Croker's view the present attractions of biography had led to characteristic

[7] "Letter to a Friend of Burns," in *The Prose Works of William Wordsworth*, ed. W. J. B. Owen and J. W. Smyser (Oxford: Oxford UP, 1974), 120. Wordsworth's complaint was aimed especially at the publication of Burns's private letters, which he thought the public had no need to see, nor ability to comprehend.

[8] Wordsworth, *Prose Works*, 121.

[9] Ibid., 122. "Such a philosophy," he warned, "runs a risk of becoming extinct among us, if the coarse intrusions into the recesses, the gross breaches upon the sanctities of domestic life, to which we have lately been more and more accustomed, are to be regarded as indications of a vigorous state of public feeling—favourable to the maintenance of the liberties of our country."

[10] John Wilson Croker, reviewing the *Memoirs of the Life of Sir James Mackintosh*, *Quarterly Review* 54 (1835): 250.

abuses and what he labeled a deterioration in the public taste. "There is nothing more easy and more worthless," Croker writes, "than a biography in the modern fashion" (250).

For Croker, as for Wordsworth, the dangers of biography had to do with the blurring of public and private matters. But Croker's apprehension was not quite the Wordsworthian (and Burkean) fear of a loss of some essential quality of Englishness founded in private manners. Rather, he argued that the spreading circles of biography were trivializing the concerns of the biographer, a consequence (it appears) of an expanding market for life writing and the consequent commercialization of the genre. "The eminence of the person—the splendour or utility of his or her life—the information it may convey, or the lesson it may inculcate, are by no means—as they used formerly to be—essential considerations in the choice of a subject."[11] Lives of second- and third-rate people have multiplied. Publishers compete to get their biographies out. Lives that used to win a few lines of eulogy in a parish church are now given full treatment, with the usual result being to leave their victim a smaller man.

The result, in Croker's view, was a kind of runaway inflation in the business of biography. With more being written about less, "it must be confessed that at this moment biography is perhaps the very lowest of all the classes of literature; it has become a mere *manufacture*, which seems in a great measure to have superseded that of *novels*—much to the damage of the *light* reader as well as the graver—the biographical *romance* being, for the most part, infinitely inferior in point of interest, and not very much superior in veracity."[12]

Croker complained that the circulating libraries were filled with the lives of second- or third-rate persons "to whom the honours of a special biography have been voted."[13] Evidently, a *true* library of biography should be thought of as a kind of national pantheon, filled only with heroes of unquestionable distinction. The "honour" should not be lightly given, nor obscured by second-rate pieties. Thus the "more serious objections" of his review are directed against what he calls "this system of *extemporaneous* and *contemporaneous* biography." Memoirs of the recently deceased, Croker charges, are written in a spirit of "amiable partiality" or "calculating prudence," a spirit that covers not only the main subject but all of the secondary figures as well. The effect is almost inevitably that historical truth is sacrificed to personal feelings.[14]

[11] Ibid.

[12] Ibid., 251.

[13] Ibid., 250.

[14] Ibid., 251–52. These objections to contemporary biography should, of course, be kept in mind in thinking about Croker's edition of Boswell, which is discussed below. His handling of the contents of Mackintosh's life is consistent with these remarks. His relationship with Mackintosh was a good one, despite the opposition of their two parties, and when he was working on the Boswell edition he expressed to Mackintosh his view that very little divided them politically. He relied on Mackintosh for information and cites him as an authority on the times of Boswell and

Pepys

In contrast, memoirs of earlier times carried none of the fears of improper revelation that were attached to contemporary lives. Indeed, distance might transform the most trivial or the most intimate of private records into an invaluable resource for imagining the textures of common life in another age. At this remove, the rootedness of these narratives in private life only conferred authority on their message. Lucy Hutchinson's sober, wifely devotion helped authenticate her account, just as Evelyn's patrician retirement lent added weight to his. Most of all, Pepys's secret cipher (as every reviewer noted) seemed a guarantee of honest detachment sufficient to enshrine his diary as the supreme history of private life in the age of Charles II.

In an earlier chapter I examined the way in which Lucy Hutchinson's editor and descendant, Julius Hutchinson, strained all his editorial efforts to depoliticize the memoir of his regicide ancestors and recast the *Life* as a family memoir of decidedly sentimental cast. Similar choices, though seldom as dramatic, faced other editors and reviewers of seventeenth-century memoirs. The reception of Pepys's diary is a case in point: in the conservative *Quarterly*, Walter Scott welcomed the publication with an easy, offhanded appreciation, while in the radical *Westminster* Pepys was greeted by a narrow, suspicious, and decidedly political review.

Scott opened his arms to the wide variety of information and pleasures the book could offer. On public affairs, readers would find much that was curious and valuable, though nothing absolutely new as evidence. "But there is much that is additional and explanatory of what was formerly known; much that removes all doubt,—that throws a more distinct and vivid light over the picture of England and its government during the ten years succeeding the Restoration."[15] This same vividness extended to all areas of society, and Scott waved his hand in turn at all the kinds of readers who would find themselves attracted: "the curious in musical antiquities," the kind of "antiquaries, who retire within ancient enchanted circles, magical temples, and haunted castles, venerated by the forefathers," as well as those "who desire to be aware of the earliest discoveries, as well in sciences as in the useful arts." "There exists a whole class of Old Bailey antiquaries—men who live upon dying speeches," Scott continued, also the "lover of ancient voyages and travels," "the lover of antique scandal," the seeker of literary anecdotes, or the student of political economy. All of these readers would find something to interest them in Pepys's diary (310–13).

Burke in numerous places. At the same time it is evident from the review that the Mackintosh he admired was the public man, and he criticized the *Memoirs* for the amount of space given to Mackintosh's literary life against his public activities.

[15] Walter Scott on "Memoirs of Samuel Pepys," *Quarterly Review* 33 (1826): 304.

Much of this, as we will see shortly, would seem infuriatingly beside the point to the readers of the *Westminster Review*, but the last thing Scott wanted was to have the diary's miscellaneousness set aside for the sake of higher literary or political ends. In comparison to Evelyn, Scott admitted, Pepys lacked the nobler ranges of sentiment. But for just that reason his diary was far more attractive than his contemporary's in "variety and general amusement." Almost inevitably, however, the closest comparison was to Boswell, whose small-minded greatness (as so many reviewers chose to see it) made his work the favorite antiquarian attic for the century that followed. "Pepys's very foibles," wrote Scott, "have been infinitely in favour of his making an amusing collection of events; as James Boswell, without many personal peculiarities, could not have written his inimitable life of Johnson."[16]

Pepys's gossip differed from Boswell's, however, in that the times that he spoke for belonged more securely to history, so that there was little sense of risk in detailing the private affairs of this more remote age. This left Pepys's belated reader free to indulge all forms of curiosity, as Scott confessed at the opening of the review:

> There is a curiosity implanted in our nature which receives much gratification from prying into the actions, feelings, and sentiments of our fellow creatures. The same spirit, though very differently modified and directed, which renders a female gossip eager to know what is doing among her neighbours over the way, induces the reader for information, as well as him who makes his studies his amusement, to turn willingly to those volumes which promise to lay bare the motives of the writer's actions, and the secret opinions of his heart. We are not satisfied with what we see and hear of the conqueror on the field of battle, or the great statesman in the senate; we desire to have the privilege of the valet-de-chambre to follow the politician into his dressing closet and to see the hero in those private relations where he is a hero no longer.[17]

James Mackintosh had used the very same image of the politician undressed to explain his dissatisfaction with the lack of real self-revelation in Gibbon's autobiography. But Mackintosh could never have managed Scott's seemingly careless acceptance of the idea that it is human nature to want to pry, that prying means not just seeing the outside, but entering into feelings and sentiments, that readers are gossips and writers are too, even when they are studious antiquarian ones, and that the ultimate prize is the valet's privilege, the chance for intimacy. All this was contained in Scott's ease with his work and himself, an ease that allowed him to acknowledge that the historian's impulse to find his way into the lives and minds of other individuals and other times is continuous with his curiosity about all sides of life.

[16] Ibid., 314.
[17] Ibid., 281.

Thanks to the play of still further historical distance, Scott's appreciation of Pepys as a social chronicle now seems only natural. For this reason, it is valuable to consult the contradictory views presented by the *Westminster Review*, which insisted on a narrowly political reading of the diary as a record of public corruption in its time. If, at the same time, the reviewer's position seems to be a negation of much of what has been said about the early-nineteenth-century interest in the everyday, this is only further reason for paying attention to the evidences of tension surrounding the reception of memoirs.

The *Westminster* reviewer was not unaware of the attractions of the genre. "The Diary of Mr. Pepys," he wrote in opening, "is the most curious of those MS. memorials of old times, which the inquisitive spirit of the present age has raked up from the dust of neglected libraries. We are not told to what circumstances we are indebted for its publication, at this particular period, after so long an interval of repose. Perhaps we owe it to the fortunate escape of Mr. Evelyn's Memoirs from the scissors, and to the celebrity which that amusing piece of autobiography has acquired."[18]

The *Westminster* saw the wider value of the diary as a barometer of public opinion, especially during great changes or public events. But despite an occasional reference to the curious details of life in Pepys's time, the reviewer was hostile to any broadly historicist appreciation of social change. Such views of history were likely to lead to good-humored indulgence: a tendency to mythologize the past and to tolerate the abuses of the present. Rather the reviewer saw the diary as the secret history of bad government; or, varying the metaphor, a light that illuminated "the darkest holes and corners of administration."[19]

For the *Westminster*, then, the secrecy of the diary had a straightforwardly political importance, since any thought of publication on Pepys's part would have resulted in the loss "of all or most of those singular confessions, unconscious exhibitions of character, and pieces of private and ministerial intelligence, which give them a rare and inestimable value."[20] Pepys, it was accepted, was an honest and efficient official, but he was no reformer. Having neither the opportunity nor temper to oppose the misdeeds of his superiors, he contented himself with a silent protest in the pages of his journal, "where, like the wife of king Midas, he breathed his secret, too big for his breast, and buried it in the closest recess of his cabinet" (428).

The case for reading Pepys from a strictly political point of view is put most strongly in a long passage in which the reviewer asks himself rhetorically whether he might be accused of overstressing the importance of the subject.

[18] "Memoir of Samuel Pepys," *Westminster Review* 4 (1825): 408. The review was probably the work of William Stevenson, the Scottish antiquary and journalist, who also contributed to the *ER* and the *Scots Magazine*.

[19] Ibid., 454, 455.

[20] Ibid., 410–11.

To the question of letting bygones be bygones—"After all, what is the reign of Charles the 2nd to the present age?"—there is a firm reply. If mankind changed its nature from age to age, history would be no more than "mere romance." But the truth is that political conditions remain much the same from generation to generation, and "the experience of former disasters"[21] can be a lesson to present times.

The central issue here is much the same as it was for Hume's critics—or at least for his critics as Hume saw them. The *Westminster*, like the Whig and Tory factionalists of Hume's day, could not allow the sort of distanciation that, for Hume at least, placed the struggles of the seventeenth century in a substantially dissimilar frame of historical reference. If history was not to become a political anodyne—a danger certainly hinted at in Scott's amiably antiquarian self-presentation—it would have to resist both sentimental coziness and ironic distance. For the reform-minded reviewer, then, the emphasis would not be on the picturesque variety of seventeenth-century life, but on underlying continuities that allowed history to be mobilized for purposes of political analysis.

The argument that history must subordinate simple curiosity to the lessons of public life has a noble ancestry,[22] but the *Westminster* could not entirely resist the interiorized understanding that marked the age. Along with his rejection of the conservative implications of historicism and his demand for a usable past, the reviewer concluded his essay with a lament that Pepys had not carried on his witness beyond the first decade of the Restoration:

> To have crept, as it were, into his breast, and read his feelings, at the conclusion of this period, which beheld a second ejectment of the family in whose service he had continued so long, and ejectment that undid the glorious work of the Restoration, in which we have seen him engage with an exuberance of joy that almost affects the reader with a like sensation, would have been a privilege capable, to use his own strong expression, of affecting us with "a glut of content."[23]

For just a moment here we encounter the language of feelings and sensations notably absent from most of this review. For the reviewer, Pepys's exuberant response to the "glorious work" of Restoration had almost been capable of affecting the reader "with a like sensation." We can only assume that the unwritten portion of his diary, chronicling the downfall of the same regime, would

[21] Ibid., 455.

[22] "Hence it comes about that the great bulk of those who read it [i.e., history] take pleasure in hearing of the various incidents which are contained in it, but never think of imitating them, since they hold them to be not merely difficult but impossible of imitation, as if the heaven, the sun, the elements and man had in their motion, their order, and their potency become different from what they used to be." Machiavelli, *The Discourses*, trans. Walker Richardson and B. Richardson (Harmondsworth: Penguin, 1970).

[23] Stevenson, "Memoir of Samuel Pepys," 454–55.

have given the reader a matching set of sensations, appropriate to this collapse. Why, then, is this secret history so much to be desired? A longer record would have had an obvious documentary value, but it could not have added anything substantially new to a record that the reviewer already saw as a complete exposure of the abuses of arbitrary royal power. Rather, the continuation of Pepys's "minutes" would have produced something of a different order: not the objective record that so far has been celebrated, but a subjective one, which would register the feelings of a loyal servant watching the collapse of the old regime.

There is certainly an edge of cruelty in this gloating over how it would feel to be able to watch Samuel Pepys watching while the regime he had served fell apart. But cruelty aside, there is something more fundamental at stake. It amounts to the idea that the events of 1688 would be more completely felt and better understood when registered subjectively in this way. The fall of the Stuarts would be that much more complete when vicariously experienced from within.

Boswell, Croker, and the Critics

Even to the *Westminster*'s severe reviewer, the violation of Pepys's long-kept privacy seemed more of a distraction than a danger. But Mackintosh's biographical conundrum was not so easy to escape for more recent works. This was especially true for Boswell's *Johnson*, a masterpiece of literary biography and the work that brought forward all the period's unease over the dilemmas of biography.

The new style of biography was hardly Boswell's creation. *The Life of Johnson* was the culmination of a century of fertile experiment. It was both an extraordinary work in its own right and a convenient shorthand for a whole episode in literary biography; all the more so when it was reintroduced to the English public in 1831 in "A New Edition with Numerous Additions and Notes, by John Wilson Croker."

After a generation of controversy about biography, readers of Croker's edition had reason to understand the implications of a life of a private man written to this length and detail. The life of Dr. Johnson, Croker wrote,

> is indeed a most curious *chapter in the history of man;* for certainly there is no instance of the life of any other human being having been exhibited in so much detail, or with so much fidelity. There are, perhaps, not many men who have practiced so much self examination as to know *themselves* as well as every reader knows Dr. Johnson.[24]

[24] John Wilson Croker, ed., *The Life of Johnson. A New Edition with Numerous Additions and Notes*, 5 vols. (London, 1831), 1:xxv–xxvi.

Whatever might be thought of subjecting any private individual to this degree of public scrutiny—and Croker takes pains to leave the question open—it was clear to him that the result was a measure of Johnson's moral greatness:

> We must recollect that it is not his *table talk* or his literary conversations only that have been published: all his most private and most trifling correspondence—all his most common as well as his most confidential intercourses—all his most secret communion with his own conscience—and even the solemn and contrite exercises of his piety, have been divulged and exhibited to the "garish eye" of the world without reserve—I had almost said, without delicacy. Young, with gloomy candour, has said "Heaven's Sovereign saves all beings but himself / That hideous sight, a naked human heart." What a man must Johnson have been, whose heart, having been laid more bare than that of any other mortal ever was, has passed almost unblemished through so terrible an ordeal! (1:xxvi)

This was meant as homage to Johnson, but it was also an uncomfortable tribute to Boswell and Boswell's art. To recognize greatness in Boswell's Johnson was a very different thing than to salute it in one of Plutarch's heroes. His was not a greatness of public doing, but a greatness in being seen. It was a kind of greatness in little things in reach of us all—and so lost by all. As Croker wrote, "Human life is a series of inconsistencies; and when Johnson's early misfortunes, his protracted poverty, his strong passions, his violent prejudices, and above all, his mental infirmities, are considered, it is only wonderful that a portrait so laboriously minute and so painfully faithful does not exhibit more of blemish, incongruity, and error."[25]

Even Croker felt that to put such knowledge in the hands of common readers was not (in the language of the times) delicate. That decision, however, was not his to make, or so he wanted to believe. "Whatever doubts may have existed as to the prudence or the propriety of the *original* publication," he stated at the opening of his preface,

> however naturally private confidence was alarmed, or individual vanity offended, the voices of criticism and complaint were soon drowned in the general applause. And no wonder—the work combines within itself the four most entertaining classes of writing—biography, memoirs, familiar letters, and that assemblage of literary anecdotes which the French have taught us to distinguish by the termination *Ana*.[26]

As a work of "amusement," then, the first publication of the life had been enormously successful, but for reasons that were not completely respectable.[27]

[25] Ibid., 1:xxv.

[26] Ibid., 1:v.

[27] "It was originally received with an eagerness and relished with a zest which undoubtedly were sharpened by the curiosity which the unexpected publication of the words and deeds of so many persons still living could not but excite. But this motive has gradually become weaker, and may now be said to be extinct" (ibid., 1:v).

It follows that the job of the new editor would be to distance his new edition as far as possible from the gossipy, intrusive curiosity that had motivated the first popularity of the biography. In accomplishing this work he could appeal to the workings of time, which had removed some of the old attractions, but also provided new ones: "and as the interval which separates us from the actual time and scene increases, so appear to increase the interest and delight which we feel at being introduced, as it were, into that distinguished society of which Dr. Johnson formed the centre, of which his biographer is the historian" (1:v–vi).

Boswell, in short, would make a new appearance as a respectable historian. But to do so he would need much help from his editor, whose labors were devoted to elaborating an apparatus of scholarship to rescue the work from "the gradual obscurity that time throws over the persons and incidents of private life." As the reviewer in the *Monthly* put it, in enthusiastic echo of Croker's own prologue: "He has succeeded far beyond any hopes which we had ventured to entertain, in arresting the progress by which one of the most entertaining memoirs in our language, was making towards the regions, not indeed of oblivion but of obscurity; and has thus, not unworthily connected his name with a work, whose claims to immortality he has most materially increased."[28]

The reviewer went on to admit that the resulting apparatus made the text less readable—made it less appealing "to those classes of readers, unhappily too numerous, who like nothing but plain sailing." But, though the bracketed additions and corrections or the "perpetual reference to the notes" might be troublesome, he was sure that there was no better way of doing the job. And had the work of rescue not been undertaken now, in a very few years the witnesses would have disappeared and the effort could not have succeeded at all.

In all this, Croker's sympathetic reviewer was perhaps deliberately missing the point. He saw the success of Croker's efforts without acknowledging the antecedent political and moral problem that gave his labors their full value. In a real sense time was more of an ally than enemy, and if the apparatus of footnotes and brackets impeded readers who were looking for "plain sailing," so much the better. From the start the editor's central purpose was to remove the *Life* from the category of amusement and position it in the higher one of instruction. In this effort the scaffolding of scholarship was undoubtedly there to shore up the crumbling building, but it also served to emphasize its status as a historical monument.

Croker was, of course, perfectly right in pointing to the ways in which time had remade Boswell's book. Isaac D'Israeli—one of those whom Croker thanks for information—recalled the controversies surrounding the original edition. "On its publication it raised a great disturbance, of which I could afford

[28] *MR*, n.s. 2 (1831): 453–54.

you many ludicrous instances. . . . So many were displeased at themselves in those volumes; so many secrets were published; so many of the malcontents found themselves unnoticed—that nothing but abuse and reading the book was heard."[29] The controversies around the new edition, however, were of a different kind. The reviewers drew different conclusions about Boswell's character as a biographer or Croker's as an editor; in one degree or another, however, all accepted Croker's premise that the "life" had become a history.

Curiously it was Macaulay, writing in the *Edinburgh Review*, who did least with the historical meaning of the work. His rivalry with Croker meant that his first wish was to demolish Croker's claims to historical scholarship.[30] Only when this was done—and done at some length—did Macaulay turn to the author himself. In Macaulay's view, Boswell was little more than a babbling fool, yet it was just this foolishness that made him the greatest of all biographers. "All the caprices of his temper," Macaulay writes, "all the illusions of his vanity, all his hypochondriac whimsies, all his castles in the air, he displayed with a cool self-complacency, a perfect unconsciousness that he was making a fool of himself, to which it is impossible to find a parallel in the whole history of mankind" (1:658).

This spectacle of egotism entertaining the world at its own expense was yet another version of Mackintosh's aphorism on the perils of biography.[31] Ironically, however, Boswell's foolishness was also taken as the guardian of his sincerity. It allowed him to be open and truthful, where wiser men were secretive or calculating. Just as Jeffrey trusted in Pepys's shorthand, so Macaulay believed in Boswell's alleged mental shortcomings:

> Of all confessors, Boswell is the most candid. . . . Those weaknesses which most men keep covered up in the most secret places of the mind, not to be disclosed to the eye of friendship or of love, were precisely the weaknesses which Boswell paraded before all the world. He was perfectly frank, because the weakness of his understanding and the tumult of his spirits prevented him from knowing when he made himself ridiculous.[32]

As an assessment of Boswell this may be silly, but John Gibson Lockhart's warm defense of Croker in the rival *Quarterly* differed only in degree. What made the Tory review very much richer was the generous spirit in which it

[29] *The Croker Papers*, ed. L. Jennings, 3 vols. (London, 1884), 2:40–41. On Croker's friendship with Isaac D'Israeli, see James Ogden, *Isaac D'Israeli* (Oxford: Clarendon, 1969), 133–37.

[30] "Nothing in the work has astonished us so much as the ignorance and carelessness of Mr. Croker with respect to facts and dates" (Macaulay, *Miscellaneous Essays*, 1:641).

[31] Macaulay's view of Boswell is much criticized by F. R. Hart in his valuable study *Lockhart as Romantic Biographer* (Edinburgh: Edinburgh UP, 1971), chap. 1. But, as I have tried to indicate, however faulty Macaulay's picture is, his view of Boswell is no more than a heightened version of what Hart himself calls "Paradoxical Theory in a Biographical Age."

[32] Macaulay, *Miscellaneous Essays*, 1:659–60.

was written and the wider view that this permitted of Croker/Boswell as a window into history. Lockhart's gentler version of the biography conundrum was his image of Boswell not as a vain fool, but as an enthusiastic naïf. "Never did any man tell a story with such liveliness and fidelity and yet contrive to leave so strong an impression that he did not himself understand it. This is, in one view, the main charm of his book."[33] Boswell, he said, was like the proverbial child in a courtroom—the most dangerous witness in a bad case, the very best in a good one. Who, he asks, would have wanted a more critical mind as the biographer of Johnson, any more than as the narrator of the Persian Wars? Who could wish that instead of James Boswell the task had been given to Edmund Burke, Johnson's only intellectual equal in the society of that time?

In his review of Sismondi a decade before, James Mackintosh had urged historians to read the old chronicles and to try to retain in their own accounts some of the naive vivacity of their sources. Lockhart's review works in much the same spirit by assimilating Boswell's book—"this charming narrative"—to the class of naive social chronicles. But Lockhart also discovered another dimension in Boswell's innocence that was not so much personal as national. Boswell, he argued, observed many things that would then have seemed too obvious to an Englishman to bother recording, though time had since made them unfamiliar to Englishmen too. Reciprocally, Johnson, for his part, was "naturally led to speak out his views and opinions on a thousand questions" that the Scotsman was able to record for posterity.[34]

Lockhart's view of Boswell's value as a witness closely parallels the way in which Walter Scott structured *Waverley* as the story of a young and naive Englishman learning the ways of the north. It may be, then, that Lockhart, who was Scott's son-in-law and biographer, owed to Scott his sensitivity to the ways in which cultural distances might produce the same effect as temporal ones. Equally, Lockhart had some of Scott's understanding of the importance of collecting a record of language and manners on their way to extinction:

> The interfusion of three nations, as to manners, opinions, feelings, and in a word, *character*, has proceeded at so rapid a pace within the last half-century, and is so likely to go on, and to end in all but a complete amalgamation before another period of similar extent shall have expired, that if it were but for having given us, ere it was too late, a complete portrait of the real native uncontaminated Englishman, with all his tastes and prejudices fresh and strong about him . . . the world would have owed him . . . no trivial obligation.[35]

[33] Lockhart on "Boswell" in *Quarterly Review* 46 (1832): 8.

[34] Ibid., 10.

[35] Ibid.

Here Lockhart echoes the language of the postscript to *Waverley* and all but bestows the novel's subtitle—*'Tis Sixty Years Since*—on the older Scottish work. But it was also Lockhart's humor to carry off a sly reversal of several generations of Enlightenment ethnographers—Johnson and Scott included. In Boswell's human laboratory, Lockhart claimed, the prize exhibition was not the usual picturesque Highlander, but the Highland visitor himself, the bearish, prejudiced, provincial "uncontaminated Englishman."

Even as a novelistic character, Lockhart added, Boswell's Johnson would have been a most precious record of its times. "But what can the best character in any novel be, compared to a full-length of the reality of genius." Thus to the alliance of novel and history forged by Scott, his son-in-law joined the still more powerful claims of biography, and concluded:

> Enlarged and illuminated, as we now have it . . . "Boswell's Johnson" is, without doubt . . . that English book, which, were this island to be sunk tomorrow with all that it inhabits, would be most prized in other days and countries, by the students "of us and of our history."

Of all the reviewers of Croker, only Thomas Carlyle would carry further Boswell's claim to be the *essential* historian of the eighteenth century.

Henry Cockburn and the Preservation of Social Memory

In Croker's Boswell, as in the belated publication of Hutchinson, Evelyn, and Pepys, new historical accounts were created by a process of editorial reframing. Texts that had been written with very different purposes in mind were reread in an enlarged social framework to feed the current interest in evoking a wider social memory. From this point it was not a long step to the memorializing of one's own life in light of the same expanded consciousness of social change. This step was taken by Henry Cockburn, the friend and biographer of Francis Jeffrey, whose *Memorials of His Time* and two further volumes of memoir are a fund of memory set aside prospectively in the midst of passing time.

In a sense, Cockburn's memorialization of his generation represented a return to the first purpose of history, which was to record recent events for the benefit of posterity. Thucydides and Caesar, Guicciardini and Clarendon all made this their point of departure. But in other ways Cockburn's *Memorials* are as far removed as possible from the public, political narratives of these statesman-historians. In this respect Cockburn's work stands closer to the methods and purposes of medieval chronicles, whose loose-jointed narratives preserved a picture of their times that was both encyclopedic and intimate—to the special delight of nineteenth-century readers.

The distinctive sense in which the *Memorials* could be described as a modern chronicle has a great deal to do with Cockburn's cultivation of both civic and personal memory. In classical histories, the historian's own perspective and experience was strenuously suppressed to avoid the imputation of partiality. But in Cockburn's re-creation of Edinburgh, personal memory is central, giving color and depth to public life and collective experience. Neither autobiography nor history, the *Memorials* tells a public story, but from a private vantage. It neither renounced public life for the cultivation of inwardness, nor rejected personality in the service of a public ideal. Rather, Cockburn's memoir attempted to preserve history not simply as a set of events, but as the experience of a generation. As Cockburn put it, "It occurred to me, several years ago, as a pity that no private account should be preserved of the distinguished men or important events that had marked the progress of Scotland, or at least of Edinburgh, during my day. I had never made a single note with a view to such a record. But about 1821 I began to recollect and to enquire."[36] Cockburn left it to his friends, however, to bring out the volumes of journals that became the *Memorials* and two further works of memoir, *Circuit Journeys* and *Sedition Trials*.

Cockburn was not the first to see the rich interest attaching to a personal chronicle of "the progress of Scotland." Alexander Carlyle and John Ramsay of Ochtertyre had done something similar. Creech and Arnot also left descriptions of the character and manners of Edinburgh, though these were not primarily autobiographical, and Scott himself planned a description of his own, only to renounce the idea when the youthful Robert Chambers published his popular volume on the traditions of the city. Nonetheless, Cockburn deservedly remains the best-remembered memorialist of early-nineteenth-century Edinburgh, nor is it coincidental that he was also an active campaigner for the preservation of the architectural and natural beauties of the city, a pioneering role continued by Edinburgh's architectural heritage association, called in his honor the Cockburn Society.

Cockburn was a devoted correspondent, and in many ways his letters are the best introduction to his life and writings. Friendship and memory, the constant preoccupation of the *Memorials*, are also the twin themes of Cock-

[36] Cockburn, *Memorials of His Time*, preface. The book was posthumously published from Cockburn's notebooks. On the composition of the *Memorials* as well as on Cockburn's correspondence, see Alan Bell's several contributions to Alan Bell, ed., *Lord Cockburn: A Bicentenary Commemoration* (Edinburgh: Scottish Academic P, 1979). See also Karl Miller, *Cockburn's Millennium* (Cambridge: Harvard UP, 1976). At an early stage of my work on Cockburn, Alan Bell very kindly made his transcriptions of Cockburn's letters available to me; all quotations from the correspondence have been checked against these transcriptions. I am deeply grateful to Alan Bell for this generosity. A selective version of Cockburn correspondence was published by Harry A. Cockburn, *Some Letters of Lord Cockburn, with passages omitted from the Memorials of his Time* (Edinburgh: Grant and Murray, 1932).

burn's correspondence. Even as a young man, he wrote pressingly about the slippage of memory and the need to preserve a treasury of personal recollection. To his friend, John Richardson, he lamented the daily loss of the memory of the ordinary feelings of everyday life. It is a pity "that so many of our feelings—and so many occurrences in existence, are daily suffered to drop for ever into irrecoverable oblivion." Why, he goes on to ask, do we part so easily

> with views and emotions, which at the time we are conscious of them, seem to us to be the only things worth living for. You have lived *nearly* 30 years—all this time your mind has been actively employed, and your heart warmly attached, to some thing or other. Yet if you will sit cross legged at the fire for half an hour, I suspect you will be able to make everything you can recollect, of past years, arise before you.[37]

Cockburn's thoughts, characteristically, turned to diary keeping, but, devoted as he was to the cultivation of memory, Cockburn had no use for what Carlyle would later call Wertherism—brooding self-love turning to moody self-hatred. His vocation as a diarist ultimately led outward, not inward, and the memories he urged Richardson to recollect at his fireside would be ones that could be widely shared:

> I know of no life, in which there is anything in the least like a true account of the feelings of a boy. I delight to hear you talk of Dalkeith school, because then I see in another the simple and actual notions I have so often felt myself, and wondered if anybody else did the same. Think what a curious volume you could make by just telling plainly what your prevailing feelings or opinions were for the 6 years you were under the beastly despotism of Bell.[38]

His own recollections of school were of a complete inability to see how reading of any kind might be pleasant, of being goaded by teachers to try harder and become ambitious, and finally of dreams of what his future might hold. Reading an old commonplace book, he had found a passage spelling out how he had imagined life would pass—"from about my 16th to my 72nd year, laid regularly out." Romantic and absurd though these imaginings were, they were also precious to him, and Cockburn concluded by announcing what amounts to a kind of vocation: "Now this brings me back to my position, that a life written with such minute fidelity to human nature, would of all things be the most interesting to the writer and the most useful to others. I am there-

[37] Henry Cockburn to John Richardson (?1806), NLS Dep. 235. Partially printed in *Some Letters*, 9–10. This melancholy sense of loss, Cockburn continues, was impressed on him by "looking over an old common place book, which revived so many facts, and strange old notions in me, notions that with all their absurdity I loved, that I began to lament I had never kept a minute diary of all the memorabilia of my days."

[38] Cockburn to Richardson, NLS Dep. 235.

fore sometimes half persuaded to record, e'er 'the glimmering landscape fade' the simple but real thoughts by the consciousness of which my past years and moments have been engaged."[39]

Autobiography is a pivot in Cockburn's later works, as in his letters. But for a man who was more sentimental than egotistical, his own biography was never an object in itself. It was always inscribed in the wider circle of friendships that made up his social world. This world was rooted in Edinburgh schoolrooms. It was nourished in the Speculative Society and in the efforts of underemployed young Whig lawyers to find briefs in a Tory-dominated city. With eventual prosperity, it grew to include country houses, Highland tours, and—for those whose careers had moved on to wider scenes—seasonal visits home.

One reason that friendship remained a central preoccupation for Cockburn was that it was always under threat. This was a group of talented provincials whose ambition and education always outran their finances and local opportunities. As distinctive a home as Edinburgh was for them—and the whole of the *Memorials* turns on this point—England was necessarily a wide temptation. Many, indeed, would leave to be "devoured by hungry London" (181). But if Richardson and other friends whose paths led away from the narrow circle of Edinburgh were not entirely lost, it was because of the enormous value these men gave to maintaining their ties. Letters, like Cockburn's, were the tokens of this continuing effort to hold their circle together; it is no wonder that his letters have a sentimental tone, or that friendship became a constant theme and a serious duty.[40]

By and large, Cockburn's group of friends was one that found success, not failure, so recollection of early adversity was warmed by the glow of eventual prosperity. When Francis Jeffrey gave up his position as lord advocate for Scotland, Cockburn keenly anticipated his friend's permanent return:

[39] Ibid.

[40] "The business of the survivors is to act and to enjoy to act, so as to diminish the misery of others; to enjoy, by cherishing the remembrance of their departed friends, and continuing keenly engaged in the virtuous associations in which they delighted. The performance of the necessary business of life; the increased cultivation of surviving friendships; and the bringing on, after our own meridian has been reached, of younger men, who may, in their turn, be our new supports and associates; these are the proper tests and fruits of a right sense of what is due to a lost friend. But Sunday tho' it be, I don't see why I should preach to you." Letter to Sir Thomas Dick Lauder, April 26, 1829, NLS Dep. 235. Extracts in *Some Letters*. Cockburn reacted to another loss (the bankruptcy and disgrace of a friend) with a similar determination to underline the value of friendship: "Amidst all these terrible examples of the precariousness of man's happiness, the reflection, How necessary it is to preserve the friendships that remain—always presses on me strongly. Some would rather say, Let them all go—since they end thus. But this is the language of desperation—and it is unnatural." Letter to Macvey Napier, July 5, 1828, BL Add. mss 34613, ff. 406–7.

> I can think of little else than the curious and gratifying result of the career you have run, since the days when I used to walk home with [you] to Buccleuch Place, from Dugald Stewart's political class, till now. This includes the period before the review began—when you were under proscription, and my worthy uncle Harry Dundas was the Autocrat of Scotland,—thro' the seditious ascendancy of that work; during 15 years of which whether you lived at Edinburgh or at Sydney, depended entirely on the pleasure of the public accuser,—till the late triumphs came thickly upon us.

"It could not be expected of Playfair," he added, "but would that Gordon and Horner had been here to enjoy this."[41]

This fragment of memory encapsulates what would be the essential theme of the *Memorials*. As we will see very shortly, that book celebrated the good humor and perseverance of talented youths in the face of prejudice in all the seats of power. For Cockburn, Jeffrey's climb—first to literary prominence in the *Review*, then to political eminence in Parliament—was not just a personal success. It was the triumph of enlightened opinion over Tory obscurantism. But Cockburn was also capable of taking a more humorous view of his friends' triumphs. When another of the circle, Andrew Rutherfurd, became lord advocate, Cockburn sent warm congratulations to his wife—a favorite correspondent. After indulging in his usual vein of sentimental recollection, Cockburn added:

> What I always think of with sorrow, is, that his mother is not here. What disrespectful jokes she and I would have had at my Lord. I met John t'other day, and said, "Well John, you're getting on. You were Mr when I first knew you; and now you're My Lord! I fancy you mean to be King soon?"—To which stutters John, "Eh! Eh! God, I wud na' wonder."[42]

The anecdotal talents Cockburn displayed in his correspondence make up a good part of the charm of his memoirs as well. But in an age that was easily alarmed by risks to privacy that same lively informality complicated the prospect of publication, and in the end Cockburn left it to his closest friends to decide the fate of his notebooks of recollection. For the *Memorials* in particular, his sense of delicacy was compounded by some uncertainty about the character of the work itself.[43] "I really wish that you and Rutherfurd would instruct me about the Red [book]," he wrote to Richardson.

[41] Letter to Francis Jeffrey, May 26, 1834, NLS Dep. 235; *Some Letters*, 36–37.

[42] Letter to Mrs. Andrew Rutherfurd, April 29, 1839, NLS Ms. 9687 ff. 105–6.

[43] In his instructions to his literary executors, he cautioned that the notebooks "have been written or collected for my own private amusement and occupation; and I abstain from destroying some of them myself because they may possibly amuse my family or friends. Any publication can only be with great caution and with the delicacy due to individuals named and to their surviving friends." About the "Sedition Trials" and the "Circuit Journal" he shows little hesitation, probably because the first was clearly public in its concerns, the second securely private. But the third seemed most perplexing: "if well selected and edited a curious work might be made out of

> He has seen only the first vol. but I suspect has not had time, during Session, to read it all. To divert his wife, I made her welcome, and she has read it all, but is so charmed with old Esky[44] that he half supersedes everything else. The sole question is, ought I to attempt to make a continuous history out of it; or ought [I] just to go on recording, and leave the mass to be put into shape by others after I shall be sodded?[45]

As we saw earlier, Cockburn said that he compiled the notebooks because he wanted to preserve a "private account . . . of the distinguished men or important events that had marked the progress of Scotland, or at least of Edinburgh, during my day." This brief summary points to three related themes. First, the book was to be an account framed in autobiographical memory—a private account as seen by an eyewitness ("in my day"). Second, it was, nonetheless, not to be a book about himself, but about others. Third, the story was to be shaped not only by its time and place, but a philosophical plot, "the progress of Scotland." Each of these elements gives the *Memorials* a part of its character. Schematically, we could say that the first provides its tone of warmth and sentiment, the second its picturesque subjects, the third its moral purpose and thematic unity.

Little needs to be said about the purely autobiographical side of the *Memorials* since much of the same ground was covered in looking at Cockburn's correspondence. The book begins as a conventional autobiography, recording the author's birth and giving some details of his family and circumstances. He recalls his father's character and occupations, his own intense love of his mother, his early days in school, and the later influence of Stewart, Playfair, and the debates in the Speculative Society. He also makes a point of the kinship, created by his mother's sister's marriage, to Henry Dundas, first viscount Melville, the most powerful Tory in Scotland.

All this is straightforward, and it is reinforced initially by the declaration that begins the second chapter. "In December 1800 I entered the Faculty of Advocates; and, with a feeling of nothingness, paced the Outer House. Being now of age, and in a position to observe things intelligently, I can speak of

---

Volumes of Edinburgh Events and recollections but this would require a very judicious hand. . . . All I say is that if these volumes had been written by another and I had the editing of them I could have made a good book out of them" (Apr. 3, 1852, NLS Ms. Acc. 3521). He also left instructions for the return or destruction of all letters, "except Jeffrey's which are too curious to let perish. But there won't be many epistles found perfidiously preserved by me. The fire has already devoured thousands of them."

[44] The reference is to Lord Eskgrove, one of a series of old and eccentric judges who preside over the early pages of the *Memorials:* "But a more ludicrous personage could not exist. When I first knew him he was in the zenith of his absurdity. People seemed to have nothing to do but to tell stories of this one man. To be able to give an anecdote of Eskgrove, with a proper imitation of his voice and manner, was a sort of fortune in society. Scott in those days was famous for this particularly" (Cockburn, *Memorials of His Time*, 118–19).

[45] Letter to John Richardson, March 19, 1852, NLS Dep. 235, and *Some Letters*, 69–70.

Edinburgh, and through it of Scotland, then and since, with knowledge of a witness, and indeed of an actor in most of its occurrences" (80). Characteristically, though the statement begins in autobiography, it ends in a far more general view. In this way the transition is accomplished from autobiographer to eyewitness; this is *not* a book about Henry Cockburn, but it is quite clearly to be Henry Cockburn's book about Edinburgh in Henry Cockburn's time.

This brings us to the second theme, the memory of "distinguished men or important events." This, the second circle of memory, is certainly the aspect of the memoir that has sustained its attractions over a long time. It is also the area in which Cockburn's own literary skills were displayed with greatest effect.

Nineteenth-century readers often read novels as if they were little more than spaces given over to the display of characters. Scott, for instance, was relished for his virtuosity in this area, which won him comparison with Shakespeare. But the taste for portraiture was not confined to novels. It figured in pathetic readings of historical works and was a force in the rage for biography, memoir, and literary anecdote. Cockburn's multitude of portraits were clearly a product of this climate, and we recall that his very first reader, Mrs. Rutherfurd, was so charmed with his portrait of an eccentric judge, Lord Eskgrove, "that he half supersedes everything else." No less eccentric, but more lovable, was Lord Hermand. "What was it that made Hermand such an established wonder and delight? It seems to me to have been the supremacy in his composition of a single quality—intensity of temperament. . . . He could not be indifferent. Repose, except in bed, where however he slept zealously, was unnatural and contemptible to him. It used to be said that if Hermand had made the heavens, he would have permitted no fixed stars" (132).

Hermand's energies were fueled by a great love of liquor, but where commonplace drinkers thought drink a pleasure, he thought it a virtue. He had "a sincere respect for drinking, indeed a high moral approbation, and a serious compassion for the poor wretches who could not indulge in it; with due contempt of those who could, but did not" (134). A case came to the court of two young friends, whose long night of drinking ended in a minor quarrel. One thing led to another and the consequence was a fatal stabbing. The other judges of the court were disposed to leniency, but not Hermand: "They had been carousing the whole night; and yet he stabbed him; after drinking a whole bottle of rum with him! Good God, my Laards, if he will do this when he's drunk, what will he not do when he's sober?" (140).

The bench provided Scotland with some its most notable eccentricities, though as Cockburn noted in the case of Eskgrove "it was unfortunate that a judicial chair was necessary for their complete exhibition" (125). But there were other classes of revered ancients that were equally characteristic of the earlier world of Edinburgh. Ten pages are devoted to the "singular race of excellent Scotch old ladies" (57–58 ff.); the literary men of that age—Stewart, Robertson, Ferguson, Alexander Carlyle—were another favorite subject.

Cockburn's primary purpose was a celebration of his own generation. But he enjoyed the sense of succession gained from the illustrious past. "Though living in all the succeeding splendours, it has been a constant gratification to me to remember that I saw the last remains of a school so illustrious and so national, and that I was privileged to obtain a glimpse of the 'skirts of glory' of the first, or at least of the second, great philosophical age of Scotland" (57). There was nothing artificial about this sense of continuity. "Our neighbour on the east, was old Adam Ferguson, the historian of Rome, and Stewart's predecessor in our morals chair—a singular apparition." In his youth Ferguson had been "a handsome and resolute man," but Cockburn's memory was of a later time:

> A severe paralytic attack had reduced his animal vitality, though it left no external appearance, and he required considerable artificial heat. His raiment, therefore, consisted of half boots lined with fur, cloth breeches, a long cloth waiscoat with capacious pockets, a single breasted coat, a cloth great-coat also lined with fur, and a felt hat commonly tied by a ribbon below the chin. . . . he generally wore the furred great-coat even within doors. When he walked forth, he used a tall staff, which he commonly held at arm's length out towards the right side; and his two coats, each buttoned by only the upper button, flowed open below, and exposed the whole of his curious and venerable figure. His gait and air were noble; his gesture slow; his look full of dignity and composed fire. He looked like a philosopher from Lapland. (48–49)

Ferguson's regimen was austere. He ate no meat and never dined out, "except at his relation Dr. Joseph Black's [the chemist], where his son . . . used to say it was delightful to see the two philosophers rioting over a boiled turnip" (50).

At the opposite end of the social spectrum were the picturesque occupations of old Edinburgh that disappeared with civic improvement. One such group was the City Guard—"Always called by the people 'The Toon Rottens' "; another were the water carriers, whose livelihood disappeared with the advent of piped water (353–55). But Cockburn did not make the mistake of thinking only the lower classes colorful, and some of the most interesting parts of the book come from his attempt to define the changes of modern manners by recollection of the features of social life in his youth—the hour of dinner, the formality of manners strangely coupled with much coarseness and drinking, the fashion for sentimental toasts, the processionals that accompanied judges to the court, the custom among the same judges of taking wine and biscuits on the bench, the wearing of buckles or wigs as signs of loyalty, and so forth.

Like Scott, Cockburn deeply relished the opportunities Scotland provided the social portraitist; like Scott, too, he also understood the underlying social transformations that made such portraiture a form of social enquiry as well as a literary diversion. Though members of opposite political factions, they shared in all essentials the same mix of nostalgia and acceptance.

> The change from ancient to modern manners, which is now completed, had begun some years before this, and was at this period in rapid and visible progress. The feelings and habits which had prevailed at the union, and had left so many picturesque peculiarities on the Scotch character, could not survive the enlarged intercourse with England and the world. It would be interesting to trace the course of this alteration, provided the description was made intelligible by accounts of our curious men and our peculiar customs. But it cannot be done except by one who lived, and was in the practice of observing, and perhaps of noting, in the very scenes, and with the very men; and consequently it cannot be done by one who only came into action when the old suns were going down. (28)

This was meant as an act of renunciation. Nonetheless it set the terms for the remaining task, which was to lay up a store of observation of the succeeding generation before it was too late.

The social changes of his own day were necessarily less dramatic than those of the previous century. Even so, Cockburn's philosophical approach dictated the recognition that his own generation was completing the powerful story of Scotland's social transformation. But for Cockburn as for Scott, the problem was how to give this philosophic history an outward form, how to make this often invisible alteration of habits and feelings "intelligible."

With these questions, though we have not by any means left behind the subject of "distinguished men or important events," we come to the theme of the "progress of Scotland." This is the widest circle of recollection in the book, comprehending both its autobiographical material and its range of eyewitness report. The growth of his own mind, the gradual awakening of his generation to a more liberal spirit, the physical expansion of the city, the disappearance of the water carriers, the foundation of the *Edinburgh Review*—these and other themes, even when given the most anecdotal treatment, move beyond simple personal history to become signposts of broader directions of social change. In this way, memory and philosophy cooperate to make the experience of a generation intelligible as history.

Two central events gave shape to the way Cockburn and his generation experienced history as a succession of generations. The first was the move to the New Town, the most visible of all signs of Edinburgh's progress. The social as well as the material fabric of the city was transformed by this physical change. "The single circumstance of the increase in the population," writes Cockburn, "and its consequent overflowing from the old town to the new, implied a general alteration of our habits. It altered the style of living, obliterated local arrangements, and destroyed a thousand associations, which nothing but the still preserved names of houses and of places is left to recall" (28).

The other moment of reference for all subsequent changes was the French Revolution. "Everything," Cockburn recollected, "rung, and was connected with the Revolution in France; which, for above 20 years, was, or was made, the all in all" (80). This was more than a generalization. It was a specific memory of the discussions around his father's table, which was a gathering point of zealous Tories. "I can sit yet, in imagination, at the small side table, and overhear the conversation, a few feet off, at the established Wednesday dinner. How they raved! What sentiments! What principles!" (46).

Elsewhere the Revolution may have been a political event, but in the Scotland of Cockburn's memory it occupied a deeper place. "Everything, not this or that thing, but literally everything, was soaked in this one event" (46). The Revolution became a social divide, separating not only Whigs from Tories, but the young from the old. Yet, at the same time, it was all an imposition. There was no revolutionary party in Scotland, and the cry of revolution was no more than a tool of faction. But if genuine Jacobinism hardly existed, "Scotch Toryism did, and with a vengeance." Yet Toryism, itself, had limited roots in Scotland. It was no more than a faction, held together by power and patronage.[46] At the center of this political monopoly stood Cockburn's uncle, Henry Dundas, the first viscount Melville. He was "the Pharos of Scotland. Who steered upon him was safe; who disregarded his light was wrecked" (87).

The dominion of narrow-minded and selfish Toryism left Scotland without genuine politics. Town councils were self-elected. The established church had no visible rival. Juries were picked at the discretion of the sheriff, and parliamentarians were elected by a franchise so narrow that it was easily controlled by bribery and patronage. "In other words, we had no free political institutions whatever" (87). But for Cockburn, as for his friend Jeffrey, the gravest sign of the country's political inanition was the lack of any genuine channel by which public opinion might express itself. "*As a body to be deferred to*, no *public* existed. Opinion was only recognized when expressed through what were acknowledged to be its legitimate organs; which meant its formal or official outlets." The "general community" had no method of expression, and the people were silent—"or if they spoke out, were deemed audacious" (88–89).

Cockburn's diagnosis of the possibilities for "progress" was true to the same "sociological" vision of politics.

[46] "This thing, however, must not be considered as exactly the same with pure Toryism in England. It seldom implies anything with us except a dislike of popular institutions; and even this chiefly on grounds of personal advantage. A pure historical and constitutional Tory is a very rare character in this country" (*Memorials of His Time*, 81).

> The only hope was in the decline of the circumstances that had sunk it. What had to be waited for was, the increase of numbers and of wealth, the waning of the revolutionary horror, the dying out of the hard old aristocracy, the advance of a new generation, and the rise of new guides. The gradual introduction and operation of these redeeming circumstances has been very interesting, and illustrates, by the example of a single place, the general principles which regulate the improvement of the world. (104)

These abstractions might have served as a preface to a philosophic history of modern Scotland rather than passing comment in a book of recollection. But there was no real contradiction. In Cockburn's memory the little group of Whig lawyers who opposed the Tory monopoly were themselves a kind of philosophic brotherhood, held together equally by sentiment and right thinking. Their rise *was* the "progress of Scotland."

The essence of their eventual triumph was simply their respect for justice, just as it was the total disregard of internal reform that undermined their Tory opposites. "The real strength of their party," Cockburn wrote of the Whigs, without any shading or hesitation, "lay in their being right, and in the tendency of their objects to attract men of ability and principle" (86). But their complete exclusion from the spoils—"this single, and most blessed fact"—was a secondary cause of their success. It gave them their closeness and spirit. "Those on the opposite side, who saw themselves excluded from everything that power could keep from them, reaped the natural advantages of this position. It gave them leisure; persecution cherished elevation of character and habits of self-dependence. Being all branded with the same mark, and put under the same ban, they were separated into a sect of their own, within which there was mirth and friendship, study and hope, ambition and visions" (149).

His friends, the bright, young, excluded lawyers of the Outer House, were the greatest concentration of talent Edinburgh had seen (176). Their ideas were nurtured in Dugald Stewart's lectures on political economy—a subject still so unusual to illiberal Edinburgh that some examined the lessons for signs of Jacobinical subversion, while to others "the word *Corn* sounded strangely in the morals class" (75). The natural outgrowth of their talents was the *Edinburgh Review*. Its first appearance in October 1802 did more than anything else to establish the new intellectual climate of the city.[47]

The *Review* was the beginning of the formation of a body of enlightened opinion without which there could be no real community or politics. When he looked back on those times, Cockburn found it impossible "not to be struck with the apparent absence of enlightened public views and capacities all over

[47] "It elevated the public and literary position of Edinburgh to an extent which no one not living intelligently then can be made to comprehend" (ibid., 166).

the community" (166). All the agitation of the times had produced nothing in the way of lasting Scottish achievement until this point. And by the same token, all their later achievements were prefigured in this first one. The public meetings and petitions, the gradual institutional reforms in law and representation, the eventual coming to power of a Whig administration (with Francis Jeffrey as lord advocate) with which the book ends—all of this was no more than a gradual but necessary unfolding of the public mind. Only the publication of *Waverley*, a dozen years later, offered a comparable moment of public awakening (282).

Everyday Life and Historical Distance

Cockburn's *Memorials* is perhaps the most striking and certainly the most self-conscious demonstration we have yet examined of the power of memoirs to evoke the textures and experiences of everyday life. For this reason, Cockburn's work stands as the best witness to that historicization of everyday life which is so important a theme of this period. This reframing of common life as a domain of pervasive historical change is particularly striking when we remember that it concerns a theater of experience that found no place at all in classical prescriptions for historical writing. Yet it is fair to say that by the early part of the nineteenth century the silent transformation of everyday things came to seem not the least, but the most persuasive evidence of history's sway over all things human. The signs of such a reconceptualization have, of course, been evident right across the spectrum of historical genres we have examined, but never so dramatically as in the case of memoir, which of all forms of writing seemed best adapted to overcome the formal restrictions that still surrounded historical narrative.

In a letter to an earlier editor of the *Life of Johnson*, John Wilson Croker articulated a concern with the loss of memory that was a fundamental part of the historicization of everyday life. "Nobody thinks of telling what everybody knows," Croker wrote, "and yet how soon does it happen that no one remembers what all the world knew a few years before? How many people are there in London who do not know where Rosamond's pond lay? Who knows what the game of the Mall was? The Northern roads are still measured from an imaginary standard of *St Giles's Pond*, of which no trace is to be found in the memory of the inhabitants of the parish."[48]

Croker's comment reverses the usual nervousness about "prying" by indicating that, as time advances, the real issue facing readers of memoir and biography has less to do with violations of privacy than with the disappearance of common knowledge. Croker, it is interesting to note, understood the implica-

[48] Croker to Alexander Chalmers, August 20, 1829, *Croker Papers*, 2:38.

tions that this process of growing loss and distance held for editorial efforts like his own, and he acknowledged that his work would need a further edition in the next generation. In this way he signaled his acceptance of the need to historicize not only the text, but its editor and its audience as well.

Croker's comments take us further into the complexities of historical distance as they affected the pleasures nineteenth-century readers found in memoirs. Without question, these works were attractive because they offered an immediacy absent from the more public and distanced accounts of historians. At the same time, it is also clear that this immediacy could seem uncomfortably close to the prying curiosity that contemporary audiences identified as the dark side of their own fascination with biography. This made the forms of distanciation that came with belated publication especially welcome. Belated publication fashioned a new relationship between reader and text in which the reader is conscious of standing outside the author's original audience and of being in possession of knowledge no contemporary could have had. Belated publication, in other words, turns every narrator into a naive one and makes every reader more knowing. This leaves the reader free not only to sympathize with the story, but also to rework it in ways that the writer could not have envisaged.

Nineteenth-century editors and reviewers were certainly aware of the shifts in distance created by this reframing of memoir as history. As we have seen, they frequently invited readers to treasure texts for this quality of historical naïveté, which (among other things) was seen as the best guarantee of the uncontaminated authenticity of the account. They understood, too, that this constructed innocence in the narrator had as its counterpart a reader who prides himself on his own critical capacities. Thus the general emphasis on Boswell's simple-mindedness, to take a prime example, clearly sets up our own distanciation as historical readers. Thanks to the passage of time, and a little editorial help, we follow the biographer's performance as a more knowing audience, appreciative of this opportunity to reexperience the past in a manner that both relishes innocence and rewards sophisticated understanding.

Twelve

William Godwin and the Idea of Commemoration

IN HER sympathetic eyewitness history of the French Revolution, Helen Maria Williams conjures up for herself a picture of the unknown pilgrims who at some future time will make their way to the sites where she herself had been privileged to witness the great moments of the Revolution. In a passage briefly cited earlier, she writes that strangers, when they visit France,

> will hasten with impatience to the Champs de Mars, filled with that enthusiasm which is awakened by the view of a place where any great scene has been acted. I think I hear them exclaim, "here the Federation was held! . . ." I see them pointing out the spot on which the altar of the country stood. I see them eagerly searching for the place where they have heard it recorded, that the National Assembly were seated! I think of these things, and then repeat to myself with transport, "I, was a spectator of the Federation."[1]

Williams's sense of historical pilgrimage is rooted in some of the oldest habits of Western culture, but it also points to a perception of history that has been increasingly cultivated since her time. The idea of public commemoration by marking "historic sites" has become a commonplace of modern life. For us, history is not only a story to be narrated; it is also an experience to be evoked, and no form of evocation is more widespread than the practice of erecting commemorative plaques and monuments. History, traditionally regarded as a book to be read, has become a scene to be revisited.[2]

This intermingling of the associations of past and place has become so pervasive that we take it for granted. But apparently this was not yet so in Britain at the end of the eighteenth century. Nearly twenty years after Williams published the first volume of her history, another English friend of the Revolution, William Godwin, outlined a proposal for evoking England's own past by raising a subscription to mark in the simplest possible manner the burial places of notable men. It is striking, however, that Godwin advanced his *Essay on*

[1] Williams, *Letters from France*, 1:107–8.

[2] For a broad discussion of this theme, see David Lowenthal, *The Past Is a Foreign Country* (Cambridge: Cambridge UP, 1985); and Patrick Wright, *On Living in an Old Country* (London: Verso, 1985). The historical resonance of place has, of course, become a major theme in contemporary historical thought and has been taken as the organizing principle for a new type of historiography, notably in Pierre Nora's *Realms of Memory: Rethinking the French Past*, trans. Arthur Goldhammer, 3 vols. (New York: Columbia UP, 1996).

Sepulchres (1809) as a kind of visionary experiment—a "speculation and solemn reverie"—whose feasibility even he could not really credit. Indeed the work, which Godwin published at his own expense, seems to have attracted very little notice, then or since.[3]

The interest of Godwin's essay, however, is not simply its anticipation of later commemorative programs. Godwin's essay was one of a number of contemporary texts that explore the emotional resonances of historic places by calling on the psychological doctrine of association. Taken together, these texts show the power of associationalism—joined with other aspects of the culture of sensibility—to promote an essentially inward response to the scenes of history. Like the emergent idea of tradition, this interest in historical places as "sites of memory" gave further impetus to the gathering desire for immediacy in historical representation.

Godwin's proposal for a program of commemoration alters history's traditional face with respect to both public and private memory. The simple grave-markers he wants to see erected cannot determine the contents or lessons of the past in the ways that are possible in more elaborate forms of commemoration. Instead, his program would create a more open theater for remembrance, which allows for a new and intensely personal dimension to history's traditional public role.[4] Godwin does not stop with the public meaning of past lives. His evocation of the historical associations of place aims to intensify the sense of inward engagement with historical experience as much as to mark a public

[3] The *Essay on Sepulchres* was published at Godwin's expense in 1809. A modern edition is now available in Mark Philp, ed., *The Political and Philosophical Writings of William Godwin*, 7 vols. (London: Pickering, 1993), vol. 6. It will be some time before this invaluable, but rather expensive edition is widely available; for this reason, I have chosen to retain the references to the first edition (London, 1809), but I have added page references to the modern edition. Graham excerpts a few, generally sympathetic notices in *William Godwin Reviewed*, 297–301, but Godwin's book seems to have attracted little notice in its time. Recent commentary, such as it is, has generally been puzzled or even hostile. One biographer, Don Locke, quotes a letter from Mary Lamb as "best" describing the work when she writes satirically that it is a "great work which Godwin is going to publish to enlighten the world once more." Locke's own view is no more positive: "In fact the great charm of this little pamphlet is the deadly seriousness with which Godwin approaches his modest, not to say silly, little suggestion. . . . Once he had suggested men might be able to conquer death by reason alone, but now he preferred to put his trust in a cross of wood and a mark on a map." *A Fantasy of Reason: The Life and Thought of William Godwin* (London: Routledge, 1980), 223–24. In fact, Mary Lamb gives a fairly detailed and, in part, sympathetic summary of Godwin's ideas, while Charles Lamb calls it a "very pretty, absurd book about Sepulchres." See *Letters of Charles and Mary Anne Lamb*, ed. E. W. Marrs, 3 vols. (Ithaca: Cornell UP, 1976), 2:286–87 and 3:14.

[4] Wordsworth's reflections on epitaphs seem relevant here: "But an epitaph is not a proud writing shut up for the studious: it is exposed to all—to the wise and the most ignorant; it is condescending, perspicuous, and lovingly solicits regard; its story and admonitions are brief, that the thoughtless, the busy, and indolent, may not be deterred, nor the impatient tired" ("Essays upon Epitaphs," in *Prose Works*, 59).

space. Like Williams's historical pilgrims, visitors to Godwin's commemorated sites would be invited to participate in a new relationship to history that is essentially spectatorial and inward. In this way, Godwin's "reverie," along with other contemporary explorations of historical association, represents a historical sensibility undergoing a transformation brought about by the value given to private experience.

Godwin's *Sepulchres*

The central idea of Godwin's *Sepulchres* is stated in its subtitle—"a proposal for erecting some memorial of the illustrious dead in all ages on the spot where their remain has been interred." Characteristically, he begins his essay on historical memory with the personal experience of bereavement, founding his sense of the value of public commemoration on sentiments of affection and loss that are both universal and private. The loss of a friend, he writes, is the greatest of all losses we can sustain; to us "his person was a little world"—and though Godwin keeps to the masculine pronoun, we inevitably think of his account of the death of Mary Wollstonecraft.[5] When a friend dies, it is impossible to separate our sense of him from reminders of his physical person. As a result, "every thing which practically has been *associated* with my friend acquires a value from that consideration; his ring, his watch, his books, and his habitation. The value of these as having been his, is not merely fictitious; they have an empire over my mind; they can make me happy or unhappy; they can torture, and they can tranquillise; they can purify my sentiments, and make me similar to the man I love."[6]

The extraordinary power Godwin attributes to these objects has nothing to do with their ordinary physical qualities or functions; their value lies in the fact that they are the survivors of the "little world" we have lost. Thus their "empire" lies entirely—and arbitrarily—in their biographical associations. Public memories, too, are governed by the same associationalist principle. But in this public context, the place of burial takes on the function of provoking recollection. For this reason, Godwin urges the importance of marking the very spot where the illustrious dead lie buried. This insistent literalness may come as a surprise to the modern reader, for whom association is a weaker, more metaphoric concept:

[5] Godwin muses on the loss suffered if the friend who died were someone with whom one had dwelled under the same roof—if she "were the wife of my bosom" (*Essay on Sepulchres*, 12–13 [Philp, 8–9]). Godwin's life of Wollstonecraft, *Memoirs of the Author of the Vindication*, stirred up a controversy that well exemplifies the anxieties about biography discussed in the previous chapter; James Mackintosh, on the other hand, found it an enormously affecting work.

[6] Godwin, *Essay on Sepulchres*, 6–7 (Philp, 8); emphasis added.

> Man is a creature who depends for his feelings upon the operations of sense. . . . When I have visited the monuments of our English kings, I study their transactions in a graver spirit than before. Portraits may be imaginary; the scenes where great events have occurred are the scenes of these events no longer; but the dust that is covered by his tomb, is simply and literally *the great man himself.*[7]

These sentiments underline the difference between Godwin's proposal and contemporary programs of memorial statuary blossoming in the patriotic atmosphere of the struggle with France. In contrast to the classically draped statues of British naval heroes that were beginning to fill St. Paul's, Godwin's plan asks only for the simplest of markers to fix the place of burial. Though he does not say so, this plainness suited contemporary psychological doctrines, which argued that the power of association would be greatest where the linkages between ideas were least subject to distracting interruption.[8] A horizontal stone, a tablet on a wall, in rural areas a plain wooden cross—these simple memorials would offer no images of the hero. Nor would the tribute be removed from the landscape to enhance a national pantheon or decorate the monuments to civic pride springing up in provincial centers. On the contrary, in Godwin's vision, everything would be left to the power of association and to the sense of place. In consequence, unlike the monuments that found official favor and changed the urban landscapes of London or Birmingham, Godwin's speculative program of commemoration finds its home in the private life of the individual mind. Sumptuousness and decoration are not required by his plan, Godwin writes; "the object is to mark the place where the great and the excellent of the earth repose, and to leave the rest to the mind of the spectator."[9]

At the heart of *Sepulchres* stands Godwin's account of his own emotional response to the places of history. Among the "accidents" that led him to his proposal was a visit to Westminster, where he found that most of the great figures he looked for had been missed out. Pilgrimage to another abbey—Thetford in Norfolk—brought out the elegiac strain in his romance of place. "As I wandered through the limits of the enclosure," writes Godwin, "I trod upon the remains of the Bigods, the Mowbrays, and the Howards," men who in their day had upheld the pride of chivalry and defied the power of kings. "Ponderous monuments graced with sculptures and diversified with copious sepulchral inscriptions, once marked the place where they lay. . . . All now was

[7] Godwin, *Essay on Sepulchres*, 66–67 (Philp, 20).

[8] For the idea that the force of association would be greatest where least impeded by distracting alternatives, see the discussion of Archibald Alison below. Regarding the monuments at St. Paul's and the civic uses of memorial statuary, see Alison Yarrington, *The Commemoration of the Hero, 1800–1864* (New York: Garland, 1988). The wider background of national feeling is given in Gerald Newman, *The Rise of English Nationalism: A Cultural History, 1740–1830* (New York: St. Martin's, 1987); and Linda Colley, *Britons: Forging the Nation, 1707–1837* (New Haven: Yale UP, 1992).

[9] Godwin, *Essay on Sepulchres*, 57–58 (Philp, 18).

speechless, and the grass grew as freely where their bones reposed, as over a peasant's grave."[10]

The politics of this elegy differ markedly from the radicalism of *Political Justice* (1793). But as he demonstrates in historical works as well as his novels, the romantic associations of the Middle Ages hold a strong attraction to Godwin. In *Sepulchres*, however, the main point is to demonstrate his own susceptibility to the historical associations that attach themselves to the landscape of old England—to offer himself, in short, as an example of the power of place at work. The Tower, the House of Commons, the scenes of battle in the Civil War: such places have a power to "call up"—to use his earlier phrase—the life of the nation:

> I never understood the annals of chivalry so well, as when I walked among the ruins of Kenilworth Castle. I no longer trusted to the tale of the historian, the cold and uncertain record of words formed upon paper. . . . The subtle, the audacious and murder-dealing Leicester stood before me. I heard the trampling of horses, and the clangour of trumpets.[11]

In imagination, Godwin has become a direct witness of the scenes of history. In this place of historical pilgrimage, he can see and hear the life of medieval England with an immediacy no narrative could match—or could only match, as Godwin does here, by a strategy that calls attention to the inadequacy of the "cold and uncertain record of words."

At other times, another voice speaks out, one not less romantic, but prophetic rather than nostalgic in its intonations: "I would say with Ezekiel, the Hebrew, in his Vision, 'Let these dry bones live!' Not let them live merely in cold generalities and idle homilies of morality; but let them live, as my friends, my philosophers, my instructors, and my guides!" Those who lived in other times, he asks, are they less important than we are? "Had their thoughts less of sinew and substance; were their passions less earnest," he continues.

> To him who is of a mind rightly framed, the world is a thousand times more populous, than to the man, to whom everything that is not flesh and blood, is nothing. . . . They are not dead. They are still with us in their stories, in their words, in their writings, in the consequences that do not cease to flow fresh from what they did: they still have their place, where we may visit them, and where, if we dwell in a composed and a quiet spirit, we shall not fail to be conscious of their presence.[12]

In these places, Godwin seems to anticipate Thomas Carlyle, and like Carlyle in *Heroes and Hero Worship*, he has heroes of the spirit uppermost in his mind. He argues for a generous and inclusive program of commemoration, but

[10] Godwin, *Essay on Sepulchres*, 45 (Philp, 15–16).
[11] Godwin, *Essay on Sepulchres*, 71–72 (Philp, 21).
[12] Godwin, *Essay on Sepulchres*, 74–78 (Philp, 22–23)

he worries that ordinary people would be drawn to military and naval figures, rather than the writers and thinkers that populate his own imagination. Great military figures like Scipio have "dwindled into a name," he insists, while the ancient poets and philosophers have come down to us entire. They "appear" before us in all their wholeness and individuality, and still have the power to illuminate our souls.[13]

Another kind of difficulty is posed by the literalness of his belief in finding the exact place of burial. There must be no room to suspect that the marker is simply a convenient fiction; such skepticism would muffle the evocative power of the actual grave. Fortunately, Godwin writes, it happens that a "spirit of antiquarian research" is one of the characteristics of the present age, and he ends the essay with a proposal that nicely combines his antiquarian and sentimentalist interests. An atlas should be created that would ensure permanence and exact knowledge of burial sites, even in times of unrest—a proviso that says much about the wider context in which his project for commemoration was conceived. In addition, there must be a catalogue. This document "might be despicable to the literal man and the calculator; but it would be a precious relic to the man of sentiment, and prove to be a Traveller's Guide, of a very different measure of utility, from the "Catalogue of Gentlemen's Seats," which is now appended to the "Book of Post Roads through Every Part of Gt. Britain."[14]

Archibald Alison and the Aesthetics of Association

As I have indicated, Godwin presents his essay as a kind of visionary proposal, one without precedent and quite probably without practicality. Even so, his tacit use of associationalist doctrines indicates an essential background to his ideas. Here Archibald Alison's *Essays on the Nature and Principles of Taste* (1790) is an important and influential text.[15]

Neither Alison's *Essays* nor his sermons show him to be a man for whom history is a central interest; nonetheless, in developing his psychology of aes-

[13] "Military and naval achievements are of temporary operation: the victories of Cimon and Scipio are passed away; these great heroes have dwindled into a name; but the whole of Plato and Xenophon, and Virgil have descended to us, undefaced, undismembered, and complete. . . . I am acquainted with their peculiarities; their inmost thoughts are familiar to me; they appear before me with all the attributes of individuality; I can ruminate upon their lessons and sentiments at leisure, till my whole soul is lighted up by the spirit of these authors" (*Essay on Sepulchres*, 109–10 [Philp, 28]).

[14] Godwin, *Essay on Sepulchres*, 112, 115–16 (Philp, 29–30).

[15] The second edition of Alison's essay, which appeared in 1811, was enthusiastically welcomed by Francis Jeffrey in the *Edinburgh Review.* Jeffrey's lengthy essay was reprinted in the *Encyclopaedia Britannica* as the article "Beauty" as well as in his popular collected essays. Jeffrey

thetic emotions, Alison gives attention to history as a rich source of associational images. This exploration of the power of historical association opens up possibilities for a new reading of history—one that might undercut history's traditional emphasis on public instruction in favor of its newly articulated powers of evocation.

Alison brings together two influential themes in eighteenth-century thought. Writers on art and aesthetics hoped to give their judgments a sounder philosophical basis by shifting attention from the qualities of objects to the processes of perception. Concurrently, Hume, Hartley, and others thought that the "association of ideas" might explain how the mind could build complex ideas out of simple perceptions. Alison systematically applied the principle of association to questions of taste, giving association wide powers over our perception of beauty. In his hands, the association of ideas becomes an immensely flexible conductor of emotional currents, with the result that all parts of life—even those little touched until now by the contemporary tendency to aestheticize experience—could be drawn into a regime of feeling.

The essence of Alison's general argument is that "Matter is not beautiful in itself, but derives its beauty from the Expression of Mind."[16] When a beautiful object is presented to the mind, we are conscious of a "train of thought" awakened in the imagination. This imaginative response is richer than anything the object alone could produce and may even have little ostensible relation to the object itself—a gap that is made up by the principle of the association of ideas.[17] Alison believes that the associative process is automatic, and he emphasizes that it is quickest and most intense where the imagination is most free and spontaneous. "It is, then, indeed, in this powerless state of reverie," he writes, "when we are carried on by our conceptions, not guiding them, that the deepest emotions of beauty or sublimity are felt, that our hearts swell with feelings which language is too weak to express, and that in the depth of silence and astonishment we pay to the charm that enthrals us, the most flattering mark of our applause."[18]

This passive and dreamy mental state is much like Kames's "ideal presence." Godwin, too (as I have already indicated) aimed at something similar

helped to give Alison a lasting influence, especially in Scotland, making his work, like Burke's, an important bridge to the next century.

[16] Archibald Alison, *Essays on the Nature and Principles of Taste* (Edinburgh, 1790; rpt. Hildesheim: Olms, 1968). For the aesthetic background, see Samuel Monk, *The Sublime: A Study of Critical Theories in Eighteenth-Century England* (Ann Arbor: U of Michigan P, 1960); and Martin Kallich, *The Association of Ideas and Critical Theory in Eighteenth-Century England* (The Hague: Mouton, 1970).

[17] "Trains of pleasing or of solemn thought arise spontaneously within our minds, our hearts swell with emotions, of which the objects before us seem to afford no adequate cause" (Alison, *Taste*, 2–3).

[18] Ibid., 14, 42.

in his choice of simple, undecorated grave-markers in which nothing would distract the spectator from the associations of place. From the standpoint of classical historiography, on the other hand, cultivating the "powerless state of reverie" undermines fundamental principles that give history its ethical value. It is a long way from Alison's dreamy spectatorialism to the humanist's claim that history instructs the active will. The suspended animation in which associationalist currents move most powerfully is a deeply private state of mind, far removed from the alertness to public lessons inculcated by exemplary history.

When Alison turns from the general mechanism of association to describe more specific sources and influences, private experience remains prominent. The "interesting recollections of childhood" bring special meaning to particular scenes or books, or perhaps to a favorite piece of music. "The view of the house where one was born," Alison writes, "or of the school where one was educated and the gay years of infancy were passed, are indifferent to no man."[19] But biographical associations of a less personal kind can also have the same effect. Scenes linked to people we admire possess an emotional resonance, even when the landscape itself has little attraction. Memories of the dead mingle with the scenery to produce a kind of sanctity of place. "There are scenes, undoubtedly, more beautiful than Runnymede," he writes, "yet to those who recollect the great event which passed there, there is no scene, perhaps, which so strongly seizes upon the imagination."

The emotions excited by historical recollection are very different from any that natural scenery by itself could produce, but they "unite themselves" with the inferior emotions in such a way that the scene itself seems charmed.[20] The Vaucluse is made more beautiful by the memory of Petrarch; the Alps become still more majestic by association with Hannibal's crossing; "and who is there, that could stand on the banks of the Rubicon, without feeling his imagination kindle, and his heart beat high?" (18).

Similarly, the field of any celebrated battle becomes sublime through association. "No man, acquainted with English history, can behold the field of Agincourt, without some emotion of this kind. The additional conceptions which this association produces, and which fill the mind of the spectator on the prospect of that memorable field, diffuse themselves in some measure over the scene, and give it a sublimity which does not naturally belong to it."

At Agincourt, as envisioned by Alison, history and landscape bleed into each other. All parts of the scene come together in a single experience that is both vivid and curiously indistinct. The mind, in consequence, is filled with a

[19] Ibid., 15. The passage continues: "They recal so many images of past happiness and past affections, they are connected with so many strong or valued emotions, and lead altogether to so long a train of feelings and recollections, that there is hardly any scene which one ever beholds with so much rapture."

[20] Ibid., 16.

new emotion, a historical sublime, in which the associations of time and place run together. The resulting view of the actual field of battle is deliberately hazy, leaving the spectator free to pursue his or her own inward vision of history.

Alison, for whom history is an illustration, rather than the passion it was for Godwin, does not limit himself to such scenes. Association springs from experience in all its forms. It is shaped by nationality, by social station, by habits of work—all of which add up to bodies of shared knowledge and experience. The more we know of any subject, he writes, the more meaning it has for us and the richer may be its effects. Thus the peasant has no sense of the beauty of a mathematical theory, nor does the habitual townsman respond to the pleasures of the countryside. Professional knowledge, similarly, endows the painter with a greater delight in the technical triumphs of a colleague than the layman can understand. For the same reasons, educated men will enjoy everything reminiscent of classical times, and the effect will be most powerful for those most immersed in antiquities. In the presence of relics of earlier ages, the antiquarian "seems to himself to be removed to periods that are long since past." His memory is filled with all that is venerable in those times, and a kind of nostalgic longing makes the whole more engaging still. Images of the past come into his mind, writes Alison, "softened by the obscurity in which they are involved, and rendered more seducing to the imagination by that obscurity itself, which, while it mingles a sentiment of regret amid his pursuits, serves at the same time to stimulate his fancy to fill up by its own creation those long intervals of time of which history has preserved no record." In this state, the "relics" of the past—its clothing, furniture, or weaponry—serve as "so many assistances to his imagination," bringing the antiquary still closer to the presence of his imagined past.[21]

On this view, the emotions of history are essentially a possession of men of the political class, who share the reading and travel that give resonance to historical events and places. This is particularly true for the classical past, and Alison comments on the "emotion of sublime delight, which every man of common sensibility feels upon the first prospect of Rome." Present-day Rome, he says, echoing Gibbon, is no more than a scene of destruction and triumphant superstition.[22] Yet this is not what the onlooker feels. "It is ancient Rome which fills his imagination. It is the country of Caesar, and Cicero, and Virgil, which is before him." Years of study have populated his imagination with images of this world. "Take from him these associations, conceal from him that it is Rome that he sees, and how different would be his emotion!"

[21] Ibid., 27–28: "The relics he contemplates seem to approach him still nearer to the ages of his regard."

[22] The echo of Gibbon seems deliberate: the Rome we picture "is not the triumph of superstition over the wreck of human greatness, and its monuments erected upon the very spot where the first honours of humanity have been gained" (ibid., 28).

In this image of the historical spectator in the wreckage of ancient Rome, Alison finds the ideal illustration of his general thesis. What better example could there be to show that objects in themselves are powerless to create the "emotions" of beauty or sublimity evoked by such sights? Even so, Alison himself shows no interest in exploring the implications of such a scene for historical studies. History is for him simply an illustration of a principle that, in its universality, is at work in all areas of emotional and aesthetic response. In this regard he treats history as a close cousin to the picturesque, which is the subject of the next section of the *Essays*. The view of Rome, like the picturesque landscape, involves the viewer with a rich trove of associations and provides the theorist with a ready laboratory of aesthetic emotions.

Within these limits, Alison's associationalism seems to point toward the sort of fusion of place and memory that Godwin later proposed. Moreover, by showing how easily the associationalist principle could be extended to history, he provides an opening to an analysis of historical writing that is passional and essentially private. Such a view would focus on the emotional responses of the reader, rather than—as traditionally—on maxims of conduct or explanations of events. When read in an associationalist frame, history might loosen its ancient tie to public action, setting the reader free to become a sort of sentimental traveler in past times.

"The Pleasures of Memory"

The fusion of historical association and place that Alison theorized and Godwin would have liked to promote left traces in other contemporary texts, especially those concerned with travel, topography, and literary history. In writings of this sort, the intensification of national sentiment brought on by the struggles with revolutionary France expressed itself in the desire to explore—and exploit—the possibility of historical commemoration.

Though its high culture remained broadly cosmopolitan, the eighteenth century showed a growing interest in ideas of patriotism and "local attachment."[23] For much of the century, the idea of intense loyalty to place was primarily associated with harsh climates and unsophisticated peoples. A favorite example, popularized by Rousseau, is the "mal du pays" of the Swiss soldier who—on hearing the particular song of his homeland—is overcome with nostalgia and loses all his famous military virtues. And the homesick mercenary was

[23] See A. McKillop, "Local Attachment and Cosmopolitanism—the Eighteenth Century Pattern," in *From Sensibility to Romanticism*, ed. F. W. Hilles and Harold Bloom (New York: Oxford UP, 1965), 191–218. On the growth of patriotic sentiment in this period, see Newman, *Rise of English Nationalism;* and Colley, *Britons*.

sometimes joined by the Hottentot and the Highlander as emblems of unshakable attachment to uncomfortable places.

On this level, the idea of local attachment serves to reinforce, rather than contradict, the predominant cosmopolitanism of the Enlightenment, since it is clear that "mal du pays" is thought of as a condition encountered in countries shaped by nature more than by history. Even so, these discussions of nostalgia gave form to the idea that, as Boswell wrote in his journals, "There are ideas attached to particular places which it is almost impossible to express."[24]

Associationalism, too, provided an opening to the recognition of the power of national sentiment. Though it was Alison's view that associationalism provides support for the universal norms of neoclassicism, it is clear that his ideas could be called upon to explain the diversity of national taste. As Alison himself pointed out, national associations provide their own particular stock of images, thus intensifying a Roman's response to Virgil, for example, in ways that moderns can not possibly share.

National sentiment and local association enter into Samuel Rogers's popular long poem, "The Pleasures of Memory" (1792). "The Poem begins," he explains in his introductory gloss, "with the description of an obscure village, and of the pleasing melancholy which it excites on being revisited after a long absence. This mixed sensation is an effect of the Memory." Rogers's explanation for this "mixed sensation" is a clear, brief restatement of the psychology of association: "When ideas have any relation whatever, they are attractive of each other in the mind; and the perception of any object naturally leads to the idea of another, which was connected with it either in time or place, or which can be compared or contrasted with it. Hence arises our attachment to inanimate objects; hence also, in some degree, the love of our country, and the emotion with which we contemplate the celebrated scenes of antiquity."[25]

In the body of the poem the link between patriotism, individual memory, and the association of ideas is developed a little further; here, too, a larger framework of historical memory is invoked, making it clear that for Rogers, as for Alison, history gives rise to some of the richest examples of the associative power of memory:

Thus kindred objects kindred thoughts inspire,
As summer-clouds flash forth electric fire.
And hence this spot gives back the joys of youth,
Warm as the life, and with the mirror's truth.
Hence home-felt pleasure prompts the Patriot's sigh
This makes him wish to live, and dare to die.
. . . .

[24] Quoted in McKillop, "Local Attachment and Cosmopolitanism," 205.

[25] Samuel Rogers, "The Pleasures of Memory," in *Poetical Works* (London, 1869), 3–4.

And hence the charm historic scenes impart;
Hence the Tiber awes, and Avon melts the heart.
Aerial forms in Tempe's classic vale
Glance thro' the gloom and whisper in the gale;
In wild Vaucluse with love and Laura dwell,
And watch and weep in Eloisa's cell.[26]

Rogers's invocation of Laura and Eloisa suggests the importance of literary history—and of the female—to the associationalist program. At the same time, Tempe and Tiber draw our attention again to the prominence of images of the classical world in these evocations of history and memory. The fusion of place and past times seems to have come most easily when the scene was classical; after all, the classical world was not simply more ancient than anything English, it also presented itself in texts that modern readers had long been accustomed to regarding as indistinguishably literary and historical.

Rogers's fusion of literary landscape and cultivated memory had a kind of precedent in the work of midcentury "gardenists," who marked their creations with urns, inscriptions, and classical temples. Such emblematic devices turned the garden into a place of contemplation, inviting the visitor to connect each place or vista to specific moral themes. These gardens were, in effect, associationalist experiments, just as Godwin hoped all England might one day become. But despite Stowe's celebration of British worthies, neoclassical taste ensured that the language of cultural memory remained idealized and Roman. For all its celebrated Englishness, the garden was a reminder of journeys elsewhere. It took some time for Englishmen, schooled in Italian travels and views of Rome, to feel the power of historical association in more ordinary settings. In this sense, the most visionary part of Godwin's idea may have been that he proposed to turn Britain itself into his landscape of memory.[27]

Gilpin and the Picturesque

Contemporary travel literature offers some valuable hints about the possibilities, and also the limits, of this extension of historical feeling to the British landscape. William Gilpin's well-known explorations of Britain in search of the picturesque illustrate this point. Gilpin's affective approach to landscape

[26] Ibid., 13–14.

[27] On eighteenth-century gardens and their use of association, see H. F. Clark, "Eighteenth-Century Elysiums: The Role of 'Association' in the Landscape Movement," *Journal of the Warburg and Courtauld Institutes* 6 (1943): 165–89; Ronald Paulson, *Emblem and Expression: Meaning in English Art of the Eighteenth Century* (Cambridge: Harvard UP, 1975); John Dixon Hunt and Peter Willis, *The Genius of the Place: The English Landscape Garden, 1620–1820*, rev. ed. (Cambridge: MIT P, 1988).

has affinities to Alison's exploration of association. It would not be hard to imagine Gilpin's travels as providing an occasion for a wider appreciation of the aesthetics of place in which history, joined to the picturesque, would add her own colors to the pictorial imagination.

In fact, Gilpin frequently mentions significant historical events connected to the places he describes, but his historical descriptions suggest something more traditional. History does not become a part of his aesthetic; rather it remains with few exceptions a separate category of interest to the traveller. "Few towns offer a fairer field to an antiquary, than Carlisle," Gilpin writes in his tour of Cumberland and Westmoreland (1786). "It's origin and history, are remote, curious and obscure." Two pages later, however, he declares: "But I mean not to enter into the history of Carlisle: it concerns me only as an object of beauty."[28] So, too, when Gilpin pauses to mention the death of Edward I, an entertainment presented for Queen Elizabeth, an incident connected to Cromwell, or an anecdote of the '45, each historical reference arises in connection with a specific place, but there is no desire to fuse historical memory and visual impression to evoke the unique experience of place (1:45, 2:97–99, 112, 199–200).

In short, picturesque beauty and historical interest remain separate categories. "The country around Newberry furnished little amusement," he reports in the *Observations on the River Wye* (1782), "but if it is not picturesque, it is very historical." But this particular passage continues with a tantalizing look toward another possibility:

> In every historical country there are a set of ideas which peculiarly belong to it. Hastings and Tewksbury; Runnemede and Clarendon, have all their associate ideas. The ruins of abbeys and castles have another set: and it is a soothing amusement in travelling, to assimulate [*sic*] the mind to the ideas of the country. The ground we now trod, has many historical ideas associated with it; two great battles, a long siege, and the death of the gallant Lord Falkland.[29]

This seems an intriguing anticipation of Alison's associationalism, but there is no follow-up to the passage, which falls at the very end of the book. We are left with no more than a tantalizing suggestion that certain kinds of places—ruined abbeys and castles, scenes of battle or of sieges—retain a special power over the mind, which accommodates itself in some way to the strong impressions formed in their presence.

[28] William Gilpin, *Observations relative Chiefly to Picturesque Beauty made in the Year 1772, On Several Parts of England; Particularly the Mountains and Lakes of Cumberland, and Westmoreland*, 2 vols. (London, 1782), 2:93, 95.

[29] *Observations on the River Wye and several parts of South Wales relative chiefly to Picturesque Beauty made in the summer of the year 1770* (London, 1782), 98.

Medieval ruins, like classical ones, were the obvious collecting points for historical sentiment. In his tour of Cumberland and Westmoreland, Gilpin writes a brief, unremarkable history of Warwick Castle, but concludes on a note of romantic nostalgia: "Such is the present state of a structure, which two hundred years ago was second to none in England. . . . But now in Ossian's plaintive language, 'It's walls are desolate: the grey moss whitens the stone: the fox looks out from the window; and rank grass waves round it's head.' "[30]

Gilpin championed the Gothic style in architecture, and it is clear that the remains of medieval England had special power for him.[31] But his feeling is less for the memorials of human life than for the works of nature. The more, in fact, a ruin becomes a part of nature—the more it can be seen simply as a physical object removed from human time—the freer he is to respond on his favorite aesthetic grounds. Nor is there the gap, which for Alison is so significant, between the physical object and its imaginative associations. "Nature has now made it her own," Gilpin writes at Tintern. "Time has worn off all the traces of the rule."[32] In another place, he declares that the proprietor who "owns" a ruin is really no more than the guardian of a sacred trust because in truth, if not strictly in law, the ruin stands outside of the human world: "A ruin is a sacred thing. Rooted for ages in the soil; assimilated to it; and become, as it were a part of it; we consider it as a work of nature, rather than of art."[33]

Where, on the other hand, medieval remains call human history rather than nature to mind, another, more guarded response prevails. Contemplating the vast ruins of Glastonbury, Gilpin recognizes the power of this "amazing combination of various buildings . . . perhaps the largest society under one government, and the most extensive foundation that ever appeared in England." Nonetheless, his description moves on inevitably to a severe dismissal of everything unenlightened in monastic life.[34] And Gilpin completes his extensive review of Glastonbury's history with a perfectly conventional anecdote of the death of its last abbot, an innocent and bewildered victim of Henry VIII's brutality.[35]

[30] Gilpin, *Cumberland*, 1:39–41, 43. On "view hunting" and the literary interest in ruins, see Ian Ousby, *The Englishman's England: Taste, Travel, and the Rise of Tourism* (Cambridge: Cambridge UP, 1990); and Anne Janowitz, *England's Ruins: Poetic Purpose and the National Landscape* (Cambridge: Blackwell, 1990).

[31] Gilpin, *Observations on the Western Parts of England relative chiefly to Picturesque Beauty* (London, 1798), 63–64.

[32] Gilpin, *River Wye*, 33.

[33] Gilpin, *Cumberland*, 2:188.

[34] "On the other hand, when we consider five hundred persons, bred up in indolence, and lost to the commonwealth; when we consider that these houses were the great nurseries of superstition, bigotry, and ignorance; the stews of sloth, stupidity, and perhaps intemperance . . . " (Gilpin, *Western Parts*, 137–38).

[35] It is worth comparing these scenes to his encounter with Stonehenge, a premedieval structure that Gilpin found alien and—despite the advantage of its ruinous condition—un-picturesque.

Pratt's *Gleanings*

It is instructive to compare Gilpin's responses to the human landscape of England with those of a slightly later traveller writing in the patriotic atmosphere produced by war with France. Samuel Jackson Pratt was a prolific man of letters whose works are something of a barometer of contemporary moods.[36] Contemporaries knew Pratt best for his books of travel, which he entitled *Gleanings*. The first volumes (1795) ranged over Wales, Holland, and Westphalia, but at the end of the decade Pratt turned to scenes closer to home with his *Gleanings in England; Descriptive of the Countenance, Mind, and Character of the Country* (1799).

As the subtitle suggests, Pratt's purpose is different from Gilpin's and his scope wider. He writes about inns and the commercial exports of Lynn, the superiority of English roads and the coldness of the English character. He talks about taste, the picturesque, and the failings of Methodism. As regards politics and literature, Pratt shows clearly which way the winds were blowing in this antirevolutionary decade. He praises the reactionary *Anti-Jacobin* review and satirizes the excesses of sentimentalism—this in a long novelistic segment portraying the devastation of the countryside that results from the unwise benevolence of an eccentric landlord.

"The point proposed," writes Pratt, "is an amusing, interesting, and true idea of England, and of Englishmen in their various classes."[37] Manners and travels are frequently paired in this way, but as a domestic traveler, Pratt is addressing an audience already largely familiar with local custom. His real purpose is celebratory. England, he says fondly, is only a little place, "which, like the ant hill, is populated by the most industrious, ingenious, and wonder working creatures in the universe" (1).

Nonetheless, he could not deny its power: "But it is not the elegance of the work, but the grandeur of the idea that strikes us. . . . To be immured, as it were, by such hideous walls of rock; and to see the landscape through such strange apertures must have thrown the imagination into a wonderful ferment. The Druid, though savage in his nature, had the sublimest ideas of the object of his worship, whatever it was" (ibid., 80).

The interest here is that the passage shows Gilpin feeling his way inside an alien landscape, trying to imagine the experiences it once held. But this was a kind of "assimulation" he seldom looked for or achieved.

[36] According to a recent summary, his works are "an accurate and energetic response to changing tastes in the writing and reading of late eighteenth-century novels." See April London on Pratt, *Dictionary of Literary Biography*, 39:362.

[37] Samuel Jackson Pratt, *Gleanings in England; Descriptive of the Countenance, Mind and Character of the Country*, vol. 4 (London 1799), 6. This is designated as volume 4 as a continuation of the previous volumes on Wales, Holland, and Westphalia.

The later chapters in particular are soaked in a patriotic spirit stirred by naval battles and threats of invasion. "War must for ever be a scourge," he writes on the news of Nelson's victories, "but the love of country, my friend, is an inborn emotion; and to preserve our birth place from invasion is a sacred principle that uplifts the filial arm throughout the globe."[38] Pratt is no mindless jingo, and there is room in his patriotic fervor to recognize doubts and legitimate dissension.[39] But patriotism casts its glow on his view of England—especially when the "Gleaner" looks out to sea. Witness the rubrics introducing chapter 22:

> Cromer—Beeston Priory—Cromer Beach—Views of the ocean in different parts of the day and evening—The Author gleaneth the Sea—Also the five late victories upon it—A retrospect of Naval Glory of England—Borrows some golden ears from living English Bards, to make his sheath-offering presented to English heroes more worthy of their acceptance.

Here, as the chapter headings clearly indicate, a conventional description of picturesque landscape becomes associated with English naval traditions and recent triumphs over the French. In short, at Cromer Beach, Pratt reimagines the sea as a specifically English "place," one resonant with patriotic associations, and he completes his description with a long praise-poem to the naval heroes of England.

Away from sea and battle, Pratt offers another kind of patriotic description in his picture of Houghton, the house of Robert Walpole. Such a house, along with the grounds and plantings around it, make an impression on the traveler who approaches knowing something of the illustrious person whose erected it. "With the rapidity of thought," Pratt writes, "your mind will go back to all you ever heard or read of the celebrated founder, and those distinguished relatives who have successively possessed and ennobled it." By comparison the actual objects it contains will seem secondary. "The simple circumstance of knowing that many of the trees in the magnificent woods were planted by Sir Robert Walpole, will carry your reflections from the plantation to the planter." The mind of the traveler will be filled with the characters and events of Walpole's administration. The history of England ("this little island") Pratt continues,

> will croud [*sic*] upon you: for awhile, woods which have long been the admiration of travellers, will shrink diminished before you, or be so subordinate to the governing idea, that you will be able to afford them no distinct notice; and the very first portrait

[38] Ibid., 489.

[39] Pratt retained some worry about the dangers of war, especially for a commercial country like Britain: "the very sight of a commercial, turned into a military, nation—as is now the case of Great Britain—while it reflects the image of public virtue, and of patriotism, mingles with it the idea of mutilated life, unnatural deaths, and a groaning world" (ibid., 566–67).

> you are shewn of this Minister, or of Horace Walpole, will engross your attention, though the keeper of the house lions, who has little time to spare for contemplative visitors, will be impatient to draw you off from Statesmen and from Bards, to her Derbyshire marble, bronze Gladiators.[40]

Though Pratt gives us something less than Godwin's excited vision of commemoration, there is certainly more to this than a conventional picture of a great house. His description has less to do with physical images than with echoes of Walpole's work as builder, planter, and minister. These echoes in turn become part of a more general account of the way in which historical associations of place work their way through the mind of the spectator. In fact, since his work is topographical, rather than theoretical, Pratt's tracing of the process of historical association is more specific than anything Alison himself has to offer. And Houghton, as a native English site, neither ruinous nor romantic—a place, in fact, with very little sense of the heroic—nicely illustrates the breadth of possibilities awaiting anyone proposing to trace the associations of history across the map of modern Britain.

Aikin, Barbauld, and the Ruins of St. Paul's

I would like to end with John Aikin and his sister, Anna Laetitia Barbauld—two writers close to Godwin in background and politics, who nonetheless arrived at an assessment of the associations of place in English history quite different from the one promoted in the *Essay on Sepulchres*.

In his *Letters from a Father to his Son* (1793 and 1800), John Aikin acknowledges the power of association in general terms, only to dismiss the particular associations of the English past. Aikin begins with a skeptical look at the century's passion for ruins, which he is inclined to see as indulgent and self-deceiving. Ruins might have some beauty as "objects of sight," but for a ruin to be worth preserving, it must be the relic of a building originally of some beauty and importance. "With respect to the *sentimental* effects of ruins," he goes on to say, "they are all referable to that principle of association which connects animate with inanimate things, and past with present, by the relation of place."[41] These associations have a powerful appeal to the imagination, says Aikin, and he illustrates the thought—as it had been illustrated so often before—with reference to battlefields, "ruined palaces," and abandoned cities. Scenes like these have the power to move every susceptible breast (268).

So far Aikin's view of the psychological effect of ruins seems no different from Godwin's, and he goes on to speak of their effect of "elevated melan-

[40] Ibid., 202 ff.

[41] John Aikin, *Letters from A Father To His Son* (London, 1794), 267.

choly" and to quote Dyer's *Ruins of Rome*. But while conceding the evocative power of such places, Aikin refuses to give in to indiscriminate sentimentalism. It is necessary, he argues, that the place and its relics "refer to somewhat really interesting." In other words, Aikin refuses to accord any sentimental value to ruinousness itself. With the same literalness, he insists that the emotions inspired by the recollected scene should not be incongruous with those that we are likely to bring with us to the spot. But he points out that this is hardly the usual situation: the "gay party" approaching the "awful pile of religious ruins" would soon lose its cheerfulness if they really felt the force of its associations. In fact, he concludes, this incongruity of emotions is proof of how little the ruin-hunters are truly affected by the scenes they visit.

Aikin's insistence that ruins not be sentimentalized, that they be taken seriously as reminders of the past as it really was, results in a conclusion that turns Godwin's proposal upside down: "Upon the principle of association it will, however, appear, that the great part of the relics of antiquity in this country can produce but trifling effects on the heart. The ideas they suggest are those of forms of life offering nothing dignified or pleasing to the mind." The castle and the monastery remind us only of stern tyranny and brutal ignorance. "We are rejoiced that their date is past; and we can have little inducement to recal them from that oblivion into which they are deservedly sunk, and which best accords with their primitive insignificance."[42]

Thus Aikin is prepared to turn his back on the dark associations of the past in the name of an enlightened present. But a decade later, his sister, Anna Laetitia Barbauld, could no longer subscribe to this hopeful view of England's progress. Her long narrative poem *Eighteen Hundred and Eleven* is a further essay on the melancholy spirit of ruins, but the broken landscape she contemplates is a relic not of the past, but of the present—a projection into the future of the wreck of contemporary Britain.

Barbauld personifies history as an erratic, unpredictable spirit: "The Genius now forsakes the favoured shore, / And hates, capricious, what he loved before." But in truth the movements of history seem to her all too predictable: "Arts, arms, and wealth destroy the fruits they bring; / Commerce, like beauty, knows no second spring."[43] Without its wealth or its spirit of liberty, England

[42] "The castellated mansion of the ancient Baron, of which nothing is left but a shattered tower, frowning over the fruitful vale, reminds us only of the stern tyranny, brutal ignorance, and gross licentiousness, which stained the times of feudal anarchy. And if we look back to the original state of our ordinary monastic remains, what shall we see but a set of beings engaged in a dull round of indolent pleasures, and superstitious practices, alike debasing to the heart and understanding" (ibid., 270–71).

Godwin, we might remember, had expressed similarly negative views of the English medieval past in his essay "Of History and Romance," written in 1797 and first published as an appendix to the Penguin edition of *Caleb Williams*, 366–67.

[43] *The Works of Anna Laetitia Barbauld*, 2 vols. (London, 1825), 1:232–50.

would join other empires past their zenith and sink into a new (wholly unromantic) dark age.[44] Still, there is consolation of a kind in the thought that the inheritance of English philosophy would live on in the New World, and some day a youth from "the Blue Mountains or Ontario's lake," might make a pilgrimage to gaze on the ruins of London:

> Or of some crumbling turret mined by time,
> The broken stairs with perilous step shall climb,
> Thence stretch their view the wide horizon round,
> By scattered hamlets trace its ancient bound
> And choked no more with fleets, fair Thames survey
> Through reeds and sedge pursue his idle way.[45]

Not surprisingly, Barbauld's dark prophecy met harsh criticism. The Napoleonic era demanded a simpler loyalty and a very different sort of vision of the British landscape. Yet thirty years later Macaulay would echo this poem in a famous passage in which he comfortably imagines a time in remote futurity when "some traveller from New Zealand shall, in the midst of a vast solitude, take his stand on a broken arch of London Bridge to sketch the ruins of St. Paul's."[46] By then the war with Napoleon was a heroic memory and the vision of time's decay, taken so seriously by both the writer and her critics in 1811, was hardly more than a flourish.

"Antient Piety"

How Godwin read *Eighteen Hundred and Eleven* I do not know, but it is clear that he would have disagreed with both of the Aikins. In a striking passage in the *Essay on Sepulchres*, Godwin argues for the choice of living in an old country, with all its richness of association, against life in the New World, surrounded only by the bounty of nature. In older lands, Godwin writes, there is on every side "some object connected with a heart moving tale" or a scene where "the deepest interests of a nation . . . have been strenuously agitated."[47] Even scenes and objects that are not truly historical can have this power: old traditions or novels, even though not strictly true, may still endow a place with a "beautiful association."

[44] "Night, Gothic night, again may shade the plains / Where Power is seated, and where Science reigns."

[45] Barbauld, *Works*, 1:241–42.

[46] See Macaulay's essay on Ranke in *Miscellaneous Essays*, 2:465–66.

[47] Godwin, *Essay on Sepulchres*, 67 (Philp, 20): The full passage reads: "I love to dwell in a country, where, on whichever side I turn, I find some object connected with a heart-moving tale, or some scene where the deepest interests of a nation for ages to succeed, have been strenuously agitated, and emphatically decided. A tale of invention, or of idle tradition merely, is of great power in this respect."

Generally we connect this embracing of the pleasures and burdens of living in the presence of history not with Godwin, but with his opponent in the Revolution debate, Edmund Burke. As a contemporary reviewer of the *Essay on Sepulchres* noted with some irony, "this *Meditation among the tombs* . . . unlike other productions of Mr. Godwin's pen, is more in the style of *antient piety* than of *modern philosophy*."[48] Perhaps so—but in light of the texts we have surveyed, it seems clear that the desire for an emotional engagement with history belonged to no one author and no single politics. And when we recall the role of associationalism in promoting the idea of historical evocation, we must conclude that "modern philosophy" and "antient piety" were not always such enemies to one another.

[48] *MR* 61 (1810): 111.

Conclusion

Historical Distance and the Reception of Eighteenth-Century Historical Writing

THE DECADE of the French Revolution has long been seen as marking the transition between two great eras in historical thought. Some have characterized the shift primarily as a matter of literary style (from classic to romantic), some as a matter of ideology (from Enlightenment progress to Burkean tradition), and others again as a question of trope and emplotment (from Humean irony to Micheletian romance). For the purposes of this book, however, it has seemed more fruitful to move across such boundaries, with the result that it has been possible to see some important continuities linking the historical writings of the mid–eighteenth century with those of the early decades of the nineteenth. Even so, any continuity thesis must eventually confront the question of its own limits. At what point, it is necessary to ask, does an accumulation of small changes amount to a new configuration? And, granting the evidence of considerable continuity, how do we account for the widespread perception of a substantial break in historical understanding?

This book has pursued three related themes that give some help with this fundamental problem of continuity-in-change. The first has to do with the late arrival of a classical moment in British historical writing; the second concerns interrelationships among the family of historical genres; the third is the neglected issue of historical distance and the emergence in the eighteenth century of new norms of distance that subsequently hardened into dogmas of historical thought. Most of this conclusion will concern itself with the last of these three issues, but first I must return briefly to the other two.

It was widely agreed in the eighteenth century that with Hume, Robertson, and Gibbon Britain had at last acquired its classical historical literature. This understanding blends two meanings of the term *classical*, since it recognized both that these writers were steeped in the influences of Greco-Roman tradition and that their own works had attained a degree of polish and authority that would make them models for later generations. But the late formation of this canonical literature is also important, because it means that by the time British historical writing had acquired this sense of canonical authority, history had, in fact, lost its classical subject and with it the clear priority of public over private life. For Hume and his contemporaries, that is, history had become wider in its concerns and more flexible in its practices than classical narrative could easily accommodate. Just like their successors in the following century (as well as in our own times), eighteenth-century historians were forced to grapple with the problem of representing worlds of social experience and inward feeling that were hard to translate into the traditional narrative conventions. Consequently, eighteenth-century narratives were already concerned with commercial life and everyday manners, with the experiences of women, "primitives," poets, and others not involved in statecraft, with histories of literature, the arts, and the sciences. But it was not simply in its thematics that eighteenth-century historical writing had moved away from classical convention. As writers and readers in all genres absorbed a sentimentalist moral psychology, historians reconceived both the mimetic and the instructive power of their art in ways that stood at some remove from humanist traditions of exemplary narrative.

The second aspect of this study that bears importantly on the question of continuity concerns genre. My argument has been that we are better served if we think of history as a family of related genres, rather than (as customarily) a simple, unitary one. Indeed, unless we think of genre in this more fluid and complex way, the substantial continuity of historical questions and interests in this period may be hidden. Reciprocally, I have argued that one of the major gains that comes from thinking of history as a family of genres is precisely that it allows us to see this continuity, since some of the characteristic questions of the period are first apparent in the so-called minor genres. Writers of memoir or biography, for example, were able to respond comparatively quickly to the sentimental interests of eighteenth-century audiences. But it is not only the minor genres that have this value as historical markers. The rise of conjectural history in this period demonstrates the way in which the emergence of new or hybrid genres, high or low, can be a revealing indicator of changing directions in historical thought.

Genre is also an important factor in historical distance, which is the third of the three themes I want to recall in this conclusion. I have argued earlier that distance is a neglected, but crucial dimension in historiographical texts; here I want to focus on one facet of the question, which bears most directly on the question of continuity and its limits: this is the question of how shifting norms of distance conditioned the reception of eighteenth-century writing both in the early nineteenth century and in more recent criticism.

Norms of distance, I have suggested, are subject to periodic shifts. From this standpoint, one could sum up many of the changes in historical writing in the eighteenth century as involving a gradual reorientation toward more proximate norms of distance—an ideal strikingly demonstrated in Godwin's plan, discussed in the last chapter, to transform England into a landscape of commemoration. The corollary of this observation from the standpoint of genre is that this preference for proximity is often most apparent in the minor genres, as indeed is the case in Godwin's essay. But I do not want to oversimplify the picture: after all, some of the most striking evidence of a desire for immediacy came from the portraiture in Hume's *History of England* as well as the literary theorizing of Adam Smith and Lord Kames.

In short, interest in more proximative forms of historical distance was both an early and a characteristic expression of historical writing in eighteenth-century Britain. Indeed, as we have seen, the desire to understand and exploit occasions for historical immediacy is already present a half century and more before the counterrevolutionary traditionalism of Edmund Burke or the "romanticism" of Godwin and Walter Scott. But this evidence for continuity only makes more compelling the question of limits with which I began. In this light, it becomes important not only to acknowledge that in some parts of his work Hume prepared the ground for a more evocative style of historiography, but also to recognize that in doing so he helped to create expectations that ultimately worked to make his own writing seem less adequate to new generations of readers.

Distance and Reception in the Nineteenth Century

The importance of preferences about distance in shaping Hume's reputation can be captured by a brief comparison of evaluations by James Mackintosh and John Stuart Mill. As we have already seen in chapter 8, Mackintosh held Hume's historical works in the highest regard. In a passage from his journals from 1811 that I quoted earlier, Mackintosh wrote: "No other narrative seems to unite, in the same degree, the two qualities of being instructive and affecting. No historian approached him in the union of the talent of painting pathetic scenes with that of exhibiting comprehensive views of human affairs."[1] For Mackintosh, evidently, it was precisely Hume's versatility and control in matters of distance, his ability to combine philosophic detachment with affective presence, that marked him as a supreme writer of narrative. But with this praise, Mackintosh mingled a measure of criticism, and he did so in terms that would be prophetic for the subsequent climate of rejection. Like later critics, Mackintosh saw Hume's skeptical and rationalist temper as a limitation on his

[1] *Memoirs*, 2:168. We should also recall that in his discussion of history and fiction Mackintosh discounts differences in genre by calling Hume and Richardson the two great "pathetic painters." It is worth underlining the fact that Mackintosh, who was a serious student of philosophy, put Hume's reputation as a historian at the front: "His greatest work, and that which naturally claims most attention, was his 'History of England,' which, notwithstanding great defects, will probably be at last placed at the head of historical compositions" (ibid.). We might note a parallel judgment by A. F. Tytler on Hume's essays on political economy, which he believed would be more lasting than Hume's philosophical work. The essays "have served as the basis of that enlarged system of polity, which connects the welfare of every nation with the prosperity of all its surrounding states" (Tytler, *Memoirs of Kames*, 2:104–5).

capacity for sympathy. Too often, he thought, Hume used his intelligence to fill the place of evidence. He "was too habitually a speculator and too little of an antiquary, to have a great power of throwing back his mind into former ages, and of clothing his persons and events in their moral dress; his personages are too modern and argumentative—if we must not say too rational."[2]

Mackintosh treated the problem of sympathy as marking a limit to Hume's historical genius. A generation later, however, John Stuart Mill set the question of sympathy at the very center of historical understanding and contended that Hume's failure on this score meant that his writings could hardly even be considered historical. Reviewing Carlyle's *French Revolution*—a work he had done a great deal to encourage—Mill writes:

> If there be a person who, in reading the histories of Hume, Robertson, and Gibbon (works of extraordinary talent, and the works of great writers) has never felt that this, after all, is not history—and that the lives and deeds of his fellow-creatures must be placed before him in quite another manner, if he is to know them, for them to be real beings, who once were alive, beings of his own flesh and blood, not mere shadows and dim abstractions; such a person, for whom plausible talk *about* a thing does as well as an image of the thing itself, feels no need of a book like Mr. Carlyle's; the want, which it is peculiarly fitted to supply, does not consciously exist in his mind.[3]

For Mill, the problem lay, self-evidently, in Hume's failure of sympathy. "Does Hume throw his own mind into the mind of an Anglo-Saxon, or an Anglo-Norman?" Does any reader feel he has gained "anything like a picture of what may actually have been passing, in the minds, say, of Cavaliers or of Roundheads during the civil wars?"[4]

Between Mackintosh's criticisms and Mill's there is considerable continuity of substance combined with a sharp difference in emphasis. This shift is reflected in Mill's tone, which self-consciously exhibits the excitement of generational change. Mill presses a new standard of historical truth, whose depth is measured by the very fact that some readers (implicitly older ones) cannot be expected to open themselves to its terms. The differences been the two commentaries, then, are not simply individual. Rather the comparison of

[2] *Memoirs*, 2:169. Francis Jeffrey seconds this opinion of Hume's limitations; see *Contributions to Edinburgh Review*, 3:673.

[3] The review appeared in the *London and Westminster Review*, July 1837; John Stuart Mill, *Essays on French History and Historians*, ed. J. H. Robson and J. C. Cairns (Toronto: U of Toronto P, 1985), 134. Significantly, Mill supported his argument with the evidence of genre: the vast production of historical plays and historical novels, he wrote, was the best evidence that such a "want" was generally felt.

[4] Mill suggests that the simple sight of a few homely implements of Anglo-Saxon life would tell us more, "directly and by inference," than everything Hume's skillful narrative accomplishes (ibid., 135).

Mackintosh and Mill nicely illuminates the way in which the preference for immediacy, so long anticipated eighteenth-century narratives and criticism, had by midcentury come to seem a new article of faith. It is not hard to show, in fact, that some of the most familiar pronouncements of "romantic historiography" concern the abbreviation of distance, and that the definition of this new norm depends upon a dramatized sense of contrast with the preceding era.

A prime example is Carlyle's definition of history as "the essence of innumerable biographies." This famous, but often misunderstood dictum speaks directly to Carlyle's desire to understand the historical process as something actual and experienced. As he puts it, his goal was to gain "some acquaintance with our fellow-creatures, though dead and vanished, yet dear to us; how they got along in those old days, suffering and doing."[5] Carlyle should not, therefore, be read as advocating biography as a shortcut to historical understanding. Quite the contrary: he believed that the political economists and other heirs of the Enlightenment rationalism ("cause and effect speculators") gave history a false transparency by distancing it from the mysteries of experience. He contrasted his own desire to evoke history's immediate presence to the aloof philosophical style of Enlightenment and post-Enlightenment historians ("those modern Narrations of the Philosophic kind"), whose lofty generalizations he compared to the resonant emptiness of an owl hooting from a rooftop.[6]

Macaulay, too, makes distance a central issue. Indeed, in his early essays, which are more romantic in tone than his later *History*, he figures the problem as defining the crucial dilemmas confronted by modern historiography. Macaulay's formulation reworks a familiar romantic trope, which sets the rationalistic, self-conscious, and divided spirit of modernity against the naive unity of thought and feeling once possessed by the Greeks. Writing history, Macaulay argues, has always involved a difficult effort to join reason and imagination, but recent times had witnessed a complete divorce between the two. Now only the greatest of historians might be able to summon up the imaginative strengths needed to overcome this modern problem of self-division.

Macaulay overlays this abbreviated history of the historical imagination with a second schematic having to do with genre, in which the competing claims of the essay and the novel stand for the dilemmas of the contemporary historian. Much like those who today talk of history and memory, burying in each unspoken assumptions about distance, Macaulay sees modern historical understanding as having suffered a sharp division between the distanciating rationality of the historian-essayist and the evocative power of the historical novelist:

[5] Carlyle, "Biography," in *Works*, 28:47.

[6] "[T]hose Modern Narrations, of the Philosophic kind, where 'Philosophy teaching by Experience," has to sit like [an] owl on housetop, *seeing* nothing, *understanding* nothing, uttering only, with such solemnity, her perpetual most wearisome *hoo-hoo*" (ibid.).

> To make the past present, to bring the distant near, to place us in the society of a great man on an eminence which overlooks the field of a mighty battle, to invest with the reality of human flesh and blood beings whom we are too much inclined to consider as personified qualities in an allegory, to call up our ancestors before us with all their peculiarities of language, manners, and garb, to show us over their houses, to seat us at their tables, to rummage their old-fashioned wardrobes, to explain the uses of their ponderous furniture, these parts of the duty which properly belongs to the historian have been appropriated by the historical novelist.[7]

To overcome this problem of loss and division, Macaulay suggests, would require more than Shakespearean powers; a truly great historian would need to combine the science of Hallam with the imagination of Scott.

Distance and Reception in the Twentieth Century

The new norms of historical distance evident in the comments of Mill, Carlyle, and Macaulay have exercised a deep and continuing influence, so that we continue to read eighteenth-century texts through nineteenth-century eyes. One reason for this remarkable persistence is that nineteenth- and twentieth-century idealist philosophies gave renewed emphasis to the idea of sympathetic insight (*Verstehen*), which came to be seen as the central feature of historical understanding. In this way, a long-standing preference for proximity was made more systematic and elevated to a principle of historical method.

It is no accident, then, that many of those who have written within this idealist tradition have continued to define their views by way of a contrast to the failings of eighteenth-century historians. In a revealing passage, the English philosopher R. G. Collingwood sums up his own historicist program as one that entails a fundamental acceptance of the self-understanding of other times. The Romantics, Collingwood writes, possessed this kind of sympathy for earlier times, but Enlightenment historiography fails this crucial test:

> A truly historical view of human history, sees everything in that history as having its own *raison d'etre* and coming into existence in order to serve the needs of the men whose minds have corporately created it. To think of any phase in history as altogether irrational is to look at it not as an historian but as a publicist, a polemical writer of tracts for the times. Thus the historical outlook of the Enlightenment was not genuinely historical; in its main motive it was polemical and anti-historical.[8]

[7] Macaulay, *Miscellaneous Essays*, 1:310. The essay, a review of Hallam, was first published in *ER* in September 1828.

[8] R. G. Collingwood, *The Idea of History* (Oxford: Oxford UP, 1956), 77.

When one compares Hume's complete lack of sympathy for the Middle Ages, Collingwood writes, with "the intense sympathy for the same thing which is found in Sir Walter Scott, one can see how this tendency of Romanticism [i.e. sympathy] had enriched its historical outlook."[9]

With such views in the background, even some of the best-informed students of the Enlightenment have been ready to replicate the same negative judgment. John Stewart, for example, in a thorough study of Hume's politics, dismisses Hume's history on grounds that once again amount to a preference for proximity over distanciation:

> The *History*, in an important sense, is antihistorical. The great stimulus to English historians, especially in the seventeenth century, had been the desire to trace up "privilege" or "prerogative" to the "ancient constitution." By demonstrating the invalidity of such a mode of argument, Hume annihilates much of the old justification for studying the past. It is notable that when he had finished his essentially negative task, he did not undertake another historical work.[10]

Stewart evidently assumes that there is only one acceptable relationship to the past, a relationship of (political) connectedness; as a result, historical knowledge that might enable a kind of *dis*engagement seems to him not simply a different sort of politics, but an illegitimate form of history. More broadly, Stewart's dismissal of a great historical narrative as essentially antihistorical depends on confidently held assumptions about what constitutes a properly historical attitude. Taking his cue from Butterfield and others, Stewart treats historiography as, by definition, a literature of recuperation, and for this reason he laments that Hume never displays "the true historian's love for the past" (298).

A surprisingly similar judgment on Enlightenment historiography prefaces Hayden White's influential *Metahistory:*

> The skeptical form which rationalism took in its reflection *on its own time* was bound to inspire a purely Ironic attitude with respect to the past when used as the principle of historical reflection. The mode in which all the *great* historical works of the age were cast is that of Irony, with the result that they all tend towards the form of Satire, the supreme achievement of the literary sensibility of that age. When Hume turned from philosophy to history, because he felt that philosophy had been rendered uninteresting by the skeptical conclusions to which he had been driven, he brought to his study of history the same skeptical sensibility. He found it increasingly difficult, however, to sustain his interest in a process which displayed to him only the eternal

[9] Ibid., 87. The historian, he writes, "must never do what Enlightenment historians were always doing, that is, regard past ages with contempt and disgust, but must look at them sympathetically and find in them the expression of genuine and valuable human achievements."

[10] John Stewart, *The Moral and Political Philosophy of David Hume* (New York: Columbia UP, 1963), 299.

return of the same folly in many different forms. He viewed the historical record as little more than the *record* of human folly, which led him finally to become as bored with history as he had become with philosophy.[11]

The vocabulary here departs from that of earlier critics, but the substance seems remarkably consistent. White's "purely Ironic attitude with respect to the past" points to the same sins Collingwood had in mind in talking of the requirement for intense sympathy or Stewart meant when he insisted on "the true historian's love for the past." All three critics want to reduce eighteenth-century practice to a single, frozen posture of distanciation, and all three arrive at this drastic simplification by privileging a romantic desire for identification as foundational for a true understanding of history. And behind what amounts to a series of caricatures, running from Carlyle's hooting owl to White's bored philosopher, is an assumption that there is one true norm of historical distance. Such an assumption, however, is clearly unhistorical and cannot hold up to a more catholic reading of the history of historiography.

Collingwood was right, of course, about Hume's general lack of sympathy for the medieval world, but his own inability to accept the standpoint of Enlightenment historiography seems an equally blatant failure. Surely Collingwood's own philosophical program would require us to look at eighteenth-century historiography, no less than any other practice or institution, as "having its own *raison d'etre* and coming into existence in order to serve the needs of the men whose minds have corporately created it." In fact, as I have indicated, the criticisms offered by Collingwood, Stewart, and White reflect a conception of historical distance that first emerged in the eighteenth century, especially in the minor historical genres, but became a consensus of European thought only in the half century that followed Hume's *History*.

My point in making these remarks is not (except indirectly) to defend Hume's reputation. Rather, by underlining the importance of unexamined assumptions about historical distance in shaping that reputation, I want simply to emphasize that these norms must themselves be understood as historically variable. It should be clear, then, that historical distance itself has a history that we will need to know more about if we are to appreciate the ways in which historical writing has served "the needs of the men whose minds have corporately created it." But just because assumptions about distance lie close to the core of history's methods and purposes, these assumptions have seldom been brought to the surface, and have more often been the subject of dogmas than of questions.

[11] White, *Metahistory*, 55.

Bibliography

Printed Primary Sources

Adams, John. *Woman. Sketches of the history, genius, disposition, accomplishments, employments, customs and importance of the fair sex, in all parts of the world.* London, 1790.

Aikin, John. *Letters from a Father to his Son.* London, 1794.

Aikin, Lucy. *Epistles on Women, Exemplifying their Character and Condition in Various Ages and Nations.* London, 1810. Reprint, Brown Women Writers Project, 1993.

Alexander, William. *The History of Women, from the earliest antiquity, to the present time.* 2 vols. Philadelphia, 1796.

Alison, Archibald. *Essays on the Nature and Principles of Taste.* Edinburgh, 1790. Reprint, Hildesheim: Olms, 1968.

Ancell, Samuel. *A Circumstantial Journal of the Long and Tedious Blockade and Siege of Gibraltar, from the Twelfth of September 1779, to the third Day of February, 1783. By an Officer.* Manchester, 1783.

Anderson, Adam. *An Historical and Chronological Deduction of the Origin of Commerce from the earliest accounts, containing an history of the great commercial interests of the British Empire . . . revised, corrected, and continued to the present time.* Continued to 1788 by William Coombe. 4 vols. London, 1801. Reprint, New York: A. M. Kelley, 1967.

Anderson, William. *The Popular Scottish Biography.* Edinburgh, 1842.

[Andrews, John]. *An Account of the Character and Manners of the French; with occasional Observations on the English.* 2 vols. London, 1770.

Anon. *Memoirs of the Life and Times of Sir Thomas Deveil, Knight, One of his Majesties Justices of the Peace.* London, 1748.

Anon. *The Trial of Warren Hastings, Esq. Late Governor General of Bengal.* London, 1788.

[Astell, Mary]. *The Christian Religion, as Profess'd by a Daughter of the Church of England.* London, 1705.

Austen, Jane. *Jane Austen's Letters.* Ed. Deirdre Le Faye. 3d ed. Oxford: Oxford UP, 1995.

Barbauld, Anna Laetitia. *The Works of Anna Laetitia Barbauld.* 2 vols. London, 1825.

Belsham, William. *Essays, Philosophical, Historical, and Literary.* 2 vols. London, 1799.

Benger, Elizabeth. *Memoirs of the Late Mrs. Elizabeth Hamilton.* London, 1818.

Bennett, John. *Letters to a Young Lady.* Warrington, 1789.

Berington, Joseph. *The History of the Lives of Abeillard and Heloisa.* Birmingham, 1787.

———. *The History of the Reign of Henry the Second, and of Richard and John.* Birmingham, 1790.

Bisset, Robert. *The History of the Reign of George III to the Termination of the Late War. To which is prefixed, A View of the Progressive Improvement of England in Prosperity and Strength; to the Accession of his Majesty.* 6 vols. London, 1803.

Bisset, Robert. *The Life of Edmund Burke*. 2 vols. London, 1800.

Blackwell, Thomas. *Enquiry into the Life and Writings of Homer*. London, 1736. Reprint, Hildesheim: Olms, 1976.

Blair, Hugh. *Lectures on Rhetoric and Belles Lettres*. Ed. H. F. Harding. 2 vols. Carbondale: U of Southern Illinois P, 1965.

[?Bolton, Robert]. *Letters to a Young Nobleman*. London, 1762.

Boswell, James. *Boswell's Journal of a Tour to the Hebrides with Samuel Johnson*. London: Heineman, 1936.

———. *The Life of Johnson. A New Edition with Numerous Additions and Notes*. Ed. John Wilson Croker. 5 vols. London, 1831.

———. *The Life of Samuel Johnson*. Ed. R. W. Chapman. Oxford: Oxford UP, 1976.

———. *London Journal, 1762–1763*. Ed. Frederick Pottle. London: Heineman, 1950.

Burke, Edmund. *Correspondence of Edmund Burke*. Ed. Thomas Copeland. 10 vols. Cambridge: Cambridge UP, 1958–78.

———. "A Letter to a Noble Lord (February 1796)." In *Further Reflections on the French Revolution*. Ed. Daniel Ritchie. Indianapolis: Liberty, 1992.

———. *Reflections on the Revolution in France*. Ed. J. G. A. Pocock. Indianapolis: Hackett, 1987.

———. *Selected Writings and Speeches*. Ed. Peter Stanlis. Chicago: Regnery, 1962.

———. *Three Memorials on French Affairs. Written in the Years 1791, 1792 and 1793. By the Late Right Hon. Edmund Burke*. London, 1797.

———. *Writings and Speeches of Edmund Burke*. Ed. Paul Langford et al. 9 vols. Oxford: Clarendon, 1981–.

Carlyle, Thomas. *The Works of Thomas Carlyle*. 30 vols. Edinburgh Edition. New York: Scribner, 1904.

Carte, Thomas. *A Collection of Original Letters and Papers, Concerning the Affairs of England, from the year 1641 to 1660*. 2 vols. London, 1739.

Chapone, Hester. *Letters on the Improvement of the Mind, Addressed to a Young Lady*. 3d ed. London, 1774.

Clarke, Stanier, and John McArthur. *Life of Admiral Lord Nelson*. 2 vols. London, 1809.

Cockburn, Henry. *Life of Lord Jeffrey, With a Selection from his Correspondence*. 2 vols. Edinburgh, 1852.

———. *Memorials of His Time*. Edinburgh, 1856. Reprint, Edinburgh: James Thin, 1988.

[Creech, William]. *Letters Addressed to Sir John Sinclair, respecting the mode of living, arts, commerce, literature, manners etc. of Edinburgh, in 1763, and since that period*. Edinburgh, 1793.

Croker, John Wilson. *The Croker Papers*. Ed. L. Jennings. 3 vols. London, 1884.

[Currie, James]. *A Letter, Commercial and Political, addressed to the right Honorable William Pitt, in which the Real Interests of Britain in the Present Crisis Are Considered, and Some Observations Are Offered on the General State of Europe*. London, 1793.

D'Israeli, Isaac. *Curiosities of Literature*. 2 vols. London, 1791. Reprint, New York: Garland, 1971.

———. *Dissertation on Anecdotes*. London, 1793. Reprint, New York: Garland, 1972.

———. *An Essay on the Manners and Genius of the Literary Character*. London, 1795. Reprint, New York: Garland, 1970.

Ferguson, Adam. *The Correspondence of Adam Ferguson.* 2 vols. Ed. Vincenzo Merolle. London: Pickering, 1995.

———. *An Essay on the History of Civil Society.* Ed. Fania Oz-Salzberger. Cambridge: Cambridge UP, 1996.

———. *Principles of Moral and Political Science.* 2 vols. Edinburgh, 1792.

Fielding, Henry. *Jonathan Wild.* Harmondsworth: Penguin, 1982.

Fox, Charles James. *A History of the Early Part of the Reign of James the Second.* London, 1808.

Gilpin, William. *Observations on the River Wye and several parts of South Wales relative chiefly to Picturesque Beauty made in the summer of the year 1770.* London, 1782.

———. *Observations on the Western Parts of England relative chiefly to Picturesque Beauty.* London, 1798.

———. *Observations relative Chiefly to Picturesque Beauty made in the Year 1772, On Several Parts of England; Particularly the Mountains and Lakes of Cumberland, and Westmoreland.* 2 vols. London, 1782.

Godwin, William. *Caleb Williams.* Ed. M. Hindle. Harmondsworth: Penguin, 1988.

———. *The Enquirer.* London, 1797. Reprint, New York: A. M. Kelley, 1965.

———. *Essay on Sepulchres.* London, 1809.

———. *Life of Geoffrey Chaucer, the early English Poet, including Memoirs of his near friend and kinsman, John of Gaunt, Duke of Lancaster: with Sketches of the Manners, Opinions, Arts, and Literature of England in the Fourteenth Century.* 4 vols. London, 1803.

———. *The Lives of Edward and John Philips.* London, 1815.

———. "Of History and Romance." In *Caleb Williams*, ed. M. Hindle. Harmondsworth: Penguin, 1988.

———. *The Political and Philosophical Writings of William Godwin.* Ed. Mark Philp. 7 vols. London: Pickering, 1993.

Goldsmith, Oliver. *Collected Works.* Ed. Arthur Friedman. 5 vols. Oxford: Clarendon, 1966.

———. *The Life of Richard Nash.* London, 1762.

Green, Thomas. *Extracts from the Diary of a Lover of Literature.* Ipswich, 1810.

Hale, Matthew. *The History of the Common Law of England.* Ed. Charles Gray. Chicago: U of Chicago P, 1971.

Hamilton, Elizabeth. *Letters on the Elementary Principles of Education.* 2 vols. Bath, 1801.

———. *Memoirs of Agrippina, the Wife of Germanicus.* 3 vols. Bath, 1804.

———. *A Series of Popular Essays, illustrative of principles essentially connected with the improvement of the understanding, the imagination, and the heart.* Edinburgh, 1813.

Hayley, William. *Essay on Epic Poetry.* London, 1782. Reprint, Gainesville, Fla.: Scholar's Facsimiles, 1968.

———. *An Essay on History, in Three Epistles to Edward Gibbon.* 2d ed. London, 1781.

Hazlitt, William. *Complete Works of William Hazlitt.* Ed. P. P. Howe. 21 vols. London: J. M. Dent, 1930–34.

Henry, Robert. *The History of Great Britain, From the First invasion of it by the Romans under Julius Caesar. Written on a New Plan*. 6th ed. 12 vols. London, 1823.

Horner, Francis. *The Horner Papers: Selections from the Letters and Miscellaneous Writings of Francis Horner, M.P., 1795–1817*. Ed. Kenneth Bourne and William Banks Taylor. Edinburgh: Edinburgh UP, 1994.

Hume, David. *Essays, Moral, Political, and Literary*. Ed. Eugene Miller. Indianapolis: Liberty, 1987.

———. *The History of England from the Invasion of Julius Caesar to the Revolution in 1688*. Foreword by William B. Todd. 6 vols. Reprint, Indianapolis: Liberty, 1983.

———. *History of Great Britain*. Edinburgh, 1754.

———. *Letters of David Hume*. Ed. J. Y. T. Greig. 2 vols. Oxford: Clarendon, 1932.

———. *A Treatise of Human Nature*. Ed. L. A. Selby-Bigge. Oxford: Clarendon, 1968.

Hutchinson, Lucy. *Memoirs of the Life of Colonel Hutchinson*. Ed. Julius Hutchinson. London, 1806.

Jeffrey, Francis. *Contributions to the Edinburgh Review*. 2d ed. 3 vols. London, 1846.

———. *Jeffrey's Criticism*. Ed. Peter Morgan. Edinburgh: Scottish Academic P, 1983.

Johnson, Samuel. *The Rambler*. Ed. W. J. Bate and A. B. Strauss. 3 vols. New Haven: Yale UP, 1969.

Kames, Henry Home, Lord. *Elements of Criticism*. 3 vols. Edinburgh, 1762.

———. *Historical Law-Tracts*. Edinburgh, 1761.

———. *Sketches of the History of Man*. 2d ed. 4 vols. Edinburgh, 1778. Reprint, Hildesheim: Olms, 1968.

Knox, Vicesimus. *Winter Evenings; Or Lucubrations on Life and Letters*. 3 vols. London, 1788.

Lamb, Charles, and Mary. *Letters of Charles and Mary Lamb*. Ed. E. W. Marrs. 3 vols. Ithaca: Cornell UP, 1976.

Logan, John. *Elements of the Philosophy of History. Part First*. Edinburgh, 1781.

Macaulay, Thomas Babington. *Critical, Historical, and Miscellaneous Essays*. 3 vols. New York: Albert Cogswell, 1859.

MacDonald, Thomas. *Thoughts on the Public Duties of Private Life, with Reference to Present Circumstances and Opinions*. Edinburgh, 1795.

Mackintosh, James. *Arguments Concerning the Constitutional Right of Parliament to Appoint a Regency*. London, 1788.

———. *Discourse on the Law of Nature and of Nations*. 3d ed. London, 1800.

———. *History of England*. 3 vols. London, 1830–32.

———. *History of the Revolution in England in 1688, prefaced by a notice of the Life, Writings and Speeches of Sir James Mackintosh*. Ed. William B. Wallace. London, 1834.

———. *Memoirs of the Life and Writings of Sir James Mackintosh*. Ed. Robert Mackintosh. 2 vols. Boston, 1853.

———. *The Miscellaneous Works of the Rt. Honourable Sir James Mackintosh*. Ed. Robert Mackintosh. London, 1851.

———. *The Trial of John Peltier, Esq. for a libel against Napoleon Buonaparte, First Consul of the French Republic*. London, 1803.

———. *Vindiciae Gallicae*. London, 1791.

Machiavelli, Niccolo. *The Discourses*. Trans. Walker Richardson and B. Richardson. Harmondsworth: Penguin, 1970.

Macpherson, David. *History of European Commerce with India*. London, 1812.

MacQueen, Daniel. *Letters on Hume's History of Great Britain*. London, 1756. Reprint, Bristol: Thoemmes, 1990.

Mason, William. *The Poems of Mr Gray, to which are prefixed Memoirs of his Life and Writings*. York, 1775.

[Mathias, Thomas]. *The Pursuits of Literature. A Satirical Poem in four dialogues*. 5th ed. London, 1798.

Mill, John Stuart. *Essays on French History and Historians*. Ed. J. H. Robson and J. C. Cairns. Toronto: U of Toronto P, 1985.

Millar, John. *Origin of the Distinction of Ranks*. Ed. J. V. Price. Bristol: Thoemmes, 1990.

Montesquieu, Charles de Secondat, baron de. *The Spirit of the Laws*. Trans. and ed. Anne M. Cohler, Basia Carolyn Miller, and Harold Samuel Stone. Cambridge: Cambridge UP, 1989.

Murphy, Arthur. *Arminius; a tragedy*. London, 1798.

———. *Works of C. Tacitus by Arthur Murphy; with an Essay on the Life and Genius of Tacitus*. 8 vols. London, 1811.

Philpot, Charles. *An Introduction to the Literary History of the Fourteenth and Fifteenth Centuries*. London, 1798. Reprint, New York: Garland, 1970.

Pinkerton, John. *Letters of Literature*. London, 1785. Reprint, New York: Garland, 1970.

Pratt, Samuel Jackson. *Gleanings in England; descriptive of the countenance, mind and character of the country*. London, 1799.

Priestley, Joseph. *A Course of Lectures on Oratory and Criticism*. London, 1777.

———. *Lectures on History and General Policy*. Birmingham, 1788.

Ramsay, John. *Letters of John Ramsay of Ochtertyre*. Ed. Barbara L. H. Horn. Edinburgh: Scottish History Society, 1966.

———. *Scotland and Scotsmen in the Eighteenth Century*. Ed. A. Allardyce. 2 vols. Edinburgh, 1888.

Reeve, Clara. *The Progress of Romance*. London, 1785. Reprint, New York: Garland, 1970.

Richardson, Samuel. *Clarissa, or The History of a Young Lady*. Ed. Angus Ross. Harmondsworth: Penguin, 1985.

Robertson, William. *The History of Scotland*. 2 vols. London, 1761.

———. *The History of the Reign of the Emperor Charles V. With a view of the progress of society in Europe, from the subversion of the Roman Empire to the beginning of the sixteenth century*. 3 vols. London, 1769.

———. *The Progress of Society in Europe*. Ed. Felix Gilbert. Chicago: U of Chicago P, 1972.

Rogers, Samuel. *Poetical Works*. London, 1869.

Roscoe, Henry. *The Life of William Roscoe, by his son Henry Roscoe*. 2 vols. Boston, 1833.

Roscoe, William. *The Life and Pontificate of Leo the Tenth*. 2 vols. London, 1846.

Russell, William. *Essay on the Character, Manners, and Genius of Women in Different Ages. Enlarged from the French of M. Thomas, by Mr. Russell.* 2 vols. Edinburgh, 1773.

———. *History of Modern Europe.* 5 vols. London, 1786.

Scott, Sir Walter. *The Letters of Sir Walter Scott.* Ed. Herbert Grierson. 12 vols. London: Constable, 1932.

———. *Periodical Criticism of Sir Walter Scott.* 5 vols. Edinburgh, 1835.

———. *Waverley.* Ed. Andrew Hook. New York: Penguin, 1972.

Sheridan, Thomas. *A General Dictionary of the English Language.* London, 1780.

Smith, Adam. *Correspondence of Adam Smith.* Ed. E. C. Mossner and I. S. Ross. Indianapolis: Liberty, 1987.

———. *An Enquiry into the Nature and Causes of the Wealth of Nations.* Ed. R. H. Campbell and A. S. Skinner. 2 vols. Indianapolis: Liberty, 1981.

———. *Essays on Philosophical Subjects.* Ed. W. P. D. Wightman and J. C. Bryce. Indianapolis: Liberty, 1982.

———. *Lectures on Jurisprudence.* Ed. R. L. Meek, D. D. Raphael, and P. G. Stein. Indianapolis: Liberty, 1982.

———. *Lectures on Rhetoric and Belles Lettres.* Ed. J. C. Bryce. Indianapolis: Liberty, 1985.

———. *The Theory of Moral Sentiments.* Ed. D. D. Raphael and A. L. Macfie. Indianapolis: Liberty, 1982.

Smith, Charlotte. *The History of England from the Earliest Records to the Peace of Amiens. In a series of letters to a young lady at school.* 3 vols. London, 1806.

Steuart, Henry. *The Works of Sallust; to which are prefixed two essays on the life, literary character, and writings of the historian.* 2 vols. London, 1806.

Stewart, Dugald. *Account of the Life and Writings of William Robertson.* 2d ed. London, 1802.

———. *Dissertation: Exhibiting the Progress of Metaphysical, Ethical, and Political Philosophy, Since the Revival of Letters in Europe.* In *Collected Works*, ed. Sir William Hamilton. 11 vols. Edinburgh, 1854.

Strutt, Joseph. *The Chronicle of England; or a compleat history, civil, military and ecclesiastical of the ancient Britons and Saxons.* 2 vols. London, 1778.

———. *The Sports and Pastimes of the People of England.* London, 1830.

Thomson, George. *The Spirit of General History, in a series of lectures, from the eighth to the eighteenth century.* 2d ed. London, 1792.

Towers, Joseph. *Tracts on Political and Other Subjects.* London, 1796.

Trusler, John. *Principles of Politeness, and of Knowing the World.* London, 1775.

Tytler, Alexander Fraser. *Elements of General History, Ancient and Modern.* Edinburgh, 1801.

———. *Memoirs of the Life and Writing of Henry Home of Kames.* 2 vols. Edinburgh, 1807.

———. *Plan and Outline of a Course of Lectures on Universal History, Ancient and Modern, delivered in the University of Edinburgh.* Edinburgh, 1782.

Waldron, George. *The history and description of the Isle of Man: viz. its antiquity, history, laws, customs, religion and manners of its inhabitants.* 2d ed. London, 1744.

Walpole, Horace. *The Yale Edition of Horace Walpole's Correspondence.* Ed. W. S. Lewis et al. 48 vols. New Haven: Yale UP, 1952.

Warton, Thomas. *The Correspondence of Thomas Warton*. Ed. David Fairer. Athens: U of Georgia P, 1995.

———. *History of English Poetry*. Ed. W. C. Hazlitt. 4 vols. London, 1871.

Wheare, Degory. *Method and Order of Reading Both Civil and Ecclesiastical Histories*. Trans. Edmund Bohun. 3d ed. London, 1678.

Wight, William. *Heads of a Course of Lectures on the Study of History; given annually by William Wight DD., Professor of History in the University of Glasgow*. Glasgow, 1767.

Williams, Helen Maria. *Letters from France*. Ed. Janet Todd. 2 vols. London, 1796. Reprint, New York: Scholar's Facsimiles, 1975.

Wollstonecraft, Mary. *Vindication of the Rights of Woman*. Harmondsworth: Penguin, 1985.

Wood, Robert. *An Essay on the Original Genius and Writing of Homer*. London, 1775. Reprint, New York: Garland, 1971.

Wordsworth, William. *The Prose Works of William Wordsworth*. Ed. W. J. B. Owen and J. W. Smyser. Oxford: Oxford UP, 1974.

———. *Selected Poems and Prefaces*. Ed. Jack Stillinger. Boston: Houghton Mifflin, 1965.

Selected Secondary Sources

Allan, David. *Virtue, Learning, and the Scottish Enlightenment*. Edinburgh: Edinburgh UP, 1993.

Ankersmit, Frank, and Hans Kellner, eds. *A New Philosophy of History*. Chicago: U of Chicago P, 1995.

Appleby, Joyce Oldham. *Economic Thought and Ideology in Seventeenth-Century England*. Princeton: Princeton UP, 1978.

Appleby, Joyce Oldham, Lynn Hunt, and Margaret Jacob. *Telling the Truth about History*. New York: Norton, 1994.

Arendt, Hannah. *The Human Condition*. Chicago: U of Chicago P, 1958.

Ayling, Stanley. *Edmund Burke: His Life and Opinions*. London: Cassell, 1988.

Ballaster, Ros. *Seductive Forms: Women's Amatory Fiction from 1684–1740*. Oxford: Oxford UP, 1992.

Bann, Stephen. *Romanticism and the Rise of History*. New York: Twayne, 1995.

Barker-Benfield, J. G. *The Culture of Sensibility: Sex and Society in Eighteenth-Century Britain*. Chicago: U of Chicago P, 1992.

Barrell, John. *English Literature in History, 1730–80: An Equal, Wide Survey*. London: Hutchinson, 1989.

Bate, Walter Jackson. *The Burden of the Past and the English Poet*. Cambridge: Harvard UP, 1970.

Bell, Alan, ed. *Lord Cockburn: A Bicentenary Commemoration, 1779–1979*. Edinburgh: Scottish Academic P, 1979.

Benedict, Barbara M. " 'Service to the Public': William Creech and Sentiment for Sale." In *Sociability and Society in Eighteenth-Century Scotland*, ed. John Dwyer and Richard Sher. Edinburgh: Mercat, 1993.

Bohls, Elizabeth. *Women Travel Writers and the Language of Aesthetics, 1716–1818*. Cambridge: Cambridge UP, 1995.

Bongie, Laurence. *David Hume, Prophet of the Counter-Revolution*. Oxford: Clarendon, 1965.

Boulton, James T. "James Mackintosh: *Vindiciae Gallicae*." *Renaissance and Modern Studies* 21 (1977): 106–18.

Braudy, Leo. *Narrative Form in History and Fiction: Hume, Fielding and Gibbon*. Princeton: Princeton UP, 1970.

Brissenden, R. F. *Virtue in Distress: Studies in the Novel of Sentiment from Richardson to Sade*. New York: Harper and Row, 1976.

Bromwich, David. *A Choice of Inheritance: Self and Community from Edmund Burke to Robert Frost*. Cambridge: Harvard UP, 1989.

Brown, Stewart J., ed. *William Robertson and the Expansion of Empire*. Cambridge: Cambridge UP, 1997.

Bryant, Donald. *Edmund Burke and His Literary Friends*. St. Louis: Washington UP, 1939.

Burke, Peter. "Reflections on the Origins of Cultural History." In *Interpretation and Cultural History*, ed. J. Pittock and A. Wear. London: Macmillan, 1991.

Burrow, J. W. *A Liberal Descent: Victorian Historians and the English Past*. Cambridge: Cambridge UP, 1981.

Burrow, J. W., Stephan Collini, and Donald Winch. *That Noble Science of Politics: A Study in Nineteenth-Century Intellectual History*. Cambridge: Cambridge UP, 1983.

Butler, Marilyn. *Jane Austen and the War of Ideas*. Oxford: Clarendon, 1987.

Cafarelli, Annette Wheeler. *Prose in the Age of Poets: Romanticism and Biographical Narrative from Johnson to De Quincey*. Philadelphia: U of Pennsylvania P, 1990.

Canary, Robert, and Henry Kozicki, eds. *The Writing of History: Literary Form and Historical Understanding*. Madison: U of Wisconsin P, 1978.

Carnochan, W. B. *Gibbon's Solitude: The Inward World of the Historian*. Stanford: Stanford UP, 1987.

Chandler, George. *William Roscoe of Liverpool*. London: B. T. Batsford, 1953.

Clark, H. F. "Eighteenth-Century Elysiums: The Role of 'Association' in the Landscape Movement." *Journal of the Warburg and Courtauld Institutes* 6 (1943): 165–89.

Clive, John. *Scotch Reviewers: The Edinburgh Review, 1802–1815*. London: Faber, 1957.

Cohen, Ralph. "History and Genre." *New Literary History* 17 (1986): 203–18.

Cohn, Dorrit. *Transparent Minds: Narrative Modes for Presenting Consciousness in Fiction*. Princeton: Princeton UP, 1978.

Colley, Linda. *Britons: Forging the Nation, 1707–1837*. New Haven: Yale UP, 1992.

Collingwood, R. G. *The Idea of History*. London: Oxford UP, 1956.

Congar, Yves. *Tradition and Traditions: An Historical and a Theological Essay*. Trans. Michael Naseby and Thomas Rainborough. New York: Macmillan, 1967.

Copeland, Thomas. *Our Eminent Friend Edmund Burke*. New Haven: Yale UP, 1949.

Crawford, Robert. *Devolving English Literature*. Oxford: Clarendon, 1992.

———, ed. *The Scottish Invention of English Literature*. New York: Cambridge UP, 1998.

Cromartie, Alan. *Sir Matthew Hale (1609–1676): Law, Religion, and Natural Philosophy*. Cambridge: Cambridge UP, 1995.

Dickinson, H. T. *Liberty and Property: Political Ideology in Eighteenth-Century Britain*. London: Methuen, 1977.

Dwyer, John. "Enlightened Spectators and Classical Moralists: Sympathetic Relations in Eighteenth-Century Scotland." In *Sociability and Society in Eighteenth-Century Scotland*, ed. Dwyer and Richard Sher. Edinburgh: Mercat, 1993.

———. *Virtuous Discourse: Sensibility and Community in Late Eighteenth-Century Scotland*. Edinburgh: John Donald, 1987.

Emerson, Roger L. "Conjectural History and Scottish Philosophers." In *Historical Papers* (Canadian Historical Association, 1984), 63–90.

Ezell, Margaret. *Writing Women's Literary History*. Baltimore: Johns Hopkins UP, 1993.

Favret, Mary. *Romantic Correspondence: Women, Politics, and the Fiction of Letters*. Cambridge: Cambridge UP, 1993.

Ferris, Ina. *The Achievement of Literary Authority: Gender, History, and the Waverley Novels*. Ithaca: Cornell UP, 1991.

Folkenflik, Robert. *Samuel Johnson, Biographer*. Ithaca: Cornell UP, 1978.

Fontana, Bianca Maria. *Rethinking the Politics of Commercial Society: The Edinburgh Review, 1802–1832*. Cambridge: Cambridge UP, 1985.

Forbes, Duncan. *Hume's Philosophical Politics*. Cambridge: Cambridge UP, 1975.

Fowler, Alastair. *Kinds of Literature: An Introduction to the Theory of Genres and Modes*. Oxford: Clarendon, 1982.

Gadamer, Hans-Georg. *Truth and Method*. Trans. Joel Weinsheimer and D. G. Marshall. New York: Continuum, 1995.

Garside, Peter. "Scott and the 'Philosophical' Historians." *Journal of the History of Ideas* 36 (1975): 497–512.

Giarrizzo, Giuseppe. *David Hume, politico e storico*. Torino: Einaudi, 1962.

Gilbert, Felix. *Machiavelli and Guicciardini: Politics and History in Sixteenth Century Florence*. New York: Norton, 1984.

Gossman, Lionel. *Between History and Literature*. Cambridge: Harvard UP, 1990.

Grafton, Anthony. *Defenders of the Text: The Traditions of Scholarship in an Age of Science*. Cambridge: Harvard UP, 1991.

Grafton, Anthony, and Lisa Jardine. " 'Studied for Action': How Gabriel Harvey Read His Livy." *Past and Present* 129 (1990): 30–78.

Graham, Kenneth, ed. *William Godwin Reviewed: A Reception History, 1783–1834*. New York: AMS, forthcoming.

Greig, James. *Francis Jeffrey of the "Edinburgh Review."* Edinburgh: Oliver and Boyd, 1948.

Guillen, Claudio. *Literature as System*. Princeton: Princeton UP, 1971.

Gunn, J. A. W. *Beyond Liberty and Property: The Process of Self-Recognition in Eighteenth-Century Political Thought*. Kingston: McGill-Queens UP, 1983.

———. "Opinion in Eighteenth-Century Thought: What Did the Concept Purport to Explain?" *Utilitas* 5 (1993): 17–33.

Haakonssen, Knud. *Natural Law and Moral Philosophy: From Grotius to the Scottish Enlightenment*. Cambridge: Cambridge UP, 1996.

———. *The Science of a Legislator: The Natural Jurisprudence of David Hume and Adam Smith*. Cambridge: Cambridge UP, 1981.

Hart, F. R. *Lockhart as Romantic Biographer*. Edinburgh: Edinburgh UP, 1971.

Haskell, Francis. *History and Its Images: Art and the Interpretation of the Past*. New Haven: Yale UP, 1993.

Hicks, Philip. *Neoclassical History and English Culture: From Clarendon to Hume*. New York: St. Martin's, 1996.

Hilson, J. C. "Hume: The Historian as Man of Feeling." In *Augustan Worlds: Essays in Honour of A. R. Humphreys*, ed. J. C. Hilson, M. Jones, and J. Watson. Leicester: Leicester UP, 1978.

Hont, Istvan. " 'The Rich Country–Poor Country' Debate in Scottish Classical Political Economy." In *Wealth and Virtue: The Shaping of Political Economy in the Scottish Enlightenment*, ed. Istvan Hont and Michael Ignatieff. Cambridge: Cambridge UP, 1983.

Howell, Wilbur S. *Eighteenth-Century British Logic and Rhetoric*. Princeton: Princeton UP, 1971.

Hudson, Nicholas. " 'Oral Tradition': The Evolution of an Eighteenth-Century Concept." In *Tradition in Transition: Women Writers, Marginal Texts, and the Eighteenth-Century Canon*, ed. Alvaro Ribeiro and James Basker. Oxford: Clarendon, 1996.

Hunt, John Dixon, and Peter Willis. *The Genius of the Place: The English Landscape Garden, 1620–1820*. Cambridge: MIT P, 1988.

Hunter, Paul. *Before Novels: The Cultural Contexts of Eighteenth-Century English Fiction*. New York: Norton, 1990.

———. "The Loneliness of the Long-Distance Reader." *Genre* 10 (1977): 455–84.

Janowitz, Anne. *England's Ruins: Poetic Purpose and the National Landscape*. Cambridge: Blackwell, 1990.

Johnson, James. *The Formation of English Neoclassical Thought*. Princeton: Princeton UP, 1967.

Jones, Chris. *Radical Sensibility: Literature and Ideas in the 1790s*. London: Routledge, 1993.

Jones, Vivien. "Women Writing Revolution: Narratives of History and Sexuality in Wollstonecraft and Williams." In *Beyond Romanticism: New Approaches to Texts and Contexts, 1780–1832*, ed. Stephen Copley and John Whale. London: Routledge, 1992.

Kallich, Martin. *The Association of Ideas and Critical Theory in Eighteenth-Century England*. The Hague: Mouton, 1970.

Kelly, Gary. *Women, Writing, and Revolution, 1790–1827*. Oxford: Clarendon, 1993.

Kellner, Hans. *Language and Historical Representation: Getting the Story Crooked*. Madison: U of Wisconsin P, 1989.

Kettler, David. *The Social and Political Thought of Adam Ferguson*. Columbus: Ohio State UP, 1965.

Kidd, Colin. *Subverting Scotland's Past: Scottish Whig Historians and the Creation of an Anglo-British Identity, 1689–c.1830*. Cambridge: Cambridge UP, 1993.

Klancher, Jon. *The Making of English Reading Audiences, 1790–1832*. Madison: U of Wisconsin P, 1987.

Klein, Lawrence. *Shaftesbury and the Culture of Politeness: Moral Discourse and Cultural Politics in Early Eighteenth-Century England*. Cambridge: Cambridge UP, 1994.

Lehmann, W. C. *John Millar of Glasgow*. Cambridge: Cambridge UP, 1960.

Levine, Joseph. *The Battle of the Books: History and Literature in the Augustan Age*. Ithaca: Cornell UP, 1991.

———. *Humanism and History: Origins of Modern English Historiography.* Ithaca: Cornell UP, 1987.

Levine, Philippa. *The Amateur and the Professional: Antiquarians, Historians, and Archaeologists in Victorian England, 1838–1886*. Cambridge: Cambridge UP, 1986.

Levy, David. "The Partial Spectator in the *Wealth of Nations:* A Robust Utilitarianism." *European Journal of the History of Economic Thought* 2 (1995): 299–326.

Lieberman, David. *The Province of Legislation Determined: Legal Theory in Eighteenth Century Britain*. Cambridge: Cambridge UP, 1989.

Livingstone, Donald. *Hume's Philosophy of Common Life*. Chicago: U of Chicago P, 1984.

Locke, Don. *A Fantasy of Reason: The Life and Thought of William Godwin*. London: Routledge and Kegan Paul, 1980.

Lowenthal, David. *The Past Is a Foreign Country.* Cambridge: Cambridge UP, 1985.

McKenzie, Lionel. "The French Revolution and English Parliamentary Reform: James Mackintosh and the *Vindiciae Gallicae*." *Eighteenth-Century Studies* 14 (1981): 264–82.

McKeon, Michael. *The Origins of the English Novel, 1600–1740*. Baltimore: Johns Hopkins UP, 1987.

McKillop, A. "Local Attachment and Cosmopolitanism—the Eighteenth Century Pattern." In *From Sensibility to Romanticism*, ed. F. W. Hilles and Harold Bloom. New York: Oxford UP, 1965.

Mayo, Robert. *The English Novel in the Magazines, 1740–1815*. Evanston, Ill.: Northwestern UP, 1962.

Meek, R. L. *Social Science and the Ignoble Savage*. Cambridge: Cambridge UP, 1976.

Miller, Karl. *Cockburn's Millennium*. Cambridge: Harvard UP, 1976.

Mink, Louis. *Historical Understanding*. Ed. Brian Fay et. al. Ithaca: Cornell UP, 1987.

Momigliano, Arnaldo. *The Classical Foundations of Modern Historiography.* Berkeley and Los Angeles: U of California P, 1990.

———. "The Eighteenth-Century Prelude to Mr. Gibbon." In *Sesto Contributo allo studio degli studi classici*. Rome: Edizioni di Storia e Letteratura, 1980.

———. *Studies in Historiography.* London: Weidenfeld, 1966.

Monk, Samuel. *The Sublime: A Study of Critical Theories in Eighteenth-Century England.* Ann Arbor: U of Michigan P, 1960.

Moran, Mary Catherine. " 'The Commerce of the Sexes': Civil Society and Polite Society in Scottish Enlightenment Discourse." In *Paradoxes of Civil Society: New Perspectives on Modern German and British History*, ed. Frank Trentmann. Providence: Berghahn Books, 1999.

Morgan, Peter. *Literary Critics and Reviewers in Early Nineteenth-Century Britain.* Beckenham, Kent: Croom Helm, 1983.

Mossner, Ernest Campbell. *The Life of David Hume*. Oxford: Clarendon, 1980.

Mullan, John. *Sentiment and Sociability: The Language of Feeling in the Eighteenth Century.* Oxford: Clarendon, 1988.

Musselwhite, David. "The Trial of Warren Hastings." In *Literature, Politics, and Theory*, ed. Francis Barker et al. London: Methuen, 1986.

Nadel, George. "The Philosophy of History before Historicism." *History and Theory* 3 (1963): 291–315.

Newman, Gerald. *The Rise of English Nationalism: A Cultural History, 1740–1830*. New York: St. Martin's, 1987.

Nora, Pierre. *Realms of Memory: Rethinking the French Past*. Trans. Arthur Goldhammer. 3 vols. New York: Columbia UP, 1996.

Norton, David Fate, and Richard H. Popkin. *David Hume: Philosophical Historian*. Indianapolis: Bobbs-Merrill, 1965.

O'Brien, Karen. *Narratives of Enlightenment: Cosmopolitan History from Voltaire to Gibbon*. Cambridge: Cambridge UP, 1997.

Ogden, James. *Isaac D'Israeli*. Oxford: Clarendon, 1969.

Okie, Laird. *Augustan Historical Writing: Histories of England in the English Enlightenment*. Lanham, Md.: UP of America, 1991.

O'Leary, Patrick. *Sir James Mackintosh: The Whig Cicero*. Aberdeen: Aberdeen UP, 1989.

Orr, Linda. *Jules Michelet: Nature, History, and Language*. Ithaca: Cornell UP, 1975.

Ousby, Ian. *The Englishman's England: Taste, Travel, and the Rise of Tourism*. Cambridge: Cambridge UP, 1990.

Patterson, Annabel. *Censorship and Interpretation: The Condition of Writing and Reading in Early Modern England*. Madison: U of Wisconsin P, 1984.

Paulson, Ronald. *Emblem and Expression: Meaning in English Art of the Eighteenth Century*. Cambridge: Harvard UP, 1975.

Peardon, Thomas Preston. *The Transition in English Historical Writing, 1760–1830*. New York: AMS, 1966.

Pelikan, Jaroslav. *The Christian Tradition: A History of the Development of Doctrine*. 4 vols. Chicago: U of Chicago P, 1971.

———. *The Vindication of Tradition*. New Haven: Yale UP, 1984.

Phillips, Mark. "Adam Smith and the History of Private Life: Social and Sentimental Narratives in Eighteenth-Century Historiography." In *The Historical Imagination in Early Modern Britain*, ed. D. R. Kelley and David Harris Sacks. Cambridge: Cambridge UP, 1997.

———. "Historiography and Genre: A More Modest Proposal." *Storia della storiografia/Histoire de l'historiographie* 24 (1993): 119–32.

———." 'If Mrs. Mure Be Not Sorry for Poor King Charles': History, the Novel, and the Sentimental Reader," *History Workshop Journal* 43 (1997): 111–31

———. "Reconsiderations on History and Antiquarianism: Arnaldo Momigliano and the Historiography of Eighteenth-Century Britain." *Journal of the History of Ideas* 58 (1996): 297–316.

———. "Representation and Argument in Renaissance Historiography." *Storia della storiografia/Histoire de l'historiographie* 10 (1986): 48–63.

———. "Scott, Macaulay, and the Literary Challenge to Historiography." *Journal of the History of Ideas* 50 (1989): 117–33.

Phillipson, Nicholas. *Hume*. London: Weidenfeld and Nicholson, 1989.

Piggott, Stuart. *Ancient Britons and the Antiquarian Imagination: Ideas from the Renaissance to the Regency*. New York: Thames and Hudson, 1989.

———. *Ruins in a Landscape*. Edinburgh: Edinburgh UP, 1976.

Pocock, J. G. A. *The Ancient Constitution and the Feudal Law: A Study of English Historical Thought in the Seventeenth Century*. 2d ed. Cambridge: Cambridge UP, 1987.

———. *Politics, Language, and Time: Essays on Political Thought and History.* New York: Atheneum, 1971.

———. *Virtue, Commerce, and History: Essays on Political Thought and History, Chiefly in the Eighteenth Century.* Cambridge: Cambridge UP, 1985.

Pomata, Gianna. "History, Particular and Universal." *Feminist Studies* 19 (1993): 7–50.

Raven, James. *Judging New Wealth: Popular Publishing and Responses to Commerce in England, 1759–1800.* New York: Oxford UP, 1992.

Rawson, Claude. *Satire and Sentiment, 1660–1830.* Cambridge: Cambridge UP, 1994.

Redford, Bruce. *The Converse of the Pen: Acts of Intimacy in the Eighteenth-Century Familiar Letter.* Chicago: U of Chicago P, 1986.

Reiss, Timothy. *The Meaning of Literature.* Ithaca: Cornell UP, 1992.

Rendall, Jane. Introduction to *The History of Women: From the Earliest Antiquity to the Present Time,* by William Alexander. 2 vols. Bristol: Thoemmes, 1995.

———. "The Political Ideas and Activities of Sir James Mackintosh (1765–1832)." Ph.D. diss., London University, 1972.

Rose, Mark. *Authors and Owners: The Invention of Copyright.* Cambridge: Harvard UP, 1993.

Ross, Ian Simpson. *The Life of Adam Smith.* Oxford: Clarendon, 1995.

———. *Lord Kames and the Scotland of His Day.* Oxford: Clarendon, 1972.

Ross, Trevor. "Copyright and the Invention of Tradition." *Eighteenth-Century Studies* 26 (1992): 1–27.

Rotwein, Eugene, ed. Introduction to *Writings on Economics,* by David Hume. Madison: U of Wisconsin P, 1970.

Samuel, Raphael. *Theatres of Memory.* London: Verso, 1994.

Scholem, Gershon. "Revelation and Tradition as Religious Categories in Judaism." In *The Messianic Idea in Judaism.* New York: Schocken, 1971.

Sekora, John. *Luxury: The Concept in Western Thought, Eden to Smollett.* Baltimore: Johns Hopkins UP, 1977.

Shaw, Harry. *The Forms of Historical Fiction: Sir Walter Scott and His Successors.* Ithaca: Cornell UP, 1983.

Sher, Richard. *Church and University in the Scottish Enlightenment.* Princeton: Princeton UP, 1985.

Shils, Edward. *Tradition.* Chicago: U of Chicago P, 1981.

Siebert, Donald. *The Moral Animus of David Hume.* Newark: U of Delaware P, 1990.

Skinner, A. S. "Adam Smith: An Economic Interpretation of History." In *Essays on Adam Smith,* ed. A. S. Skinner and T. Wilson. Oxford: Oxford UP, 1975.

Smith, Dale. "Impolite Atoms and Polite Histories: Tobias Smollett, Contemporary History, and the Republic of Letters in Eighteenth-Century Britain." M.A. thesis, Carleton University, Ottawa, 1996.

Smith, R. J. *The Gothic Bequest: Medieval Institutions in British Thought, 1688–1863.* Cambridge: Cambridge UP, 1987.

Spencer, Jane. *The Rise of the Woman Novelist: From Aphra Behn to Jane Austen.* Oxford: Blackwell, 1986.

Stafford, William. "Narratives of Women: English Feminists of the 1790s." *History* 82 (1997): 24–42.

Stauffer, Donald. *The Art of Biography in Eighteenth Century England*. Princeton: Princeton UP, 1941.

Stein, Peter. *Legal Evolution*. Cambridge: Cambridge UP, 1980.

Stewart, John. *The Moral and Political Philosophy of David Hume*. New York: Columbia UP, 1963.

Struever, Nancy. "Topics in History." In *"Metahistory": Six Critiques*. History and Theory Beiheft 19. Middletown: Wesleyan UP, 1980.

Suleri, Sara. *The Rhetoric of English India*. Chicago: U of Chicago P, 1992.

Taylor, Charles. *Sources of the Self: The Making of the Modern Identity*. Cambridge: Harvard UP, 1989.

Todd, Janet. *Sensibility: An Introduction*. London: Methuen, 1986.

———. *The Sign of Angellica: Women, Writing, and Fiction, 1660–1800*. London: Virago, 1989.

Turner, Cheryl. *Living by the Pen: Women Writers in the Eighteenth Century*. London: Routledge, 1992.

Ty, Eleanor. *Unsex'd Revolutionaries: Five Women Novelists of the 1790s*. Toronto: U of Toronto P, 1993.

Vance, John. *Samuel Johnson and the Sense of History*. Athens: U of Georgia P, 1984.

Van Sant, Anne Jessie. *Eighteenth-Century Sensibility and the Novel: The Senses in Social Context*. Cambridge: Cambridge UP, 1993.

Watson, Nicola. *Revolution and the Form of the British Novel, 1790–1825: Intercepted Letters, Interrupted Seductions*. Oxford: Clarendon, 1994.

Weinbrot, Howard. *Augustus Caesar in Augustan England*. Princeton: Princeton UP, 1978.

Wellek, Rene. *The Rise of English Literary History*. Chapel Hill: U of North Carolina P, 1941.

Welsh, Alexander. *The Hero of the Waverley Novels: With New Essays on Scott*. Princeton: Princeton UP, 1992.

Wendorf, Richard. *The Elements of Life: Biography and Portrait Painting in Stuart and Georgian England*. Oxford: Clarendon, 1990.

Westerman, Pauline. "Hume and the Natural Lawyers: A Change of Landscape." In *Hume and Hume's Connexions*, ed. M. A. Stewart and J. P. Wright. University Park: Pennsylvania State UP, 1994.

Wexler, Victor. *David Hume and the History of England*. Memoirs of the American Philosophical Society, vol. 131. Philadelphia: Philosophical Society, 1979.

Wheeler, David, ed. *Domestick Privacies: Samuel Johnson and the Art of Biography*. Lexington: U of Kentucky P, 1987.

Whelan, Frederick. *Edmund Burke and India: Political Morality and Empire*. Pittsburgh: U of Pittsburgh P, 1996.

White, Hayden. *Metahistory: The Historical Imagination in Nineteenth-Century Europe*. Baltimore: Johns Hopkins UP, 1973.

White, James Boyd. *Acts of Hope: Creating Authority in Literature, Law, and Politics*. Chicago: U of Chicago P, 1994.

Winch, Donald. *Riches and Poverty: An Intellectual History of Political Economy in Britain, 1750–1834*. Cambridge: Cambridge UP, 1996.

Womersley, David. *The Transformation of "The Decline and Fall of the Roman Empire."* Cambridge: Cambridge UP, 1988.

Wood, Paul. "Hume, Reid, and the Science of the Mind." In *Hume and Hume's Connexions*, ed. M. A. Stewart and J. P. Wright. University Park: Pennsylvania State UP, 1994.

———. "The Natural History of Man in the Scottish Enlightenment." *History of Science* 27 (1989): 89–123.

Woolf, Daniel. "A Feminine Past? Gender, Genre, and Historical Knowledge in England, 1500–1800." *American Historical Review* 102 (1997): 645–79.

———.*The Idea of History in Early Stuart England: Erudition, Ideology, and the "Light of Truth" from the Accession of James I to the Civil War*. Toronto: U of Toronto P, 1990.

Wootton, David. "Hume, 'the Historian.' " In *The Cambridge Companion to Hume*, ed. David Fate Norton. Cambridge: Cambridge UP, 1993.

Wright, Patrick. *On Living in an Old Country*. London: Verso, 1985.

Yarrington, Alison. *The Commemoration of the Hero, 1800–1864: Monuments to the British Victors of the Napoleonic Wars*. New York: Garland, 1988.

Yerushalmi, Yosef. *Zakhor: Jewish History and Jewish Memory*. Seattle: U of Washington P, 1982.

Zimmerman, Everett. *The Boundaries of Fiction: History and the Eighteenth-Century British Novel*. Ithaca: Cornell UP, 1995.

Zwicker, Steven. "Reading the Margins: Politics and the Habits of Appropriation." In *Refiguring Revolutions: Aesthetics and Politics from the English Revolution to the Romantic Revolution*, ed. Kevin Sharpe and Steven Zwicker. Berkeley and Los Angeles: U of California P, 1998.

Index